FAMILY LAW & PRACTICE

Frances Burton, LLB, LLM
Senior Lecturer in Law
London Guildhall University

Cavendish
Publishing
Limited

First published in Great Britain 1997 by Cavendish Publishing Limited, The Glass House, Wharton Street, London WC1X 9PX.

Telephone: 0171-278 8000   Facsimile: 0171-278 8080

British Library Cataloguing in Publication Data

Burton, F
Family Law & Practice
I. Title II. Series
344.10615

ISBN 1-874241-91-0

Printed and bound in Great Britain

Contents

Table of cases

Table of statutes

Section 1

The divorce process – professional attitudes, law and procedure

Chapter 1

Divorce law

Introduction

For reasons too obvious to mention, family law in general, and divorce law in particular, cannot be regarded as just another aspect of civil litigation, although until comparatively recently there were few practitioners who realised this and fewer still who adopted an approach to family law work which reflected such a view.

After more than 25 years of limited progress since the last fundamental reform to the law of divorce, during which bodies such as the Solicitors Family Law Association have attempted to introduce a constructive and civilised approach to the resolution of legal matters following matrimonial breakdown, the Family Law Act 1996 has finally incorporated the proposals of the 1995 White Paper, *Looking to the Future: Mediation and the Ground for Divorce*, and this will, when the Act comes into force, introduce a true 'no fault' divorce system. This change envisages as the norm a cooperative process depending heavily on mediation. How this will emerge in the form of legislation and rules of procedure and practice is not yet clear, but we can safely say that if you want to make a success of family law work you must familiarise yourself with the contemporary non-adversarial approach which will permeate and influence your work in this field.

Note

The existing law, which is largely contained in the Matrimonial Causes Act 1973, as amended, will continue in force until the divorce provisions of the Family Law Act 1996 are fully implemented, which is expected to be in about two years' time. This may seem confusing to the trainee, but there are in fact certain benefits to be extracted from each system, according to the needs of the particular client. The trainee who understands both will be able to advise whether that client should proceed under the existing law or wait until the Family Law Act 1996 is fully in force.

1.1.1   **The Solicitors Family Law Association**

Both under the old law and the new, it is now universally accepted that the legal resolution of marital problems is not conveniently achieved by a predominantly litigious approach, even where a firm has no specialist family department.

One way of consciously changing gear from the usual approach of the civil litigator is for family law experts to join the Solicitors Family Law Association (SFLA). This was established in 1982 to take family matters, as far as possible, out of the atmosphere of contentious litigation with the aim of achieving agreed solutions which, while not substantially different from what the court would order if the matter were acrimoniously contested, might with cooperation be achieved at less cost, emotionally as well as financially. The philosophy has become much more important since the passing of the Children Act 1989 (CA 1989), which establishes the concept of *parental responsibility* and encourages divorcing parents to continue good parenting regardless of the fact that they are no longer married.

However, whether or not you join the 3,000 strong membership, the Law Society recommends that *all* solicitors practising family law observe the SFLA's principles and Code of Practice, adherence to which is not a sign of weakness and which does not in any way place the client at a disadvantage. (The Code is reproduced in Appendix 1.)

Note

If you have the misfortune to encounter a solicitor who does not observe the Code, and who insists on conducting matters in an aggressive and acrimonious manner, you should stick firmly to its principles and not give in to the obvious temptation to retaliate in kind. There are in fact a few such solicitors, whose identity is well-known in the profession, and whose approach is unfortunately still rooted in the pre-1969 law which was entirely adversarial and fault-based. Experience has shown that the best response is one of increased politeness and courtesy backed up where necessary by immediate and decisive court action which is in no way precluded or inhibited by the Code. SFLA principles merely require that litigation should not be the first resort, where matters may be conveniently negotiated first and formalised procedurally afterwards.

Terminology in divorce suits   1.1.2

By way of emphasising the difference between the law of divorce and the course of ordinary litigation, the procedural terminology is distinct:

- the parties are known as the petitioner and the respondent (not plaintiff and defendant);
- they proceed by petition (not statement of claim or particulars of claim);
- a party defending files an answer and, where appropriate, cross-petition (not defence and counterclaim).

The primary source of the law of *divorce* is the Matrimonial Causes Act 1973 as amended (MCA 1973) – the statute which consolidated the Divorce Reform Act 1969 from which the contemporary 'reformed' law of divorce derives – and the main procedural source is the Family Proceedings Rules 1991 (FPR 1991).

There are other primary sources – in particular those dealing with other aspects of family and divorce practice and procedure, and with special topics such as jurisdiction, occupation of the home, financial provision without dissolution of the marriage and child matters – but the basic working knowledge of divorce law and procedure which you require may be obtained from the MCA 1973 and the FPR 1991, which are conveniently reproduced in the *White Book* and in the leading practitioner text, *Rayden and Jackson* (often simply referred to as *Rayden*).

The first year of marriage – absolute   1.2
bar on divorce

It is not possible to *petition for divorce* during the first year after the celebration of the marriage: s 3(1), MCA 1973 (inserted by s 1, Matrimonial and Family Proceedings Act 1984).

This is an absolute bar to which there are no exceptions, and the bar still applies even where early presentation of the petition is inadvertent: *Butler v Butler* [1990] Fam Law 21, in which the contravention of the rule occurred where the petition was originally presented (quite properly within the year) for judicial separation, and later amended for divorce. This proved fatal, since the date of *presentation* of the amended *petition* was technically that of the original petition for judicial separation, and there was no remedy but to present a new one.

1.3   Alternatives open to the client

There are a number of other options open to the client, although with the exception of obtaining a nullity decree none will permit remarriage (which is probably what the client wants at the time of consulting the solicitor even though there may be no potential new spouse yet in view). Often, clients merely want a finite dissolution of the existing marriage so that new attachments may be formed with a clear conscience and with the bad experience firmly in the past. You should make use of whatever scope there is for putting your client's affairs in order in a sensible manner.

Under the new provisions incorporated into the Family Law Act, a year's wait will still be required. Thus, because it would probably be foolish for most clients with one failed marriage behind them to be in a position to contract another before the first anniversary has been reached, the year's wait is not in practice much of a drawback. You should concentrate on pointing out to your client the various alternatives available, some of which may apply in your client's case, and on either taking emergency or temporary action where appropriate or else in disposing in the intervening year of the 'baggage' which it will be undesirable to take into any new relationship (particularly as statistics show that many second and subsequent marriages fail because of unfinished business of one sort or another left over from the previous one).

1.3.1   Judicial separation or nullity

It often comes as a surprise to clients to learn that divorce is not the only decree available, and that the alternatives of judicial separation (under s 17, MCA 1973) or nullity (under ss 11 and 12, MCA 1973) may be applicable. Either of these decrees may be applied for if appropriate within days of the marriage ceremony and in the case of nullity, a lengthy delay in presenting a petition can even be fatal.

A detailed knowledge of these alternative decrees is outside the scope of the average LPC syllabus, but you should be aware of their usefulness for those clients who oppose divorce on religious grounds, or for those for whom it is important to achieve a formal break with a spouse where dissolution of the marriage by divorce is temporarily either:

• not possible (due to s 3) or, even when the initial year is up;

- not advisable, eg due to an unresolved property dispute affected by the termination of the status of marriage, such as where steps must be taken to retain the client's rights under a pension scheme.

You should therefore be prepared to look up the relevant law on nullity in the latest edition of *Rayden and Jackson* and advise accordingly where necessary.

However, some general knowledge of the subject will be helpful to enable you to judge whether either of these alternative decrees might be suitable to a client.

Judicial separation

A decree of *judicial separation* can be obtained on the same facts as divorce save that it is not necessary to prove irretrievable breakdown of the marriage: see Chapter 2.

> *Note*
>
> This may in particular satisfy the client who wants to achieve a formal break where the marriage has obviously ended for all practical purposes but divorce is not yet possible. A further advantage is that such a decree records the separation which can later be used for a divorce decree when the year is up, ie it preserves the evidence. However, judicial separation is not to be recommended where the client's real objective is to remarry, since the decree will inevitably cost money to obtain and by the time it is obtained it is likely to be time to petition for divorce.

Nullity

A decree of *nullity* can be obtained where the marriage is either *void* or *voidable*.

A decree of nullity in respect of a *void* marriage can always be obtained on proof of the relevant fact on the basis of:

- defective formalities;
- one of the parties already being married;
- the parties not being respectively male and female; or
- its polygamous nature, provided one of the parties is domiciled in England and Wales.

> *Note*
>
> There is no time limit for petitioning on any of these grounds since the marriage is void anyway and strictly no declaration to that effect is actually necessary for it to be regarded as void. A void marriage can *never* be valid *whatever* the parties wish. Sometimes, however, an actual decla-

ration *is* required, eg trustees of a settlement may wish to know whether to treat a marriage as void or voidable. If any of the grounds apply which make a marriage void, therefore, the sooner a petition is presented the better, so that the matter may be formalised.

A decree of nullity can be obtained where the marriage is voidable (until which time it is a good marriage, valid for all purposes) on the basis of:

- incapacity to consummate: s 12(a), MCA 1973;
- wilful refusal to consummate: s 12(b), MCA 1973;
- lack of consent due to mistake, duress, unsoundness of mind or otherwise: s 12(c), MCA 1973;
- mental disorder: s 12(d), MCA 1973;
- venereal disease in a communicable form at the date of the ceremony: s 12(e), MCA 1973;
- pregnancy at the date of the ceremony by someone other than the petitioner: s 12(f), MCA 1973.

In the last four cases a petition must be presented within three years of the marriage and in the case of the first two a delay in petitioning might give rise to the defence of approbation of the marriage, ie that the petitioner acted as though he or she was willing to honour the marriage regardless.

Note

Where a marriage is *voidable*, it is too late to dissolve it after the death of one of the parties. The marriage will have subsisted as a valid marriage until death and will therefore by that stage have been dissolved by death, upon which the surviving partner will have the status of widow or widower in the normal way.

1.3.2   Separation agreements

Some clients are surprised to discover that a decree is not essential to effect a formal separation and that a separation agreement can deal formally with all matters over which the court has jurisdiction without the necessity of going to court, save only for ultimately dissolving the marriage when the parties are finally ready and able to seek a decree of divorce.

Separation agreements have the additional advantage over court proceedings in that it is possible with very few limits to insert into them virtually any provisions which the parties desire, although care needs to be taken to remember that financial agreements may have a subsequent influence on provision which the court may order on dissolution of the marriage. This is therefore an important opportunity for good drafting to secure a favourable result for your client, and such drafting is one of the matrimonial solicitor's most vital skills.

Note

It is of course open to the parties merely to separate, by informal mutual agreement or by the unilateral decision of one of them, without either decree or formal separation agreement, save only that if one leaves the other without just cause that party will technically be in desertion and might ultimately be divorced for it: see Chapter 2, para 2.4.

Sources of funds

1.3.3

If the real reason behind the client's consulting you is because the break-up of the marriage has caused financial problems, there are three possible sources of funds without the need to petition for any decree whatsoever (four if the parties have children):

- ss 2, 6 and 7, Domestic Proceedings and Magistrates' Courts Act 1978 (DPMCA 1978): see 14.1 below;
- s 27, MCA 1973: see 14.5;
- welfare benefit advice: see Chapter 13;

and if the parties have children

- the Child Support Agency (CSA): see 7.5 and 18.6.

Alternatively, it might be possible to negotiate voluntary payments from the other spouse. Much will depend on the reason for the marital breakdown and on whether the separation was consensual.

Children Act proceedings

1.3.4

Very often the catalyst bringing the client into the office talking about divorce is a problem about the children. In this case a free standing application can be brought under the Children Act 1989 (CA 1989) to resolve such problems without taking any proceedings in relation to the marriage. For example, a residence order may be obtained if there is a sufficient dispute as to where a child should live, or a contact order if contact is being denied, or a specific issue or prohibited steps order in relation to urgent decisions in relation to important matters such as medical treatment, education or religion: see Chapter 6 below.

1.3.5   Injunctions and declarations

Similarly an act of violence or a dispute as to occupation of the family home may be the immediate reason why the client has consulted you.

The law in this area is at present contained in the Domestic Violence and Matrimonial Proceedings Act 1976 (DVMP 1976), the DPMCA 1978, and the Matrimonial Homes Act 1983 (MHA 1983). The courts (both the High Court and the county court) also have inherent powers to grant injunctions ancillary to any suit before it so that injunctions are also available ancillary to divorce proceedings, wardship or CA 1989 proceedings, and if such another suit is already on foot it will usually be expected that any injunction will be granted ancillary to those proceedings.

Note

The present law will be repealed and replaced by the provisions of Part IV of the Family Law Act 1996, which is expected to come into force sometime in 1997: see Chapters 15 and 17.

1.3.6   Advice to the client

The best advice to the client is probably that, unless there are grounds for nullity, it is probably futile to consider a decree in the first year since a year soon passes and it will probably be more cost-effective to prepare a divorce petition to file as soon as possible rather than to waste time and money obtaining a temporary decree of judicial separation which will ultimately need to be superseded by one for divorce in order to leave the client free to remarry.

You should therefore suggest:

- making use of any of the remedies described at 1.3.3–1.3.6 which suit your client's circumstances;

and to concentrate on such practical matters as;

- money to live on;
- somewhere suitable to live; and
- absence of any harassment, interference or violence from the other spouse.

A petition for divorce on the basis of either adultery (see Chapter 2, para 2.2.1 below) or behaviour (see Chapter 2, para 2.3) can be presented one year and a day after the ceremony, regardless of how early in the marriage the matters relied upon occurred. Despite the ban on actually *petitioning* during the first year of marriage, any matters *occurring* during that year may still be relied on as the substance of the petition: s 3(2), MCA 1973.

Example

Following the marriage the husband commits adultery with an air hostess on the honeymoon flight to the Seychelles. The wife may petition for divorce on this single act of adultery as soon as the year is up, or for judicial separation immediately.

Self-assessment questions

1 What is the SFLA and what role does it play in the practice of family law?
2 What are the parties to a divorce suit called? What are the pleadings which are used in divorce suits?
3 Are there any advantages in obtaining judicial separation during the first year of marriage?
4 What grounds make a marriage void?
5 What grounds make a marriage voidable?
6 What proceedings are available during the first year of marriage to a spouse who is unable to present a *divorce* petition?
7 Is it necessary to wait for a divorce to obtain a residence order in respect of a child of both parties to the marriage?
8 What is the advantage, if any, of a separation agreement while the parties are unable to divorce?
9 What are the consequences, if any, of the parties separating informally?
10 Is domestic violence protection available prior to presenting a divorce petition?

Chapter 2

The ground for divorce

The ground for divorce and the five facts

2.1

Theoretically, there is only one *ground* for divorce – irretrievable breakdown of the marriage: s 1(1), MCA 1973. As this is the sole ground, it is technically incorrect to speak of 'the grounds' for divorce. However, in order to *prove* the ground in s 1(1) it is necessary to prove one (or more) of the five *facts* evidencing that irretrievable breakdown which are specified in s 1(2)(a)–(e). Thus, both practitioners and clients tend to speak of 'the grounds for divorce' by which they mean the s 1(1) 'ground' of irretrievable breakdown *and* the fact or facts by which the technical ground will be proved.

Note

'Facts' in this sense are usually written with a capital F to distinguish them from the factual scenario of the case, and are referred to as Facts A–E to correspond with the five facts detailed in s 1(2)(a)–(e).

The facts are:
- Fact A – adultery;
- Fact B – behaviour;
- Fact C – desertion;
- Fact D – two years' separation with consent of the respondent;
- Fact E – five years' separation.

Note

All references in this chapter are to the Matrimonial Causes Act 1973 unless stated otherwise.

2.2

Proof of the ground

Sub-sections 1(1) and (2) are separate requirements which must be individually satisfied, one without the other will be insufficient: see *Buffery v Buffery* [1980] 2 FLR 365 and *Richards v Richards* [1972] 1 WLR 1073, [1972] 3 All ER 695 (irretrievable breakdown but no fact proved), and *Biggs v Biggs* [1977] 1 All ER 20 (fact but no irretrievable breakdown). No link is, however, necessary between the two requirements: *Stevens v Stevens* [1979] 1 WLR 885.

Note

Inability to satisfy both s 1(1) and (2) occurs more often than might at first be thought. It is common for marriages made in haste to be repented fairly quickly also, but undoing them is more difficult. If a couple separate early in the marriage, for example out of boredom with each other, and when neither has committed adultery nor could be said to have been guilty of sufficient 'behaviour' for a successful Fact B petition, they will need to wait for two years before being able to use Fact D for a successful separation petition. Although both may be quite sure that the marriage has irretrievably broken down, it will not be possible to prove any Fact, so no decree will be possible until it is. Your advice in these circumstances, if tactful enquiries do not reveal the slightest chance of a case of behaviour that the other spouse would not defend and the parties are unwilling to wait, may be that someone should go and commit adultery as soon as possible! It is immaterial which party petitions as no tactical advantages are to be gained by petitioning or being petitioned against where both parties want a divorce.

The court has a duty to enquire, so far as it reasonably can, into the facts alleged by the petition, balanced by a philosophy of avoiding pointless enquiries into conduct and fault which modern divorce law is designed to escape from: *Grenfell v Grenfell* [1977] 3 WLR 738, [1978] 1 All ER 561.

If the court is satisfied, therefore, that one of the Facts has been proved, then unless it is satisfied on all the evidence that the marriage has *not* broken down irretrievably, it has a duty, subject to the restrictions of s 5 (see 3.2.2), to grant the decree of divorce: s 1(4). In other words, proving a Fact leads to a presumption of irretrievable breakdown.

2.2.1

Adultery: Fact A

The requirement to establish this Fact is that the respondent has committed adultery and the petitioner finds it intolerable to live with the respondent: s 1(2)(a). Note that there are two separate elements to this Fact:

- the act of adultery; and
- that the petitioner also finds it intolerable to live with the respondent, *not necessarily because of the adultery*.

The act of adultery   2.2.2

Adultery means voluntary sexual intercourse between a married person and a person of the opposite sex, whether married or not, who is not that married person's spouse. It is necessary to consider the meaning of the individual words of the section in this definition.

Voluntary

A wife who has been raped does not commit adultery: *S v S* [1962] 3 All ER 816; neither does a child who cannot consent voluntarily to intercourse, but this will not stop the adult party being guilty of adultery: *Barnett v Barnett and Brown* [1970] 2 All ER 33. However, once intercourse is established it is for the respondent to show that it was not voluntary: *Redpath v Redpath* [1950] 1 All ER 600. Being intoxicated is generally not an excuse for adultery: *Goshawk v Goshawk* (1965) 109 SJ 290.

Sexual intercourse

There must be some penetration although a complete act of intercourse is not required: *Dennis v Dennis* [1955] 2 WLR 187, [1955] 2 All ER 51, where an impotent respondent spent a night in bed with a woman, giving rise to an inference of adultery which was nevertheless rebutted because he could prove he was incapable of penetration. Sexual familiarities short of intercourse, such as might have applied in the last case, are not enough: *Saps-Ford v Saps-Ford* [1954] 2 All ER 373. However, such an association might be a basis for a Fact B behaviour petition: see 2.3 below.

Note

In this country adultery is not possible with a person who has changed sex because a person's biological sex is regarded here as established at birth by chromosomes which cannot be artificially changed by a later sex change operation; a different view pertains in some American jurisdictions: *Corbett v Corbett* [1970] 2 All ER 33. It has also been established that the UK view does not violate the European Convention on Human Rights because of the UK's traditional concept of marriage as between persons of the opposite biological sex: *Rees v UK* [1987] Fam Law 157, *Cossey v UK* [1991] Fam Law 362.

Proof of the act of adultery   2.2.3

Proof of adultery may be something of a mechanical exercise in contemporary divorce suits since it is unusual for divorces to be defended and the most common way of proving adultery is therefore by the respondent's admission for which provision is made on the Acknowledgment of Service form (which is sent out to the respondent by the court with the petition). See 5.6 below.

However, should it be necessary to prove adultery, in the absence of clear evidence you should consider whether there is any other Fact which could be relied upon instead. This is because the standard of proof required (which would certainly apply in a contested case) is not the general civil standard of proof but a higher (not precisely specified) standard based on the lingering historical background which has always regarded adultery as a serious accusation which used to be, at best, a grave offence and at worst a crime. This is curious as adultery is now generally regarded as a symptom rather than a cause of marriage breakdown. Nevertheless, it means that where it is not going to be admitted it is not sufficient merely to allege adultery without some seriously credible evidence: *Bastable v Bastable* [1968] All ER 701, where the husband petitioned on the basis of a mere suspicion of adultery due to the wife's persistent association with another man. His petition was dismissed.

Methods of proof

The most useful method of proof is DNA testing, which is much more reliable than the blood tests formerly used. However, as these are expensive, cannot be *ordered* if not undertaken voluntarily and will not be *directed* by the court merely to establish adultery, the more old fashioned methods may have to be considered first. These are:

1 *Circumstantial evidence,* ie inclination and opportunity to gratify it: *Farnham v Farnham* (1925) 153 LT 320. A rebuttable presumption will be raised by the parties spending the night in the same room: *Woolf v Woolf* [1931] P 134 but this presumption may be rebutted by evidence such as in *Dennis* above.

2 *Confession statement,* a method once much used, and still useful if adultery is not admitted on the Acknowledgment of Service form but strong suspicions of adultery are confirmed, eg by a private detective sent to watch the parties, who may also invite the parties to volunteer a formal written confession.

Note
Respondents will often do this if they realise that it they do not the private detective will give acceptable evidence anyway, especially if by giving the confession the respondent is able to keep the name of the third party involved out of the suit as is now possible: see 4.4.12 below.

3   *Birth of a child* as a result of the adultery, which may be proved by entry on the birth register if the third party has signed the Register of Births in place of the father: *Jackson v Jackson and Pavan* [1961] 2 WLR 58, [1960] 3 All ER 621 and even by no entry in the space for the father's name in the Register: *Mayo v Mayo* [1948] 2 All ER 869.

4   *Living with another partner*, one of the easiest methods of all since, whether or not the new partner is named in the petition (see drafting advice at 4.4.12) if the court sees that the respondent has set up house away from the petitioner with a new partner adultery will be presumed, especially if a child has also been born.

5   *Findings in other proceedings*, eg where the respondent is *named* as co-respondent or party cited in other divorce proceedings and adultery is proved, or where there are successful proceedings against the respondent spouse under the Children Act 1989, Schedule 1 for property transfer or a lump sum (see Chapter 18, para 18.3.3), or a conviction of rape against a respondent husband, or where adultery has already been used to obtain a decree of judicial separation, which by s 4(2) enables the judicial separation decree to be treated as proof of adultery.

There is, however, a *strong presumption of legitimacy* and, in the absence of proof of adultery, a child born in wedlock or within nine months of the last possible date for married intercourse is presumed legitimate, although this may still be rebutted by proof of non-access. Rebuttal of the presumption is on a balance of probabilities: s 26, Family Law Reform Act 1969 (FLRA 1969) but the standard of proof in such a case is a heavy one: *Serio v Serio* (1983) 4 FLR 756, *W v K* [1988] 4 FLR 756 (a wife-swapping case).

Example

In *Preston-Jones v Preston-Jones* [1951] AC 391, [1951] 1 All ER 124 – still the classic case on non-access – the wife was of a serious and sober disposition and there was no evidence of any associations or loose behaviour on her part. Adultery was still established, however, as her husband had gone abroad between six and 12 months before the birth. Thus the period of gestation was entirely incredible and adultery was held to be established.

If these alternative methods of proof are unpromising, then there will be no alternative to blood tests or DNA fingerprinting, both of which may be directed, although the court's power is limited to giving a *direction* and they may not *order* a test against the will of the parties to be tested. A person with care of a child must consent on behalf of the child whose blood or genetic sample is required for a test: s 20(1), FLRA 1986. Neither of these tests may be directed to *establish* adultery: *Hodgkiss v Hodgkiss* [1985] Fam Law 87, but only to discover true parentage, where that is in the interests of the child, which it usually is: *S v S* [1972] AC 24, [1972] 3 All ER 107, HL. In that case, Lord Hodson said this was rarely not the case in modern times as there is some psychiatric evidence that children need to know their true origins. If, however, a test is directed to establish parentage and it shows adultery must have been committed, *then* the results may be used to *prove* that adultery. Tests may be *directed* on the application of any party or on the court's own motion, but if the application is contested the direction may only be given by the judge.

Note

Inferences may be drawn if a test is not taken: s 23(1), FLRA 1969. In particular, an applicant for financial relief is likely to have the application dismissed if a test is refused: s 23(2), FLRA 1969 and see *McVeigh v Beattie* [1988] 2 All ER 500 where a man's refusal to take a test was held to be corroboration of the assertion of the woman in an affiliation case that the child was his. However, sometimes there are good grounds for refusing a test, eg *B v B and E* [1969] 3 All ER 1106 where the mother did not raise the question of the child's parentage until he was three years old and the father established that it was reasonable for him to rely on the presumption of legitimacy after such a long period of believing the child was his.

Unfortunately only the DNA fingerprinting test is virtually 100% reliable, blood tests can only exclude (and not identify) any party as a parent of the child. Generally, the result of the latter test, unless a rare blood group is involved, will only indicate whether a person could or could not be a parent of the child, and indicate within what percentage of the population such a person falls as a potential parent.

Note

If adultery cannot be proved, because there has apparently been no sexual intercourse, the non-adulterous association might be sufficient for a behaviour petition presented on the basis of Fact B (see 2.3). This is because it has been accepted by the Court of Appeal that such a relationship may be more destructive of marriage than an act of adultery, since adultery is now seen as a symptom rather than a cause of marriage breakdown: *Wachtel v Wachtel* [1973] 3 WLR 366, [1973] 1 All ER 829, CA.

Proof of the intolerability element of Fact A   2.2.4

The petitioner must also find it intolerable to live with the respondent. The actual act of adultery and the fact that the petitioner finds it intolerable to live with the respondent are construed independently, although it is doubtful if this is what Parliament intended when the Divorce Reform Act 1969 was passed. The matter was raised in *Goodrich v Goodrich* [1971] 1 WLR 1142, [1971] 2 All ER 1340, where it was held that the two requirements were independent of each other, and also that whether it was intolerable for the petitioner to live further with the respondent was a *subjective* test for that particular petitioner. As a result, if the actual adultery alleged is proved and the petitioner states that further cohabitation with the respondent is intolerable, the court has no option but to grant the decree.

The independence of these two elements of Fact A has since been confirmed in *Cleary v Cleary* [1974] 1 WLR 73, [1974] 1 All ER 498, CA, and *Carr v Carr* [1974] 1 WLR 1534, [1974] 1 All ER 1193, CA. In the former case the intolerability sprang from the wife's going out leaving the husband to baby-sit and by corresponding with another man, although neither of these actions was linked to the adultery, and in the latter by the wife's treatment of the children, which similarly had no connection with the adultery.

Note

Adultery only remains a valid basis of petition for divorce for six months after it is discovered by the potential petitioner. Thus, if the parties continue to cohabit after an act of adultery is *discovered*, then after a *total period of six months* of such continued cohabitation a petition will not be possible on the basis of that particular incident of adultery – some renewal of the adulterous association, or some fresh act of adultery with another person will be required: s 2(1). This is designed as a reconciliation provision, so that the parties may attempt to overlook such incidents of adultery, even possibly separating and then resuming cohabitation) following the initial discovery that adultery has been committed. Many couples do this because they are not sure if the marriage is really over.

This ambivalence is *completely irrelevant*, no matter how many times they separate and then change their minds and decide to try again, until there has been six months *actual* cohabitation since the adultery in question was discovered, as periods of *separation* are not counted in the total six months which finally bar a petition under s 2(1).

Remember that it is the *discovery* of the adultery, not the date of its commission, which is relevant to the continued ability to petition, so it is still possible to petition on the basis of an act of adultery which took place many years before, provided discovery was more recent and the s 2(1) bar does not apply.

2.3 Behaviour: Fact B

The requirement to establish this Fact is that the respondent has behaved in such a way that the petitioner cannot reasonably be expected to live with the respondent: s 1(2)(b).

There is no finite list of conduct which does or does not constitute sufficient 'behaviour' for this Fact, so that it is a less straightforward Fact to use than that of adultery. On the other hand, behaviour does provide an opportunity for an immediate divorce on the basis of the petitioner's complaints against the respondent. Indeed, given that the marriage will have broken up for some reason or reasons which have given the petitioner (and possibly the respondent also) cause for dissatisfaction with it, and given that there is such a low incidence of defended divorces, it may still be possible to obtain a divorce on the basis of quite slight behaviour, provided the allegations are not too trivial for the court to allow and provided the respondent does not defend. It is not therefore surprising that behaviour and adultery usually between them account for the largest number of decrees.

Note

If you suspect that a petition might be defended, greater care will need to be taken in advising a client to petition on Fact B than if it is likely to go undefended: see below 2.3.1, 2.3.4, 2.7 and 4.4.12.

You will need to acquire a good grasp of what is and what is not behaviour within the meaning of s 1(2)(b), gain a working knowledge of the main groupings of behaviour where case law has established that such behaviour qualifies, and also appreciate the role of intention in such qualifying behaviour, as it is now established that behaviour for Fact B does not have to be either deliberate or positive. In practice, it is very unlikely that cases you encounter will be on all fours with those which have appeared in the law reports: it is therefore essential for you to be able to distinguish between what is worth pleading in a petition and what is really too feeble an allegation to succeed, especially if the petition is defended, and also to hone your drafting skills to make the most of such material as is available for the petition. Provided the suit is undefended, good drafting can obtain a decree on the basis of initially quite unpromising material, as consultation of a good collection of precedents will indicate!

The test for behaviour

2.3.1

The test by which the court will decide whether any conduct is or is not behaviour is a hybrid one, partly subjective and partly objective.

Remember that the Fact is not one of 'unreasonable behaviour' – and it is incorrect to speak of Fact B in this way – because, as the Court of Appeal stated in *Bannister v Bannister* (1980) 10 Fam Law 240, CA, the behaviour contemplated by the working of the section is significantly different from 'behaving unreasonably'. In *Carew-Hunt v Carew-Hunt* (1972) *Times* 28 June, Ormrod J confirmed this view and added that it was not up to the court to pass moral judgments and to say whether a person's behaviour was 'right or wrong, good or bad'.

The proper test for this Fact is generally regarded as that stated in *Buffery v Buffery* (1980), namely (to paraphrase the judgment):

Can this petitioner (looking at the petitioner's own behaviour) be expected to live with this respondent (looking at the respondent's behaviour) taking into account the kind of people they are and also whether there has been any provocation, deliberate or otherwise, eg through antisocial conduct or even illness.

This test builds on the much earlier judgment of Bagnall J in *Ash v Ash* [1972] 2 WLR 347, [1972] 1 All ER 582, a case of violence and alcoholism, where the judge suggested that like can always be expected to live with like, eg the violent/alcoholic/sport addicted petitioner with the like respondent, so the situation where each party is as bad as the other might result in neither being able to obtain a divorce as, logically, there ought to be some disparity in the parties' conduct.

However, in practice this situation does not arise because most petitions are not defended and the court will not know that the petitioner's behaviour is just as bad as that complained of in the respondent. If the allegations are *objectively* of the type that a petitioner might reasonably complain of, a decree will be granted.

Dunn J put this in a nutshell in *Livingstone-Stallard v Livingstone-Stallard* [1974] 3 WLR 302, [1974] 2 All ER 776 when he suggested a 'jury approach', ie 'what would the right thinking man conclude' about the behaviour complained of. The case also established that although the behaviour relied on should not be absolutely trivial overall, a weight of trivia taken together may be sufficient.

Example

In *Livingstone-Stallard* the husband, a much older man, had basically nagged, bullied, criticised and irritated his younger, rather nervous, wife to the point where she lacked all confidence and could no longer stand living with him, and her petition succeeded.

O'Neill v O'Neill [1975] 1 WLR 118, [1975] 3 All ER 289 affirmed this approach and also stressed that no other extraneous concepts should be imported into the test, such as that the behaviour should be 'grave and weighty' (as it used to have to be under the pre-1969 law, which involved the completely different concept of cruelty).

The modern approach, therefore, is primarily concerned with assessing any conduct which is not utterly trivial and in looking at that conduct objectively in the light of its effects on the particular petitioner (thereby importing the subjective element of the hybrid test). A good recent example of this approach is *Birch v Birch* [1992] 1 FLR 564, where the petitioner insisted that the behaviour complained of affected her particularly badly and her assertion was accepted.

The role of intention

From these developments you can see that intention has progressively assumed a more minor role. In the early 70s there was a discernible backward-looking tendency in decisions which adhered to the philosophy of the old entirely fault-based law and which seemed to insist that intention must play a major part in any 'behaviour'. However, when *Katz v Katz* [1972] 1 WLR 955, [1972] 3 All ER 219 and *Thurlow v Thurlow* [1975] 3 WLR 161, [1975] 3 All ER 979 came before the court, the approach changed significantly. Previously, it seemed that the court had always been influenced by the concept of marriage being 'for better for worse, for richer for poorer, in sickness and in health' – particularly in sickness and in health – so that obtaining a decree based on the respondent's involuntary behaviour due to mental and/or physical illness was problematic.

Then, *Katz* established that mental illness of even a relatively minor sort could be sufficient to obtain a decree if after making full allowances for the respondent's disabilities, the temperament of both parties and the obligations of marriage, the type and seriousness of the behaviour was such that the petitioner should not really be called upon to endure it.

Thurlow however, was really the watershed in establishing a sufficient degree of mental or physical illness combined, in that case, with a depressing degree of deterioration, as 'behaviour' within the terms of Fact B. In particular, *Thurlow* established that such 'behaviour' was nevertheless acceptable for Fact B despite its being *involuntary*, and despite the ordinary connotation of the word 'behaviour' suggesting something positive and active, rather than unavoidable and passive. The judge decided that it was for the court to say in each case whether despite the obligations of marriage the petitioner could be called upon to withstand the stress imposed by the respondent's condition, in particular considering the length of time the condition had existed and the effect on the petitioner's health.

Some types of Fact B behaviour

Each case turns on its own facts but it is helpful to look at cases where sufficient behaviour has been found to establish the fact.

* violence, physical and verbal, including false accusations (especially if combined with alcoholism);

- insensitivity;
- lack of communication;
- excessive unsociability;
- general neglect;
- bullying;
- constant criticism;
- financial irresponsibility;
- excessive financial restrictions;
- obsessive DIY.

Note

The above classes of generally unpleasant behaviour may be expected to recur with some regularity and if a potential petitioner's initial statement does not disclose enough material to petition (since clients are sometimes extraordinarily reticent in providing detail, though others will give a blow-by-blow account) it is worth checking whether any of the less obvious ones apply.

The following effects on the petitioner are unlikely to qualify, unless they can be firmly linked to a cause in the respondent's behaviour, though they might be sufficient if *injury to health* results and if the incidents relied on are carefully pleaded to link them to some identifiable fault on the respondent's part:

- emotional dissatisfaction (but is there *neglect*? *insensitivity*? *selfishness*?);
- sexual dissatisfaction (but is this neglect or caused by the *respondent's serious illness*?);
- desertion (but is it *neglect*? or the respondent *not appreciating the commitment of marriage*?);
- boredom or growing apart (but is it *insensitivity*? *inability to communicate*? *general neglect*?).

It is essential in these latter cases to be able to show that the respondent has breached some marital obligation, even if that is only the mutual enjoyment of each other's company socially, and the affection and moral support which one spouse is entitled to expect from the other.

Violence

Where there is actual physical violence it is best if the petitioner has reported the matter to the doctor or police. Not doing so will not necessarily lead to the conclusion that such violence has been tolerated but evidential problems might arise: *Bergin v Bergin* [1983] 1 All ER 905. Any psychological violence, such as what used to be referred to as mental cruelty, should also, if possible, be substantiated by medical or psychiatric evidence.

Insensitivity, lack of communication, excessive unsociability or general neglect

If any one of these is alleged it is essential that some conduct can be imported to the respondent and tied to incidents which can be given as examples.

Example

In *Buffery* this did not succeed as the parties had really each gone their own ways and neither was more to blame than the other. However, in *Bannister* the petition was successful because it could be said that the husband never took the wife out and never told her where he was when he went out himself, sometimes at night, and indeed never spoke to her if he could avoid it! Good detail obtained in interviewing the client and good drafting to present a picture of unacceptable behaviour can overcome this problem.

Bullying or constant criticism

Bullying or constant criticism which fall short of violence, or strong verbal abuse which might otherwise appear to be trivial, will also need to be carefully particularised to show an overall picture which is unacceptable. In *Livingstone-Stallard*, for example, the incidents individually were insufficient but together presented such a horrible picture of life in the Livingstone-Stallard household that the court had no difficulty in drawing the right conclusion.

Financial irresponsibility or excessive financial restriction

This is established Fact B behaviour, especially where it adversely affects the family and causes stress: *Carter-Fea v Carter-Fea* [1987] Fam Law 131, and this might also be 'conduct' within the meaning of s 25(2)(g) which would reduce the respondent's entitlement in subsequent ancillary relief proceedings (see 7.2.9 below), especially if it has had the effect of dissipating the family assets.

Similarly, excessive financial restriction will usually be behaviour but will need to be carefully pleaded with some concrete examples since the wives' cry of 'not enough money' is often seen as a classic 'sitcom' joke, and if a wife has managed to live frugally despite the husband's parsimony this may have repercussions in establishing what she needs for the purposes of ancillary relief.

Obsessive DIY

The classic case on obsessive DIY is *O'Neill v O'Neill* (1975), where the court at first hesitated to decide that two years of 'home improvement' was not something that the wife and daughter should have been called upon to endure – although this was a particularly bad instance of living in discomfort for the sake of financial gain, since it included mixing cement on the living room floor and leaving the lavatory door off for eight months (which particularly embarrassed the teenage daughter). At first instance, the petition was unsuccessful as the incidents complained of were said to be no more than the ordinary wear and tear of married life undertaken for the benefit of the family as a whole, but the Court of Appeal eventually accepted that the situation went beyond such a mundane description and did not require such stoic endurance! However, it may be that what really tipped the balance was that in addition to making life so physically uncomfortable, the husband also cast doubt on the paternity of the children of the family. (In the absence of some evidence this is never regarded as good matrimonial conduct and would also qualify as bullying or verbal abuse.)

Emotional dissatisfaction

This has not done well in Fact B case law to date, the leading case being *Pheasant v Pheasant* [1972] 2 WLR 353, [1972] 1 All ER 587, but this was probably because the wife in that case had done absolutely nothing wrong in matrimonial terms, and to say the least the husband was a little strange, as he claimed that he needed an excessive amount of demonstrative affection due to his particular nature and personality, and that his wife had failed to provide it.

In the circumstances, it can probably be safely said that in the ordinary case, if a petitioner were able to show emotional dissatisfaction linked to some aspect of the respondent's conduct which could be said to breach a matrimonial obligation, while the petitioner remained a committed, if perhaps less than sparkling, spouse, then there is no reason why emotional dissatisfaction (which is, after all, the usual reason for marriages breaking up) should not be a basis for a successful petition. However, such emotional dissatisfaction should be *evidenced* by the normal 'distress' which every well drafted behaviour petition alleges the petitioner suffers as a result of the respondent's unacceptable behaviour.

Note

In cases of emotional dissatisfaction, you must look for instances of insensitivity, selfishness, and general lack of the mutual consideration which in any civilised relationship one spouse is entitled to expect from the other.

Sexual dissatisfaction

Although not found sufficient in *Dowden v Dowden* (1977) 8 Fam Law 106, sexual dissatisfaction is probably in a similar category to emotional dissatisfaction. In *Dowden* the wife's petition was unsuccessful, despite her claims of frustration and tension as a result of the husband's lack of interest in sex. However, in view of the decisions in *Katz* and *Thurlow*, had the petition alleged some disorder on the part of the husband which had caused the conduct complained of, as well as emphasising the effect on the petitioner, it is difficult to see how, in the light of the now established proper test for Fact B behaviour, the petition could have failed.

Desertion

It goes without saying that ordinary cases of desertion are not behaviour and should therefore be pleaded as Fact C and not Fact B: *Stringfellow v Stringfellow* [1976] 1 WLR 645, [1976] 2 All ER 539 where the parties' falling out and going their separate ways were said to be only the steps preparatory to separation rather than what is normally understood by the word 'behaviour' which suggests some actual positive conduct. Again this might be a little harsh in the light of the modern test for behaviour, since if the parties grow apart from each other, go their separate ways and in the process are *inconsiderate, insensitive, neglectful* and *boorish* there is logically no distinction where that happens immediately prior to separation than if it happened years before – parties in this situation want a divorce, and provided the petition is properly pleaded and not defended it should succeed. What is essential is to *avoid pleading* the actual finite incident of *desertion*, where the respondent leaves and does not return to the matrimonial home, as an instance of *behaviour*. If previous instances are pleaded of being constantly away from home, eg staying out late, not telling the petitioner of the respondent's whereabouts, apparent lack of appreciation of the nature of marriage and commitment to it and so on, there should be no problem.

Boredom and growing apart

Where these are relied upon, again you should avoid confusion with simple desertion by detailing enough incidents prior to the actual departure to make it clear that the petitioner has some actual behaviour to object to irrespective of desertion, which will usually have not yet qualified for Fact C by not having lasted for two years: see 2.4. Such a case where the pleading was probably to blame was *Morgan v Morgan* (1973) 117 SJ 223.

Note

1 The same reconciliation provisions as for adultery apply to behaviour, save that by s 2(3) if the parties live together for more than six months after the last incident of behaviour relied upon it will not *automatically* constitute a bar to obtaining a decree based on that behaviour, but the period of cohabitation will be *taken into account* by the court in deciding whether or not it is reasonable for the petitioner to be obliged to live with the respondent, given that the behaviour in question will have been tolerated for at least the six months of the cohabitation. In any case, *any* cohabitation will be disregarded if the petitioner has no where else to go as in *Bradley v Bradley* [1973] 1 WLR 1291, [1973] 3 All ER 750 where the wife could not get rehoused until after decree.

2 The cohabitation bar applies even after decree nisi and the decree will not usually be made absolute if the parties are still living together when it is applied for.

3 If the parties have cohabited briefly and then separated again between the two decrees, usually this will not affect decree absolute. Very often, the cohabitation is irrelevant anyway, since much 'behaviour', such as selfishness, insensitivity, verbal abuse, financial irresponsibility etc, is of a continuing nature.

Example

1 In *Savage v Savage* [1982] 3 WLR 418, [1982] 3 All ER 49 the court refused to make the decree absolute because the parties resumed cohabitation three months after decree nisi and were still living together three and a half years later.

2 In *Court v Court* [1982] 3 WLR 199, [1982] 2 All ER 531, however, the court took the point that it had already been held at decree nisi stage that it was unreasonable for the petitioner to have to live with the respondent, so the fact that the parties had resumed cohabitation and then separated again if anything underlined this finding; thus the subsequent delay and cohabitation did not change the situation.

2.3.4   Drafting behaviour particulars

It is obvious from the above account that good drafting is essential to the uncomplicated success of a behaviour petition. This is the more so because of the nature of the 'Special Procedure' (see Chapter 5, para 5.10) by which, contrary to the suggestion in the name, most divorces are now processed entirely on paper without an oral hearing of any kind. Thus, if the particulars of behaviour pleaded in the petition give the court any cause for wondering whether the ground and the fact have been made out, queries will arise and delay will be inevitable. If this does happen, it is nearly always possible to get the suit back on track, either by amending or by supplying further evidence, but this will mean that additional costs will be incurred.

In theory, while you are a trainee, mistakes of this kind will be picked up by the principal responsible for supervising your work, but even this is not good for your image so a simple well-tried formula should be followed for behaviour drafting which should automatically result in errors being avoided and possibly even in a good drafting habit which should remain with you throughout your career.

It is generally agreed that behaviour particulars should not follow the form of Booker Prize literature, still less the purple prose of the indignant old fashioned advocate. Instead, they should be factual, *unemotional* and, as far as possible, *precise*.

This is, in fact, the spirit of the SFLA approach but the style and format of such drafting in behaviour petitions has an earlier origin. In the opinion of the late distinguished family judge Sir Roger Ormrod, if neither party had committed adultery (the easiest Fact to use for an immediate divorce desired by both parties), what he called 'the mild behaviour petition' was the next best choice. What he meant by this was that the petition should both show the *minimum safe level for the grant of a decree under Fact B* (in other words it had to meet what is now the *Buffery* test) and at the same time not be *unnecessarily offensive* to the respondent.

In making this suggestion, Ormrod, who was an early champion of civilised divorce suits, thought first of the desirability of not making it impossible for the parties ever to speak to each other again (as was often the case under the pre-1969 law and obviously a consideration where the existence of children mean there must be ongoing parenting) and only second of the benefit to divorce procedure if behaviour particulars are kept within a sensible framework.

The original Ormrod suggestion was that behaviour particulars should ideally be limited to about three incidents. These he categorised as 'the first, the worst and the last'. The phrase has subsequently often been expanded by practitioners to the 'first, worst, last and witnessed' and it is generally accepted that the most extensive particulars should not detail more than about six incidents; more and the court may think that the petitioner's case must be somewhat weak if so many incidents have to be relied on. In any event dates, times, places and any other details should be as specific as possible. Thus, a good precis may be necessary in some cases, particularly where the marriage has been long and the parties have apparently soldiered on against the odds for some time.

For further drafting advice see Chapter 4.

2.4   Desertion and constructive desertion: Fact C

To establish this Fact the respondent must have deserted the petitioner for a continuous period of at least two years immediately preceding the presentation of the petition: s 1(2)(c).

You need to know about this Fact since it remains a possibility along with the other Facts in s 1(2) as the basis for proving that a marriage has irretrievably broken down. However, unless the case is extremely clear cut and definitely will not be defended, it is rarely used by practitioners because of its technical requirements. Moreover, a respondent who has deserted a petitioner for two years as required for Fact C is unlikely to resist a request to consent to a divorce on the basis of Fact D, ie the same two years separation plus the respondent's consent to the decree: see 2.5.

In theory, 'desertion' under Fact C can take two forms, either simple desertion, where the petitioner is left by the respondent without just cause and without the petitioner's consent, or 'constructive desertion', where it is actually the petitioner who leaves the respondent, but there is just cause for the petitioner's departure. However, 'constructive desertion' is even more rarely used in practice as a basis for divorce than actual desertion itself and there have been very few reported cases since the early 70s. This is because any petitioner who can show constructive desertion can also show behaviour under Fact B and, in fact, more easily so since, apart from being able to present such a petition immediately without waiting for two years to accrue, the test for behaviour (see 2.3.1) is much easier to satisfy than that for constructive desertion. For constructive desertion the standard of conduct must be 'grave and weighty' which, as was expressly stated in *O'Neill v O'Neill* (1975), is not necessary for a successful behaviour petition. The reason for this is precisely because desertion increasingly fell out of use following the introduction of Facts B and D in the Divorce Reform Act 1969 and thus, unlike behaviour which also used to be interpreted as needing to be 'grave and weighty', missed being modernised by developing case law.

The four elements of desertion   **2.4.1**

The following must be separately established:
- actual separation;
- intention to desert by the respondent;
- lack of consent to the separation by the petitioner;
- that the separation is without just cause.

Actual separation   **2.4.2**

This is often clear because one party has left the other and gone to live elsewhere. Sometimes it is less clear because there is coming and going, or the parties consider they are separated but they live at the same address.

Establishing that actual separation has occurred is important not only for desertion but also for Facts D and E (see 2.5. and 2.6) especially where the parties are still living in the same house. The principles are the same for Facts C, D and E, namely that it is essential that the parties, even if living at the same address, are in truth living in separate 'households' (more in the style of flat-sharers living independent lives rather than in a cohabitational sense as husband and wife). A distinction is drawn between one 'unhappy' household, where there may be little contact, and two separate households where the parties are usually only still occupying the same premises because there is no alternative. Thus, desertion may be available in situations where at first sight it appears not to be.

Example

In *Naylor v Naylor* [1961] 2 WLR 751, [1961] 2 All ER 129 the wife removed her wedding ring and decided never to perform any domestic services for the husband again, while he in turn gave her no housekeeping money. They shared no family or communal life and the wife was held to be in desertion.

Naylor is the basic situation which will suffice for separation to be established where the parties are still living under one roof. Other cases fall one side or the other of the shared life marker and accordingly either amount to sufficient separation or not.

Basically, the fatal flaws to check for in an alleged separation under the same roof are:

- *Mending, washing or cooking done by the wife* specifically for the husband: see *Le Brocq v Le Brocq* [1964] 2 All ER 464 where the parties had separate bedrooms and sexual intercourse had ceased as the wife bolted the husband out of her bedroom, they did not speak to each other and communicated by note only when essential, but where the wife did carry on cooking her husband's meals – which proved fatal to her claim of having separated from him.

Note

A wife who *returns* to domestic tasks which she has abandoned will bring her separation to an end even if she refuses to resume sexual intercourse: *Bull v Bull* [1953] 2 All ER 601.

- *Shared cleaning*, as in *Mouncer v Mouncer* [1972] 2 All ER 65 where the parties were held *not* to be separated because they shared the general housework despite the fact that the wife did no laundry for the husband, the parties were on bad terms and had separate bedrooms.
- *Communal life*, especially eating meals with the family: see *Hopes v Hopes* [1948] 2 All ER 920, where no domestic services (as in *Le Brocq*) complicated the issue, and there was no shared bedroom or sexual intercourse, but where there was a certain amount of communal life, including eating meals with the family in the dining room and sharing the remainder of the house. The separation was held to be insufficient, as Lord Denning said, because there were not *two separate households* but *one unhappy* household in which there was chronic discord and gross neglect.

Note

One aspect of the shared (albeit inharmonious) life which convinced the court that the parties were not separated in *Mouncer v Mouncer* was that while the husband had no desire to remain in the house, he in fact did so in order to help look after the children. This case was, of course, decided long before the Children Act 1989 put into statutory form an expectation that parents would remain good parents in the interests of the children. As there clearly was only one unhappy household and not two separate ones in *Mouncer*, it is unlikely that the case would now be decided differently merely because of the more recent concept of parental responsibility. However, if a party does engage in a certain amount of communal life in the interests of the children, it may be that if the parents are otherwise living discernably separate lives under the same roof, helping to look after the children would *not* be fatal to establishing separation, especially if the parties have nowhere else for the children to spend time with the parent in respect of whom a separate life is claimed.

This must be especially so in view of the fact that in some cases separation has been recognised where the petitioner had nowhere else to go, as in *Bartram v Bartram*, [1949] 2 All ER 270, where the parties had separated, but were forced to resume living under the same roof, even sleeping in the same bed and eating at the same table, without sharing any common household tasks (although it is fair to say that Mrs Bartram made her feelings clear by treating her husband like a lodger whom she cordially disliked!).

Advice to clients petitioning in these circumstances must be that *scrupulous* care must be taken to show separation under the same roof save for occasions for the specific benefit of contact of the other parent with the children.

Bona fide residence in the home as a lodger will always qualify as separation.

Example

In *Fuller v Fuller* [1973] 2 All ER 650, the parties separated in the normal way, the wife leaving the husband for another man and taking the children with her. When subsequently the husband went to live with them as a lodger (he had been told that he had a terminal illness and only a year to live during which he should not be alone), the separation was held to have continued, even though he shared the entire life of the household, having all his meals with them and his laundry done by the wife, as this was in his capacity as a lodger. (In the event, he turned out not to be terminally ill after all, which was presumably why the decree was ultimately necessary!)

Intention to desert by the respondent   2.4.3

The intention to desert permanently is called the *animus deserendi*. It can be formed when the parties are already apart without having originally parted with the requisite intention, and can continue even if the respondent gets into a situation where the intention could not be demonstrably revoked, eg where the respondent is sent to prison.

Example

The first point was demonstrated in *Beeken v Beeken* [1948] P 302, where the parties were prisoners of war. The wife started an affair with another man and ceased sexual intercourse with the husband who knew of the association. When she was moved to another camp and told the husband she had decided never to return to him she was held to be in desertion.

The latter point was demonstrated in *Drew v Drew* (1838) 13 PD 97, where the husband had deserted his wife and was then arrested and sent to prison, and where it was held that he would not have returned to her even if he had been free to do so.

Clearly, a person who is insane cannot be in desertion as the *animus deserendi* cannot be formed: *Crowther v Crowther* [1951] 1 All ER 1131, and whether an insane person who formed the intention before becoming insane will remain in desertion depends on what evidence there is that the intention would have been sustained if insanity had not supervened.

Note

This is just one example of the technicalities of desertion which encourages practitioners to keep away from Fact D unless there is no alternative.

2.4.4   Lack of consent to the separation by the petitioner

There are two elements of this lack of consent:
- no agreement to the respondent's leaving;
- no refusal of a reasonable offer to return.

No agreement to the respondent's leaving

This first element is not as straightforward as it looks at first sight. Clearly there must be no *express* agreement, but there must also be no indirect agreement. This therefore precludes:
- a decree of judicial separation because this will end the duty to cohabit and desertion will therefore be impossible;
- a deed of separation for the same reason, though

not a maintenance agreement which does not contain a clause that the parties expressly agree to live apart: *Crabtree v Crabtree* [1953] 1 WLR 708, [1953] 2 All ER 56;

Note

Where there is a deed of separation precluding or ending desertion, this can be cured by repudiating the agreement. This can have unintended results. In *Pardy v Pardy* [1939] 3 All ER 779, for example, the parties had separated by agreement due to the husband's drinking. When the husband stopped paying maintenance under the clause requiring him to do so, the wife tried to effect a reconciliation, but the husband refused. This had the effect of him repudiating the agreement, so *he* was then, quite unintentionally, in desertion.

• any conduct implying consent to separation, eg changing the locks on the matrimonial home, as this would stop the respondent returning, or obtaining a Jewish religious divorce which, although not valid to dissolve the English civil marriage, indicates that the party obtaining it does not want the other spouse back: *Joseph v Joseph* [1953] 2 All ER 710. An exclusion order obtained against a violent spouse does not, however, terminate desertion: s 4(4).

Note

It does not matter that the petitioner is relieved at the respondent's departure, or even helps with the packing, provided it is not actually encouraged in any way: *Pizey v Pizey* [1961] 2 All ER 658. However, the petitioner must not do anything which suggests regarding the marriage as over until the two years are up, eg there must be no celebration of the respondent's departure by starting up an adulterous relationship with a third party, as the essence of desertion is that the petitioner is complaining of breach of a matrimonial obligation to cohabit and so must in theory expect the respondent back any time during the ensuing two years. Entering into a new relationship (unless it were not adulterous – which would not be much fun in the circumstances!) would end the respondent's desertion by providing just cause for staying away. (See 2.4.5.)

Agreement to the respondent's leaving, initially given for good reason, may be revoked if that good reason no longer applies and then the absent party will be in desertion.

Example

In *Nutley v Nutley* [1970] 1 WLR 217, [1970] 1 All ER 410, the husband consented to his wife living with her parents so she could look after them, but when she refused to return on their death she was in desertion. However, she was only in desertion from their deaths when she told him she was not returning as, although she had formed the intention earlier she had not communicated it, so he had had no chance to revoke his consent.

Desertion can also be ended by implied consent to separation deduced from conduct.

Example

In *France v France* [1969] 2 All ER 870 the parties separated, the wife having constructively deserted the husband by falling in love with another man and asking the husband to leave the home. Later, the husband fell into the habit of visiting her and having sexual intercourse with her, although they did not resume cohabitation. This was held to end any desertion since the separation had thereby become subject to their agreement that the husband could come and go as he pleased.

Such sexual intercourse will not always end desertion however, if, as in the case of *Mummery v Mummery* [1942] 1 All ER 533, it does not establish a regular course of conduct.

No refusal of a reasonable offer to return

This second element is quite straightforward. Basically, it must be a *bona fide offer of reconciliation on a proper cohabitational basis* with no unreasonable conditions attached. It will not do, for example, that the offer is subject to the condition that the wife should merely return in the capacity of a housekeeper as in *Slawson v Slawson* [1942] 2 All ER 527, or that the wife should agree to join a commune run by the Tramp Preachers Movement as in *Fletcher v Fletcher* [1945] 1 All ER 382.

The offer must also be sincere: see *Everitt v Everitt* [1949] 1 All ER 903, where the wife did not believe in the husband's offer as she believed he was still committing adultery with the women for whom he had left her. However, if it is apparently a sincere offer, and it is turned down for the petitioner's own reasons, the petitioner can then be in desertion even if it turns out that the offer might in fact have been insincere: see *Day v Day* [1957] 1 All ER 848, where the husband had been committing adultery but the wife did not give this as her reason for rejecting his offer to return, and was held then to be in desertion herself.

That the separation is without cause   2.4.5

As have already explained in relation to the alternative of constructive desertion, to establish a case of desertion under Fact B the separation must be without just cause on the part of the respondent. This means that while constructive desertion may not now actually be pleaded by the party who left, since if a divorce is desired Fact B would be more appropriate, if the conduct of a petitioner has not been above reproach the respondent will have a defence and desertion will not therefore be made out. However, a respondent may not actually make use of such a defence because in practice divorces are not normally now defended by parties who wish to obtain a decree since there is no longer any stigma to being divorced on whatever basis, and the decree will usually have no effect whatever on the outcome of future proceedings for ancillary relief (see Chapter 7) or in proceedings under the Children Act 1989 in respect of child matters (see Chapter 6).

Note

A separation that starts out as being without just cause when the potential respondent leaves may become one for which there is just cause if the potential petitioner then does something to give the respondent a good excuse to stay away, eg commits adultery. This is fatal as it brings the desertion to an end.

There is a good deal of case law on what is and what is not just cause for leaving (another good reason for avoiding Fact C). All the usual reasons which would suffice for Fact B will probably be just cause for leaving and therefore both constitute a defence to a desertion petition and also enable a petitioner who has left to establish a case of constructive desertion if serious enough.

Example

- keeping 30 dirty cats so that the house is uninhabitable: *Winans v Winans* [1948] 2 All ER 862;

- being overbearing, dictatorial and violent: *Timmins v Timmins* [1953] 2 All ER 187;

- being lazy and slovenly to the extent of driving out a moderately civilised spouse: *Gollins v Gollins* [1963] 2 All ER 966;

(Although all the above cases were fought hard at the time they were decided.)

- contracting a second polygamous marriage even where the first wife was also a Moslem – here the decision was also logical because the parties were westernised and the first wife had expressly requested that this not be done: *Quoreshi v Quoreshi* [1985] FLR 760 (one of the few modern cases of constructive desertion).

However, problem areas still remain. It was, for example, held in *Buchler v Buchler* [1947] 1 All ER 319 that a wife who left her husband, who had formed a strange relationship which fell short of homosexuality with one of his farm hands, did not have just cause for leaving (and therefore she was in constructive desertion) although she was upset by it, embarrassed by local gossip and felt 'left out' and starved of affection. This is an old case which might have been decided differently today, but in any event she could now have easily obtained a Fact B decree on the basis of such allegations, *Wachtel* having in any case now established that non-adulterous relationships can be more hurtful than adultery itself.

Similarly, there is some dispute as to whether refusal of sexual intercourse is just cause for leaving. In *Weatherly v Weatherly* [1947] 1 All ER 563 the wife was held not to be in desertion for such refusal, but in *Hutchinson v Hutchinson* [1963] 1 All ER 1 it was held that a wife could leave a husband who refused to have sexual intercourse. Despite the decision in the behaviour case of *Dowden* (see 2.3.1) it is probably the case that refusal of sexual intercourse if coupled with other insensitive and non-communicative behaviour is now sufficient for Fact B, a further reason, if refusal of sexual intercourse must be relied upon, for avoiding desertion and choosing behaviour.

Insane delusions will not always be just cause for leaving, as in *Kacmarcz v Kacmarcz* [1967] 1 WLR 317, [1967] 1 All ER 416, where the wife believed her husband was committing a grave sin by having sexual intercourse with her, though in *Perry v Perry* [1963] 3 All ER 766 the wife's delusion was that the husband was trying to murder her, which enabled the court to decide that she was not in desertion herself since she should be judged as if her delusion were true. If delusions are not insane, but based on flimsy and unreasonable grounds, then usually there will not be just cause for leaving and such petitioners will be in constructive desertion themselves, see *Marsden v Marsden* [1967] 1 All ER 967 where the husband deluded himself into believing, on no serious basis, that the wife was committing adultery so he was not only unable to petition successfully, but also put himself into constructive desertion.

Note

Although a spouse must not normally lock out a deserting spouse or desertion will be brought to an end, and also the spouse who excludes the other will be in desertion instead, it is permissible to exclude a spouse whose conduct is frightening to the other party and/or children of the family without that spouse being in desertion as such behaviour will constitute just cause for leaving (and therefore the locking out): see *G v G* [1964] 1 All ER 129, where the husband was mentally ill and the wife waited for him to go away on a journey before taking her opportunity to change the locks!

It goes without saying that any conduct which is said to be just cause for leaving must actually have acted upon the mind of the spouse when deciding to leave: see *Herod v Herod* [1938] 3 All ER 722 where the husband had actually committed adultery, but the wife did not know and so was uninfluenced by it, thus herself being in desertion when she decided to leave.

Note

1 The two-year period relied on for Fact C must immediately precede the presentation of the petition (or cross-petition if desertion is alleged in the Answer), although if a decree of judicial separation has already been obtained on the basis of an existing period of two years and the parties have not resumed cohabitation, that period can be relied on as if it had immediately preceded the presentation of the petition: s 4(1).

2 There are similar reconciliation provisions to those in connection with Fact A, in that the parties may live together for a period or periods totalling less than six months and no account will be taken of any periods of cohabitation in calculating the necessary two-year period to found desertion under this fact.

Problems in relation to the location of the matrimonial home   2.4.6

There are sometimes problems in relation to where the matrimonial home should be regarded as being located and as to who has the right to decide that point. Basically this is usually a point for behaviour under Fact B rather than a desertion matter and should probably be dealt with as an instance of lack of commitment to the marriage, both for simplicity and for all the reasons that Fact B is preferable to rely on in comparison with Fact C.

First, desertion is withdrawal from a state of affairs and not from a place. Thus, there may be desertion even though there is currently no matrimonial home and even where there has never been a matrimonial home, as in the case of members of the Armed Forces. In *Milligan v Milligan* [1941] 2 All ER 62, for example, the husband, who had lived with his wife in a series of hotels and in rented accommodation was held to be in desertion as soon as he left her to live alone in the officers' mess and refused to return to her. This situation can also apply to domestic servants who live in their employers' homes, as in *Bradshaw v Bradshaw* [1897] P 24 where the parties visited each other at the husband's employer, and they even had children together; however, the husband was in desertion as soon as he refused any longer to have her to visit or to maintain the children.

Alternatively, where there is supposed to be a matrimonial home, problems sometimes arise because the parties cannot agree where that should be, so if the impasse persists it is difficult to decide who has deserted whom. Even prior to the modern practice of presuming equality between the sexes and of regarding marriage as a partnership of equals, it was not necessarily the husband who had the right to dictate the location of the matrimonial home even if he was the breadwinner. There may be other reasons why the choice of residence may realistically only be the wife's.

Example

In *Dunn v Dunn* [1918] 2 All ER 822, the wife was acutely deaf and very shy and did not want to move from the place where the parties had first set up home when the husband's posting in the Navy required him to live elsewhere. Due to her reasonable cause for refusing to move, the wife was held not to be in desertion, whereas the husband was as he had unreasonably refused to agree to the location of the matrimonial home.

This is clearly the sort of situation which while technically possibly desertion is more amenable to Fact B than Fact C and should be treated accordingly.

Two years' separation with consent of the respondent to the decree: Fact D

The requirement to establish this fact is that the parties have lived apart for a continuous period of at least two years immediately preceding the presentation of the petition and the respondent consents to a decree being granted: s 1(2)(d).

Living apart

The principles used to decide in desertion cases whether the parties when living at one address are living in one household or two (see 2.4.2) also apply to cases under Fact D, save that the statute provides that the parties are to be treated as living apart unless they are living with each other in the same household: s 2(6).

Fact D requires living apart plus recognition that the marriage is at an end and when the parties are already living apart when that decision is taken some evidence of the changed status of the marriage will be required.

Example

In *Santos v Santos* [1972] 2 All ER 246, the husband lived in Spain and the wife in England, although they visited each other. It was held that a mental element was required to indicate the changed circumstances of the separation, that the two years could only start when one party recognised that the marriage was over, but that once that had been done there was no need actually to communicate the decision.

However, it will be necessary if the decision is unilateral for the petitioner to pinpoint the moment when he or she decided the marriage was over and for there to be some evidence of that. In practice, this means no more than that the petitioner is able to say in the affidavit in support of the petition both when the decision was made and when the separation began if, as is usually the case, that was at a different time.

Sometimes there is actual evidence of a positive step, eg one party writing a letter, or at least a change in the pattern of behaviour, eg discontinuing visiting a spouse who is in prison or in hospital or elsewhere away from home, a cessation of communication with a spouse working overseas, or setting up home with a third party.

Consent of the respondent to the decree

Positive consent is required and *not* mere failure to object.

Example

In *McGill v Robson* [1972] 1 All ER 362 the husband was living in South Africa and the wife's solicitors in serving the papers somehow managed not to send him a form of acknowledgment of service for him to consent to the decree. He nevertheless acknowledged service and wrote saying that he wanted the proceedings completed as soon as possible – but in the absence of a specific written consent no decree could be granted.

One drawback of using Fact D instead of risking the complications of Fact C is that, as consent must be positive – and the suit simply cannot proceed under Fact D without it – the respondent can exact conditions in return for the essential consent. The common condition is that the respondent will pay no costs as in *Beales v Beales* [1972] 2 WLR 972, [1972] 2 All ER 667, but as it is now usual in Fact D cases for each party to pay their own costs this is not of far-reaching importance.

A more tedious condition can be that the respondent wants to exact a sharp deal on ancillary relief but in general, if both parties want a divorce and the respondent sees that one will not be obtainable without some sort of suitable ancillary relief package, consent will usually be forthcoming. If the marriage has broken up anyway, the alternative might be to risk a petition being served on a fault based Fact, such as behaviour. As allegations need not be profoundly shocking for such a petition, it would usually not be possible or desirable to defend such a petition successfully. However, costs, unlike in Fact D cases, might legitimately be asked for, especially if the respondent has refused to consent to a Fact D decree. In these circumstances your best course is to suggest that all outstanding matters are agreed before a Fact D petition is filed and then the agreed ancillary relief package can go ahead by consent.

Note

A respondent must have *capacity* to consent to a Fact D decree: see *Mason v Mason* [1972] 3 All ER 315 where it was established that the test for capacity is usually the same as for contracting marriage. This test, established in *In the Estate of Park* [1953] 2 All ER 1411 is basically 'Is the respondent capable of understanding the nature of the contract in to which he is entering?' In case of any doubt it will be up to the petitioner to establish that the respondent had capacity.

A further hazard of Fact D is that there is power to withdraw consent at any time before decree nisi and also power to apply for rescission of the decree nisi where the respondent has been misled in relation to any matter taken into account in deciding whether to give consent: s 10(1). (See Chapter 3, para 3.2.1.)

Note

Fact D requires a period of separation of at least two years prior to the presentation of the petition. *Warr v Warr* [1975] 1 All ER 85 shows that this period is *crucial* – the day of separation was included in the calculation of the two years in that case and a new petition had to be served – so it is good practice not to file the petition until two years and one day from the separation.

The usual reconciliation provisions apply to Fact D and the parties must not cohabit for more than six months so as not to break the period of separation. No account will be taken in calculating the two years of any periods which do not qualify because the parties were cohabiting: s 2(5).

Five years' separation: Fact E   2.6

The requirement to establish this Fact is that the parties have lived apart for a continuous period of at least five years immediately preceding the presentation of the petition: s 1(2)(e).

This Fact is substantially the same as Fact D save that the period of separation must be five years and no consent is required from the respondent who, subject to some slight financial protection, may be divorced regardless unless able to use the defence of 'grave financial or other hardship' provided by s 5(1) to preclude the grant of a decree in certain cases (see Chapter 3, para 3.2.2).

Grave financial or other hardship   2.6.1

This special defence applies only to Fact E cases (and not to those brought under Fact D) and *only* where no other Fact is alleged in the petition. It is of limited application, therefore, because the number of cases where grave financial or other hardship can successfully be shown is very limited.

Note

Grave financial hardship is now virtually entirely limited to loss of pension rights cases, and only here where the petitioner cannot make alternative provision to compensate for lost pension rights which will terminate for the defending spouse with the status of marriage. The importance of this defence has recently been further reduced when the Pensions Act 1995 came into force in July 1996: see Chapter 7.

The defence is also limited because where such marriages have broken down more than five years previously and the respondent has been obstructive in refusing consent to a Fact D decree, the petitioner often feels inclined at that stage, even if this was ruled out before, to petition on the basis of a fault-based Fact which the respondent will at least be put to a lot of trouble to defend. Moreover, the respondent will be precluded both from defending the petition on the fault based Fact and from cross petitioning, as once the five-year separation period is admitted there is no room for the respondent to obtain a decree because the petitioner is already entitled to one: *Parsons v Parsons* [1975] 1 WLR 1272, [1975] 3 All ER 344.

In order to invoke the defence the respondent must file a defence to the petition (called an Answer), thus making the suit defended and, unlike most divorce suits, eligible for legal aid: see 5.1.4.

It must be shown that it would be wrong in all the circumstances to dissolve the marriage, which, of course, would not be possible if the petitioner can also rely on Facts A, B or C, and which is why the defence is exclusively reserved for petitions brought under Fact E alone. The rationale for this was that when the law was fundamentally changed in 1969 to introduce Fact E, it was realised that special arrangements would have to be made to avoid injustice either to petitioner or respondent. Fact E and s 5 were therefore combined to achieve two separate but linked results:

- to enable spouses to petition who were previously unable to obtain decrees, because (usually having left to form other relationships but not having divorced their spouses) they were technically the 'guilty' party with no possibility of petitioning under the law which provided no separation decrees; and
- to protect the elderly, and especially financially dependent, spouses (usually wives) who could now be divorced against their will from being cast off without proper provision at least being made for them.

The reason for combining the new Fact E with the s 5 defence was because Fact E was at the time regarded as something of a 'Casanovas' charter', enabling as it did those husbands who had traded in faithful, if boring, middle-aged wives for a newer model to bestow a marriage certificate (and the future status of widow entitled to their pensions) on the 'bimbo' whose existence the wives had always refused to recognise by declining to take the divorce proceedings only they had grounds for.

A further class of spouses whom s 5(1) was intended to protect were those for whom religious objections to decrees were a serious consideration, especially in relation to foreign ethnic communities where divorce was said to be a social disgrace, but these cases have never really had much success, and have only infrequently been brought since the 1970s.

However, Fact E is now largely irrelevant as the stockpile of old cases where it benefited the errant husbands and the second families they had set up were all worked through in the 70s, so s 5(1) defences are usually now only employed as a bargaining tactic where divorce is likely to be inevitable and the only question is whether better financial terms can be exacted in return for truncating the delay and expense which a s 5(1) defence will cause. Generally, as good if not better terms can be secured at the earlier stage of consenting to a Fact D decree: see 2.7 and Chapter 3, para 3.2.1.

Note

The Family Law Act 1996 considerably strengthens the position of a respondent claiming hardship, including on religious grounds, so clients should accordingly be advised:

- if petitioner to petition now without delay;
- if a potential respondent to prolong negotiations for a Fact D decision in the hope that a Fact E petition is not presented before the MCA 1973 is repealed by the Family Law Act 1996 coming into force.

Choosing the strongest Fact on which to proceed

2.7

As most divorces are undefended, it is best to proceed on the Fact which is the most easily and inexpensively proved, and to remember that most Facts can be proved without difficulty *as long as the suit remains undefended*. Esoteric points of law are usually only going to arise if the respondent disagrees so violently with the Fact on which the decree is sought that an irresistible desire to defend arises which cannot be headed off either by the respondent's own good sense or second thoughts or your advice combined with that of friends.

2.7.1 Multiple Facts

If there are multiple Facts on which a petition could proceed, it is not actually a good idea to proceed on the basis of more than one Fact even if the situation qualifies, as this merely makes the petitioner's case look weak. Thus, the strongest one should be selected. If the case is weak, using more than one Fact will usually make it look weaker, except in the case of using both a fault-based Fact and also Fact D in the hope that the respondent will consent to the Fact D decree and the other Fact need not be proceeded with.

Some practitioners advocate following this course, but a better view is that if there is a fault-based Fact available, a draft petition shown to the respondent or respondent's solicitors before it is served may result in an agreement that consent will be forthcoming to a Fact D decree. If, on the other hand, the respondent is actually felt to be untrustworthy, then it may be better to plead the two Facts in the alternative, and if the desired consent is then given the petition can be amended to delete the other Fact and particulars of it, rather than having to change Facts after filing, which always looks rather foolish. This may be done without leave unless an Answer has been filed in the suit: see 5.8.

2.7.2 Fact D

If the parties are on good terms and it appears that everything will be agreed, Fact D is the most civilised, although it does have drawbacks if the respondent might drive a hard bargain in return for the necessary consent. (For how to deal with such a situation, see 2.5.2.)

If Fact D is not available, or is thought to be problematic, and there is more than one Fact available, then a choice will have to be made.

2.7.3 Adultery

Adultery, if available, should always be the first choice, since it is the most straightforward Fact:
- provided there is proof when there will be no defence; or
- where an admission is likely.

And of course the suit is unlikely to be defended!

Defended adultery is not to be recommended. However, the chances of a defended adultery suit must be at an all time low since it is not now necessary to name a co-respondent. Thus, the names of any new partners can be kept out of the suit. This may be desirable if there are children and the new relationship is to be permanent. (See 4.4.12 for suitable drafting where a co-respondent is not to be named.)

Officially, no stigma is now attached to being divorced for adultery, even where a co-respondent is named because adultery is best considered as a symptom rather than a cause of marriage breakdown. However, you should always *check* the position with your client in case they hold different views and in case there might be any unforeseen complication which the client has neglected to mention, eg the respondent or co-respondent is a clergyman or holds a church job. *If in doubt*, the Solicitors Family Law Association code gives clear guidance – *discourage* the naming of a co-respondent without good reason.

While there is no defence if there is proof, divorcing a respondent for adultery if there is likely to be some strong dislike of it may make agreeing ancillary relief and/or child matters more difficult and expensive in both emotional and financial terms.

Behaviour   2.7.4

Behaviour is likely to be your next choice, preferably the 'mild behaviour petition' as envisaged by Ormrod restricted to no more than three to six carefully drafted paragraphs. Most respondents do not mind this, especially if the allegations are not too exaggerated, since it seems to be accepted (particularly for some reason by men, which is as well as statistics show that most petitions are filed by women!) that spouses who want to complain about their marriages and to obtain a decree against their partners will be able to do so under the existing law, and that there is little point in resisting the determined petitioner in this case. In particular, it seems to be accepted that women habitually complain about and divorce their husbands for relatively trivial reasons and most men are therefore unlikely to defend a behaviour petition which restricts itself to moderate language and what men regard as run of the mill 'women's complaints'.

This is, therefore, a good choice of Fact if your client's statement shows reasonable material on which a good piece of drafting can be done to establish the minimum safe level for a behaviour decree. It will obtain the decree quickly and easily without fuss and should not prejudice the ancillary relief and/or child matters.

2.7.5   Other Facts

Once the above Facts are exhausted, the practitioner enters the danger zone. For all the reasons explained in 2.5.2, Fact C should be avoided like the plague unless the case is absolutely straightforward and the respondent will not defend. Fact D can be dangerous if the respondent is grasping but Fact E should only be used if there is no better and earlier alternative, or the respondent is very sweet natured. This is because a potential respondent's failure to agree to a Fact D petition long before the two years separation necessary for such a decree is established will usually be because that respondent anticipates being to cause a lot of trouble to the petitioner when a Fact E petition has to be brought after five years. Usually, such a respondent can extort a high price for Fact D consent (as otherwise the petitioner will have to wait three more years and still face a costly ancillary relief package to secure a decree after the further delay). Moral (for petitioner and respondent alike): *use Fact D if you can*. It is rare that *any respondent* gets a *better deal* after having kept the petitioner waiting five years: it is better to threaten the three year delay at Fact D stage and stand out for a good financial package in return for consent, than to be on the defensive after the five years (when the respondent has nothing to bargain with).

Example

Mr and Mrs A are fed up with each other, and are basically bored and restless after 20 years of marriage. Each complains about the other incessantly to anyone who will listen. They think of divorce but never get around to it although good drafting could probably package the complaints of one or the other to obtain a Fact B decree. Then their life looks up as they go to a wife-swapping party! Both commit adultery, Mr A with a 'page three model' for whom he promptly leaves Mrs A to set up house elsewhere. Mrs A is suddenly sad and wants him back, though she is not too pleased when he writes to say that he was never so bored in his life as during their 20-year marriage, he wants a divorce and that he is never going to see her or the children, whom he never wanted, ever again. Mrs A still misses him but if there is going to be a divorce she wants a quick and easy decree so she can obtain generous financial orders on ancillary relief before the 'page three model' spends all Mr A's savings. Adultery is the obvious answer – Mr A will probably admit it, but if not there are witnesses from the party. Anyway, he is now living with the 'page 3 model' and although Mrs A really wants him back she has no difficulty showing that she would find it intolerable to live with him because she dotes on the children and could not cope with Mr A's now overt dislike of them which is one of the things that has always annoyed her about him anyway.

Self-assessment questions

1 Can a decree be obtained in England and Wales against a respondent who has committed adultery with a person who has had a sex change operation?
2 Can DNA or blood tests be ordered by the court?
3 Can these tests be used to prove adultery?
4 What is the test for 'behaviour' which qualifies for a decree of divorce?
5 What is the effect of cohabitation after the last incident of behaviour relied on in a petition?
6 Can the respondent's involuntary behaviour qualify for a decree?
7 Can leaving the other spouse ever qualify as behaviour?
8 May a spouse lock out the other who has left the matrimonial home?
9 Can spouses who are still living in the matrimonial home qualify for a Fact D decree?
10 What is the s 5 defence, who can use it and in what circumstances?

Chapter 3

Practical considerations

Introduction

Divorce is not a field of law which can usefully be studied academically and in isolation from practice, especially on the LPC, since while the MCA 1973 provides a legal framework for the grant of decrees, other provisions of the Act, and also Divorce Practice and Procedure, significantly limit the impact of the purely substantive law in MCA ss 1 and 2. It is therefore essential for you to understand the way in which the law works in practice or advice you will give which although *technically* correct on a reading of ss 1 and 2 will in fact be way off what a practitioner would advise, knowing as the practitioner does what actually *happens* when a petition is presented and then goes through the various stages of divorce procedure as regulated by the Family Proceedings Rules 1991 (FPR 1991). The interaction of the ground for divorce with other sections of the MCA 1973, as amended, will often have a profound influence on the conduct of the divorce suit and ancillary relief or other related proceedings.

Example

A petitioner presents a petition on the basis of behaviour under s 1(2)(b). It is weak and an academic with little or no experience of practice might truthfully say to a University class that it is highly doubtful whether there is sufficient behaviour to establish Fact B, since there is room for intellectual argument as to whether the test in *Buffery* (see 2.3.1 above) is met. The *practitioner* however knows that *provided the particulars of behaviour are carefully drafted so that it appears on the face of the petition that the petitioner could be entitled to a decree, and provided the respondent also wants a divorce and does not mind being divorced on the basis of that particular Fact, so that the petition remains undefended*, it will almost certainly succeed. Moreover it is entirely proper, despite the weakness of the allegations, for the practitioner to present such a petition. There are also good reasons for having chosen Fact B, despite the possibility that the respondent might have been coaxed into consenting to a decree under Fact D, because if Fact D had been chosen instead the respondent could have attached unwelcome conditions – which *cannot* be used in a Fact B suit – so that the necessary consent before the petitioner could obtain a Fact D decree might have become unduly expensive.

You should therefore bear in mind at all times a number of practical considerations which are relevant to the successful attainment of the decree of divorce which will enable the client to remarry, and understand how this goal fits together with other matters with which the client and his advisers may be concerned on the way to the successful conclusion of the case.

3.2 Financial protection for reluctant respondents

Every divorce will usually provide some fair financial provision for both parties on decree of divorce, and this is built in under the ordinary law of ancillary relief, where the court (which is usually not in any way influenced by the fact on which the decree was obtained) will seek to divide the assets as cleanly and fairly as possible, irrespective of which party technically 'owned' them while the parties were married. However, the two 'separation' Facts, Fact D and Fact E, have their own protection, since prior to their inclusion in the present divorce law decrees were possible only on proof of fault, so it was thought that if such a radical change as a separation decree was proposed – either on the sole basis of a short separation and consent, or a lengthy separation and against the respondent's will – such a decree should only be granted if the respondent could be sure that the post decree financial position was definitely going to be satisfactory. This is achieved in different ways for Facts D and E.

3.2.1 MCA 1973 s 10

The first important provision of s 10 may or may not have any connection with financial protection, but is an extremely powerful bargaining chip where the petitioner wants a divorce badly and has no other fact to rely on, so it may well be used in a financial context.

Since consent to a Fact D decree must be positive and not merely amount to the respondent's not objecting, the respondent will have had to signify consent on the Acknowledgment of Service form for this Fact to result in a decree at all, and the consent can be withdrawn, for any reason, at any time up to pronouncement of the decree nisi which conditionally dissolves the marriage: see 2.5.2.

Note

Decree Nisi ('DN') is the first of *two decrees* required fully to dissolve a marriage, and must be distinguished from the second, which is called *Decree Absolute* ('DA') after the issue of which the parties are both free to remarry (which they are not, in any jurisdiction in the world, *between* DN and DA although this sometimes not stopped people claiming they believed themselves to be free to remarry at this stage and doing so bigamously!) There is normally a *minimum* period of six weeks between the two decrees, largely for the court's administrative purposes, although it can in practice be much longer at the will of the parties if there are good reasons, eg hard bargaining in the ancillary relief context, especially where there is no satisfactory compensation for pension rights which depend on the continued status of marriage. In financial terms, this limbo period can be used to good tactical effect both by petitioners and respondents.

First, if it transpires in a Fact D divorce that the respondent has actually been *misled* in any way, in relation to any matter which was taken into account when consent was given, s 10(1) even permits the consent to be withdrawn after pronouncement of *decree nisi*, provided action is taken before the decree becomes final at the *decree absolute*: see 5.11 and 5.12. The section permits such a respondent even to apply to have the decree nisi rescinded (so that if the petitioner still wants a decree another Fact will have to be used, or a new deal negotiated with the respondent!).

This is obviously a powerful weapon in the hands of the respondent and in theory can apply to any condition which might be expected, no matter how ridiculous, although there are no reported cases on the degree of absurdity to which this might be taken.

By s 10(2), however, Fact D respondents who cannot claim to have been misled in any way and also Fact E respondents unable to defend the Fact E petition: see below at 3.2.2, can still hold up the final decree dissolving the marriage by applying to have their financial position specially considered by the court, and this too can be a powerful weapon if the petitioner is in a hurry to remarry. Indeed the petitioner in a hurry to remarry who has to rely on Fact D is giving hostages to fortune all along the way, and obviously only uses Fact D if there is no fault based Fact available.

By s 10(3) the court will consider the s 10(2) application and will not allow the decree nisi granted on the basis of the respondent's consent to be made absolute until they are satisfied that either the

- petitioner does not need to make any such financial provision, for the respondent; or

- financial provision made for the respondent is reasonable or fair or the best that can be made in the circumstances.

By s 10(4) the petitioner can rescue the position – which may be desperate if, for example he has promised early marriage to a pregnant new partner who insists on being married at the birth, or where the respondent or the new partner has a terminal illness – by applying to the court to relax the provisions of s 10(3). In order to do this the petitioner will have to show that:

- there are circumstances which make it desirable to make the decree absolute without delay; and
- he will make such financial provision for the respondent as the court may approve, *and give an undertaking to the court to that effect.*

The case of *Grigson v Grigson* [1974] 1 All ER 478 shows that any undertaking must be sufficiently precise to be useful (in that case the general formula 'such provision as the court may approve' was rejected and precise proposals required) and the case of *Parkes v Parkes* [1971] 3 All ER 670 shows how important it is that the s 10(3) power exists as the agreed provision in that case was not sufficiently clearly defined to prevent the petitioner from exploiting ambiguities and in effect depriving the respondent of the fruits of the agreement. Had there been no s 10(3) power enabling the respondent to insist on the petitioner keeping the spirit as well as the letter of the agreement the respondent would have lost out significantly.

On the other hand, the case of *Lombardi v Lombardi* [1973] 3 All ER 625 shows that some applications are entirely unnecessary (in that case no more was awarded than the approximate offer under the one third rule already made by the husband) and the case of *Krystman v Krystman* [1972] 3 All ER 247 was even more absurd (where the wife Fact E respondent was better off than the husband and the parties had cohabited for only two weeks out of a 26 year marriage! Not surprisingly, the court decided that this hasty and long abandoned wartime marriage should be dissolved without further provision).

By s 10(3) this consideration of the respondent's financial position is a thorough stocktaking of that position as it will be *after* decree absolute and if the petitioner should die first, taking into account such matters as the age, state of health, conduct, earning capacity, financial resources and financial obligations, exactly as under

MCA 1973 s 25 in relation to ancillary relief: see below Chapter 7. Indeed a s 10(2) application and the usual comprehensive claim for ancillary relief are usually heard together, supported for convenience by one affidavit, although the FPR 1991 require a separate 10(2) application to be lodged on Form M12 alongside Form M11 or M13 one of which, depending on the procedural circumstances of the applicant, will be used to activate the ancillary relief stage of the divorce: see Chapter 7.

It is thus hard to see the need for the technically separate procedure, as all the form Ml2 does is to alert the court hearing the ancillary relief application to the fact that the case is a s 10(2) situation, and that the ancillary relief package is not satisfactory to the respondent, the court the decree finally dissolving the marriage will have to be held up unless the court relents pursuant to s 10(4).

A s 10(2) application is therefore a useful delaying tactic which tends to secure better financial terms in many cases. Even where it may not actually work at the substantive hearing, it will still have a nuisance value in that the final decree will be held up at least until that hearing, whereas otherwise the marriage might have been dissolved on the respondent's application for the final decree earlier than the financial hearing could be arranged. This is because it is impossible to obtain a court date for such a hearing until the parties' advisers can say they are fully prepared and how much court time will be required for the hearing, from which point the state of court lists generally means the wait for a hearing will be some months.

However s 10(2) can *only* be used where Fact D or E is the *sole* basis of the petition so in practice it is not available where a fault based Fact can be used, and a petitioner who fears s 10(3) trouble from the respondent therefore petitions on a fault based Fact if at all possible.

MCA 1973 s 5   3.2.2

On the other hand, instead of merely a useful delaying tactic, s 5 provides an actual *defence* which if successful will stop a decree being granted at all, and this one applies in Fact E cases only – it is *not* available to Fact D respondents. Thus Fact E respondents who cannot use s 5 can *still* obtain some tactical advantage by using s 10 above to *delay* a final decree which they know they cannot ultimately *prevent* in due course.

The section provides that the respondent may oppose the grant of a decree under s 1(2)(e), despite proof of five years' separation, if it can be shown that the dissolution of the marriage will result in *grave financial or other hardship* to the respondent *and* that it would be *wrong in all the circumstances* to dissolve the marriage: MCA 1973 s 5(1). If the respondent is successful the court will have to dismiss the Fact E petition.

Obviously it is only worth using the defence if the petitioner cannot rely on any other Fact as if the Fact E petition is dismissed the petitioner is only likely to present another one, this time on Facts A, B or C.

In order to use the defence, an Answer will have to be filed in response to the petition: see 2.6 and 5.13.2. For technical reasons, it is never possible to *cross-petition* on a s 5 defence, so this will be a simple Answer without Cross Petition incorporated for decree on any other Fact, even if one exists. This is because, as shown by the case of *Parsons v Parsons* [1975] 1 WLR 1272, [1975] 3 All ER, once the five year separation period is *admitted*, which is essential in order to invoke the s 5 defence at all, there is no opportunity for the respondent to petition since the petitioner is already *entitled* to a decree. The whole purpose of s 5 is to ask the court not formally to grant the decree to which the petitioner has shown entitlement by proving the five years' separation – the sole requirement of s 1(2)(e) – because of the special circumstances afforded by s 5 (if the respondent can prove that they apply in the particular case).

Note

Where a five year separation already exists and one party petitions not on Fact E but on a fault based Fact (eg Fact B) the respondent can defend the Fact B petition and cross-petition on Fact E, but in that situation, as is shown by the case of *Grenfell v Grenfell* [1977] 3 WLR 738, [1978] 1 All ER 561, the original *petitioner* will not be able to use the s 5 defence against the Fact E cross-petition, the reason being that that petitioner cannot then say that she does not want a divorce nor that it would be wrong in all the circumstances to dissolve the marriage, since it will not be possible logically to object to a Fact E petition when, as in the case of Mrs Grenfell, a petitioner has herself already petitioned for divorce! Mrs Grenfell's s 5 defence was struck out as an abuse of the spirit of the defence.

Section 5 defences rarely succeed, except in cases where the respondent can show that the dissolution of the marriage will have adverse financial effects which cannot be compensated for, eg where lucrative pension rights will be lost. It is usually impossible to show 'other hardship' in the sense of some social disadvantage, even in the lives of ethnic minorities where divorce is a disgrace which impacts on children's marriage prospects, since this does not usually apply in a Westernised context and in most overseas communities divorce is either now tolerated or it is the separation, not the actual dissolution of the marriage, which has usually already done the damage complained of. The court usually looks to terminating such empty marriage ties, as in the case of *Talbot v Talbot* (1971) 115 SJ 870, a case of a Catholic husband wanting to marry his mistress with whom he lived in Italy, by converting his decree of judicial separation into one of divorce. The wife was young, employable and not losing any pension rights. The court could not see any argument for not ending the marriage.

Wives' pension cases may still succeed, as the complex rules of pension schemes often preclude the wife sharing in the husband's pension rights where they cannot be split and the scheme may not agree to pay his benefits to the ex-wife. In these circumstances a decree of divorce may be undesirable because it ends the status of marriage, but if there is nothing in the pension scheme to preclude the wife receiving the widow's pension on the husband's death regardless of whether they live together, judicial separation will mean that the wife will still be provided for as the marriage is not dissolved.

However usually the husband is able to provide for the wife in another way so as to compensate for the lost pension rights and in this case the s 5 defence will fail, as in the case of *Dorrell v Dorrell* [1972] 1 WLR 1087, [1972] 3 All ER 343 where the parties were both over 60 and the wife was living on welfare benefits. However, although the husband claimed she could quite well manage on this without the widow's rights from his small local government pension, the defence was upheld as the court said that the amount – tiny as it was – was a significant part of her small income and as there was apparently no way of compensating her the marriage should not be ended. The same happened in *Julian v Julian* (1972) 116 SJ, a case of a police pension where the husband could not close the gap between what was lost and what was required to compensate, and nearly happened in *Le Marchant v Le Marchant* [1977] 1 WLR 559. [1977] 3 All ER 610 where there was a Post Office pension and only at the last minute was the husband able to take out an insurance policy to compensate the wife, though the court would not make the decree absolute until he had actually done it.

Sometimes welfare benefits can be sufficient as in the case of *Reiterbund v Reiterbund* [1975] 2 WLR 375, [1975] 1 All ER 280 which was complicated by the fact that the parties were in their 50s and the wife could not show that she was likely to suffer hardship by the husband dying before her and also before she became entitled to her own pension at age 60. The court thought this remote possibility could be covered temporarily by welfare benefits if it arose.

The s 5 defence will not work where the wife is young and/or the marriage has been short as in the case of *Mathias v Mathias* [1972] 3 WLR 201, [1972] 3 All ER 1, where the parties were in their 30s and the marriage had lasted only three years. There was a discretionary Army pension at stake as well as the state pension, but the court said the wife was young and employable and retirement was too far into the future for the pension to be a significant consideration.

Nor will the defence succeed where the respondent cannot establish that it would be wrong in all the circumstances to dissolve the marriage, ie where the respondent has to shoulder some blame for the breakdown of the marriage, although the decree is sought under Fact E. This was the situation in the case of *Brickell v Brickell* [1973] 3 All ER 508, where the wife had no difficulty establishing financial hardship on the loss of a Ministry of Defence pension, but her behaviour during the marriage was fatal, since she had had an obsessive belief that the husband had committed adultery with someone who worked in their business which had so adversely affected the business that it had had to be closed down.

Note

Despite various initiatives to achieve a fair division of the husband's pension rights on divorce, this problem of compensating the divorced wife for lost pension rights still subsists, although there is now a limited improvement effected by the Pensions Act 1995 s 166 of which came into force on 1 July 1996. This enables a share of the spouse's pension to be 'earmarked' for the other spouse when the spouse with the pension ultimately becomes entitled to draw it, although the pension cannot usually at present be divided at the time of the actual divorce. Some pensions can be split as in the case of *Brooks v Brooks* [1995] *Times*, 3 July, where Lord Nicholls of Birkenhead accepted that some such pensions could be varied under MCA 1973 s 24(1)(c) as a post-nuptial settlement.

The wife's solicitors have a duty to obtain an actuarial variation of the pension rights and to seek a substantial sum in compensation, or run the risk of a suit for negligence. Above all, whether or not s 5 is invoked they should never seek a final decree dissolving the marriage except on express instructions of the client where pension rights may be lost as a result, since while application may be made for all available forms of ancillary relief at a subsequent ancillary relief hearing, leverage will have been lost if the marriage is already dissolved and the pension rights have actually gone.

Cases of financial hardship other than on the basis of pensions are not common, but in the case of *Lee v Lee* (1973) 117 SJ a divorce was refused due to inability to provide a satisfactory ancillary relief package outside a pension context. In that case the problem was the financial and other demands made on the wife by a seriously ill son and since the husband could not give the wife enough money for her to cope in this situation the court declined to dissolved the marriage.

Note

Such successful defences will undoubtedly increase when the Family Law Act 1996 comes into force as it will multiply the opportunities for objecting to a decree on the basis of hardship. Conversely, the Act will reduce the opportunity to object on the basis of loss of pension rights, although further legislation is necessary (and has been promised) to enable all pension rights to be split.

The effects of cohabitation following marriage breakdown   3.3

The practitioner must be aware of the operation of the reconciliation provisions in MCA 1972 s 2 on the different Facts when choosing which one to petition on.

Adultery   3.3.1

Cohabitation of six months or more after discovery by the petitioner of the last act of adultery will be fatal to the success of the petition. However, it should be noted that it is after the petitioner finds out about the adultery, not six months after the last act of adultery has actually been committed, so as long as the petitioner leaves immediately after finding out about it, very old adultery indeed may suffice for a decree. Another act of adultery is however required once the six months' cohabitation is completed: MCA 1973 s 2(1), see 2.2.4. Where cohabitation was for less than six months, this must be mentioned in the petition: MCA s 2(2), see 4.4.12.

3.3.2   Behaviour suits

Cohabitation of six months or more after the last act of behaviour is *not* necessarily fatal to the success of the petition, for two reasons:

- the behaviour may be of a continuing nature, so that there may still be a sufficient case without relying on the older incidents;
- in any case, cohabitation is not an absolute bar to the use of incidents prior to renewed cohabitation in the petition, since cohabitation is only relevant to consideration of whether the petitioner may be 'reasonably expected' to live with the respondent. Moreover, as in the case of *Bradley v Bradley* [1973] 1 WLR 1291, [1973] 3 All ER 750, especially if the petitioner is a woman without independent resources she may only still be technically cohabiting because she genuinely has nowhere else to go: MCA 1973 s 2(3), see 2.3.3.

3.4   Desertion and separation suits

Cohabitation of six months or more since the start of the two year desertion or separation periods will break the continuity of the period and the two years must be started again. However, less than six months (whether the cohabitation was in one or more periods) will not break the accrual of the total two year period required to petition, although any months cohabiting will not count towards the total of two years' desertion or separation required. MCA 1973 s 2(5), see 2.4.5.

Where there is cohabitation, for the purposes of these Facts the circumstances of the cohabitation should be examined carefully in accordance with the principles in *Mouncer v Mouncer* and *Hopes v Hopes* above at 2.4.2, since it may be that the parties can be said not to be cohabiting at all. Obviously, the court must not be deliberately misled or deceived: see PCS 21.07, since this would be a matter of professional misconduct, but the Act does address the point by providing that the parties are treated as living apart unless *living together in the same household*: s 2(6).

Note

There will be an opportunity for the petitioner to establish that the parties have been living apart under the same roof in that the printed form of affidavit in support of the

petition asks for details of living arrangements to be specified in such circumstances, including details of whether the
parties have shared a bedroom, whether they have taken
their meals together, what arrangements have been made
for cleaning the accommodation and what arrangements
have been made for paying the household bills. There may
be a perfectly bona fide case to be made out for their living
apart at the same address.

Children in divorce   3.5

Although clients coming to the office to seek a divorce
will often have problems (and arguments with their
spouses) concerning their children, the resolution of
these now has very little impact on the actual *divorce*
process, although, as in any adversarial case, giving
clients' spouses what they want may make agreement in
other areas, such as over money, rather easier. For
example, if the mother wants a good ancillary relief
package from the father, for herself and the children,
human nature being what it is he is likely to be more
cooperative if matters are agreed about contact with the
children (he may want more, less or none depending on
the approach to parenting of the particular father!) or
where they should live or go to school, than if the mother
insists on taking him to court under the Children Act
1989 for a formal order with which he does not agree.

   Although there is a minimal formal requirement for
approving *agreed* ongoing arrangements for children
whose parents are divorcing: see 5.4 and 5.10, where at
the stage the petition is filed the parties are in fact
already locked in combat over the children, the conduct
and outcome of such battles is specifically excluded from
the divorce suit and decided in Children Act 1989 proceedings completely outside the divorce process. Thus
the only matter with which the court granting the *divorce*
will concern itself is that of what is to be done where supposedly *agreed* ongoing arrangements for the post
divorce lives of the children (or at least arrangements
which are not formally being litigated) are *not* such as a
conscientious non-interventionist judge, applying the
non-interventionist philosophy which is dictated to
divorce judges by the Children Act 1989, can reconcile
with common sense.

   This is a big change in the pre-1991 position which
the lay client, and the trainee with an ordinary regard for
the welfare of children, may at first have some difficulty
in taking on board.

Before 1991 when the Children Act 1989 came into force it was *impossible* to obtain even a *decree nisi* of divorce unless the court was satisfied of the arrangements for the children of the family and pursuant to s 41 of the MCA 1973 *issued a certificate*, which was by no means rubber stamped, to that effect. This was called the 's 41 certificate' and also had to *specify* who had 'custody' of the child, ie the power to decide everything of importance in the child's life, who had 'care and control', ie the management of the child's day to day life, and who had 'access' and sometimes even *when*, ie and whether this was to be arranged on a 'reasonable' basis or was 'defined' by the court, eg 'every other Sunday between 10 am and 4 pm with four weeks staying access per year during the usual school holidays'.

This approval of child arrangements still survives in an emasculated form in the amended s 41, a new version of which came into force in 1991 to reflect the non-interventionist policy of the Children Act 1989. As a result, whereas the previous paternalistic approach of the court often kept the parties up to scratch by close enquiry and intervention in their arrangements, by *automatically* making formal orders for custody etc and *refusing* even *decree nisi* unless *satisfied* about the children, the *right* to a *decree nisi* is now always certified, if the petitioner is entitled to one, *before* the position of the children is considered at all.

Nowadays, again pursuant to the ethos of the Children Act 1989, there are *no* formal orders unless they simply cannot be avoided, and it is now *rare* for the court to refuse even a *decree absolute* on the basis of concern about the children, although in an appropriate case the final decree actually dissolving the marriage and permitting remarriage *may* be held up because of the children if the court has sufficient grounds to do so.

Thus whatever the position in respect of the children, the decree nisi which ends the first stage of the divorce process is now *completely independent of child matters*: although it is not actually pronounced in open court until after the s 41 certificate has been issued in one form or another, technically the decision has *already been taken and recorded* in the District Judge's certificate that the petitioner is *entitled* to a decree *before* the position of the children is addressed and the *s 41 certificate* dealt with at all: see 5.10. Thus most divorces are already a *fait accompli* by the time the court even begins to consider the arrangements for the children and therefore you generally need not worry that the children may hinder the divorce suit as such.

This situation is supposed to be a good thing and was brought about due to the non-interventionist policy of the Children Act 1989, pursuant to s 1(5) of that Act, which enshrines the charming if sometimes naive idea that parents are the people who will know what is best for their children and that they will be likely to observe the principle of parental responsibility created by the Act which requires them to continue in the role of parents despite the formal dissolution of their marriage partnership: see 6.2.

As a result, *no routine formal orders* are now made concerning either residence arrangements or contact with children following the divorce of their parents, which is the complete opposite of the earlier situation where someone had to have a formal order for what was then termed *custody* and someone else usually had to have an order for *care and control* or the child was felt to be living in an undesirable vacuum!

The modern position is therefore that the court will wish to look at a statement, called the Statement of Arrangements, jointly prepared by the parents in most cases, of the proposed living and educational arrangements for the children, and will then wish to *certify* that it does not need to exercise any of its powers under the Children Act 1989 (which do permit it to make formal orders for residence and contact in cases where the parents have not sorted the matter out themselves in the approved manner so as to obviate the need for a formal order). This is meant to place the responsibility on the parents, and enable the court to assume a role which is lightly supervisory but which does not cut across the non-interventionist policy of the Children Act 1989.

However, if this idealistic position is in fact *not* the situation in any particular case, the court may then reluctantly involve itself in a number of ways to regulate matters for children who fall within the court's s 41 jurisdiction so as to bring the position disclosed in the Statement of Arrangements into line with what is felt to be reasonable.

Children to whom s 41 applies   3.5.1

The children with whom the court will concern itself are those termed *children of the family*. This has a technical meaning, being defined in MCA 1973 s 52 as amended by the CA 1989 as:

- a child of both parties to the marriage, including a child of both born before their marriage; or
- any other child, not being a child who is placed with the parties to the marriage as foster parents by a local authority or voluntary organisation, who has been treated by both the parties as a child of the family.

A stepchild may thus *not* be a child of the family. Only children under 16 are strictly the province of the court, or children under 18 if they are still in full time education or training, though the court may decide if there are any other children in each case, eg an older disabled child not in full time education or training, over the age of 16 to whom s 41 should apply.

Note

If there are no children of the family the court must still issue the certificate which will simply certify that there are no children of the family to whom s 41 applies.

3.5.2   The satisfactory situation

Where both parents sign the form of Statement of Arrangements and the details provided in the form give the court no cause for concern, the court will automatically, without any further evidence, issue the s 41 certificate indicating that the court knows the identities of the children concerned and that it does not wish to intervene in the parents' arrangements for them. Prior to 1991 there was a formal oral hearing before the judge of the court (not the district judge whose jurisdiction did not extend so far) which had to be attended by the parent with whom the children lived. Now neither has further involvement unless the Statement of Arrangements is plainly unsatisfactory.

If, however, when the district judge, pursuant to FPR 1991 r 2.39 considers the Statement of Arrangements which is filed at court with the petition, and feels that there is a problem with, eg the accommodation, education, health care, financial provision or some other similar matter, or that there are any other potential snags in future arrangements, the district judge may be unwilling to issue the s 41 certificate. If this is the case, the court can invite the parties to file further evidence, order a welfare report or exceptionally call the parties before it in an effort to resolve the matter. If, however, this still produces no satisfactory solution, then the certificate will take a particular form reserved for such cases, because the district judge will apply the cumulative test in s 41(2), deciding that because:

- the circumstances of the case require the court to consider the exercise of its powers under the Children Act;
- the court cannot do so without further considering the case; and
- there are exceptional circumstances which make it desirable in the interests of the child that the court should give a direction the decree of divorce (ie the final decree dissolving the marriage and permitting remarriage) should not be made absolute until the court directs otherwise.

It is clear from this cumulative test in s 41(2) that delay of the final decree is considered to be an exceptional step.

Mostly this sort of situation can be headed off by proper preparation of the Statement of Arrangements and filing with it any further documents which will deal with any potential area of difficulty, eg where there is a child with a chronic illness a medical report, where there is an accommodation problem, a letter from the local authority promising future accommodation as soon as possible etc: see 5.4.

Where the matter is to go direct to a Children Act 1989 hearing for a formal order

3.5.3

Where the petition discloses that the parties are in any event seeking a formal order for residence or contact or in relation to another matter (called a 's 8 order') or where there is such an application already pending when the divorce suit is started the district judge is excused from considering the arrangements for the children since they will be considered in the separate Children Act proceedings: see 5.4.2 and 6.5.

Grey areas

Where no *formal application* has been made for a s 8 order, but the district judge is not too happy with the arrangements, because for example there is a dispute about where a child shall live, some district judges will call the parties in to court to explain what orders might be applied for so that the matter might be formally resolved between the parties, and the court welfare service will often be involved if it is felt that they might help in resolving the parties' differences and putting them off the formal procedure under the Children Act pursuant to the non-interventionist policy of that Act. If an application is then made, the matter will pass as in 3.5.3 to the

3.5.4

court hearing the s 8 application. However, if nothing is done, and if the district judge feels thoroughly unhappy then a choice must be made between directing that the final decree be held up until the children's future is settled by the court making orders itself and asking for further evidence which might enable the issue of a satisfactory s 41 certificate, eg if doubtful accommodation is at the root of the problem, the district judge might ask the court welfare office to inspect it or for a letter from the local authority specifying when the party with care of the child will be adequately housed.

It will however be obvious from the above that the future of the children is very unlikely now to have any impact on a divorce suit, so that the children are unlikely to be a problem in relation to the *suit* itself, although there may well be hotly contested and emotionally charged child proceedings under the Children Act: see Chapter 6.

Note

The SFLA Code will always influence the conduct of divorce suits, but is nowhere more obvious in its application than where the parties have children and of course will be of even more vital importance than usual in connection with any child matters, either within the divorce suit or in proceedings under the Children Act 1989.

Jurisdiction

3.6

Jurisdiction in matrimonial suits is conferred by either habitual residence or domicile of the parties seeking a decree. By the Domicile and Matrimonial Proceedings Act (DMPA) 1973 s 5 the court will have jurisdiction in suits for divorce, judicial separation and presumption of death and dissolution of the marriage if either of the parties:

- is domiciled in England and Wales on the date when the proceedings are begun; or
- was habitually resident in England and Wales throughout the period of one year ending with that date.

In the case of the suit for presumption of death: see 3.7, the same conditions apply but obviously in respect of the petitioner alone, since the petitioner in that suit is seeking a declaratory decree in respect of an absent respondent who is thought to be dead and whose whereabouts are unknown: DMPA 1973 s 5(4).

Nullity is slightly different, in that by s 5(3) the same domicile and habitual residence conditions apply where the marriage is voidable only, but where it is claimed to be void and one of the parties who would have satisfied the jurisdictional requirements is already dead (ie a declaration of status is therefore sought for some good reason to make clear that the marriage was void and the surviving partner does not satisfy the ordinary jurisdictional requirements of s 5(3)) then the court will have jurisdiction if that deceased party was domiciled in England or Wales at death or habitually resident in England and Wales for one year immediately prior to the death.

Note

The jurisdictional requirements for orders from the magistrates' (now called the Family Proceedings Court) are quite different and distinct. This is because the magistrates do not grant any of the principal decrees, but confine themselves to financial, domestic violence and Children Act orders. The magistrates have jurisdiction based on presence in their commission area: see Chapter 14.

In practice there is rarely any difficulty in satisfying one of the appropriate DMPA 1973 jurisdictional conditions.

Note

The court can dissolve overseas marriages providing the jurisdictional requirements for starting proceedings are met, although there will be special procedural requirements, ie translation of the foreign marriage certificate, and affidavit of the translator that the translation is a true one.

Domicile   3.6.1

Domicile must be distinguished both from *residence* or *habitual residence* and from the concept of *nationality* which has no relevance to the English law of divorce. The concept of domicile is a complex one but it is essential because of DMPA 1973 to be able to classify an individual for jurisdictional purposes in the law of divorce as either domiciled or habitually resident here. A person must be *domiciled* in a single system of law, eg in England or Wales, not Great Britain, or in a single US state not 'in the USA' as a whole.

Every person has a domicile throughout life and it is not possible to be without a domicile at any time. Nor is it possible to have more than one at once, although more than one *residence* is perfectly possible and entirely normal for people who live an international life, such as businessmen with multi-national interests and film stars who are constantly on the move across borders and continents.

The first domicile a person acquires is their *Domicile of Origin*. This is taken at birth from the domicile at the time of the *father* of a legitimate child born in wedlock, and of the *mother* of an illegitimate child. The place of birth has no relevance to *domicile* though it may confer nationality, possibly an additional nationality to that of the father, mother or parents. Domicile of origin can be changed for another domicile, which will then be either a *domicile of choice* or *domicile of dependence*, but it is the strongest species of domicile, since if at any time in life a person appears to have no domicile, the domicile of origin will always revive to fill the vacuum if the individual cannot be said to be domiciled anywhere else.

Once an individual is 16, the domicile of origin can be changed at will, whereupon the new domicile will be called the *domicile of choice*. At age 16, when the power to change the domicile first arises, the domicile of origin may be regarded as the first domicile of choice unless and until changed. Acquiring a domicile of choice is simple, since the individual simply needs to move to a territory (within which there is a single system of law as explained above) and decide to live there with the intention of remaining *indefinitely*, either in the sense of *permanently or at least without contemplating any future departure*. As soon as the individual is bored of that domicile of choice, it may be changed simply by leaving without intending to return to live. If no new country is chosen for the next domicile of choice, provided it can be shown that the existing domicile of choice has actually been given up and not retained, the domicile of origin will revive until a new domicile of choice is in fact selected and effectively assumed.

Note

It is not possible to assume a new domicile of choice without actually going and taking up residence in a country with the requisite intention: intention alone is not enough, just as taking up residence alone is not enough. Moreover, no preparatory acts – such as buying the ticket to travel, or even failing to complete an abortive journey – will be enough.

While an individual is under the age of 16, whatever domicile that individual's parents have will also extend to their child as a *domicile of dependence*. To begin with this will be whatever was the child's *domicile of origin* acquired at birth, but if the parents move countries with the requisite intent, taking the child with them, thus themselves selecting a new domicile of choice, their new *domicile of choice* will be their child's *new domicile of dependence* which will be retained until the age of 16, when a domicile of choice may be independently selected by the child. Of course if the family moves again with the requisite intent on the part of the parents before the child is 16, it will be the *final* pre-16 domicile of dependence which will become the child's first domicile of choice when the sixteenth birthday is reached.

Note

If the father dies while the child is under 16, or if the parents separate and the child lives with the mother, the child's domicile will change with that of the mother not that of the father: DMPA 1973: s 4.

Thus an individual always has a domicile and can always tell if it is possible to petition for one of the principal decrees in England of Wales based on domicile. Once domicile is established, it will not be affected by departure elsewhere, no matter for how long, provided existing connections are not severed, ie there is some reason to come back, and there is in fact both an intention to return and no intention to establish a domicile of choice elsewhere.

Example

Hugo is an ambitious young business man who takes on overseas building contracts for his multi-national company. They pay him well to spend extended periods in countries with fast developing tourism, building and managing time share projects at an enhanced salary which is topped up with bonuses at the end of each contract. He receives generous expenses to make up for his enforced absence from Europe. He has a British passport having been born and educated in England, where he has also spent much of his adult life, but his father, also an international businessman, was actually German and Hugo's domicile of origin was German until he changed it to an English domicile of choice in his late teens. Since then he has taken up a new domicile of choice in each of the countries where he has gone to work, in each place finding it cheaper to buy a house rather than rent, and settling in for the duration. Usually he keeps the houses for investment when he leaves, as his sites usually do so well they create a thriving tourist trade where there is a demand for luxury self-catering villas.

In the Middle East he met, lived with and had a child by a Turkish girl, whom he reluctantly married following the birth and just before returning to England at the end of a three-year contract spent building a holiday complex near Bodrum. After a few months in England, where the three of them lived in his flat in Docklands (which was bought in the English domicile of choice phase, and is treated as an investment, being used when he is in the UK and then normally rented out again for the period for which he is overseas on contracts) they decided the marriage was a mistake and that they should obtain a divorce and go their separate ways before Hugo has to set off on his next contract, this time to the South Pacific where he will probably remain for five years.

There may well be a problem about establishing jurisdiction for the divorce on the basis of domicile as Hugo does not seem to have a domicile of choice anywhere at the moment, his domicile of origin, which in this case will have revived, is German not English, and his wife has certainly not established a domicile of choice here as she does not intend to stay without Hugo: they may have to wait to petition until one of them can use one year's habitual residence. As Hugo is off again, his wife will have to start proceedings as soon as she qualifies for one year's habitual residence.

3.6.2   Habitual residence

Habitual residence is much easier to establish since it is not significantly different from the concept of 'ordinary residence' which exists in other areas of law, any voluntary residence with a settled purpose qualifies, and valid reasons for settlement may be business, education, health, family reasons, or simply enjoyment of the country or its way of life.

Note

It is possible to be resident in more than one country, and temporary absence (eg for holidays) will not break the qualifying residence.

3.7   Alternative decrees

Sometimes it is not possible to decide whether to petition for divorce or nullity, or divorce or judicial separation. There is also a decree of presumption of death and dissolution of the marriage under s 19 of the MCA.

Divorce or nullity

There may well be an overlap between these two decrees, for example:

- venereal disease at the time of the marriage or pregnancy *per alium* (for which a nullity decree under MCA 1973 ss 12(e) and (f) respectively would be available) might be a better alternative to trying to establish adultery under s 1(2)(a) if the venereal disease was probably contracted or the pregnancy arose before rather than after the ceremony;
- mental disorder at the time of the marriage (for which a nullity decree under s 12(c) may be available) might be better than trying to establish behaviour under s 1 (2)(b) where mental or physical illness might not be sufficient to qualify under Fact B;
- invalidity of the marriage may be an alternative where there is only a weak basis for divorce and the first year is not up: see 1.3.

Should the alternative of nullity seem more appropriate the trainee must be prepared to consult Rayden for a detailed account of the relevant law to establish whether a decree is in fact available in the particular case, since there are bars to nullity.

Divorce or judicial separation

Judicial separation is sought by people who object to divorce on religious or other grounds (eg that it would end the marriage and therefore the wife's right to a pension or other property) or where the parties have not been married for a year. Where there is a decree of judicial separation is in force and the parties remain separated, if either party dies intestate his or her real and personal property devolves as though the other party were dead: MCA 1973 s 18(2).

A decree of judicial separation may subsequently be accepted by the court as evidence of the ground on which it is sought in future proceedings for divorce, provided evidence is given by the petitioner: MCA 1973 s 4(2). Thus such a decree, irrespective of why it was sought at the time it was granted, has the additional advantage of preserving the evidence for future divorce if that is likely to be required.

The court has the same powers as to ancillary relief as after divorce and nullity decrees, and the same s 41 certificate will have to be issued if there are children. A judicial separation suit may be defended in the same way as a suit for divorce.

The same five Facts as enable a divorce petition to be presented will also suffice for a petition for judicial separation. The only difference between the two suits is that–
- judicial separation may be sought within one year of the celebration of the marriage;
- there is no need to establish irretrievable breakdown: MCA 1973 s 17(1);
- a decree of judicial separation does not end the marriage, only the duty to cohabit: MCA 1973 s 18(1) or desertion, so there is only one decree (instead of DN and DA). Because of the termination of the duty to cohabit there will also be a presumption of non-access so adultery, which might later found a decree of divorce, is easy to establish, though since a Fact will already have been established in order to obtain a decree of judicial separation that should not be strictly necessary since s 4(2) permits the court to grant a decree of divorce on the basis that there is already a decree of judicial separation provided the petitioner gives evidence.

Should judicial separation seem more suitable to a divorce for any client, the trainee should suggest it. Many clients do not realise that judicial separation still exists, or know much about its effects and possible advantages. Judicial separation is retained by the Family Law Act 1996 and the only change is in the name since the existing decree will be replaced by a 'separation order'.

3.8 Review of essential practical considerations in the law of divorce

Advice to a client may be much influenced by the above practical considerations:
- where Fact E might be thought to be the cleanest basis for a divorce it sometimes cannot be used because of the fear of a protracted s 5 defence (so a fault based Fact must sometimes be used instead to exclude s 5);
- where Fact D might also otherwise be favoured, because the respondent also wants a divorce (but not necessarily on the petitioner's terms) a fault based Fact must be used to exclude reliance on s 10 (whereby the respondent might apply for rescission of the DN under s 10(1) or apply for consideration of their post DN financial position under s 10(2), risking delay of the DA under s 10(3);

- availability of any of the five Facts may be precluded by cohabitation where that has been such as to result in an absolute or discretionary bar to a decree, and this may influence choice of Fact on which to petition where more than one is available;

- poor post divorce arrangements for children might exceptionally delay DA (but have no effect on DN, and formal Children Act proceedings have no relevance to the progress of the *divorce suit*);

- jurisdiction problems may arise because of lack of English domicile of both parties (but can always be cured after a maximum wait of one year to establish habitual residence of one party to the marriage – it is irrelevant whether that party is petitioner or respondent);

- sometimes a case may disclose a situation which is too weak to prove any Fact on which to petition for divorce (but a decree of nullity may alternatively be available on the same evidence);

- sometimes a divorce may not be advisable on status grounds, eg for financial reasons (but judicial separation, available on the same facts, would not have the same objections as it terminates the duty to cohabit and preserves the evidence for a later divorce if desires, but does not end the married status).

You will therefore need to review any potential divorce suit in the light of these practical considerations before taking a decision to petition. If this is not done it may later be found necessary to amend, the need for which seldom reflects well on the practitioner, or, worse, to withdraw a petition and start again.

Self-assessment questions

1 When and how may a s 5 defence be invoked?
2 Does the respondent have any alternative to fall back on if the s 5 defence fails?
3 Is there any way out of the delay occasioned by the respondent's making use of ss 10(2) and 10(3)?
4 Will cohabitation necessarily preclude a successful petition on the basis of adultery? behaviour? desertion or separation for two or five years?
5 Is it possible to delay a divorce suit by being obstructive about arrangements for the children?

6 How does the philosophy of the Children Act 1989 influence divorce suits generally?

7 Is jurisdiction likely to be a problem in bringing an English suit for divorce for an international businessman with several homes around the world (including one in England) who wants to avoid the unfriendly jurisdiction of California where he is domiciled because the Californian court will give half his fortune to his wife?

8 When might a decree of nullity be a useful alternative to one for divorce?

9 When would you recommend a decree of judicial separation?

10 Is it possible to prove adultery when the parties are judicially separated? Will that be strictly necessary?

Chapter 4

Drafting

Introduction

Apart from the ubiquitous influence of the SFLA Code, which will certainly extend to drafting in encouraging the practitioner to produce non confrontational documents, (especially where the children might be directly or indirectly affected if the respondent is unnecessarily annoyed), good drafting in family matters is in principle no different from drafting in other civil suits.

However, as in litigation generally, you will find that mastering a range of basic drafts will be an important confidence builder, and you should aim to be able to produce a useful portfolio of acceptable documents which demonstrate a solid familiarity with every day law and practice. While *excellence* in drafting is not expected at the trainee's stage of development, a knack of handling difficult points which do not generally arise on a regular basis will come automatically with years of experience.

Not only is the avoidance of fundamental error more important at this stage than flashes of brilliance, but since the majority of divorce suits now proceed to final decree via the so-called Special Procedure (see below at 5.10) good *routine* drafting is absolutely essential or avoidable mistakes will clog the system. Moreover, not only will *poor drafting* invite swift retribution, since professional opprobrium will almost certainly be accompanied by unnecessary delay and expense occasioned by queries raised by the district judge processing the case under the Special Procedure, but the practical result may well be avoidable amendments punishable by costs, and perhaps even a wasted costs order against the practitioner personally!

All these unwelcome consequences may be avoided by the acquisition of a good drafting habit at the outset. Coincidentally, the basic petition, which is usually the simple document on which students cut their teeth, is a convenient vehicle for this initial learning process in family drafting.

Drafting a petition

Every divorce suit must be commenced by petition: FPR 1991 r 2.2.

There is no set *wording* or even *format* for a petition although its essential *contents* are governed by the FPR 1991 r 2.3 and Appendix 2 to those rules. Thus a petition to start proceedings in a divorce suit may be drafted from scratch, like any other pleading, or a pre-printed form may be completed with the necessary particulars, and adapted where necessary if, rarely, there are minor peculiarities in the case which do not quite fit the form. Basically, so little time is now wasted on obtaining the actual decree that only in a very esoteric case would it be necessary to draft specially from scratch. It has been truthfully, if flippantly, said in the press that divorce is now a 'mail order business', and this is certainly true of the actual divorce suit which obtains the decrees ending the marriage, since unless there are complications these are obtained by post from the Court office with no judicial hearing. Having settled the paperwork for the grant of the decree, the practitioner's effort is therefore almost entirely concentrated on sorting out the financial and child caring and rearing consequences of the divorce.

However, you would be ill advised to exercise any cheap originality in departing from the format generally used for the petition, whether drafting from scratch or using the printed form, since the latter, which is based on the standard format which petitions had begun to assume before printed forms were used, sets out the contents required by the FPR in the order in which those rules recite those requirements, and generally (unless the case is super-complicated) it will be appropriate to use a pre-printed form obtainable from law stationers. These are generally ordered in bulk by all firms regularly practising family law so a petition drafted from scratch would usually only be needed if the supply had run out for some reason, since in a genuinely complex case the petition would probably be sent out to counsel for drafting.

The precise version of the pre-printed form which you will find in the firm's stationery cupboard will depend on which law stationers that firm patronises, since various law stationers print forms under licence from the Lord Chancellor's Department, each employing slight variations in design (and usually carefully appending their name and copyright to that version in a conspicuous place on the form).

Note

Up to 1976 petitions were almost always drafted by counsel but following the introduction of the Special

Procedure this became solicitors' work unless the case was unusual and this remains the position today. A thin case of behaviour which, if not carefully pleaded, might fall below the 'minimum safe level' on which a district judge could reasonably consider the petitioner entitled to a decree or a complex case of desertion where the respondent might defend would both fall into this latter category, because in such cases the rare occurrence of a hearing in open court might follow, in which case it is traditional that the advocate conducting such a hearing should have the drafting of the petition.

Checklist of the essential contents of the petition

While there is no set way in which a petition must be drafted, there is no getting round the inclusion of the following matters specified in Appendix 2 to the FPR and trainees should be familiar with this list in paragraph 1 of the Schedule which, despite length, is for convenience set out virtually verbatim as a checklist against which a petition should be carefully compared for compliance:

(a) the names of the parties to the marriage and the date and place of the marriage;

(b) the last address at which the parties to the marriage have lived together as husband and wife;

(c) where it is alleged that the court has jurisdiction based on domicile:
(i) the country in which the petitioner is domiciled; and
(ii) if that country is not England and Wales, the country in which the respondent is domiciled;

(d) where it is alleged that the court has jurisdiction based on habitual residence:
(i) the country in which the petitioner has been habitually resident throughout the period of one year ending with the date of the presentation of the petition,
(ii) if the petitioner has not been habitually resident in England and Wales, the country in which the respondent has been habitually resident during that period with details in either case, including the addresses of the places of residence and the length of residence at each place;

(e) the occupation and residence of the petitioner and the respondent;

(f) whether there are any living children of the family and if so:
(i) the number of such children and the full names (including surname) of each and each child's date of birth or (if it be the case) that any child is over 18,

(ii) in the case of each minor child over the age of 16, whether that child is receiving instruction at an educational establishment or undergoing training for a trade, profession or vocation;

(g) whether (to the knowledge of the petitioner in the case of a husband's petition) any other child now living has been born to the wife during the marriage and if so, the full names (including surname) of the child and the child's date of birth or, if it be the case, that the child is over 18;

(h) if it be the case, that there is a dispute whether a living child is a child of the family;

(i) whether or not there are or have been any other proceedings in any court in England and Wales or elsewhere with reference to the marriage or to any children of the family or between the petitioner and the respondent with reference to any property of either or both of them, and if so:

(i) the nature of the proceedings,

(ii) the date and effect of any decree or order, and

(iii) in the case of proceedings with reference to the marriage; whether there has been any resumption of cohabitation since the making of the decree or order;

(j) whether there have been any proceedings in the Child Support Agency with reference to the maintenance of any children of the family and if so details as appropriate;

(k) whether there are any proceedings continuing in any country outside England and Wales which relate to the marriage or are capable of affecting its validity or subsistence and, if so:

(i) particulars of proceedings, including the court in or tribunal or authority before which they were begun,

(ii) the date when they were begun,

(iii) the names of the parties,

(iv) the date or expected date of any trial in the proceedings, and

(v) such other facts as may be relevant to the question whether the proceedings on the petition should be stayed under Schedule 1 to the Domicile and Matrimonial Proceedings Act 1973

and such proceedings shall include any which are not instituted in a court of law in that country, if they are instituted before a tribunal or other authority, having power under the law having effect there to determine questions of status, and shall be treated as continuing if they have been begun and have not been finally disposed of;

(l) where the fact on which the petition is based is five years' separation, whether any, and if so what, agreement or arrangement has been made or is proposed to be made between the parties for the support of the respondent or, as the case may be, the petitioner or any child of the family;

(m) in the case of a petition for divorce, that the marriage has broken down irretrievably;

(n) the fact alleged by the petitioner for the purposes of s 1(2) of the Act of 1973, or where the petition is not for divorce or judicial separation, the ground on which relief is sought, together in any case with brief particulars of the individual facts relied on but not the evidence by which they are to be proved;

(o) any further or other information required by such of the following paragraphs and by rule 3.11 as may be applicable ...

Note

A petition not for divorce or judicial separation may be for nullity or for a declaration of presumption of death and dissolution of the marriage under s 19 of the MCA 1973.

FPR r 3.11 deals with polygamous marriages.

The FPR continue in paragraph 4 of the Schedule:

Every petition shall conclude with:

(a) a prayer setting out particulars of the relief claimed, including any application for an order under any provision of Part I or Part II of the Children Act 1989 with respect to any child of the family, any claim for costs and any application for ancillary relief which it is intended to claim

(b) the names and addresses of the persons who are to be served with the petition, indicating if any of them is a person under disability

(c) the petitioner's address for service, which, where the petitioner sues by a solicitor, shall be the solicitor's name or firm and address. Where the petitioner, although suing in person, is receiving legal advice from a solicitor, the solicitor's name or firm and address may be given as the address for service if the solicitor agrees. In any other case the petitioner's address for service shall be the address of any place in England or Wales at or to which for the petitioner may be delivered or sent.

Note

Under FPR 1991 r 2.4. a petitioner who seeks to rely on a conviction under the Civil Evidence Act 1968 s 11 or 12 (eg of rape, in an adultery case) must give appropriate details in the petition: see 2.2.3 above.

Under FPR 1991 r 2.5 a petition should be signed by the person drafting or settling it, ie by counsel, solicitor or petitioner in person as appropriate, except if actually *drafted* by the solicitor for the client advised under the Green Form where the petitioner is acting in person, it should be signed by the client.

Under FPR 1991 r 2.7 a person with whom it is alleged the respondent has committed adultery should be made a party to the action unless that person is not *named* in the petition, or is dead, or the Court otherwise directs, and if some other improper association is alleged, ie a homosexual one, the Court may direct that that person be made a party.

Under FPR 1991 r 10.21 the petitioner may obtain leave to exclude his or her address if there is a real threat of danger if the respondent discovers it, and in this case will give the address to the Court on a separate form instead.

4.4 Completing the pre-printed form of petition

A common form of petition and the accompanying notes are reproduced in Appendix 2 together with a sample precedent for a self-drafted petition.

Pre-printed forms usually come complete with explanatory notes cross referenced to the number paragraphs. These are in theory intended for member of the public acting in person, who may obtain a form of petition including the explanatory notes from the Court to commence the divorce suit in person, but in fact the notes are as useful for the trainee solicitor or the solicitor in general practice whose daily routine does not include regular family work, since they act as a prompt to relate the rules to the form so as to avoid the omission of vital information at the correct place. They are also useful in checking for deficiencies petitions served on a solicitor's client.

Note

The printed form comes ready labelled in the alternative for use in a divorce county court or in the Principal Registry of the Family Division of the High Court. Your first task therefore is to decide which of these to strike out. If a divorce county court is preferred, by FPR 1991 r 2.6 any county court so designated by the Lord Chancellor may be used, usually the one nearest to the petitioner's residence, although as there is no residential requirement as such, any divorce county court may in fact be selected – for example, because the petitioner does not want to use one in the district where he or she resides – though not all county courts are divorce county courts. If Children Act 1989 proceedings are anticipated, however, it would be advisable to start the divorce in a divorce county court which is also a Family Hearing Centre, or the child proceedings will have to be transferred at a later stage: see Chapter 6 below. If the Principal Registry is preferred then by FPR 1991 r 1.4 and the Matrimonial and Family Proceedings Act 1984 (MFPA 1984) s 42 this is treated as a divorce county court.

You will not fill in the 'No' of the action in the top right hand corner of the form since this is the identifying number allocated by the Court in the Court books when the petition is filed.

Paragraph 1   4.4.1

This paragraph recites the details of the marriage and should be taken *exactly* from the original or certified copy of the marriage certificate, which will need to be obtained for filing with the petition. The full names of the parties therefore need to be given but it is no longer necessary to give the wife's former or maiden name although older practitioners often do it (exercising their right not to observe any particular form of words for the petition!) because it used to be a requirement.

Note

The *county* in which the marriage took place should be included (although it can be left out in the case of marriages in London, where a marriage might be in a Register Office 'in the City of Westminster) but traditionally the postcode is omitted.

Paragraph 2   4.4.2

The *full* address at which the parties *last* lived together as man and wife should be given in this paragraph, including the county and city postal district if applicable, but again not the postcode. This *may* be the same as the original matrimonial home but is obviously not always necessarily so. All *earlier addresses* at which the parties have lived are *irrelevant* to this paragraph, irrespective of the relative periods spent by the parties at those addresses.

Paragraph 3   4.4.3

The simple situation here is that the Court's jurisdiction is based on domicile of the parties, which statement is already printed on the standard form, but if another basis is to be used, eg the domicile of the respondent/habitual residence of the petitioner/respondent, a suitable amendment will need to be made.

Note

If habitual residence is relied upon, and the matter is at all complex, requiring the inclusion of a number of addresses, such violence will have to be done to the printed form to accommodate the extra details that drafting the petition from scratch may put the matter more clearly. In practice, you should not worry about your capability to do this, as this is not work that a very junior trainee would normally be asked to do alone.

The paragraph also requires the present residential addresses of the petitioner and the respondent to be given including the county but if either or both of these have been stated before at paragraph 2, only the first line of the address need be repeated, followed by the word 'aforesaid'.

Example

If paragraph 2 states that the parties last lived together at 1 High Street, Blankton in the county of Blankshire, in paragraph 3 it will be sufficient, if that address appears again as the address of one (or both) of the parties, to write '1 High Street, Blankton aforesaid'.

Note

If it is desirable to omit the petitioner's address from the petition because of fear of violence or molestation, while the solicitor's address may be given for service, there will still be a requirement for the petitioner's actual private address to be included in this paragraph unless application is made to the district judge for leave to omit it under FPR 1991 r 2.3. In this case it will be necessary for the petitioner to establish a need for protection as the district judge's discretion will not be exercised merely because the petitioner would like to start a new life free from any more mundane and trivial interference from the respondent!

The procedure is for the petitioner to apply to the district judge *ex parte* under rule 10.9, following the procedure laid down for this purpose in the Practice Direction of 11 April 1968 [1968] 1 WLR 782 and 8 May 1975 [1975] 1 WLR 787. These Practice Directions require the petition to be drafted and *filed*, omitting the petitioner's address, after which the *ex parte* application should be made for leave for service notwithstanding the omission of the address. The application should be supported by affidavit exhibiting a copy of the petition, with the address left blank. If the application is granted the petition will be served in the

normal way with a copy of the district judge's order, while
a note of the petitioner's address will be placed on the
Court file in a sealed envelope.

Obviously, if leave to omit the petitioner's address is
granted this will also have repercussions on other documents, such as the form of Statement of Arrangements,
see 5.4.2, and in ancillary relief proceedings where affidavits will have to be filed, see Chapter 11 at 11.4.2.

If leave is *refused*, the district judge will make an
order that the petition is *amended* by inserting the petitioner's address, see 5.8.

This paragraph also requires the occupations of both
parties to be stated. If the wife has no occupation outside
the home, she may simply be described as a *housewife*, or
wife and homemaker. If she is professionally qualified or
has skills or experience appropriate for some occupation,
this should be stated especially if she actually makes use
of that occupation, or could do so, in some part time
capacity. On the other hand, the husband will usually
have a profession or occupation which is actually being
deployed in gainful employment, or in some cases
would be if he was not temporarily unemployed, and is
less likely to be able to claim to be described as a 'homemaker' or the like, but the trainee should of course be
aware that in these politically correct times, in theory the
parties are equal in this respect before the law! If a
husband is merely temporarily out of work it is usually
best to give his usual occupation and to add *currently
unemployed*, but the rare husband who does not work at
all may be described as of *independent means*.

The parties' occupations are not in fact an unnecessary detail in the petition because they are relevant in
three contexts:

- where there are children, so that a Statement of
  Arrangements must be filed with the petition,
  because their parents' work will be part of the
  general picture which the district judge needs to
  decide whether the Court needs to exercise its
  powers under s 8 of the CA 1989;
- where there is domestic violence and an injunction is sought, because the Court will need to
  know the parties' employment situation in order
  to apply the criteria in s 1(3) of the Matrimonial
  Homes Act 1983 so as to decide which party could
  best afford alternative accommodation;
- in ancillary relief proceedings, where the earning
  capacity of the parties will be highly relevant.

Note

Tactics will play a part in deciding what to put in the petition at this point. Unless the wife is a feminist who is inordinately proud of her qualifications and experience, it will usually be better to describe her as a 'housewife' etc. if she has young children, wants to be maintained so as to be able to stay at home with them, and has not worked since before the marriage (or possibly not at all since gaining her qualifications and/or experience). This is more difficult to do without misleading the Court where she is professionally qualified and is using or has used the qualification recently, but can sometimes be justifiably done on the basis that the rules technically ask for occupation and no more.

4.4.4   **Paragraph 4**

Those who are new to family law drafting are often confused by the negative format of this paragraph which is normally written as 'There are no children of the family now living *except* ...' and sometimes amend it unnecessarily to produce a positive statement introducing a list of the children of the family whom they consider to qualify under s 52 of the MCA 1973 as amended by the CA 1989. This is not to be recommended because it ignores the *purpose* behind the paragraph, namely that it should be formally stated for the avoidance of any doubt in the matter that there are no other children of the family, save those whose names appear in that part of the petition, into whose interests the Court should enquire in pursuance of its duty to oversee the welfare of children whose parents are to be divorced by the Court's decree.

It is for this reason that all such 'children of the family should still be named even if they are over 18, since such over 18s may still have special needs, and whereas by s 41 of the MCA 1973 the Court always had a duty to look after the interests of all children under 18, by the amendment to s 41 effected by the Children Act 1989 this duty is now formally extended to inquiring into the interests of any child over 18 who is still dependent on the parties to a suit for divorce, for example because of mental or physical handicap.

Where a child is not the natural or adopted child of both parties, that child's parentage should be stated, together with the fact that that child 'has been treated as a child of the family', although this will not stop the respondent denying that the child in question is a child of the family if that be the case, for example because the respondent wishes to be excused financial liability for that child.

Where children of the family are under 18 their dates of birth should be given. Where such children are *over 16* (ie the minimum school leaving age) their particulars should be followed by a statement as to whether they are still receiving full time education or training for a trade, profession or vocation, though no further details need be given here, since that is for the Statement of Arrangements to be filed with the petition; see 5.4.2.

Note _____

The rules require that the full names of all children of the family be stated, including *surnames*, so it is actually *wrong* to omit their surnames even if that gives no cause for confusion.

_____

It is sometimes difficult to ascertain whether children are children of the family or not. However the following are not included in the definition:

- children *not yet born*, as an unborn child cannot be 'treated as' a living child, so if a husband behaves affectionately towards his wife while she is expecting a child which he thinks is his, that will not make it a 'child of the family': thus a child of another man cannot surreptitiously join the children of the family in this way either: *A v A (family; unborn child)* [1974] Fam 6;
- children *born after the 'family' has ceased to exist*, ie after separation prior to divorce or after divorce, so a child of another man born after the separation also cannot join the family in this way: *M v M* (1980) 2 FLR 39;
- children boarded with the parties by the local authority (s 52 expressly excludes them).

The following *are* included as children of the family:

- children who have actually been *born* and have been *treated* as children of the family when the husband mistakenly believes that any such child is his: *W(RJ) v W(SJ)* [1972] Fam 152. The rationale behind this is that such a child is nevertheless a child of the other party, irrespective of who its father is and may be treated as a child of the family like any other child of the other party, such as a child of a previous relationship.

If there are no children in the case, the word except at the end of the printed paragraph should simply be deleted and a full stop inserted so that Paragraph 4 reads 'There are no children of the family now living'.

4.4.5   **Paragraph 5**

There is also often confusion about paragraph 5 since it is not always appreciated how it differs from paragraph 4. Most children will be included at paragraph 4, which covers natural and adopted children of *both* parties (the first limb of s 52 MCA 1973), and *children of the family* within the meaning of the second limb of s 52 MCA 1973. The only children left are any not falling into any of these categories, and this paragraph is designed to cater for any such children whose inclusion in paragraph 4 cannot be justified in one way or another, for example a child whose father is and always has been accepted or alleged to be *not* the husband, whoever else the father might be and where the husband has *not* accepted a child as a child of the family. The purpose of the paragraph is therefore to bring within the court's notice any dependent child whose interests the Court might otherwise overlook and fail to safeguard before a DA is pronounced.

Children to be included in this paragraph might therefore be all or any of the following:

- any children born to the wife as a result of an extra marital affair whom the husband has categorically *not* accepted as children of the family (ie usually children put in this paragraph by husband petitioners – the wife petitioner will of course usually try to slip them into paragraph 4, unless the circumstances are very unusual, eg where the wife cannot do this because the child has never lived with the family, having spent all its life with its natural father, perhaps because the husband insisted on this as a condition of not ending the marriage earlier on the basis of the adultery resulting in the child's birth);
- any child of the wife's who is not a child of the husband, and who apparently qualifies as a stepchild, but does not qualify as a child of the family because the husband has categorically refused to accept that child as a child of the family.

These two situations are both rare but not entirely unknown, especially in the case of short marriages where the man may have married a woman who was already pregnant categorically telling her that he accepts responsibility for her but not for her unborn child, or alternatively not specifically addressing his mind to the issue.

Since the Child Support Act 1991 came into force, this issue is not likely to be one of substance unless the natural father has disappeared and cannot be traced so that he cannot support the child.

Note

The overall effect of both paragraphs 4 and 5 is to establish the identities of *any* relevant children whose lives might be affected by the dissolution of the marriage. However, stepchildren can still conceivably be excluded from both paragraphs if the husband has categorically refused to treat them as children of the family. In this case they will not qualify under paragraph 4 and if already born at the date of the marriage cannot qualify under paragraph 5 either (which is for children, not being children of the family, born to the wife *during the marriage*). Nevertheless, this is *very* difficult for a husband to establish, even after a very short marriage, as when it was tried in the case of *Day v Day* [1988] 1 FLR 278, the Court decided with both speed and asperity that Mr Day had perfectly understood his obligations to Mrs Day when he had married her, ie that the natural fathers of both her children had disappeared so that she was unable to call on them for support for either, and that in the circumstances he was taking on the obligation of supporting the children as well as her. They therefore declined to release him from his responsibilities although, after a much longer period of cohabitation, the marriage had collapsed after only six weeks.

If any child born during the marriage *is* to be included at paragraph 5 instead of paragraph 4, the petitioner should state who is alleged to be the father.

Note

If the petitioner is the husband the words 'so far as is known to the petitioner' qualify the statement to the best of his knowledge and belief (which is all that a husband is technically able to state unless he kept his wife under lock and key throughout the marriage). If the *wife* is the petitioner then these words should be *deleted* since she is presumed to *know* whether she has had other children during the course of the marriage who are not included at paragraph 4!

If there are no children to enter here, again delete the word except and insert a full stop.

4.4.6   Paragraph 6

This paragraph requires the inclusion of all previous proceedings, about which the Court which will pronounce the decree of divorce should know, anywhere in the world:

- *any* proceedings previously begun, dismissed or adjourned, even if an order was not ultimately made, relating to the *marriage, property of the parties or the children of the family*, eg dismissal of a previous divorce petition;
- *any* proceedings in the Family Proceedings Court under the DPMCA 1978, or in the High Court or county court, under MCA 1973 s 27, s 17 MWPA 1882;
- *any* proceedings for a domestic violence exclusion or non-molestation injunction;
- *any* proceedings in respect of a *child of the family*, eg for adoption or a care order.

As in the case of complications envisaged in 4.4.3, there might be a case for not using the printed form but for drafting from scratch, if such proceedings are complex and will occupy more white space than the form conveniently provides. However, again, this is not a case in which you should worry, since it would be highly unusual for any junior member of a firm's staff to be left to undertake such drafting without supervision. In any case in which you are (quite properly) asked to prepare such a draft *for approval by a superior*, careful reference should be made to the exact nature of the particulars required by the rules: see 4.3 above, and little difficulty should be experienced in practice in producing something suitable.

Note

If there is nothing to include under this paragraph again simply strike out the word except at the end, and insert a full stop in its place so as to make sense of the printed wording.

4.4.7   Paragraph 7

This paragraph is a relatively new addition to the required contents of the petition, since it requires detail to be included of CSA assessments, which are clearly vital to the Court's proper understanding of the

Statement of Arrangements, and of its duty under s 41 of the MCA 1973. If there are no details to enter here, again strike out the word *except* and insert a full stop.

Paragraph 8

This paragraph requires details to be included of any continuing foreign divorce proceedings, for the obvious reason that where there are other proceedings pending, the Court must consider whether the English proceedings should be stayed under the Domicile and Matrimonial Proceedings Act 1973 Schedule 1. The rules make it clear that 'court proceedings' include those before any tribunal or other authority which has the power to affect status, and that proceedings are 'continuing' until finally disposed of. Should details need to be given under this paragraph, close reference should be made to the rules to be sure to include everything that the Court would wish to know so as to decide on the question of a stay of the English proceedings, such as the Court where the proceedings are continuing, the names of the parties to those proceedings (which may not be the same parties as those in the English suit, eg where one party is alleged to be still married to someone else. Complex drafting of this paragraph by a trainee is subject to the same remarks as at 4.4.6 and 4.4.3. Again it should be finished off with a full stop and the word *except* deleted where appropriate.

Paragraph 9

Unless the divorce is based on s 1(2)(e), ie 5 years separation, paragraph 9 should simply be deleted and the subsequent paragraphs renumbered 9 *et seq*. If the divorce is under s 1(2)(e), succinct details of any arrangement entered into should be given, eg if the matrimonial home is to be transferred or capital or income payments made. This is because of the statutory defence to a petition brought under s 1(2)(e) afforded by s 5 of the MCA 1973: see 3.2, and of the protection to respondents afforded by s 10 of the MCA 1973: see 3.2.1, where the s 5 defence is unsuccessful. The Court will clearly need to know whether such a defence or such protection might be applicable.

Paragraph 10 (otherwise 9)

Unless the divorce is under s 1(2)(e) (when the paragraph numbering may be left as printed) this paragraph will be renumbered paragraph 9, and all the subsequent paragraphs renumbered accordingly. The substance of the paragraph can in any case be left untouched, since this is the allegation, as required by s 1(1), which is the *uniform and sole ground* for divorce, namely that the marriage has irretrievably broken down.

4.4.11   **Paragraph 11 (otherwise 10)**

This paragraph is left blank in all versions of the printed form, and is for the insertion by the person drafting the petition of the correct Fact relied upon as the basis of proof of the *sole ground* of divorce, namely irretrievable breakdown of the marriage. The most relevant Fact should be selected from ss 1(2)(a)–(e) of the Act and the allegation inserted into this blank space should follow the precise wording of the relevant sub-section of the statute as follows, and *nothing more*:

For adultery – Fact A: s 1(2)(a)

The respondent has committed adultery and the petitioner finds it intolerable to live with the respondent.

For behaviour – Fact B: s 1(2)(b)

The respondent has behaved in such a way that the petitioner cannot reasonably be expected to live with the respondent.

For desertion – Fact C: s 1(2)(c)

The respondent has deserted the petitioner for a continuous period of at least two years immediately preceding the presentation of the petition.

For two years separation and consent – Fact D: s 1(2)(d)

The parties have lived apart for a continuous period of at least two years immediately preceding the presentation of the petition.

For five years separation – Fact E: s 1(2)(e)

The parties have lived apart for a continuous period of 5 years immediately preceding the presentation of the petition.

> *Note*
>
> It is not normal to allege more than one Fact since to do so gives an impression of indecision, or alternatively either of a weak case or of overkill. Proof of one Fact alone will suffice for a decree so that the only case in which an exception might be made would be where a fault based Fact is to be used as a long stop in case the respondent cannot be relied upon to give consent, or to give consent and sustain it until DN, or without causing a great deal of trouble in relation to s 10(1) or s 10(2) and (3): see 3.2.1.

If any of these points might be a problem, not only does the inclusion of a second Fact in such a case permit the petition to proceed without delay or amendment if the respondent turns difficult, but it may even be instrumental in securing the respondent's consent, since if the respondent sees that divorce is inevitable anyway on the basis of another Fact if the required consent is not forthcoming or is withdrawn, any sensible person will cut their losses to try to drive as beneficial a bargain as possible by *consenting in return for a good overall severance package* (either of ancillary relief alone or ancillary relief and residence, contact and/or other agreements in relation to the children and will be anxious not to annoy the petitioner by withdrawing that consent.

Where two Facts have been used in the case of such an untrustworthy respondent, once the consent has been obtained on the Acknowledgment of Service, the petition may be amended (which may be done without leave before an Answer has been filed) to delete the fault based Fact so as to proceed on Fact D alone. This in most cases is preferable if Fact D is genuinely available without complications, especially if children are involved and a post-divorce relationship is desirable.

The printed form of petition can easily be adapted to allege the two Facts in the alternative, and the two sets of particulars can be entered one after the other in the space left for paragraph 12 (otherwise 11). For precedents in the rare cases where two Facts are to be relied upon, see the usual practitioners' loose-leaf works.

Paragraph 12 (otherwise 11)   4.4.12

Usually a page, or the best part of a page, is left blank in printed forms for particulars of the Fact relied upon. This should afford sufficient space to detail any one of the five Facts pleaded in paragraph 11 (including behaviour under Fact B, which is obviously the most potentially voluminous). There will not usually be a good reason for resorting at this stage to a petition drafted from scratch for reasons of space here and you should take the hint and not without extremely good reason exceed the area of paper allocated for the detailing of particulars of the chosen Fact!

A minimalist approach should ideally be adopted. *Careful thought resulting in concise, succinct details of the matters relied on* (but not the *evidence* by which they are to be proved) rather than an acreage of paper covered will result in a *strong* draft on the basis of which the district judge will be able to decide that the petitioner is entitled to obtain a decree.

It will be convenient to look at drafting of the five Facts separately, since each requires a different approach, although a common factor is that in each case the *particulars must support the statement in paragraph 11* (or 10 if the paragraphs have been renumbered following deletion of paragraph 9) *of the Fact in s 1(2) on which the divorce is based*. If you look carefully at the *precise wording* of s 1(2) which is *being pleaded* to the resulting draft should not go far wrong.

Adultery: s 1(2)(a)

Paragraph 10 (renumbered from 11 after the deletion of 9 since it is not a Fact E petition) will have stated 'The respondent has committed adultery and the petitioner finds it intolerable to live with the respondent'.

Paragraph 11 (now renumbered downwards from 12 to follow on from 10) must *specify* if possible *dates, and places* (or if these are not known exactly *the period over which* and if possible *at least one location* where the adultery was committed, eg the address at which the respondent and the third party, whether named as co-respondent or not, have been or are cohabiting). If there is a child as a result of the adultery this should be stated and will be powerful evidence, but by FPR 1991 r 2.7(1) it is *no longer necessary* to *name* the alleged adulterer and this may well be preferred by the respondent who may wish to marry that third party.

Ideally, a suitable adultery particulars paragraph would read: 'On the   day of   the respondent committed adultery with AB at   .'

Failing this, it would be perfectly acceptable to alleged that 'On the   day of   at a place or places unknown but including the Bag o' Nails Night Club, Brighton, Sussex the respondent committed adultery with a woman known to the petitioner only as "Fifi".' (or 'with a woman whom the petitioner could identify if called upon to do so').

Alternatively, it is even possible to plead 'On a day or days unknown at a place or places unknown the respondent committed adultery with a woman unknown'.

The reason for the acceptability of such apparently imprecise statements is of course that these allegations in the petition are only *allegations* and have still to be proved by *evidence*. This may be afforded by the petitioner's affidavit in support of the petition which requires the petitioner to detail that evidence on oath. As the affidavit is *sworn* the petitioner's own evidence may be sufficient and the divorce be granted on no more than the petitioner's own statement that following suspicions on which he or she challenged the respondent, the adultery was frankly admitted. Alternatively, the respondent may admit the adultery in question on the Acknowledgement of Service form: see 5.6.

The perfect situation is of course where the respondent and the third party are living and cohabiting at an address which the petitioner states in the petition, which together with the fact of the birth of a child whose parentage is detailed on the birth certificate leaves no room for argument! Even should there be no child, where the alleged adulterer is named and made a party as co-respondent in the suit, when the district judge sees that the respondent and co-respondent live at the same address, the case will generally be taken as proved since adultery will be inferred from the cohabitational relationship. A suitable paragraph in such circumstances (where the respondent is the wife) would be 'The respondent has since the day of 199 lived and cohabited and regularly committed adultery with the co-respondent at

and as a result of this association a child was born to the respondent of whom the petitioner is not the father'.

Note

Should there have been cohabitation for less than six months since the last act of adultery relied upon, then pursuant to s 2(2) MCA 1973 (see 3.3.1) this must be stated. A further paragraph will be needed to deal with this and should either be numbered consecutively to the rest of the petition 12 (following on from the renumbered 11) or alternatively paragraph 11 may be sub-divided into 11(i) and 11(ii) as follows:

'11(i) On the day of 199 the respondent committed adultery with   at the Grand Hotel, Brighton, Sussex.

11(ii) The petitioner resumed cohabitation with the respondent at 1 High Street, Blankton, Blankshire from 1st December to 31st December 199 a period amounting to less than six months.'

Note

The petitioner does not have to plead either the fact that, or any particulars of why, in addition to the adultery committed, living with the respondent is intolerable, although this is a salient part of the Fact. This is a matter of evidence for the petitioner to swear to in the affidavit in support of the petition: see 5.9.2 below.

Behaviour: s 1 (2)(b)

In the case of this Fact paragraph 10 (renumbered from 11 after deletion of paragraph 9) will have stated 'The respondent has behaved in such a way that the petitioner cannot reasonably be expected to live with the respondent' and paragraph 11 must justify this statement in terms of the law on what does and does not constitute behaviour: see 2.3.

With the possible exception of desertion, which can present technical problems, behaviour particulars can be the *most* difficult to draft *well*, although there is a world of difference in the skill and precision required depending on whether it is anticipated that the suit might be *defended* or whether (as is usually the case if the allegations are not too outrageous) the respondent intends to let the matter go through *unopposed*. In this latter case, and fortunately less than one per cent of petitions are defended, no great skill is required, as is daily demonstrated by the freehand drafts regularly produced unaided by members of the public on the basis of a set of forms and an information pack obtained from the Court or even the well known high street stationers. However, it has been observed that the brighter members of the public no longer pay good money to high street stationers, but go direct to the Court where they obtain the forms and an explanatory booklet, stop for a chat with the clerks in the Court office, and if necessary return with a list of queries and a pencil draft before finalising the fair copy, ultimately filing something very creditable. As such no lawyer can afford to be unable to do as well, and the profession, even at trainee level, is forced to do superior work!

However, where you can score over unqualified members of the public is in *learning from experience* and in *developing a polished drafting style*. Talented members of the public, even if getting divorced as regularly as allowed within the restraints of MCA 1973 s 3, necessarily have infrequent chances to hone their drafting skills, whereas if you adopt the first principle of drafting good behaviour particulars, namely that an up to date professional approach is required to match the material available in the client's statement to what is required to obtain the decree, a little practice should soon produce near perfection.

As in the case of adultery, dates and detail help and should be included where possible, but nowhere is a minimalist approach more to be recommended than in the production of a good set of behaviour particulars. What is required is not a catalogue of callous cruelty but a *minimum* of three and usually a maximum of about six sub-paragraphs, into which paragraph 11 should be divided, detailing conduct which can be said to be:

- objectively unacceptable; and
- subjectively damaging to the petitioner.

There are occasional *exceptions* to the suggested maximum but they are few and far between and as a general rule an excessive number of paragraphs only tends to show unnecessary prolixity, since the object of the particulars is only to indicate to the district judge that the petitioner is *entitled* to the decree, *not* to gain the district judge's sympathy, nor that of anyone else, for an ill used petitioner.

Thus if the petition is *unlikely* to be defended, the *safe minimum level* of behaviour for a decree is what is required and indeed over-egging the pudding may only inspire an unexpected desire to defend in an otherwise mild and malleable respondent, with disastrous consequences in terms of cost and delay.

If it is thought that the respondent *might* defend, (though mostly even those who initially think of doing so do not in the end if properly advised) then the particulars will need to be even more carefully drafted than usual, to show if possible:

- an unanswerable case of behaviour; but
- nothing gratuitously annoying.

This generally means that they do not need to be either *longer* or *nastier* than the norm. Indeed, nasty particulars only tend to inflame even those respondents who do not feel any desire to defend, to the point where they are instead obstructive about something else, such as ancillary relief or child matters, neither of which is desirable for all of the obvious reasons.

The only exception to this rule might be where there has been violence upon the basis of which a non-molestation and/or ouster injunction might have to be sought, in which the petition would of course be exhibited to the applicant's affidavit in support. In this case the position will need to be clearly and comprehensively set out. Nevertheless, this may still be done with economy and restraint, since the position may further be amplified in the affidavit if necessary: see Chapter 17.

While the suggested 'minimum of three' is the 'rule of thumb' which dates from the late Sir Roger Ormerod's idea that using a minimum of three incidents or allegations – 'the first the worst and the last' – in drafting a behaviour petition should be *sufficient* for a decree, at least if the suit was undefended, it is not a rule written in stone. The basic aim is that the petition should not give unnecessary offence to an otherwise potentially cooperative respondent, but if more sub-paragraphs are genuinely needed they should be used. A more recent trend is to add if possible another incident which is 'witnessed' – because of the potential value of third party evidence – so that the 'rule of 3' may become an ideal of 4. However, if there is no 'witnessed' incident and the three paragraphs seem weak alone, a further general paragraph to start with, alleging some overall unattractive behaviour – selfishness, self-centredness, lack of commitment to the marriage or the family – will usually suffice without reaching the suggested maximum of 6 incidents except in the gravest cases. The effect must be to make a *statement which cannot be ignored* but at the same time *avoids overkill*.

There is no closed list of 'behaviour' so you must look at the file note and extract from it whatever looks promising. The following is a basic checklist:

- violence:
  - if serious: at least one incident;
  - if less serious: two or three incidents which cumulatively are sufficient;
- any other anti-social behaviour, eg:
  - financial irresponsibility;
  - lack of participation in family life;
  - drunkenness, especially coupled with violence;
  - alcoholism, drug taking, especially if coupled with addiction;
  - criticism, especially constant, cumulative if petty;
  - abusive language or conduct;
  - selfish, self-centred, inconsiderate or unfeeling conduct;
- illness, mental or physical, if serious, prolonged, or having a bad effect on the petitioner.

Note

If *all* of these exist in one case, using every single one is manifestly unnecessary! If a defence is *anticipated* select the strongest; if a divorce is *mutually desired* select the *weakest* so as not to give unnecessary offence to a respondent who may then spontaneously cooperate in ancillary matters. What you will usually need to do in any case is to:

- review the client's statement taken at the first interview: see 5.2;

- select a list of points to be made;

It will probably be best to divide them into:

- allegations of general and/or continuing conduct; and

- specific incidents with an actual or approximate date.

Finally, arrange the whole into some sort of order.

Usually, it will be convenient to place the *general* allegations (selfishness, moodiness, financial irresponsibility, lack of participation in family life etc) *first*, and then *itemised incidents* arranged in *chronological order* afterwards, culminating in the *last and most recent*.

Some practitioners like to place the general allegations all together in the initial sub-paragraph 11(i), taking care not to stretch the district judge's credulity too far by claiming the respondent is a complete monster about whom no good word could be said, and then to start the second sub-paragraph with a statement such as 'The following are examples of such conduct', and then to set out the three or four specific incidents which are relied on, setting them out as 11(2)(a) (b) (c) and (d), and then ending with a final sub-paragraph 11(3):

'As a result of the matters aforesaid the petitioner left the respondent on the   day of 199 and the parties have not since resumed cohabitation'.

This last sentence is useful to establish that the petitioner finds the respondent's behaviour unacceptable, although if the parties have since resumed cohabitation this paragraph will have to be adjusted accordingly.

If sub-paragraphs and sub-sub-paragraphs do not appeal, it is not actually essential that all the particulars should be confined to paragraph 11, and all the remaining material entered in and after the renumbered paragraph 11 can simply be divided into further paragraphs and numbered consecutively from 12 onwards: there is generally at least a page or a page and a half of white space available to fill if required, since the next text following is the prayer.

Note

It must be emphasised that *good* drafting of particulars is a skill which comes only with practice acquired over time. It is therefore essential that you should make a start on *actually drafting* particulars as soon as possible, since a mastery of the theory is absolutely useless without the ability to produce a satisfactory draft when called upon to do so. Guidance can be given but essentially as with all drafting you have to *learn alone from experience*.

Desertion: s 1(2)c

Paragraph 10 (renumbered downwards 11 after deletion of paragraph 9) will have stated 'The respondent has deserted the petitioner for a continuous period of at least two years immediately preceding the presentation of the petition'.

The particulars in paragraph 11 must therefore support this statement and must show two years or a total of two years *up to the date of presentation of the petition* and where appropriate that any periods of cohabitation do not exceed a total of six months within the *total* period relied on for desertion. It goes without saying that desertion requires that there should have been an intention to desert: see 2.4.3 above, although there is no need to include any such statement to that effect in the *particulars* of desertion in the petition, since this will be made clear in the petitioner's evidence in the affidavit in support of the petition: see 5.9.2 and such matters only really become relevant if the petition is defended.

A general paragraph for desertion might therefore read 'The respondent informed the petitioner on the day of 199 that he was leaving her to live elsewhere and would not be returning to the matrimonial home, since which day the parties have lived separate and apart'.

If there has been cohabitation since the initial desertion, this can be stated by tacking on at the end of such a paragraph the *words*:

'... save that cohabitation was resumed for the following periods namely:

From 1st January to 1st February 199 and from 1st April to 4th April 199 at [address] which periods amount to less than six months in all'.

In the case of desertion the necessary drafting will usually therefore be short and to the point.

Constructive desertion should in general *not* be attempted, since any case of constructive desertion can be better pleaded as *behaviour* and without waiting for two years to elapse: see 2.4.5 above.

Two years' separation and consent: s 1(2)(d)

Paragraph 10 in this case will have stated 'The parties have lived apart for a continuous period of two years immediately preceding the presentation of the petition and the respondent consents to a decree being granted'.

Again, the particulars must support this statement by demonstrating two years' separation and claiming the respondent's agreement. No details of the latter need be given since the respondent will in due course be required *personally* to sign the form of Acknowledgment of Service indicating consent, which is evidence of that agreement: see 2.5.2 and 5.6.

A suitable particulars paragraph might therefore read 'The parties separated by agreement on the   day of   199   since which day they have lived apart.'

Again, if there has been any subsequent cohabitation short of six months this may be pleaded by adding to the existing paragraph the words '... save that cohabitation etc' in the same format as for desertion above.

Five years separation: s 1(2)(e)

Paragraph 10 will have stated 'The parties have lived apart for a continuous period of five years immediately preceding the presentation of the petition'.

A suitable particulars paragraph might therefore read 'On the   day of   199   the petitioner left the matrimonial home since which day the parties have lived separate and apart'.

The prayer   4.4.13

The prayer is always the same in the printed form of petition and should not be altered in any way by striking out any of the forms of ancillary relief claimed (unless any are definitely *not* required), eg claims for the children where there are *no* children, since if that is done, eg the claim for a lump sum order is struck out because it is thought that it will not be required, the petitioner will be precluded from seeking that form of ancillary relief without amendment, which may be complex: see 5.8.

Any claim for an order under the Children Act 1989 should be specifically inserted, but this is now rare since formal orders are rarely sought in divorce proceedings and may be claimed entirely independently if required: see Chapter 6.

Claims for costs are also now rare in undefended suits, although costs might be claimed against a co-respondent, the only situation in which an alleged adulterer actually needs to be named. In other undefended cases, it is common for the parties to pay their own costs, at least of divorces based on facts which are not fault based, unless a party is paying privately or is in receipt of full legal aid (not when only on the Green Form as such costs would only be those of a litigant in person): see 5.1.3 and 5.1.4.

4.4.14   Service details and backsheet

Filling in these details is perfectly straightforward. All the necessary details must be included and will be taken from the client's initial statement. The solicitor's address may be used by a Green Form client in which case the petitioner's name should appear at the bottom of the backsheet where a space is left for the purpose and the address should be expressed as c/o the firm.

4.4.15   Other family drafting

For drafting in defended divorce see 5.13.3, for Children Act 1989 applications, see Chapter 6, especially 6.8.3, for ancillary relief, see 8.4 and 11.5.1, 11.10, and for domestic violence orders see Chapter 17.

Self-assessment questions

1 What restrictions, if any, are there on the drafting of a petition?
2 What previous proceedings need to be mentioned in a petition for divorce?
3 What is a child of the family?
4 How do children over the age of 18 who may have special needs come to the attention of the divorce court?
5 What type of child should be mentioned in paragraph 5 of the printed form of petition?
6 When *must* there be a co-respondent to an adultery petition?
7 Is it *essential* to give *precise* details of the dates on and places at which adultery was committed?
8 How long and detailed should particulars of behaviour be?
9 Should the standard form of prayer of the petition be edited to remove those claims which will probably not be pursued?
10 If they are removed can such claims still be pursued if the petitioner has a change of mind and if so how?

Chapter 5

Divorce procedure

Financing the suit, ancillary proceedings and child disputes

5.1

As far as the solicitor is concerned, divorce procedure begins almost at the moment at which the new client enters the office.

This is because, since there is no legal aid available for obtaining straightforward divorce decrees, a decision on how to finance the actual suit (as opposed to any ancillary relief, child or domestic violence proceedings) is an essential pre-requisite of any work done, and the decision as to how the solicitor's work will be paid for will affect how the divorce suit is handled, ie by the solicitor on behalf of the client, or by the client acting as a litigant in person, advised by the solicitor under the Green Form Scheme.

Before opening a new file in any case it is essential to determine whether the client will be a *private client* (when the solicitor will have the whole conduct of the case in return for the usual fees charged by the firm) or whether the client will be on *legal aid*, ie either full civil legal aid or the Green Form (when depending on the nature of the work to be done, the solicitor will either have the whole conduct of the case or essentially be advising a litigant in person).

There are, moreover, professional conduct implications of this aspect of taking on a new client, since it is incumbent on the solicitor to make it clear to the client where legal aid (including Green form) is available or PCS 5.01 and 13.10 will be breached. Where the client is a private client, then all the usual client care rules must be observed, including information about costs, which should either be on the basis of applicable fixed fees or alternatively the best estimate which can be given in accordance with hourly rates. These will of course vary from firm to firm and between different levels of staff, and usually be subject to additional charges in relation to the importance of the case and other criteria. However, nowhere is the obligation more important to give detailed financial information than when the solicitor is working on legal aid because of the statutory charge: see below at 5.1.6.

As an LPC student who has already completed the compulsory part of the course before embarking on any optional subjects you will already be familiar with the distinction between the Green Form and full civil legal aid. For divorce purposes a mixture of these distinct types of legal aid may be used.

5.1.1   The divorce suit

The divorce suit will usually have to be conducted under the Green Form, since there is no civil legal aid for *divorce suits* as such, ie the process leading to the grant of DN and DA, save in exceptional circumstances, irrespective of whether the client qualifies on financial grounds, which is a separate matter. The client will therefore need to be clearly told this at the outset and it is the solicitor's obligation to make it clear. The exceptional circumstances in which full civil legal aid *is* available are where:

- the suit is defended: see 5.13;
- there is to be a hearing in open court: see 5.10.1;
- the petitioner is physically or mentally handicapped.

Note

The latter could include being unable to speak adequate English.

Other proceedings

Other proceedings *connected with the divorce* may be conducted on full legal aid. The most common proceedings thus covered are those for *ancillary relief.*

Other proceedings *not necessarily connected with the divorce* but which may surface at the same time may also be conducted on full legal aid. This category comprises contested Children Act 1989 applications: see Chapter 6 and domestic violence injunctions: see below Chapter 17, both of which may be started and pursued without divorce proceedings necessarily being on foot, though in the latter case if a divorce suit is already in process the application should, for technical reasons, normally be made latched on to the divorce suit.

Note

This does not mean that the *divorce suit itself* suddenly becomes eligible for legal aid! The suit itself will continue to be financed up to DA by whatever means was originally decided, unless there is a change of circumstances affecting that decision, while the ancillary relief, CA 1989 or domestic violence proceedings are separately paid for by the Legal Aid Board.

Green Form and legal aid distinguished 5.1.2

Most clients needing legal aid will therefore use the Green Form to obtain the divorce decree, with an *extension* for certain complications, such as service problems, but will use legal aid if any of the qualifying situations arises (eg the suit becomes defended) also routinely for ancillary relief, and for CA 1989 and domestic proceedings if these matters arise. Green Form advice may also be the first step in protection against domestic violence or CA 1989 applications.

Green Form 5.1.3

What is covered

The use of the Green Form is governed by the Legal Advice and Assistance Regulations 1989 as amended and will cover the following *divorce suit* work:

- preliminary advice on whether the client has grounds for divorce, effects on the client's status, arrangements for children, income, division of assets, housing and what to do about the matrimonial home (in other words the complete stock-taking comprised in the first interview with a divorce client): see 5.2;
- drafting the Petition and the Statement of Arrangements for the children and filling in all the necessary forms;
- advising the client how to file the forms and documents at court and on the relevant procedure, particularly on tricky points such as service: see 5.6;
- advising the client about any attendance before the district judge on a s 41 appointment if there are unusual circumstances in connection with the children: see 3.5.
- advising the client how to obtain the decree absolute.

The solicitor is allowed a total of two hours for this work, three if the petition and supporting documents are drafted, but an extension can of course be applied for for good cause. *No* court attendances are permitted, not even before the district judge on a s 41 appointment if the petitioner is asked to attend for that purpose: see 3.5.

Note

The Green Form Scheme will also of course cover any other *advisory* work *outside* the divorce suit, for example where the client is also suffering from domestic violence or wishes to make a CA 1989 application. In theory *only one Green Form per divorce* case is allowed but in practice practitioners often manage to have more than one on foot for different elements, eg the divorce suit and the children or the domestic violence and particularly use separate ones for different property proceedings and get each of these Green Forms discharged, ie the file formally closed when the proceedings are disposed of. This is beneficial to the client in not allowing a cumulative legal aid bill to develop which might result in the fruits of a later action for recovery or preservation of property to be eroded by past costs: see 5.1.6.

Technically, by Regulation 17 two forms should not be used, but an extension of the existing one probably be sought instead but there is sometimes a grey area as to whether matters are really separate or should be regarded as all one. However, by Regulation 16 if a client comes from another solicitor, it is essential to obtain prior authority to take over the case and to obtain any required extension, since the time already used counts towards the total even if for one reason or another the new solicitor has to do everything again. An extension may be obtained from the Area Manager on form GF3, although prior telephone authorisation is available by giving all the GF3 information orally and later completing the form.

Application

Application for Green Form advice and assistance is made on the appropriate form completed in the solicitor's office, after the practitioner has used the accompanying key card to determine financial eligibility and this needs to be done at the first interview: see 5.2.

Financial eligibility

This is determined in divorce cases in the same way as for any other use of the Green Form, except that obviously the spouse's resources will not be taken into account since if they divorcing (or applying for judicial separation) they will clearly have a contrary interest. This is in fact a normal exception noted on the key card, so should come as no surprise.

Your costs

Solicitors recover their own costs under the Green Form:

- First from any costs paid to them on behalf of their client as party and party costs;
- Next from any costs paid to their client, the legally assisted person, by any other person, eg the opponent, pursuant to the charge in the solicitor's favour afforded by LAA 198 s 11(2), and from any property recovered or preserved;
- Last from the legal aid fund.

There is a certain connection between the last two. A solicitor may assign the benefit of the s 11(2) charge to the Legal Aid Board who will thereupon pay over the costs to the solicitor` or the solicitor can apply to the area committee for authority not to enforce the charge in certain circumstances pursuant to Regulation 33. Generally these latter situations are not going to apply in Green Form divorce, since the ancillary relief proceedings, where the property will be recovered or preserved will be funded by legal aid, but occasionally it is possible to deal with other family property proceedings on the Green Form.

Note

Assistance by representation (ABWOR) – although this is inappropriate in *divorce* proceedings, it may be useful for matrimonial matters outside the divorce suit, eg to enable the solicitor to go to the magistrates' (Family Proceedings Court) on behalf of the client in connection with domestic violence or CA 1989 applications.

You will recall that where ABWOR is granted financial limits on charges are relaxed although the practitioner must still exercise suitable restraint or the Legal Aid Board may not meet excessive costs incurred, and approval will need to be sought from the Area Manager for large items of expenditure, such as instructing counsel or engaging experts: Regulations 22 and 23.

Financial limits are higher for the grant of ABWOR than for the Green Form, but otherwise the Green Form will need to be completed in the normal way, plus an application form for ABWOR setting out precisely, in sufficient and suitable detail to enable the Area Manager to judge whether ABWOR is appropriate, in what sort of proceedings ABWOR is required and why.

The criteria for granting ABWOR is the same as for legal aid, and it is often preferred by the Legal Aid Board for, eg domestic violence where perfectly satisfactory protection can in most cases be obtained from the Family

Proceedings Court instead of incurring the extra cost of legal aid in the county court: see Chapter 17. In urgent cases emergency ABWOR may be obtained over the telephone, although as ABWOR is granted more quickly than legal aid (because the solicitor assesses financial eligibility) this may not always be necessary. The solicitor has a duty to inform the other party and the court of the grant of ABWOR but there is no special form, so a letter will normally be used for this purpose: Regulation 24.

5.1.4   Legal aid

The use of Legal Aid is governed by the Legal Aid Act 1988 (LAA 1988) as amended and the Civil Legal Aid (General) Regulations 1989. It has not been available for the normal undefended *divorce suit* since 1977, although it is still available for exceptional situations: see 5.1 above. Briefly, the practitioner will use legal aid in the divorce suit for:

- a defended divorce; and
- where physical or mental disability makes it impractical to proceed without;
- for a hearing in open court;

and will use legal aid outside the divorce suit for;

- Ancillary relief proceedings;
- CA 89 proceedings;
- Domestic violence injunctions.

Note

Obtaining legal aid *for the respondent* in a defended divorce suit will be an uphill task. It will be necessary to satisfy the Area Manager that there is some real reason why the suit should be *defended*. By Regulation 29 the Area Manager can always refuse legal aid if although the applicant has a good case in law the benefit which would accrue from success in the proceedings would be trivial and is likely to be refused.

Emergency legal aid is available under Regulation 19 where appropriate. This differs from ordinary civil legal aid in being available much faster in emergency situations, since it can take up to six weeks to process an ordinary legal aid application and some cases cannot wait that long. Situations in which this is required in *divorce suits* are likely to be rare, but not impossible, since as in other cases an emergency certificate will be granted in divorce if:

- the applicant is likely to satisfy the usual criteria (ie as to financial eligibility and the case being a proper one for legal aid to be granted); and

- it is in the interests of justice that the applicant should be granted legal aid.

As in other case, emergency legal aid can be obtained by telephone, the solicitor undertaking to send the fully completed form confirming the information given orally in the emergency telephone application: Regulation 19. The emergency certificate will be likely to be limited to a short period, an extension of which can be granted if the full civil legal aid certificate has not arrived by the time that the emergency certificate is about to expire. The client should, as in all case, be told the consequences if full legal aid is *not* ultimately granted, ie the client will *never* have been an assisted person and will have to pay the solicitor not only at the legal aid rate the solicitor would have received under a full legal aid certificate but *also* the *difference between that figure and the private client rate*.

Application

Application is made on the appropriate LAA 1988 forms (which the practitioner may help the client to complete as part of the Green Form work). The form now in use for *divorce* is CLA 2 plus the appropriate means form, chosen from CLA 4A, B or C or form L17. Form CLA3 will be needed for an emergency legal aid application. If legal aid is being used for domestic violence or CA1989 proceedings it will depend on whether those proceedings are technically *within* the matrimonial proceedings (which they are if a divorce suit has been started) whether CLA 3 should still be used or whether, eg CLA5 should be used because the CA1989 proceedings are technically a free standing application since divorce proceedings have *not been started*. There are special legal aid provisions for Children Act 1989 proceedings: see Chapter 6.

Financial eligibility

This is governed by LAA 1988 s 15 and follows the normal legal aid rules.

The drawback of legal aid   5.1.5

The problem with using legal aid in matrimonial cases is that although the grant of legal aid results in the fund assuming responsibility for paying all the legal costs of the assisted person while the case is going on, the Legal Aid Board has a duty to seek reimbursement of the money laid out in financing the case. Moreover where, as in most divorces, money or property is recovered or pre-served in ancillary relief proceedings, the Legal Aid

Board will have first call on both to pay the cost, *not only* of the ancillary relief proceedings, but also of any *other* costs incurred, such as of Children Act 1989 proceedings or proceedings for domestic violence protection, and by LAA 1988 s 16(9) even the cost of the Green Form work. This means that legal aid is certainly not a *gift* and is usually not even a very generous *loan*. This is because although there is power to *postpone* the payment of the bill where the property in question is to provide a home for the assisted person and dependants, there is *no* power to *forego* collection of the money owed, no matter how much hardship that may cause. The result is that the 'statutory charge' – like a second mortgage – is placed on the assisted person's home where that has been 'recovered or preserved' in the course of proceedings financed by the Legal Aid Board.

This is the reason for hard things sometimes said in reported cases by judges about the foolishness of parties litigating on legal aid and running up a bill out of all proportion to the costs incurred, instead of settling in a sensible and cost effective manner before the costs run out of control.

The way in which the reimbursement of the fund for legal aid costs work is as follows. The Legal Aid Board has a duty to recoup costs:

- first from any costs paid by the other party;
- next from the assisted person's assessed contribution (if any);
- last from money or property recovered or preserved in the proceedings, which may result in the application of the statutory charge under LAA 1988 s 16(6), ie in exactly the same order as your costs are paid: see 5.1.3.

Note

If the three sources above do not fully reimburse the Legal Aid Board for their costs, they will generously bear the deficit themselves! Thus if the proceedings financed are child proceedings where there has been no order for costs, no contribution from the assisted person (and obviously no property recovered or preserved) the Legal Aid Board has to pay the whole bill.

Moreover, if the assisted person's assessed contribution *exceeds* the amount of the costs bill in any case, the Board will repay the excess to the assisted person: LAA 1988 s 16(4).

For the definition of property 'recovered or preserved' see Property which is 'in issue' at 5.1.6.

The statutory charge: LAA 1988 s 16(6)   5.1.6

Where it applies, there is no way of escaping the application of the statutory charge, on which simple interest will have to be paid at the rate of money in court except possibly by advising the client who has the credit status to do so to refinance the debt elsewhere at a better rate of interest than will be charged by the Legal Aid Board. When the mortgage rate is low this may be a realistic option for some clients, though not for those who have a cash flow problem, since one of the few advantages of the statutory charge is that, once the charge takes effect, interest on the amount outstanding is not paid monthly, as a mortgage would have to be, but only in the future when the house is finally sold and the legal aid bill defrayed.

This however will be the only possibility of helping the client, since the solicitor is under a duty to inform the Area Manager of any property recovered or preserved in the proceedings, so there is no concealing it, and it has been repeatedly held that the court should not even tailor its order to evade the statutory charge artificially, by, for example, making orders in favour of children, who are not the 'assisted person' within the meaning of the regulations, as was unsuccessfully tried in the case of *Drascovic v Drascovic* (1981) 11 Fam Law 87.

Note

Nevertheless, district judges in ancillary relief proceedings often do indirectly take the statutory charge into account, since they usually require an up to date statement of the costs position of each party before making orders, and then in practice take them into account so as not to make a futile order from which the applicant will receive no real benefit.

However, there are steps which can be taken to mitigate the effect of the charge:
- restricting the property which is technically 'recovered or preserved' in the action by ensuring that it is not 'in issue' in the proceedings: *Hanlon v Law Society* [1981] AC 124;
- using the available exemptions within the meaning of Regulation 94.

Property which is 'in issue'

It was held in the *Hanlon* case that where there is a dispute over *title* to a property which is jointly owned beneficially but not legally, and neither side agrees that the other owns at least a half share, the value of the *entire* property is in 'issue' because the successful party who achieves a transfer of the property from the legal owner has (i) recovered that party's share and (ii) preserved their own. Thus the *whole* value of the property is available to secure the debt of the successful party's costs in favour of the Legal Aid Board (otherwise they might have suffered a deficit in the settlement of their total bill if only *half* the house value had been available for their legal charge to attach to).

The case of *Curling v Law Society* [1985] 1 All ER 705 confirmed that even if there is no dispute as to *title* to the property (in this case the parties agreed they owned the home half each) the property will *still* be 'in issue' if there is a dispute as to when one party may realise their half share (in this case the husband sought a property adjustment order as he wanted to remain in the house but the wife wanted an order for sale, and the compromise that the husband would buy out her share without a sale on the open market was held to be a sufficient dispute to put the property 'in issue' for legal aid purposes). This principle has been further confirmed in *Parkes v Legal Aid Board* [1994] 2 FLR 850 where in a case of two unmarried parents compromising an action so that the woman and child of the relationship should remain in the house where the man sought a sale order, the right to remain in a house with exclusive possession over a long period of years was said to be a 'property right' within the meaning of s 16(6) of the LAA 1988.

Thus whether a property has been 'in issue' must be determined from an examination of the pleadings, evidence and judgment (merely including a complete prayer for all forms of available ancillary relief in the petition is insufficient to bring all the parties' property into issue). Where there has been *any* argument over property this usually means that the property has been in issue, and the only remaining point to settle will be whether the *whole* property has been in issue or only part (eg if one party has at least agreed that as a minimum the other owns a half or other proportional share).

Note

By LAA 1988 s 16(7) property recovered or preserved as a result of a compromise is still subject to s 16(6).

The exemptions from the statutory charge under Regulation 94

If the court can be persuaded to confine its orders to the following, no liability to the statutory charge will apply at all to:

- periodical payments or maintenance, whether in favour of a spouse or children;
- the first £2,500 of any money or property recovered or preserved.

Note

This money or property may be recovered or preserved in proceedings other than ancillary relief after divorce, eg those brought under s 17 Married Women's Property Act 1882: see below 16. 1, s 27 MCA 1973: see below 14.5, ss 2 and 6 DPMCA 1978: see below 14.1.2 or the CA 1989: see Chapter 6. Thus where a client is on legal aid applying for financial or property orders the same considerations apply to trying to get the order made in a form which will make best use of the exemptions regardless of which proceedings are being taken. Moreover, where there are different sets of proceedings it is a good idea if at all possible to obtain separate Green Forms and legal aid certificates for *each separate matter*, and then to get them discharged separately, since then costs from one action (which may or may not have been successful) will not impact on another where significant property may have been recovered or preserved as the costs of one Green Form or legal aid certificate will not be carried over into another subsequent one: *Watkinson v Legal Aid Board* [1991] 2 All ER 953, CA.

Where the statutory charge *does* apply, it is important when the order of the court is drafted to ensure that it contains the appropriate recital to ensure that postponement of the payment of the Legal Aid Board bill for costs is achieved. This is done by inserting a formal certificate on the face of the order, detailing that the money or property has been recovered or preserved for the purpose of providing the assisted person with a home in accordance with the Practice Direction of [1991] 2 FLR 384: see 8.4.

Note

If the assisted person wants to move from the house which is the subject of the statutory charge without repaying the Legal Aid Board, this can be achieved by asking them to agree to the transfer of the charge to the new property to be acquired, providing there is sufficient equity in that new house: Regulation 98.

The first interview   5.2

The first interview with any client is always important but never more so than in the case of family matters. This is because it is essential for a matrimonial practitioner to establish a good rapport with the client since there will inevitably be matters at various stages which must be dealt with in a sensitive manner when the client is feeling particularly vulnerable and depressed, which is usually not conducive to the efficient despatch of business (though there are exceptional clients who take refuge in an even more businesslike approach than usual, and whose incisiveness at this critical moment in their lives takes one's breath away).

All clients are different but generally speaking at some stage or other during the divorce process, perhaps if there are contested child proceedings or if the financial matters are particularly hard fought, they will either rely heavily on the solicitor's expert advice to see them through a difficult period or they will completely switch off and it may be very difficult to obtain instructions from them. Both these common situations are more easily dealt with if the solicitor has established a good working relationship – a professional one, not a quasi friendship – so that there is client confidence in the solicitor's judgment and good lines of communication along which to 'sell' the client a solution where necessary. This will quite often arise in matrimonial cases, where for example the case has reached a stage where a settlement is vital to bring a long running struggle to an end, to save both costs and sanity for the client and the family as a whole. It is very often at this stage that clients' common sense desert them and they cannot see what is plainly good for them. In this situation, strong advice from a trusted solicitor will usually avert disaster if the professional relationship has been positive throughout.

Note

If the solicitor is also a trained counsellor as well as a qualified lawyer, there are no circumstances in which the two roles should be confused, as the solicitor cannot possibly wear these two hats at once. Although a solicitor who is a trained mediator or ADR practitioner or who has other formal training or experience in counselling will always benefit from acquaintance with this extra dimension, which at the very least will probably have heightened all the interpersonal skills which are in constant use in matrimonial matters, the client who actually needs more than a good lawyer should be referred to a trained counsellor if that appears to be necessary (and it may well be *essential* at the beginning of the case in order to obtain any coherent instructions at all). No attempt should be made take long-term decisions until the client is in a sufficiently rational and calm state to do so.

Clients who are so distressed that they break down should be offered a cup of tea or coffee or a glass of water, tears should be met with a box of tissues and a reassuring manner (including possibly allowing the client to release inevitable tension by the solicitor making the smallest possible fuss and not even attempting to stop the tears until they recede naturally, which despite initial alarming appearances they usually do quite quickly) and the client should also be assured that such incidents are all in the day's work. Actual physical contact should usually be avoided in case of a later claim of assault, but a certain matter of fact warmth of manner will usually be successful in settling the client down to business.

Matters to be considered at the interview   **5.2.1**

There are a number of specific points which need to be covered in the first interview in a matrimonial case, in addition to taking formal notes in order to open the file. Most firms have a checklist, which usually contains about a dozen items which need to be addressed, not always in the same order. Some firms have a pre-prepared client instruction sheet, with first a structured section (leaving space for formal details in answer to the obvious questions such as name, address, children etc which will need to be recorded) and secondly some white space for the interviewer's more unstructured notes (for example as to why the marriage went wrong and a brief history of the personal and financial relationship).

Formal details

Formal details will include
- client's name, address, and telephone numbers (home and work) plus any special arrangements about writing/telephoning (eg is there any problem about ringing either number, or writing to the home, ie if the parties are still living together – a relative's home may be a better address for correspondence in this case);
- client's marital status, date of marriage, where-abouts of marriage certificate;
- name, address and telephone numbers of the client's spouse, spouse's solicitors if any, and whether the solicitor is to write to the spouse

immediately (which should not be done unless the client knows about it, and knows what is in the letter, especially if the parties are still living together).

Note

The SFLA Code of Practice recommends writing to the other side before issuing any proceedings, eg, filing a petition, and if the solicitor belongs to the Association or observes the Code without actually being a member, this is a good time to explain this to the client.

Other details

These will cover:

- how the work will be paid for, on Green Form or legal aid, or if the client is paying privately (in either case the Legal Aid Board's charge must be explained or private costs detailed as appropriate, and if the latter a payment on account must be discussed);

Note

This is *not* an insult since matrimonial cases sometimes go on for a long time and the firm would be bankrupt if it had to act completely free for a couple of years before receiving anything at all.

- precisely what it is that the client needs, ie is it a divorce at this stage or is the client unsure, is counselling needed, might there be a reconciliation, or is emergency action (eg an injunction, child proceedings or urgent financial help) needed first? If the client is not *sure* about divorce, the solicitor should in any event draw attention to the existence of the various marriage guidance agencies, such as *Relate*, through whom the parties might explore whether divorce is inevitable. If the client is sure that divorce is right, the parties may nevertheless wish to avail themselves of one of the conciliation services which seek to bring to divorcing couples a better understanding of the possibilities afforded by life after a cooperative divorce, especially where there are children. *Relate*, which is by no means restricted to holding marriages together at all costs, may be able to help in this case as much as in a case where the parties wish to stay together if possible, or alternatively one of the agencies specialising in human relations generally and in particular family therapy, such as the Tavistock Clinic, could be approached;

Note _____

Where there is to be a divorce, the solicitor should explain to the client what the forthcoming change of status will mean, especially in relation to the home, any other assets and continuing bank and credit card accounts. These points must be considered again in relation to the practical steps which may need to be taken.

- if it is divorce, all the necessary details to complete the formal part of the petition so as to commence proceedings, ie everything for the *Petition* and *Statement of Arrangements* (vital so as not to waste expensive time going back to the client to obtain such details later when these documents have to be prepared for filing – in order to avoid omissions, you should of course be thoroughly familiar with these two forms and to begin with may find it helpful to have both forms out on the table at the interview and then if there appears to be any problem, eg insufficient information about the children, the precise format of the questions can always be checked in front of the client and the right information for a suitable answer obtained and recorded);

Note _____

Divorce may *not* be inevitable – a separation agreement might be more suitable, and the solicitor should always consider what might be achieved by agreement instead of by taking proceedings; the latter inevitably increase costs as well as embittering the parties and possibly putting a strain on what might otherwise be an amicable relationship.

- details of previous proceedings, essential for the formal part of the petition, but also in case any might be relevant to the conduct of the proposed suit, eg a jurisdiction problem or a child in care or subject to an existing English or foreign order (always establish whether child matters are likely to be dispute);
- details of which fact or facts apply, and of evidence likely to be required;
- details of client's financial position, including of (i) income and whether there are any significant

short-term debts, eg utility bills, and (ii) capital and whether there are any debts which will have to be defrayed from this, eg loan for double glazing or conservatory (iii) mortgage/rent including whether it is up to date and whether any charge needs to be registered to protect client's occupation of the home, see 15.1.2, and 15.2.3, whether any valuable chattels should be placed in safe keeping to prevent unilateral disposal or whether a joint tenancy should be severed, see 15.1.1, or credit card and joint bank accounts closed;

Note

Prudent steps such as the above will obviously vary according to the personalities of the parties involved. There is nothing like divorce for bringing out the worst in people. It might be unwise to leave a spouse in a position where bank accounts can be cleaned out and huge credit card bills run up. A husband's agreement that a wife can 'buy a new car' because the household runabout is due to be changed is unlikely to mean a Ferrari when the normal purchase is a small Fiat, but wives suddenly seem to get the urge to go upmarket when a divorce is in process and they still have access to accounts they would never have dared to raid for anything but a new sit-on lawn mower during the marriage. The husband who expresses himself imprecisely and leaves the wherewithal to make an unusually extravagant purchase in the joint building society account thus has only himself to blame (especially if he is the one who has traded the wife in for a new model of the flesh and blood variety).

- details of spouse's financial position, and whether there is already or is likely in due course to be an agreed financial package: if there will inevitably be contested ancillary relief, you should consider whether to apply for legal aid immediately since the actual divorce suit may be over fairly quickly, depending on the workload at the court chosen, so that it will often be possible to commence ancillary relief proceedings – available as soon as DN is pronounced – as soon as the legal aid certificate is available: see 5.1.4;
- practical steps to be taken immediately – if income is required, you should consider voluntary payments, welfare benefits, or a court order (maintenance pending suit or a magistrates' court

order under the Domestic Proceedings and Magistrates' Courts Act 1978), you should also consider whether any urgent letters need writing to the mortgagee or utility companies, see 5.2.2, whether the client wishes to make a new will, whether any proceedings need to be taken to seize assets or obtain financial information: see 9.1.1 and 9.1.2;

Finally

- Tell the client what will happen next.

Note

It is desirable to take a written signed statement from the client, although this will have to be written up after the interview and signed by the client at a later stage.

A signed written statement has three functions:
- it provides an account of the situation for anyone else in the firm taking up the file;
- it confirms your instructions if the client later disputes what was said at the interview (and confirms the position as to, eg beneficial ownership of the matrimonial home if the client suddenly dies);
- it is already prepared more or less contemporaneously so that memories will not later have to be searched and details verified when, eg it is necessary to instruct counsel.

Green Form practitioners often say they have not got time to do this under the tight time allowance of three hours for divorce, but it does not actually take very long to dictate a statement and to have it typed up at leisure and is probably more cost effective than leaving it till later.

Follow up action   5.2.2

Following the interview, the solicitor will have various tasks to complete, mainly letters to write including a letter or letters:
- to the client confirming instructions, and dealing with the usual client care matters in accordance with Practice Rule 15; if the client is a private client, a letter will need to be sent about costs (this type of letter is normally kept in the word processor and sent out as routine in appropriate cases – it should specify if possible a figure for fixed costs, but failing that the hourly rate for the person responsible for the client's matter, plus the

hourly rates of any other person who will regularly work on the file, together with such other details, eg of any 'uplift' which it is usual to add to the hourly figures);

- to any witnesses who may be needed in behaviour cases;
- to obtain any necessary reports, eg medical reports in respect of a child or children for the Statement of Arrangements;
- to obtain a marriage certificate if necessary;
- to ask for copy court orders where there have been previous proceedings;
- to the client's spouse if that has been agreed; and
- to the mortgagee or utility companies or other creditors if appropriate.

5.3   Preparing the petition

For drafting the petition, see Chapter 4. It should be remembered that particularly where the petition is based on behaviour it is good practice to let the other spouse know that a petition is to be presented and to supply a copy of the draft to the spouse personally or to his or her solicitors where they have been instructed. The SFLA Code in any event recommends telling the other spouse before proceedings are commenced.

You should have no difficulty in preparing a petition from the information gathered in the first interview, providing the interview was conducted in the structured way recommended and a good note taken.

5.4   Supporting documents

Apart from the petition itself, either three or four documents, as appropriate, will also be required, the:
- marriage certificate;
- Statement of Arrangements for the children;
- reconciliation certificate, if appropriate;
- court fee, or a certificate of exemption.

Some points must be made about each of these.

5.4.1   The marriage certificate

This means the original marriage certificate or a certified copy: FPR 1991 r 2.6(2). Only one copy is required, since the certificate forms part of the court file and is not served with the other papers on either the respondent nor any co-respondent.

Note

For a foreign marriage, the original or a certified copy will be required as usual *plus* a translation if the language in which it is recorded is not English, together with an affidavit from the translator verifying the translation.

The Statement of Arrangements for the children 5.4.2

This is submitted in Form M4: FPR 1991 r 2.2 which provides that 'if practicable' the form should be agreed and both parents should sign it to indicate agreement in the arrangements detailed, and most parents do both sign, but if the respondent refuses to do so, the form may still be filed signed by the petitioner alone, with a covering letter explaining the circumstances.

Note

Form M4 must be signed personally by the petitioner and the respondent. The solicitor cannot sign for either of them. It is the petitioner who has the duty of filing the form but where the children are *not* living with the petitioner it may not be possible for all the information required to be supplied on the form unless the respondent cooperates.

Where a Form M4 appears to be deficient in such information it is considered good practice for the respondent to file a separate M4 when returning the Acknowledgment of Service: see below at 5.6 and if this is not done the court may ask the respondent to supply any further information in the form of a letter: FPR 1991 r 2.38.

However, it appears that the rules are deficient in not being able to *require* the respondent to do this if it is not done voluntarily. Nevertheless, the district judge is by no means left powerless in this situation since the ultimate solution is to direct that the court welfare office should prepare a welfare report giving details of the respondent's arrangements for the children, in the same way as a district judge dissatisfied with the arrangements disclosed in a fully completed Form M4 might do so before issuing a s 41 certificate in a doubtful case: see 3.5.2.

The form covers the following:
- accommodation;
- education;
- child care arrangements (particularly where the parent with whom the children reside is employed);
- financial matters, including maintenance orders and the Child Support Agency assessments;

- contact for the non-residential parent;
- health (where a doctor's letter or a full medical report will be necessary if there is anything unusual to include, unless the health problem has been present from birth and there is nothing new to add).

Note

Only one form is required regardless of the number of children of the family. If extra work is done to enable the form to be filled in properly, a Green Form extension will be available: Legal Advice and Assistance Regulations 1991, regulation 21(1).

The form, which is daunting to clients, despite having been redesigned in recent years with heavy use of the 'multiple choice' style requiring the answers 'yes' 'no' or a tick in a box, is relatively straightforward for the solicitor unless there is a serious problem with the family which needs careful presentation. Where this is the case, there are two (sometimes apparently conflicting) rules:

- As much *useful* information as possible should be included since, unless the district judge finds the form provides a wholly inadequate account of essential matters and asks for further information – which will in any case delay the s 41 certificate: see 3.5.2 – this is the court's *only* means of acquiring a picture of the post-divorce lifestyle of the children. The exercise may be compared to filling in a criminal legal aid form where legal aid is often refused because of inadequate information in the relevant boxes. However, care should be taken not to cram the form full of *more* information than is actually necessary. A fairly laconic style, just the right side of minimalist, is the correct goal, except where there is unusual information to be imparted in answer to one of the questions, such as in relation to the children's health; failure to file a medical report in such a case which obviously needs one is a common reason for the district judge asking for further information before issuing the s 41 certificate. A similar situation might arise where there have been proceedings in relation to one or more of the children and the copy order is not filed with the Form M4. If the district judge does take exception to any such omission, he will say precisely why and what is missing and at the same time ask the petitioner to renew the request for directions for trial: see 5.9;

- The overall aim should be to present a factual picture of a settled and stable life, tending even towards the *dull*. District judges exercising their supervisory powers, like the majority of children whose future lives they oversee, tend towards the ordinary and conservative: one cannot say *normal* because children living in single parent families are not living a *normal* life, despite the unfortunate contemporary incidence of divorce, since children were obviously originally meant to have two resident parents at home, but it should appear to be as normal as possible in the circumstances.

Where you are trying to strike a balance between giving the impression of a sad and solemn household bereft of the absent parent with all the attendant handicaps and deprivations (eg mother always at work because of no maintenance and chronic financial problems, clutch of childminders or children at different neighbours after school each day of the week) or of a swinging establishment where the custodial parent, usually the mother, is trying too hard to compensate (eg new toyboy, new progressive school, new flat in trendy much younger and predominantly singles district, endless other distractions) you should remember the old Chinese curse: 'May you live in *interesting* times' – this is *not* how children in an unobjectionable Statement of Arrangements which will raise no queries should live! As far as possible the child should continue an uneventful childhood already in place before the divorce, and you should aim to tick the answer No to any question asking whether it is anticipated that arrangements will change. Wherever the answer Yes must be used, details must follow in the white space provided.

Note

If there is to be an application for a formal order under s 8 of the Children Act 1989 for residence or contact, this should be stated on the form. The district judge will then be excused consideration of the children's arrangements at this stage: see 3.5.3.

5.4.3

Reconciliation certificate: Form M3, FPR 1991 r 2.6(3)

This only applies where the solicitor is acting, ie for a private client, and only requires the solicitor to indicate *whether* reconciliation has been discussed with the client and not whether it has been attempted or how or what the result was.

Note

The solicitor is not acting where the client is being advised under the Green Form Scheme, because the Green Form client has the status of a litigant in person.

It is generally thought that this reconciliation certificate provision was intended in the early stages of the 1970s divorce reform to be developed so as to be an effective encouragement to reconciliation, but somehow it fell by the wayside and now exists only in the curious formality of the solicitor's obligation to file the form when technically acting for a client in the divorce proceedings.

5.4.4   Certificate of exemption

If applicable, a certificate of exemption from paying the filing fee will be required (alternatively a fee of £150).

Clients on the Green Form or income support can claim partial exemption from the fee, which will require the filing of the form of exemption for payment.

The above documents are the standard ones to commence a suit. You should also look out for cases where:

- a *legal aid certificate* might need to be filed, ie in a case where legal aid is granted for the suit;
- *local practice directions* apply, as to which the supervising principal will doubtless draw them to your attention where applicable.

5.5   Filing

Filing is achieved by taking or sending all the above and the petition, with copies of the petition and Statement of Arrangements for service on the respondent, and a further copy of the petition for service on any co-respondent, to the chosen court: see 4.4 as to which court that might be in any particular case.

The court will then enter the case in the court books and assign it a number (which is its identity tag for the remainder of the suit and must be quoted on all contact with the court) and the petitioner, or the petitioner's solicitor where appropriate is notified. At this stage, in the unattractive language of the press, the petitioner 'has filed for divorce' but the proceedings are not yet properly on foot before service is achieved.

5.6   Service: FPR 1991 rr 2.9(1) and 2.24

The documents to be served are
- the petition;
- form M4 (plus a copy of any medical report);

- the notice of proceedings: Form M5 (ie notice to the respondent);
- the Acknowledgment of Service: Form M6.

Service is normally effected by the court, generally by second class post, but since this obviously displays a touching faith in both the reliability of the postal system and the rectitude of the respondent (who could quite well put the papers in the dustbin and pretend they had never arrived if they are sent in the normal way) there are other methods:

- bailiff service (also called personal service by the bailiff);
- personal service (ie other than by the bailiff);
- substituted service.

Alternatively service may be *deemed* or *dispensed with*: FPR 1991 r 2.9(11).

The third method of putting the proceedings into active mode regardless of the respondent's non-cooperation is *for exceptional circumstances only*, but may have to be used if the Acknowledgment of Service does not come back duly completed, either by the respondent or a solicitor acting for the respondent, since then the petition cannot be taken to be duly served pursuant to FPR r 2.9(5) and the suit cannot proceed. In order to obviate difficulties, one of the first two methods might be selected from the start. It will be convenient to look at the various methods in turn.

Bailiff service   5.6.1

This is also called 'personal service through the bailiff' to distinguish it from 'personal service through, but not *by*, the petitioner', for which see below at 5.6.2.

The district judge will direct bailiff service if the petitioner applies on the appropriate form, and it is suitable where the petitioner can supply an address where the bailiff may find the respondent and a photograph for identification. There is a fee unless the petitioner has already filed a certificate of exemption from fees, and this is the cheapest way of effective service and therefore suitable for clients on the Green Form. The bailiff attempts to obtain a signature from the respondent, files a certificate stating how the respondent was identified, and if the respondent then does not return the Acknowledgment of Service due service can be proved by the petitioner identifying either the respondent's signature or the photograph used by the bailiff to identify the respondent on whom the papers were served. The petitioner may do this in the affidavit in support of the petition.

This method can be used by private clients as well as those on the Green Form but in that case the requirements of the *Practice Direction* of 7 March 1977 [1977] 1 All ER 845 will have to be complied with to show why bailiff service is chosen instead of the more usual (more expensive) alternative for private clients of personal service.

5.6.2   Personal service

The rules allow the petitioner to request personal service through, but never by, the petitioner: FPR r 2.9(2)(b). This is suitable where postal service might not be satisfactory for the reasons explained above at 5.6 and bailiff service is inappropriate because the petitioner cannot say where the respondent might be found – the bailiff cannot go searching for a respondent in a variety of places. While the *petitioner* cannot ever serve the documents personally: FPR r 2.9(3), the petitioner's *solicitor* can do so, or alternatively an inquiry agent or professional process server can perform the task. This method can be used by Green Form clients where bailiff service is unsuitable because of the elusiveness of the respondent, and it is a proper expense for an extension.

Again the person serving the papers will attempt to obtain a signature, and if no Acknowledgment of Service is returned due service can still be proved by the petitioner's identifying either signature or photograph of the respondent as in the case of bailiff service. However, the server does not file a certificate like the bailiff but must swear and file an *affidavit* stating how the respondent was identified: FPR r 2.9(7).

Note

Personal service by an inquiry agent may have to be used because the inquiry agent must first actually *locate* the respondent. If this is necessary, eg (as a prelude to asking the court for substituted service or to dispense with service altogether) the *Practice Direction* of 13 February 1989 [1989] 1 All ER 765 should be followed. Basically, where the petition includes a claim for maintenance or there is an existing maintenance order, this enables the court to request a search of the Benefits Agency and Passport Office records, or where the respondent is in the Armed Forces the petitioner's solicitor may request an address from their records.

Obviously the solicitor would pursue all possible leads –
eg employers, clubs, trade union, friends, relatives etc –
before resorting to these more formal methods and if the
petitioner indicates at the first interview that there may
be a problem with location of the proposed respondent
the solicitor should arrange tracing before filing the petition and will think of how best to effect service *before*
ordinary postal service has proved ineffective.

Substituted service   5.6.3

Where all efforts to trace the respondent's actual address
have failed, an order may be sought from the court for
substituted service. There are various ways in which this
might be effected, which basically fall into two categories:

- where the respondent is known to be around
  somewhere but always manages to elude personal service, even at an address or addresses
  which are not the respondent's own but which the
  respondent is known to visit;
- where the respondent has effectively disappeared
  but has been seen in a certain area and is thought
  still to be there.

In the first case instead of persisting in personal visits at
great expense, the papers might be posted by way of substituted service authorised by the court to one of the
addresses which the respondent is known to visit. In the
second service by advertisement might be authorised.

It is essential in both cases that the court is convinced
that the petitioner has made all reasonable efforts to
effect service. If there is to be an advertisement, the court
will need to be convinced that the advertisement has a
reasonable chance of coming to the respondent's notice
and the court will settle the advertisement and decide
where it shall be placed: FPR r 2.9(9). Application is
made *ex parte* on affidavit. Exceptionally, the court might
authorise an advertisement to be placed other than by
itself, in which case the publications concerned containing the advertisement must be filed at court: FPR
r 10.5(3). This might be done in the case of advertisement
in a foreign newspaper, eg where the respondent was last
seen in Brazil and is thought to be still having a good
time there, but despite his sometimes being briefly seen
in public places no one has any idea where he lives
between the sightings.

5.6.4 Deemed service

Deemed service is for the type of respondent, mentioned above at 5.6 who puts the papers in the dustbin. If the petitioner knows and can show that the petition and supporting documents have come to the attention of the respondent, even if he cannot be shown actually to have destroyed or discarded them, deemed service should be available. By FPR r 2.9(6) the district judge must be *satisfied* that the papers have come to the respondent's notice, and this may be proved in any way in which that can be shown, but district judges no longer usually grant deemed service on the unsupported evidence (even sworn on affidavit) of the petitioner alone. They have had too many irate respondents appear out of the woodwork asking for the deemed service to be set aside on the basis that the petitioner knew perfectly well where they were and merely pretended not to do so. Accordingly, an affidavit from another relative or friend will be required, eg to the effect that the respondent was seen with the papers whether or not he threw the papers away in that person's presence, or told that person over the telephone that he had had them but that nothing was going to make him cooperate.

5.7 Dispensing with service

This is governed by FPR r 2.9(11) and requires the district judge to make an order dispensing with service in cases where in the district judge's opinion service is impracticable for some reason or for other reasons that it is necessary or expedient to dispense with service. Application is again *ex parte* on affidavit and the affidavit should set out in full all the attempts to serve the petition. Obviously, the quality of the affidavit will be vital here since if the order is granted the respondent may be divorced without knowing anything about it. Thus the petitioner will need to satisfy the district judge that even substituted service is not appropriate. Nevertheless, where the respondent has gone off and the petitioner cannot find him despite exhaustive efforts, the order may well be made.

5.8 Amendments

Once any service problems are dealt with, the next stage will normally be to request directions for trial, but before proceeding further, it may be advisable to consider whether any amendments are required to the petition, and if so how to effect them.

Amendments to petitions often appear to the inexperienced to be difficult, but in practice they are not. There are various sorts:

- simple amendments (basically, red ink on the existing text as in civil litigation generally), eg deleting allegations, adding a new s 1(2) fact arising *before* the date of the petition which you wish to amend;
- supplemental petitions (new document, read into the existing petition, rather like the White Book supplements), eg adding further allegations to particulars of a fact already pleaded which have arisen *after* the date of the petition you wish to amend;
- fresh petitions (you start again, usually having *discontinued or had dismissed* the existing petition, usually because you want to change facts and rely on a new one not included in the original petition).

By FPR r 2.8 you will not need leave to file another petition if the first is already dismissed or discontinued. By r 2.6(4) you *will* need leave if the existing petition is still in existence through not having been finally disposed of in one way or another.

Note

There are sometimes technical reasons for keeping the existing petition alive till the new one is on foot. You should not worry about this too much at this stage as this is not work which you would be expected to do unsupervised.

Thus the *date* of the existing petition will be important and also the *nature of the amendment* to be made. It is a question of what is already in existence in relation to the date of the petition to be amended. Clearly you cannot logically allege at the later stage of amendment a basis of divorce which must be inserted into a document with an earlier date! (Although you can bring the court up to date with current detailed developments.)

If you want to allege a *completely new Fact*, then if it arose *before* the date of the petition, this can be done by simple amendment (red ink). If it arose *after* the date of the petition, then a *fresh petition* will be required, as it will not be possible to amend the existing one in any way, not even by supplemental petition, to allege a Fact which did not exist at the date of the existing petition.

Example _____

You want to allege a separation Fact where the relevant period had not been completed at the date of the earlier petition. A *fresh petition* will be required.

If, however, all you want to do is to add *fresh allegations* to the *particulars* of the existing petition, you can do that by building on to that existing petition either with a *simple amendment* (if the new information dates from *prior* to the petition) or with a *supplemental petition*, which is technically part of the existing petition although it is contained in a separate document (if the new information arose *after* the date of the petition). Here you are adding on further up to date particulars of a Fact which has already been alleged, not asking the court to indulge in time travel.

Note _____

The standard red ink procedure is set out in FPR r 2.11. You need no leave until the suit has reached the stage at which an answer is filed and since few Answers are filed, this occasion of leave is rare: r 2(11)(1)(b). However leave will always be required once directions have been given: see 5.9.1, so amendments at a later stage will always require leave: r 2.14. In theory amendments may be made up to DA but are unusual after DN. Application is made for leave ex parte if the respondent consents in writing to the amendment, otherwise an application will need to be made on notice. For *very minor amendments* at the directions stage see 5.9 – this can be done, eg to correct a child's birth date, or add a missing middle name, correct a spelling etc, in the petitioner's affidavit in support of the petition.

The amended petition is filed at court and re-served in the normal way.

5.9   The directions stage and the role of the Acknowledgment of Service

Directions may be requested as soon as due service can be proved. This is normally achieved by proof of service in one of the ways mentioned in 5.6.1 or 5.6.2 or by return by the docile respondent of the completed Acknowledgment of Service (Form M6) sent out with the petition and accompanying documents: see 5.6. If none of these apply an interlocutory application will have to be made for substituted or deemed service, or for service to be dispensed with before the suit can proceed further. In the vast majority of cases the Acknowledgment of Service is returned and it is this standard procedure with which you will need to be primarily familiar.

The ordinary cooperative respondent should have no difficulty with return of the Acknowledgment of Service which should be received back by the court within eight days of the receipt of the petition and accompanying documents by the respondent: r 10.8(2)(a). Like the other standard forms designed for 'mail order' divorce, it is in question and answer format, and it is fully explained in the accompanying Notice of Proceedings (Form M5) which always goes out with it, see 5.6 above. While sometimes respondents do not get it back on time, in which case the court will usually send a reminder – and another copy of Form 6 in case the original is now at the bottom of the respondent's 'letters to answer' pile – late return is more likely to be due to forgetfulness or disorganisation rather than difficulty in answering the questions.

There are three points of particular importance to note about this form:

* the respondent's solicitor, if any, can sign the form for the respondent unless the divorce is on the basis of either Fact A or Fact D and the respondent is either admitting Fact A adultery or giving Fact D consent: r 2.10(1);
* although the form asks if the divorce will be defended, the respondent is not actually bound by the answer given in reply to this question and can ultimately not defend after all if wiser counsel subsequently prevails, since the result of answering this question in the affirmative is merely that the proceedings will be held up after receipt by the court of the Acknowledgment of Service to allow time for an Answer to be filed, but this in no way prevents the respondent doing absolutely nothing about filing an Answer so that the divorce will eventually proceed as undefended if no Answer is filed within the time allowed: see 5.13;
* similarly there is no obligation to follow through any other intention expressed on the form, such as in relation to the children, so that expressing no intention of asking for an order in respect of the children does not mean that a Children Act order cannot afterwards be applied for after all.

When the court receives the Form M6 it sends a photo-copy to the respondent or the respondent's solicitor if appropriate: r 2.9(8). If the form has indicated an intention to defend, the court will wait at least 28 days before the case will proceed further, so as to give an adequate opportunity for an Answer to be filed: r 2.12(1). If no Answer is filed the case proceeds as if undefended all along, unless of course a respondent subsequently obtains leave to file an Answer out of time, which is not unknown: see 5.11. However, in the vast majority of cases the suit is clearly undefended from the start and receipt of the M6 means that the case can proceed immediately to directions.

It is only in the minority of cases that where no M6 is received steps will have to be taken to deal with this in accordance with the resolution of service problems: see 5.6.

5.9.1   Directions

The directions stage does not start automatically, as Directions must be requested. Moreover, 'giving directions' in Special Procedure divorce amounts to no more than the district judge acting on the petitioner's written request for directions, entering the case in the Special Procedure list and ultimately considering the papers in an administrative manner.

This stage may be entered by requesting directions once due service can be proved: r 2.24(1)(a) and it is certain that the case is undefended, ie the M6 says it will not be or if notice to defend has been given and the time for filing an Answer has expired: rr 2.12(1) and 2.24(1). There is a standard form on which Directions are applied for by the petitioner's solicitor or the petitioner personally where a litigant in person on the Green Form: r 2.24(1.) It will be necessary for the district judge to be satisfied that all time limits have been complied with, so the first possible time for requesting directions will be eight days after service.

Although seeking directions might seem a simple and routine matter, in fact if the divorce is to proceed smoothly, directions is the next most vital stage after the skilful drafting of the petition, when a crucial document if well drafted will ensure success. In this case the crucial document is the affidavit in support of the petition which must accompany the request for directions. In the absence of an oral hearing, the affidavit is the only evidence on which the court can base a decree, although there may sometimes be exhibits to that affidavit by way of corroboration, eg medical reports in a violent behaviour case or witness statements in an adultery case. It follows that if the affidavit is not well done problems may arise. It will therefore be convenient to examine the contents and purpose of the affidavit in detail.

The petitioner's affidavit   5.9.2

A pre-printed form is normally used, although this is not obligatory, but if the affidavit is drafted from scratch it should follow the layout of the printed form so that matters are dealt with in the same order and providing the same information: r 2.24(3). You might avoid the printed form and draft from scratch if the case is exceptional, eg you are alleging Facts in the alternative, a fault based Fact plus Fact D. The pre-printed forms are Forms M7(a) to (e), each respectively tailored to Facts A to E.

Besides comprising the evidence of the Fact relied on, the affidavit also serves the purpose of providing formal confirmation of various matters:

- since the petitioner is required to swear that everything in the petition is true, the affidavit conveniently provides an opportunity to correct minor errors not worth the more formal amendment described at 5.8, eg correction of birth dates or names, without requiring the petition to be reserved since the district judge will usually treat it as standing subject to the corrections;

- since the signature of the respondent will have to be identified on the Acknowledgment of Service for that document to be acceptable as evidence that the petition and accompanying documents were duly served, and of any Fact where the respondent's signature is necessary (ie Fact A, admission of adultery, and Fact D, consent to the decree) the affidavit provides an opportunity for the petitioner to identify the respondent's signature;

- since the Statement of Arrangements is vital to the Special Procedure, the affidavit provides an opportunity to confirm the accuracy of the Statement of Arrangements and to correct any inaccuracies or add any further information, and also for the petitioner to identify the respondent's signature on that document;

- since a claim for costs may have been made in the petition by the petitioner (and resisted by the respondent, sometimes giving reasons, in the Acknowledgment of Service) the affidavit provides an opportunity for the petitioner to state whether it is really intended to pursue this claim.

However the most important function of the affidavit is to persuade the district judge that it is just to grant the decree sought, and in this respect the solicitor's skill in drafting the relevant sections of the affidavit will be paramount. There are two distinct points here:

- how best to present the petitioner's evidence;
- is any corroboration required?

5.9.3   The petitioner's evidence

It is essential that the solicitor drafting the petitioner's answers to the relevant questions in the affidavit for each Fact should bear in mind the substantive law in each case, ie the requirements of MCA 1973 ss 1(2)(a) to (e), and in particular the case law so that the petitioner's case is shown to fall squarely within what is established as sufficient for each Fact: see 2.1 to 2.6 inclusive.

A particular danger area will be where the fact relied on requires the parties to have been living apart, or where periods living together might amount to cohabitation exceeding that permitted by MCA 1973 s 2: see 2.4.2 and 3.4 where great care should be taken to show that the parties *were living apart in the same house but not the same household* if circumstances required them to live under the same roof. This is particularly so where the parties are still living under the same roof when the affidavit is filed!

The aim should be to show unequivocally that the parties have used separate rooms (if possible not simply separate bedrooms) or have used the same rooms at separate times, that meals have not (or have rarely) been shared, that no household services were performed by one for the other: you should look carefully back to the case law on this subject at 2.4 to 2.6, in particular the cases of *Mouncer v Mouncer* and *Bartram v Bartram* which point up the distinction between one and two households, and show what may be done with the situation where the petitioner is obliged unwillingly to live in the same household as the respondent since it will usually be possible to deal with this satisfactorily in the affidavit.

Where corroboration might be required

The district judge needs to apply a two part test before granting a certificate of entitlement to a decree nisi pursuant to rule 2.36(1)(a):

- would the particulars in the petition if true entitle the petitioner to a decree (this is a matter of law and if decided in the affirmative will entitle the petition to be in the Special Procedure list, on which point the district judge's decision is final): *R v Nottingham County Court ex parte Byers* [1985] 1 All ER 735;
- are the details in the petition in fact true – this is a matter of fact and evidence, which is where corroboration may be helpful.

Normally in an undefended divorce the petitioner's statements will be sufficient. After all the affidavit is on oath. There are three danger areas where corroboration would obviously be helpful:

- adultery cases where the respondent admits the adultery but the co-respondent does not (rare now, since co-respondents themselves are rare now they no longer need to be named and joined as parties in the suit);
- behaviour cases where the allegations are weak and insubstantial;
- separation cases where the parties have remained under one roof and are alleging two households.

It should be noted that standards and practices are different from county court to county court and some district judges are notoriously strict while others are not unduly demanding about corroboration. You should follow the local practice as a yardstick of what is likely to be required.

Provided a suitable affidavit is supplied with the request for directions the Special Procedure should follow automatically without hitches. It follows that great care needs to be taken in preparation of the affidavit as an ounce of prevention here may be worth a ton of cure once the district judge is alerted to any query as to whether the divorce ought be granted at all.

The special procedure

Most divorces are now obtained via the Special Procedure, which ought thus really to be called the normal or routine procedure, although it was 'special' in 1976 when it was inaugurated, since prior to that date a court hearing, however brief and formal, was essential, with sworn evidence given by the petitioner in the witness box. Now the district judge considers the papers filed, on a private administrative rather than even *ex parte* basis, usually taking a number of files to deal with each morning before beginning the day's list. Unless the papers suggest some problem as soon as the district judge begins to consider them (which will result in the case being withdrawn from the Special Procedure) the district judge's consideration of the petition and the supporting documentary evidence now take the place of the oral hearing and it will be obvious from the preceding sections above that the petition and the affidavit in support should always be prepared bearing this in mind, because the papers will be all the court (ie the single district judge alone in his private room) will have to go on in deciding whether the petitioner is entitled to a decree or not. It is therefore essential that each of these documents deals properly with the petitioner's case.

5.10.1 Consideration by the district judge of the evidence: r 2.36

If the district judge is *satisfied* with the evidence a certificate will be completed to that effect, a day will be fixed for pronouncement of the decree in open court and a copy of the certificate will be sent to each party to notify them, although neither need attend and normally they will not do so.

Note

Although decree nisi, the first decree on the route to ending the marriage, is the effective moment at which the marriage is conditionally dissolved *unless cause to the contrary is later shown*, the district judge's certificate is virtually as important. Indeed, it has been described as tantamount to the decree nisi itself, lacking only the public element of pronouncement in open court, which is undertaken either by the Judge or by the district judge (possibly the same district judge as issued the certificate, though not necessarily so, depending on how the work is allocated at the particular court).

In theory decree nisi can be stopped before it is pronounced, eg because the respondent wants after all to defend, but it will be first necessary for the district judge's certificate to be set aside and this is no easy matter, as is demonstrated by the case of *Day v Day* [1979] 2 All ER 187, where the husband kept changing his mind as to whether to defend or not, and finally turned up on the day designated for pronouncement of the decree nisi to ask to file an

Answer out of time! The judge acceded his request, at the same time removing the case from the Special Procedure list, but on appeal this was held to be wrong, since once the wife had proved her case the court was bound to pronounce the decree unless the respondent could show that there were substantial grounds to indicate that the decree had been granted contrary to the justice of the case. In the particular instance this did not apply since the husband had had ample time to defend if he had seriously wanted to and there was no injustice.

The decree nisi is thus virtually a certainty at this stage, *before* the district judge has even looked at the Statement of Arrangements. Thus the impact on the suit of the children in any case is now limited, if relevant at all, to delaying the *decree absolute* and not in any way to obtaining the *decree nisi*: see Chapter 3.

Before dealing at all with the children, however, the district judge must decide any question arising in connection with the costs. The respondent and co-respondent are entitled to make representations about costs which are governed by rule 2.37.

Normally costs will only be asked for in fault based cases, and sometimes not even then unless the suit becomes defended. If costs are asked for the district judge will consider the claim and include an order for costs in the certificate: a Green Form client can obtain costs even though a litigant in person, though obviously only those small costs appropriate to such a case: Litigants in Person (Costs and Expenses) Act 1975.

If the petitioner has asked for costs, it is essential that the respondent contests them on the Acknowledgment of Service form, giving good reasons, or the district judge will usually grant the petitioner's claim. If the respondent's reasons are insufficiently full for the district judge to decide on the claim for costs, a further written statement can be required setting out more fully the reasons for the respondent's objections to paying the costs: r 2.37(1), and the petitioner will receive a copy of this.

The petitioner can withdraw the claim for costs at any time, and may well do so between the petition and the directions stage, because, eg the parties have reached an agreement that the respondent will consent to a Fact D decree if costs are not claimed, and in this case it would be in time for the petitioner to indicate change of mind in the affidavit in support of the petition. If this opportunity is missed, a letter can be sent to the district judge withdrawing the claim for costs at a later stage. If this is not done, and the district judge cannot decide the question of costs on the spot at the same time as considering the case for decree, costs will be referred to the judge and dealt with at the time that decree nisi is pronounced. This means that on *that* occasion when decree nisi is pronounced it *will* be necessary for one of the parties at least to turn up, namely the respondent to argue the question of costs, and the petitioner may also wish to do so to defend the decision to claim costs, but need not do so. This is because if the respondent does not attend, the question of costs will at that stage be decided in favour of the petitioner.

Note

It is also possible that the district judge will incorporate a financial agreement into a court order at this stage, if the parties have reached agreement on financial matters, either permanently or temporarily.

If it is desired to do this, perhaps because the parties want an interim order anyway pending resolution of all outstanding matters at the usual ancillary relief stage, application should be made before the district judge gives directions.

This procedure is governed by rule 2.61 and like other ancillary relief orders, the order will technically be made only after pronouncement of the decree nisi and will become effective (unless superseded) upon decree absolute: see Section III for the ancillary relief stage.

Finally, pursuant to rule 2.39, the district judge considers the Statement of Arrangements for the Children, and if *satisfied* will issue a certificate to that effect, but if *not satisfied* can do no more at this stage to protect the children than to hold up decree absolute if the cumulative test in MCA 1973 s 41 is applicable: see 3.5 for how this works. Normally, an agreed approach by the parents and a properly completed Statement of Arrangements signed by both will automatically produce a *satisfied* certificate. Where an application is already on foot for an order under the Children Act 1989 the district judge is excused from considering the Statement of Arrangements at all, since their future will be considered by another court: see 3.5.3 and Chapter 6.

The above is the normal procedure for undefended divorce decrees and applies in the vast majority of cases. However, some do not go smoothly.

If the district judge is *not satisfied* the petitioner can be asked to file further evidence or alternatively (and if the further evidence is not filed or is still insubstantial) the district judge can remove the case from the Special Procedure list and list it for hearing before the Judge in open court. The district judge has however no power to *dismiss* the petition – only the judge can do that, if ultimately it becomes necessary. If the case is listed for hearing in open court, legal aid will be available: see 5.1.1.

Decree nisi 5.11

When decree nisi is pronounced in open court by the Judge or district judge on the day appointed, a copy will be sent, by post by the court, to both parties. This does not finally dissolve the marriage, which is still a marriage until decree absolute.

Decree absolute 5.12

This is the final decree which permits the parties to remarry. By s 1(5) of the MCA 1973 this may not usually be granted until six weeks after decree nisi, although there is a rarely used power to expedite decree absolute in urgent cases, eg terminal illness so that one of the parties can remarry urgently. Such urgent applications are the subject of a *Practice Direction* [1977] 2 All ER 714.

However, expediting DA is not regarded as good practice, since six weeks is short enough in any case, and is intended for the purpose of establishing that everything is in order to terminate the status of marriage, a step which may have far reaching consequences, so the better practice is for the solicitor to expedite the decree nisi by proceeding expeditiously at that stage instead, and having expedited the preparation of the petition and accompanying documents, writing to the court to press the urgency of the case, which will usually enable the court to save most or all of the six weeks between the two decrees at this earlier stage by expediting both the giving of directions and the pronouncement of the decree nisi.

Otherwise, in the ordinary course of events, the *petitioner* may apply for decree absolute six weeks after the grant of decree nisi, whereas pursuant to s 9(2) of the MCA 1973 the respondent must wait a further *three months after that*, ie *a total of four and a half months after decree nisi*, before applying if the petitioner has not done so. The petitioner's application is made on form M8 pursuant to rule 2.49(1) and Appendix 1 of the FPR. No notice need be given to the respondent but another fee is due, unless the petitioner is fees exempt.

The work to be done by the district judge on receiving the application gives some indication of why the 6 weeks between the two decrees exists at all. Pursuant to r 2.49(2) the district judge must search the court records to: check that:

- the court has complied with its duty under s 41 MCA 1973 in relation to the post divorce future of the children and that there is no direction under s 41(2) delaying the decree absolute;
- no one is trying to upset the decree nisi already granted and that no appeal or rehearing is pending;
- no one is intervening pursuant to ss 8 or 9 of the MCA 1973 to show cause preventing the decree being made absolute.

Note

By s 8 the Queen's Proctor, an official much more prominent in former times before Fact D and the agreed approach to divorce generally became the norm, may intervene to show such cause if there is any irregularity, eg a collusive divorce based on fabricated evidence, and by s 9 any third party may also intervene if there are material facts not brought to the attention of the court.

If the results of these enquiries are satisfactory, the district judge will make the decree absolute and will issue a certificate to that effect, copies of which will be sent to both parties. If the district judge does not search the court records and grants the DA regardless it will be a nullity: *Dackham v Dackham* (1987) *Times* 12 February, CA. The certificate is in Form 9 in Appendix 1 of the FPR indicating the date on which the marriage officially ended.

If the respondent has to apply for the DA this will be on four days notice to the petitioner, by application to a judge or district judge: r 2.50(2). There will be a short hearing, where the reasons for the petitioner's not having applied will be considered and if found reasonable, eg that ancillary relief orders are not in place and such security is required, perhaps because of the necessity to compensate the petitioner for benefits to be lost with the status of marriage, the DA will not be granted, unless some way is found of satisfying the petitioner's objections.

Note

If DA is not applied for after 12 months from DN an affidavit will have to be filed with Form 8 to explain the delay and in particular to deal with whether:

- the parties have resumed cohabitation since DN and if so between what dates;
- any child has been born to the wife in the interim, and if so stating the relevant facts, in particular as to whether the child might be a child of the family.

The reasons for this are obvious and the district judge can require any relevant facts to be verified on affidavit by the applicant. By r 2.49(2) the district judge must pay particular attention to whether MCA 1973 s 41 has been complied with in respect of any child born since DN.

Defended divorce

5.13

Defended divorce is most uncommon but occasionally you will come across cases which ought properly to be defended.

The cost

5.13.1

The first most important point in relation to defended causes is whether the respondent can *afford* to defend. Although legal aid is available in defended cases the respondent must still satisfy the legal aid committee that there is a case worth defending. In other words, the respondent must show reasonable grounds for defending at all and also that it is not unreasonable for legal aid to be granted, ie is there a chance of *winning*?

Even if there is a chance of winning, it must also be shown that it is reasonable to fight it all out at public expense, and that it is not reasonable that a divorce is obtained some other way, eg under Fact D. If these points are not established in the respondent's favour, legal aid will not be granted. the respondent must also be within the financial limits, so the first point is basically entirely a financial exercise. Of course it may be that the respondent wants to pay privately, in which case the solicitor can do nothing but advise against a fruitless or futile defence.

Notice of intention to defend

5.13.2

This should be given on the Acknowledgment of Service: see above at 5.9, but leave to file an Answer can be given later, and can even be applied for well out of time provided that is done before DN, but as in the case of *Day v Day* [1979] 2 All ER 187 can be difficult to obtain, because this would involve setting aside the district judge's certificate (not something district judges like and technically not possible as held in the *Day* case). The only case where this really might be worth doing is if the respondent has for some reason received no direct notice of the date of pronouncement of the decree nisi, and if a DN is pronounced without that notice being received the DN itself would be set aside as it would be a nullity: *Walker v Walker* [1987] 1 FLR 31, CA.

Most respondents should be dissuaded if at all possible from defending and this should be done as early as possible in the suit. It is not necessary to defend to contest child matters or ancillary relief and the only case in which it might be worth defending is if the respondent expects an application for a domestic violence injunction and the petition already alleges serious violence. There is also some slight risk that such violence might be prejudicial in later child proceedings if not contested in the petition but this is less so, unless an interim order under the Children Act 1989 is anticipated, since there is usually plenty of time to deal with exaggerated petitions in later child proceedings without having had to defend them earlier.

The solicitor who dissuades a respondent from defending is usually doing that respondent a service, since defending usually achieves no purpose and is expensive in terms of legal costs, painful emotion and inordinate delay in disposing of the matter. Sometimes, respondents think they should defend 'so the truth is known' perhaps by the children, the public or third parties. As the press are not very interested in divorces any more unless the parties are famous or the suit extraordinarily colourful, this is pointless, since even the judge who hears the contested case is not interested in why the parties' marriage broke down, the children are unlikely to read newspapers which report such things anyway, and if the suit is undefended only the district judge (and again not the children or third parties!) will read the petition containing the petitioner's allegedly specious allegations.

Many clients do not realise this until it is painstakingly explained to them, and if the children are the real concern the client should be advised to talk to them in suitable terms at the next opportunity for contact. Ideally parents should not have to do this sort of thing individually because recent research indicates that children appreciate being *kept informed* of any fundamental step affecting them, such as the divorce of their parents, but that they prefer not to be involved in their parents' adversarial activities after proceedings are begun. You should therefore always strongly advise a client to tell the children what is happening, and how new arrangements will affect them, and that if possible this should be done *jointly* by both parents.

Talked to sensibly on these lines, most clients will agree that defending is pointless. Some men can be persuaded that it is practically routine to be divorced by their wives for conduct which they see as more macho than socially unacceptable, and most do not mind being divorced for adultery as they often think that that reflects well on them too! Women might be more difficult, but since most petitions are brought by women this is less of a problem.

Truly valid reasons for defending, where the determined client should not be dissuaded, include:

- wishing to dispute the grant of a decree at all, possibly if there is a s 5 defence, or for religious reasons;
- wishing to cross-petition, ie to seek a divorce on an alternative basis, where the respondent *really cannot accept* the basis on which the divorce is sought by the petitioner;
- *sound* reasons for disputing the basis on which the divorce is sought, eg a clergyman might object to being divorced for adultery since he would almost certainly lose his living and not be able to obtain any other clerical post.

The Answer   5.13.3

An Answer should be filed within 21 days of the date of giving notice of intention to defend: r 2.12. A co-respondent can file an Answer as well as a respondent.

Drafting an Answer (and Cross Petition if there is one) is similar to drafting a Defence and Counterclaim. Normally, solicitors will send this out to counsel, and will normally involve counsel immediately where legal aid is needed since the legal aid certificate will almost certainly be limited to counsel's opinion to start with, but some firms insist on doing everything themselves, so the trainee should know how to do one. The precedent books will be found helpful but a sample Answer and Cross Petition appears in Appendix 3. The general rules are as follows:

- the heading is taken from the petition, and if there is another party cited by the respondent as having committed adultery with the petitioner this person will be called in the heading the 'Party Cited' (not Co-Respondent which is for petitions only). Although it is no more necessary to name adulterers in the Answer than in the petition, third parties do tend to get named more in Answers than in petitions because the respondent obviously needs to be cross enough to file an Answer at all and so will probably not stop at naming names and seeking costs whatever the advice of the SFLA solicitor!

The body of the document should then be drafted as follows:

- all *formal* paragraphs should be dealt with, together as numbered paragraphs en bloc unless there are individual inaccuracies;
- whether the marriage has or has not broken down must be pleaded in the affirmative or negative, depending on whether the respondent's defence includes a desired decree or not, eg s 5 respondents will *not* want one, whereas a cross-petitioning respondent will;
- each allegation must then be pleaded to as required, just as in a Defence and Counterclaim, and then the Cross Petition embarked on immediately afterwards (no separate heading, the numbered paragraphs simply carry on sequentially);
- the respondent ends with a prayer, comprising what the respondent wants, exactly as in a petition except that the respondent will of course ask for the prayer of the petitioner's petition to be rejected!

Signature and service details are as for a petition.

Note

In pleading a bare denial is possible: *Haque v Haque* [1977] 1 WLR 888 but it is usually better to confess and avoid individually, especially where behaviour can have more than one interpretation: *Andrews v Andrews* [1974] 2 All ER 643.

A Reply is possible from the petitioner: r 2.13 but this is even more unusual than an Answer and Cross Petition.

Note

By far the greatest value to a solicitor in knowing how to draft an answer is in appreciating what a good draughtsman can do with apparently effective particulars of behaviour, and if this is learned by drafting one or two Answers and Cross-Petitions for experience, and the skill is never required again, it may be endlessly effective in concentrating the mind when drafting good behaviour particulars in petitions which will be unassailable by the drafting skills of the respondent's advisers.

Self-assessment questions

1 What is the scope of the Green Form for matrimonial work?
2 When may legal aid be available for the divorce suit itself?
3 For what other matrimonial work is legal aid routinely available?
4 What drawback is there of using legal aid in matrimonial matters?
5 What follow up action will you take after the first interview?
6 How do you start divorce proceedings?
7 When might a Green Form extension be available to solve service problems?
8 How and when can you amend a petition already filed and served?
9 What is the Special Procedure?
10 Which decree terminates the status of marriage?

Section 2

Children –
Handling child-related
issues on marriage
breakdown

Chapter 6

The Children Act 1989

A new approach to child disputes 6.1

The Children Act 1989 made major changes in both the public and private law relating to children. Following the marginalisation of the divorce suit itself – so that it is now more often than not a process handled, albeit under the advice of the solicitor, by the client as litigant in person, now forms a major part of the specialist family lawyer's workload. This significant workload is divided between private law (cases about the respective rights and duties of children and parents *inter se*) and public law (cases about the duties of the local authority in respect of children living in their area, and of the rights of children and parents in relation to the local authority). While there are specialist child law solicitors who aim to do all their own work without the aid of counsel except in rare cases, child matters will also probably be the most common area, apart possibly from ancillary relief, in which the ordinary general practitioner will both want to get a good deal of simple work done within the firm and also need to instruct counsel in a number of more complex matters. Principals can allow trainees to go to the district judge on solicitors' appointments so this is a fruitful area for opportunities in advocacy and for handling files independently. Thus, as a keen trainee you will need:

- a sound working knowledge of at least the private law aspects of the Children Act;
- some outline knowledge of how the public law provisions might impact on advice to clients consulting you about the private law;
- an ability to watch trends and appreciate the importance of the latest cases (because of the lack of application of the doctrine of precedent – so that decisions are only a guide to how a court might interpret the exercise of its duty within the statutory framework – child work can be a fast moving field) and;
- an ability to research the law quickly where necessary in order to decide whether counsel should be instructed.

At trainee level, the *decision* to instruct is unlikely to be left in the trainee's hands, but *preparation* of suitable Instructions to Counsel *is* more than likely to be trainee's work, albeit under supervision, and the 'no delay 'principle of the Act (see 6.3) often means you have to do it at the double. The first step is a good working knowledge of the law and practice, so as to identify the *questions* that need to be asked, even if you do not know the *answers* to the more specialised and complicated ones, which fortunately does not matter, since that is what counsel, who is supposed to be a specialist, is *for*. However, for good results from counsel, it is essential to be able to prepare competent Instructions. Otherwise many counsel will not appreciate what is needed and will give less than adequate advice, and better counsel will ring up with an embarrassing list of questions, which will be the solicitor's fault.

The Children Act 1989 came fully into force on 14 October 1991. An overview of how the radical new system now works may be helpful to students who otherwise might be confused by reading reports of old cases, which are often still a useful guideline to the likely interpretation of the contemporary statutory provisions, but of course contain the old terminology.

Part I of the Act confirmed the basic principle that the child's welfare is paramount in both public and private law. The former concept of parental *rights* and duties (which had its roots in time immemorial in both historical and religious contexts) was replaced with a more modern one of *parental responsibility*.

Part II then completely restructured the private law of children. It abolished the outdated concepts (and unhelpfully emotive wording) of *custody, care and control* and *access,* and replaced them with a power for the court to make individual orders to regulate the less emotive and more specifically practical issues of a child's *residence,* ie where and with whom the child should have a *home,* and *contact,* ie when and how the child should keep in touch with the non-residential parent or other relatives. It then provided for special orders to be made with regard to any *specific issue* or *prohibited steps,* in respect of which the court was empowered to make individual one off decisions *without* making any other changes in the child's arrangements.

This package, and the fresh air it has blown into this area of the law, has in the past five years contrasted very favourably with the former position, where in order to make a simple point about a self-contained decision, such as where a child went to school, or what religion the child should practise, a parent had to embark on a full blown custody application, since under the old law the parent with custody had the right to make such major decisions and impose them on the child and the other parent, whose only recourse was to go back to the court to ask for custody to be changed so that that parent could take over major decisions in the child's upbringing.

Note

The new orders are provided by s 8 of the Children Act 1989 (CA 1989) and are thus usually referred to collectively as 's 8 orders'.

The new structure owes much to concepts derived from the wardship jurisdiction of the High court, see 6.9, for which it was designed to be an easier and cheaper alternative.

Parts III, IV and V reorganised the general powers and duties of local authorities in relation to children, also reorganised the emergency protection of children and created a new *emergency protection order* and *child assessment order*, which both together and separately assist the local authority to carry out their duties in relation to the protection of children in their area.

Procedural support for the Act alongside that for other family law matters is to be found in the two new sets of rules brought out in 1991:

- for the High Court and county court these are contained in the FPR 1991, with which the student will already be generally familiar;
- for the magistrates' court (renamed the Family Proceedings Court by the Act) the Family Proceedings (Children Act 1989) Rules 1991.

The rules are in fact much the same save for obvious procedural differences applicable to the two distinct sets of courts.

The overall effect is designed to achieve a completely new approach to child disputes, in which the *rights* of the child and the *duties* of parents and the local authority are emphasised, together with the *non-interventionist* policy of the law and the court, and the principle that in child cases there should be *no delay* in the resolution of the problem which has invited the court's involvement.

Note

The concept of a child having *rights* rather than duties, and the of the parent having *duties* instead of rights was not new in 1989, but rather traces its history back to a report of the law reform society JUSTICE in the early 1970s, which caused a stir at the time of its publication, but nevertheless took rather a long time to work its way through onto the statute book.

However, even in the short time since the implementation of the Children Act, it is clear that the new approach is largely successful. While it may take more than an Act of Parliament to confer on some feckless, damaged or inadequate parents the parental responsibility envisaged by the Act, the system clearly encourages better relations between parents, since it is no longer necessary in divorce for either parent to insist on having *custody* or indeed any sort of order at all, which in bitterly contested cases often meant merely obtaining legal possession of the children at all costs, usually for all the wrong reasons, in order for parents to get their own way in a relatively self-contained area of the child's life.

Moreover, while joint residence orders are not encouraged, on the basis that a child should generally have one home and not two unless it is already an established fact that that child divides the week entirely amicably between the parents, for example where there is a shift arrangement which is working, the provision of the system of residence, contact and specific issue or prohibited steps orders means that the child *can* often share time more fairly between both parents, who may thus *both* continue to influence a child who is living with one parent and having generous contact with the other.

The court can then contain any subsidiary arguments by deciding on any specific (educational or other) issue, *without* a pitched battle necessarily having to break out. This obviates the previous need to disrupt everything simply because one parent or the other had strong views on some point and wished to enforce them if possible.

For those parents who can agree everything without recourse to the court, actual *orders* may thus never be necessary at all, while for those for whom losing *custody* would have meant *losing face*, a generous *contact order* plus the right to go for a *specific issue order* if necessary may be entirely satisfactory. This often proves to be so, even where the other parent obtains a residence order which was not initially acceptable until the full potential of 'generous contact' was appreciated by the parent who lost the residence order application.

All these innovative concepts need to be examined in detail.

Parental responsibility   6.2

Parental responsibility is 'all the rights, duties, powers, responsibilities and authority which by law a parent of a child has in relation to the child and his property': CA 1989 s 3(1). It is central to the concept of parental responsibility that a person with parental responsibility may not *surrender or transfer* any part of that responsibility: s 2(9). It may however be wholly or partly *delegated*, for example to a child's school or to the local authority, or *qualified* or *curtailed*, for example as between the parents of the child either informally or by order of the court (ie by a s 8 order).

Note

When parental responsibility is delegated the parents remain responsible for the omissions of the person with delegated parental responsibility.

Parental responsibility is not simply a philosophical concept but actually requires the parent to assume various responsibilities towards the child to:

* *care for and control the child* till the child is 18, marries, enters the armed forces or is adopted – as far as control goes, *moderate and reasonable punishment* is allowed but any excess is assault: *R v Smith* [1985] Crim LR;

Note

As all parents know this duty tends to be reduced to giving advice as the child grows older and (hopefully) matures, as is shown by the case of *Gillick v Wisbech Area Health Authority* [1985] 3 All ER 402, where a Catholic mother took exception to the family GP giving contraception to her teenage daughter, and the House of Lords, up to which Mrs Gillick fought the case, decided there was nothing wrong with this if the girl in question had sufficient understanding to consult the doctor for proper and necessary medical treatment without informing the mother. A child with this level of understanding is now called *Gillick competent*.

* consent to the child's marriage;
* consent to medical treatment;

Note

Over l6s consent themselves: Family Law Reform Act 1969, s 8(3). Under 16s consent if *Gillick* competent, but doctors can always give emergency treatment without parents' consent anyway.

- *maintain* the child *financially*;

Note

This is enforced by various statutes including the MCA 1973, ss 23 and 24, CA 1989 Schedule 1, Domestic Proceedings and Magistrates' Court Act 1978, Social Security Act 1992, s 106 and Child Support Act 1991, s 1(1)

- protect the child from physical and moral harm;

Note

This means not doing anything to cause such harm to the child *carelessly* (which would be manslaughter which is a crime) nor *deliberately* as in cruelty to children (which is also an offence where a person over l6 having charge of a child assaults, neglects, ill treats or abandons a child or exposes a child to harm so as to cause unnecessary suffering or injury within the meaning of s 1 of the Children and Young Persons Act 1933. See *R v Lowe* [1973] 1 All ER 805 (a case of simple medical neglect where a father of low intelligence failed to appreciate that his nine week old baby was ill and failed to call a doctor, so the baby died of dehydration and malnutrition); and *R v Shepherd* [1981] AC 394, [1980] 3 All ER 899.

As far as *moral* harm goes, the parent should be aware of the Sexual Offences Act 1956, ss 10 and 11 (incest), ss 14 and 15 (indecent assault) and ss 25, 26 and 28 (permitting the use of premises by young girls for intercourse or encouraging them in prostitution etc – probably a good excuse not to buy your 16 year old daughter a flat to live in when she goes to university, regardless of the extortionate rents to which you may have to contribute or the potential investment value when she leaves three years later!)

- ensure that the child receives education, enforceable under s 36 of the Education Act 1944 by a school attendance order or under s 39 for failing to send the child to school, or by using other sanctions such as the local authority threatening a care order if the child is suffering 'significant harm' within the meaning of s 31 of the CA 1989.

The Children Act 1989 permits the court to make a 'prohibited steps order' to stop a parent taking any undesirable step in carrying out parental responsibility in one of these ways: see 6.5.3 or where appropriate the High Court could also make a wardship order so as to take over from the child's parents the task of making decisions in these matters: see 6.9. The recent case involving a 13 year old schoolgirl allowed by her parents to contract marriage with a Turkish waiter is an example of just such an appropriate case, although wardship is rarely used now since the prohibited steps and specific issue orders were expressly created so as to obviate the need to resort to wardship, which is an expensive High Court remedy only, whereas all the s 8 orders are available in all courts which have jurisdiction under the Children Act 1989.

Persons with parental responsibility   6.2.1

Parents who were married at the time of the child's birth, or who have married since, and thus, pursuant to the Family Law Reform Act 1987 s 1 have legitimated the child, will have *joint parental responsibility*: ss 2(1) and 2(3).

Mothers, where the parents are not married, will have parental responsibility.

Fathers not married to the mother (often called '*unmarried fathers*') do not automatically have parental responsibility.

However the 'unmarried father' can obtain parental responsibility in one of five ways, by:
- making a *parental responsibility agreement* with the mother: s 4(1)(b) in the *prescribed form* (which is regulated by the Parental Responsibility Agreement Regulations 1991);
- applying to the court for a parental responsibility order: s 4(1)(a);
- applying to the court for a residence order in which case if the residence order is granted the court will automatically also make a parental responsibility order under s 4(1)(a);
- being appointed the child's guardian by the court;
- being appointed the child's guardian by the mother or by another guardian: s 5;

or, of course, by marrying the mother and thus legitimating the child under the Family Law Reform Act 1987 s 1 as mentioned above, since this will result in the marriage's technically dating back for legitimation purposes to the time of the child's birth, and giving the father parental responsibility in the process.

It is not uncommon for fathers to apply for parental responsibility and the court will consider whether it is in the child's best interests for the father to have it. Naturally it will be necessary for the father to satisfy the court that he is the father, and this will be on the ordinary civil standard, namely on a balance of probabilities. The court will take into account any evidence of commitment: *Re P (A Minor) (Parental Responsibility Order)* [1994] 1 FLR 578 and it is important for a father seeking an order to be able to show that commitment in some way or other.

The case of *Re H (Illegitimate Children: Father: Parental Rights) (No 2)* [1991] 1 FLR 214, CA shows that in addition to commitment and the degree of such commitment, two further points need to be satisfactorily demonstrated in the father's favour, namely the degree of attachment between the father and the child and the reasons for his applying for the order, although the welfare of the child will be paramount and the award of parental responsibility is not 'a prize for good behaviour'!

Neither lack of actual contact between the father and the child as in *Re H (A Minor) (Parental Responsibility)* [1993] 1 FLR 484, CA nor friction between the parents as in *Re P (A Minor) (Parental Responsibility Order)* [1994] 1 FLR 578 is therefore in itself a reason for refusing a parental responsibility order if the three point test in *Re H* is satisfied. Similarly, the fact a father does not obtain a contact order for any reason (eg because he is convicted of possessing obscene literature) does not preclude his having parental responsibility, which is about duties and responsibilities and does not entitle the father to interfere in the child's day to day life: *Re S (Parental Responsibility)* [1995] 2 FLR 648, CA. Parental responsibility can always be terminated if the father does anything which obviously harmful to the child (eg assaulting the child): *Re P (Terminating Parental Responsibility)* [1995] 1 FLR 1048.

Note

If either parent misuses parental responsibility, the other can always apply for a prohibited steps order to stop this: see 6.5.3, and s 2(8) in any case prevents a parent with parental responsibility from acting in any way incompatibly with another order, eg a s 8 residence order.

Step parents do not acquire parental responsibility on marriage to the child's biological parent although a step parent caring for a child and treating that child as a child of the family will create the usual obligations towards such a child of the family, such as in respect of ancillary relief claims: see 7.5, irrespective of whether the step parent has parental responsibility: s 3(4)(a). A step parent without parental responsibility who has care of a child may do whatever is reasonable to safeguard or promote the child's welfare irrespective of having parental responsibility or not: s 3(5) as may any person who has *de facto* care of a child.

Other persons (including step parents) may acquire parental responsibility as follows:

- guardians, who are thus equated with natural parents: s 5(6);
- adopters, when the adoption order is made in their favour (since they are then parents, and the biological parents will at the same time lose their parental responsibility);
- local authorities acquiring a care order: s 33(3), though the parents will also retain theirs;
- any person acquiring a residence order, however only for the duration of the order: s 12(1) and 12(2).

The termination of parental responsibility   6.2.2

Parental responsibility acquired by an order of the court or by agreement ends when the child is 18 as of course it would do automatically in the case of any child reaching majority. Parental responsibility is thus somewhat like a smile – it can be given out generously to all and sundry without necessarily diminishing the original supply, since despite delegation and even increase in the numbers of persons who technically have it, parental responsibility can be *lost* only on *death* or *adoption*.

Note _____

Where more than one person has parental responsibility each has power to act alone: s 2(7) unless there is some specific requirement necessitates the consent of more than one, eg to adoption. But s 2(8) prevents any unilateral action incompatible with another order.

The non-intervention and no delay principles: CA 1989 ss 1(5) and 1(2)   6.3

These two principles are deeply rooted respectively in the philosophy of and in the historical background to the Act.

The *non-interventionist* principle is also sometimes referred to as 'the presumption of no order', and s 1(5) provides that 'where a court is considering whether or not to make one or more orders under this Act with respect to a child, it shall not make the order or any of the orders unless it considers that doing so would be better for the child than making no order at all'. This is a principle generated by the belief that parents are (or should be) the right people to decide what is best for their children.

Technically, it is *not now possible to make s 8 orders by consent* (as the old custody, care and control and access orders sometimes were, especially in relation to joint custody where the parents were agreed that that was the best thing in their particular circumstances and the court approved). The way that the court gives effect to agreements ultimately made at the door of the court is to make no order, which would have been what had happened if the parents had been able to agree in the first place. This is because the court prefers the parties to observe the spirit of the Act in negotiating and observing a proper parenting relationship.

The court therefore only goes on to make an order in such circumstances, ie after the parents have agreed to settle their differences, when for some reason everyone thinks a formal order would actually help, and though the court in such circumstances will put into the order whatever the parents have agreed, *technically* it is *not* a consent order as such but an order handed down by the court for the purpose of providing certainty. This may be splitting very fine hairs, but there is good reason for it in that any order is regarded as, if not precisely a failure on someone's part, at least *undesirable if it can be avoided*, and so strictly reserved for when it *serves some useful purpose*.

Sometimes orders are made, despite the no order principle, where it is necessary to give practical status, eg a residence order in favour of a non-parent.

Note

Mediation services are widely used to attempt to avoid having to make orders, and there is a procedure for a meeting before a district judge with a welfare officer present: *Practice Direction* [1992] 1 FLR 228.

The *no delay* principle is stated in s 1(2) and requires that 'in any proceedings in which any question with respect to the upbringing of the child arises' that the court should have regard to 'the general principle that delay in determining the question is likely to prejudice the welfare of the child'.

The section owes its existence to horror stories of the past, such as the case of *J v C* [1969] 2 WLR 540, [1969] 1 All ER 788, where delay in deciding the future of a Spanish boy brought up by middle class foster parents in an English green belt area resulted in his being unable to return to the working class background of his natural parents in a poor urban quarter of Madrid as it had taken nearly 10 years to reach a final hearing. As a result s 11 requires that a timetable be drawn up to progress s 8 orders (and s 32 makes a similar provision in relation to care and supervision orders in the public law part of the Act). The court takes this seriously, expecting the timetable to be adhered to and sometimes for example proceeding in the absence of some reports if the consequent delay to wait for them outweighs the disadvantage of delay. This is currently posing a dilemma in many cases as in some areas there is at least a 15 week wait for a welfare report to be prepared by the court Welfare Service.

The welfare principle: CA 1989 s 1(1)   6.4

This section provides that whenever a court determines any question with respect to the:
- upbringing of a child;
- administration of a child's property or the application of any income arising from it;

the welfare of the child shall be paramount.

There is no conflict with:
- MCA 1973 s 25 in the law of ancillary relief ('It shall be the duty of the court in deciding whether to exercise its powers under s 23, 24 or 24A above and, if so, in what manner, to have regard to all the circumstances of the case, *first* (author's italics) consideration being given to the welfare while a minor of any child of the family who has not attained the age of eighteen') nor with;
- MHA (Matrimonial Homes Act) 1983, s 1(3) in the law of domestic violence and occupation of the matrimonial home ('On any application for an order under this section the court may make such order as it thinks just and reasonable having regard to the conduct of the spouses in relation to each other and otherwise, to their respective needs and financial resources, and to the needs of any children and to all the circumstances of the case...').

Note

It is established that paramount in s 1(1) means 'the welfare of the child should come before any other consideration in deciding whether to make an order' (*Hansard*, HL vol 503, col 1167). However there is no guidance where more than one child is involved and their interests conflict.

A child is anyone under 18: CA 1989 s 105, but no s 8 orders are made for children over 16 unless the case is exceptional: s 9(7). This is for the obvious reason that at this age, which is also the school leaving age, such a 'child' might not observe them and cannot be compelled to remain in a parent's house nor to see an absent parent against the child's will. For the same reason public law orders (ie for care or supervision) are not made for children over 17 (16 if the child is married).

Welfare means, or so it is thought, as the term is nowhere expressly defined – the body of issues relevant to a child's satisfactory upbringing which now appear in the *statutory checklist* under s 1(3) of the Act: see 6.7. This statutory checklist of welfare points to be taken into account in reaching decisions has now assumed crucial importance in making all s 8 orders, and was specifically referred to in order indirectly to define welfare in a 1995 case in the court of Appeal by a judge skilfully emerging from a horrendously complex appeal against the denial of contact for a mother against the wishes of her children: see *Re M (Contact: Welfare Test)* [1995] 1 FLR 274, CA.

6.5   Section 8 orders

There are four s 8 orders:
- Residence order (RO);
- Contact order (CO);
- Prohibited steps order (PSO);
- Specific issue order (SIO).

Note

Watch out for and distinguish 'COs' in another context – it also commonly means (financial) consent order in the context of ancillary relief. A major bloomer practised by students, especially those using old precedent books, is to place purportedly agreed residence and contact orders in these financial consent orders. As the court making a consent order in ancillary relief proceedings now has no *power* to make such an order in respect of a child – as that court did prior to 1991 – this is a serious mistake not calculated to win admiration during the training contract (since despite the varied catalogue of mistakes made by allegedly experienced practitioners in the drafting of such consent orders which are routinely reported by district judges on social occasions, it is hoped that trainees' principals will know better and spot the trainees' howlers before the district judge is obliged politely to suggest some amendments in the draft Minutes of Order submitted on such occasions).

A residence order

This settles where a child shall live and no more. Parents will still share parental responsibility even if one obtains a residence order, and even if a non-parent obtains a residence order (which will give that person parental responsibility also) the parents will still retain their own parental responsibility.

Note

Although the court likes children to have one settled home, there may be (in appropriate established circumstances or where such a routine is likely to work) an order in favour of more than one person. This is variously called a *split* or a *joint* residence order. The opposite terms ought to mean distinct orders, but seem to be different ways of expressing the same idea, namely that the child will have a settled home with *each* parent and where the parties are (obviously!) not living together the order can detail the periods to be spent at each house. Recent cases where such orders have been made include *Re H (A Minor) (Shared Residence)* [1993] Fam 463, and *G v G (Joint Residence Order)* [1993] Fam Law 615.

A contact order

This requires the person with whom the child lives (who may or may not have a residence order) to allow the child to visit or stay with a named person (which is sometimes called *staying contact*) or for that person and the child to have contact with each other in some other manner. The extent of such contact may either be left unspecified or alternatively be more precisely stated as *reasonable contact* or even *defined contact* if the parents cannot agree a programme and want the court to order it in detail for them.

Note

This is a complete change from the former system of access, which could be only by physical presence – now the court may order that letters and telephone calls may be exchanged, though they generally *cannot* order the parent with whom the child resides actually to perform any particular action, eg personally to take any positive action in writing progress reports to or communicating with the other parent if children do not do so themselves (or cannot do so, eg if they are too young to speak on the telephone or write!). This was attempted in the case of *Re M (A Minor) (Contact: Conditions)* [1994] 1 FLR 272, and the court held the view that such an order could not be made although it was deemed that a custodial parent *could* be ordered to *keep the other parent informed* of the child's whereabouts, so that contact can actually take place.

However, the case of *Re O (A Minor) (Contact)* [1995] 2 FLR 124, CA, did approve a mother being asked to *send* photographs, medical reports and nursery school reports, inform the other parent of serious illness of the child and accept delivery of presents and cards for the child, which clearly only really involves the ordinary civilised behaviour which might be expected of a custodial parent towards the other with whom the child does not reside.

Technically, any conditions which are acceptable so as to achieve indirect contact where direct contact is for some reason impossible may be attached pursuant to s 11(7) which permits conditions to be attached to all s 8 orders. This power must be read in the light of the new concept of promoting indirect contact as an alternative to actually seeing the child, but not carried to extremes which require so much of that parent that the concept of contact with the *child* is distorted into a back door requirement for contact with the carer *parent*, which was not the intention of the statute!

Contact orders will usually always be granted in the case of biological parent-child relationships, even though there is no statutory presumption to that effect, on the basic principle that it is for the good of the child living with one parent to remain in contact with the other parent: *Re W (A Minor) (Contact)* [1994] 2 FLR 441, CA, where the court of Appeal made an order for contact despite a mother's hostility to the applicant (as she had remarried and was teaching the child to regard her new husband as the natural father). They allowed an appeal against the judge below who had *not* made an order, *inter alia* because the mother had said she would disobey it if it were made, so that judge had understandably thought that to make an order in that climate would only destabilise the child and not be in any child's interests. However the Court of Appeal said he had abdicated his responsibility!

This must therefore be taken to be the contemporary trend, and that in the absence of complications, such as sufficiently implacable hostility of either the custodial parent or of the children themselves to raise a query as to whether contact is not for the child's welfare, there *is* a basic presumption of some sort of a right to contact. This *can* and *will* however be displaced by expressly showing (with reference to the statutory welfare checklist) that the 'fundamental emotional need of every child to have an enduring relationship with both its parents '– as contemplated by s 1(3)(b) – is outweighed by the depth of harm which in the light, *inter alia* of the child's wishes and feelings – under s 1(3)(a) of the checklist – the child would be at risk of suffering – ie within the meaning of s 1(3)(e) – by virtue of the contact order'.

Contact is therefore likely to be refused if that is absolutely necessary and in the child's interests: *Re B (Minors: Access)* [1992] 1 FLR 140, *Re H (Minors: Access)* [1992] 1 FLR 148 especially if the *child* personally opposes it and is of an age when the child's ascertainable wishes and feelings, within the meaning of the statutory checklist, are taken into account: *Re F (Minors) (Denial of Contact)* [1993] 2 FLR 677.

Whether an order should be made is less obvious where the hurdle is the *custodial parent's* implacable hostility to the contact for the child, making the child potentially at serious risk of emotional harm if contact is compelled because it will have such a bad effect on the objecting parent: see *Re D (A Minor) (Contact: Mother's Hostility)* [1993] 2 FLR 1, *Re F (Minors) (Contact: Mother's Anxiety)* [1993] 2 FLR 830, *Re J (A Minor) (Contact)* [1994] Fam Law 316.

On the whole, courts do not like parents being obstructive about contact and in the past have indicated that a parent's attitude to contact might influence them to make an order for residence in favour of the other parent: see, eg *D v M* [1982] 3 WLR 891, [1982] 3 All ER 897 (where the father was reluctant for the mother to have contact and the court was reluctant to let him have the children as a result) and *Re S* [1990] 2 FLR 166 where the children (two boys) lived each with one parent, and the court said that if the mother did not allow the boy in her care to visit the father and the other child (as she was depriving the boys of *each other's* company as well as the father of the company of the boy in her care) she might have to give up the boy with her unless she became less recalcitrant. Attitude to contact is therefore very important in a s 8 order application.

Note

Contact orders do *not* confer parental responsibility so, like a step parent without parental responsibility, a person with a contact order and no parental responsibility can do anything which safeguards and promotes the child's welfare during the contact but should not exceed that duty by doing anything which would be appropriate in a person exercising parental responsibility. It should be remembered that apart from the case of parents with automatic parental responsibility, the key to other relations and associates of the child having parental responsibility is not the relationship as such but whether that person has a residence order which does confer parental responsibility on anyone who has such an order: see 6.2.1.

6.5.3   A prohibited steps order

This order is one which can prohibit a parent from taking any step which could be taken in meeting that parent's parental responsibility towards the child. They are not intended to prevent parents doing other things which do not amount to a step in meeting their parental responsibility, as is shown by the case of *Croydon Borough Council v A* (1992) 136 (LB) 69 (FS), where the local authority had removed children from their home under an emergency protection order and placed them with foster parents because the father had sexually abused one of them. When the authority applied to the magistrates for an interim care order the court refused the interim care order and instead for some reason made two prohibited steps orders, the first preventing the father from seeing the children and secondly prohibiting him from having contact with the mother. On appeal the second order was overturned because it did not fall within the statutory definition of a parent taking a step in meeting his parental responsibility, and the authority got their interim care order.

Similarly in the case of *Re H (Prohibited Steps Order)* [1995] 1 FLR 638 a judge made a prohibited steps order to forbid contact between a mother's former cohabitee and her children who were living with her, and over whom the local authority had supervision orders because the children had been sexually abused by the former cohabitee, and he also attached no contact conditions to the supervision orders. On appeal the court of Appeal held that the prohibited steps order was wrong because it contravened s 9(5)(a) of the CA 1989, which specifically forbids a court to make a prohibited steps order as a back door means of achieving a desired result which could, and properly should, be effected by a residence or contact order, and that although conditions could be attached to the authority's supervision order (such as for medical or psychiatric examination) a condition for no contact could not be so attached, although the supervisor has other means under Schedule 3 of the CA 1989 of achieving the same result.

A specific issue order

This order, as the name suggests, enables the court to give directions to decide a dispute as to any major decision to be taken in relation to a child's future, eg a change of surname, school or religion, or whether a child should or should not have a particular medical treatment, such as a blood transfusion (where one or even both of the parents are against it for religious or other reasons) or sterilisation or abortion, eg where the child is advised not to have children for some sufficient medical reason.

The court either takes the decision itself or directs that a particular person should take it, eg where treatment is directed by a specified doctor as the doctor deems appropriate. Such orders may be sought by non-parents, eg a local authority concerned for the child's welfare.

The same restrictions apply to these orders as for prohibited steps orders.

Note

All s 8 orders may be made as interim orders and ss 11(3) and 11(7) permit conditions to be attached or allow the court to delay implementation, restrict the effect of the order to a certain period or attach conditions.

Tactically, an interim order is usually in the client's interests, because of the *status quo* element in the statutory checklist: see 6.7 and the additional value of an interim residence or contact order is that it may cement a relationship thus strengthening other statutory checklist points in the client's favour, for example, such as the child's ascertainable wishes and feelings in favour of remaining with the client if temporary arrangements are working out well.

Enforcement can be a great problem in the case of both residence and contact orders. Both may be enforced by using the FLA 1986 s 34, formerly used to enforce old style custody and access orders, but expressly referred to in the CA 1989 Schedule 13 for enforcement of residence and contact orders. Schedule 14 of the CA 1989 also affords another method whereby such an order may be enforced under s 63(3) of the Magistrates' Court Act 1980 by serving a copy of the order and requiring production of the child.

However, while fathers are often committed for contempt for failing to observe orders, mothers tend not to be (as then children might have to go into the care of the local authority if there is no one else available to look after them) but committal is not really suitable and is only used in the last resort: see *Re N (A Minor) (Access: Penal Notices)* [1992] 1 FLR 134. The remedy is really to re-educate the parents into observing the philosophy and spirit of the Act, and to use of one of the charity contact centres so the parents do not have to meet. A Directory of all such centres may be obtained from the Network of Access and Child Contact Centres at Nottingham.

6.5.5 | **Who may apply for s 8 orders**

Certain persons are entitled to apply as of right:
- any parent or guardian of the child: s 10(4);
- anyone who has a residence order in respect of the child: s 10(4);
- any person with an old style custody, care and control or access order, called an 'existing order': Schedule 14.

Note

A father who is not married to the mother will be classed as a parent, and will not require leave, but only if he can show that he is the father. Alternatively he may have resided with the child for three years (see below) and thus not need leave for that reason.

The following are entitled to apply for residence and contact orders only, ie any:
- party to a marriage (whether or not the marriage is still subsisting) in which the child was a child of the family as defined in s 105(1);
- person with the consent of all those with residence orders (or 'existing orders') or parental responsibility in respect of the child;
- person who has the consent of a local authority which has a care order;
- person with whom the child has resided for three years (not necessarily continuously, but beginning not more than five years before the application is made).

Rules of court may extend this list: s 10(7).

Other person can still apply but will need leave of the court, eg grandparents or any other relatives with whom the child has not established a three year residence qualification.

Note

The child itself may apply if of sufficient understanding: s 10(8), and a number of such applications by teenage and sub-teenage girls have succeeded; a solicitor may accept instructions from such a child and obtain legal aid in order to pursue the child's application. It is clear, since children picked up the idea of 'divorcing their parents' that this may be a practice growth area.

Acting for children has become a specialism in itself and, owing to the potential complexities, all such s 8 applications must be heard in the Family Division of the High Court. See *Practice Direction* [1993] 1 All ER 820.

It is incidentally, of course, *impossible* for a child to divorce its parents, since parental responsibility is for life or at least until adulthood or adoption of the child, though the child may of course obtain a residence order to go to *live* with other relatives, or with anyone suitable, and maintenance may be obtained from the natural parent(s) to enable this to happen: see 7.5. Recently a child succeeded in making her own application in her parents' s 8 proceedings: *Re C (Child's Application for Leave)* [1995] 1 FLR 927.

If leave *is* required the court will base its decision on the following:
- the nature of the proposed application for a s 8 order;
- the applicant's connection with the child;
- any risk there might be of the application's disrupting the child's life so that the child would be harmed by it;
- if the child is being looked after by the local authority, the authority's plans for the child and the wishes and feelings of the child's parents.

Note

Applications are often made in the course of a divorce, but this is in no way necessary: see 3.5, since application may be made at any time on a completely free-standing basis and the same form is now used irrespective of whether there is a divorce in process.

The court will have jurisdiction if the child is either habitually resident in England and Wales or present and not habitually resident elsewhere on the date of application or hearing. Jurisdiction is excluded if there are matrimonial proceedings elsewhere in the UK unless the other court has waived its jurisdiction, or stayed proceedings so that the matter might be heard in England and Wales: FLA 1986 s 3 though if the court thinks that the matter would be better determined outside England and Wales (ie in any other jurisdiction) it has the power to direct that no order be made: FLA 1986 s 2(4)

6.5.6   **The alternative to a s 8 order: the Family Assistance Order: CA 1989 s 16**

This is a short-term alternative to a s 8 order, though it may be used for many purposes, such as even when a s 8 order has already been made and the parents need extra support. The order was introduced by the CA 1989 and is specifically designed to help at times of matrimonial breakdown. Such an order is only made in the most *exceptional* circumstances, and merely enables a social worker to give general advice and assistance. Everyone involved except the child must consent to the order: ss 16(3) and 16(7).

So far, there has not been great use of the Family Assistance order, though it has come in useful where it was held that a s 11(7) condition of supervision of contact could not be attached to a contact order: see *Leeds County Council v C* [1993] 1 FLR 269 where Booth J used a Family Assistance Order to achieve supervised contact.

6.6   **Change of name or removal from the jurisdiction: s 13(1)**

The prohibition of these two acts by s 13(1) provides an instant example of the use of the prohibited steps order to stop a parent misusing parental responsibility by taking a step with which objectively the other parent cannot necessarily be expected to agree, thus making unilateral action clearly inadvisable. Where a residence order is already in force, ie where the parents have already had recourse to the court for one reason or another, the section prohibits:

- changing the child's surname;
- taking a child out of the jurisdiction;

in either case without the written consent of every person with parental responsibility or the leave of the court. The reasons for this are obvious.

6.6.1   **Removal from the jurisdiction**

Here the person with the residence order may in fact take the child for a holiday of up to one month *without leave* and if leave is required for longer it is likely to be given by the court if the other parent will not consent provided the holiday is not obviously intended as a cover for permanent removal beyond the reach of the court's authority. Moreover a parent who had totally unreasonably withheld consent might find that he or she has to pay the costs.

The way to deal with this in practice is to have in place either a general direction attached to the residence order to enable removal of the child whenever convenient subject to a return to the jurisdiction whenever required, or a general undertaking may be given to the court by the parent wishing to remove the child, eg a father living abroad whom the child will visit regularly.

Note

Beware trips to Scotland and Ireland – these are outside the jurisdiction of England and Wales and are just as much 'foreign' as Outer Mongolia.

Permanent removal is more difficult, as this might in practice cut off all contact for the other parent. However, the court is aware of the difficulties which may arise if the parent with the residence order is thwarted in an attempt to emigrate, with consequent unhappiness for the whole family, as is shown by the cases of *Chamberlain v de la Mare* (1983) 4 FLR 434 and *Lonslow v Hennig* [1986] 2 FLR 378.

The court sometimes does refuse leave if the future picture presented is unsatisfactory, but generally will not, as in *Re F* [1988] 2 FLR 116, if a parent is remarrying, if the new partner seems to be good news and if there is a good relationship between the applicant parent and the child or children and other positive indications. The key to a successful application is that the applicant parent should already have a residence order or a settled *status quo* whereby the children are and have been for some time living happily with that parent. Applications for leave to take the children out of the jurisdiction to emigrate are obviously not best placed where the relationship between the applicant parent and the children is already slender and the other parent conversely has established a satisfactory lifestyle for them, especially if that includes an existing or interim residence order.

Lengthy more temporary removal may be a problem as is shown by the case of *Re K (A Minor)* [1992] 2 FLR 98 where the court would not allow a mother to take the child to the USA for her postgraduate study because it would seriously disrupt contact with the father, which does show that each case will genuinely turn on its circumstances as is intended by the requirement to balance the child's interests in accordance with the statutory checklist.

6.6.2

Change of surname

Here either formal change by deed poll or informal change (eg by instructing a school that a child is to be known by a certain name) is equally forbidden by the section and if the other parent will not consent application will again have to be made to the court.

The court tends to stick out against consenting, because of the importance of preserving the formal link with the absent father and of the importance of his name as part of the child's identity regardless of the mother's new associations. The children's own wishes count exceptionally little in this situation, and much less than they might in others *because* of the importance placed by the court in the continuing connection with the father, as is shown by cases such as *W v W* [1981] Fam 14, [1981] 1 All ER 100 where the family were all emigrating to Australia and the 12 and 13 year olds wanted to take their mother's new name, which was of course that of their new stepfather.

With the general tendency towards serial monogamy and cohabitation, embarrassment at having a different name (or even several in the reconstructed family) is now unlikely to be felt by the children, or at least believed by the court, so that the chances of the court's agreeing to a change appear slimmer than ever, and the older cases where they did agree (except perhaps because of a *fait accompli*) are now probably out of date and no longer even a guideline. In particular, as in the case of *L v F* (1978) *Times* 1 August, where the father is a person of stature and able to make a positive contribution to the children's lives the court is unlikely to approve the loss of his name, especially as contemporary psychiatric evidence shows that children need to know and acknowledge their biological origins. Conversely, a parent's best chance of success might be if the father were notorious (as has been successful in one well known case in the USA).

Note

By CA 1989 s 10(8) a child of sufficient understanding could make its own application to the court to seek or prevent a change of surname.

6.7   The statutory checklist: s 1(3)

The Act for the first time reduces to statutory form the various matters which courts have always taken into account when making orders in relation to the custody, care and control of children, and access to them for the non-residential parent. However, the case law from which the new checklist was derived may still afford guidelines as to how the court interprets that checklist.

However the court's primary duty is now simply to work through the checklist itself, which is *mandatory* when making, varying or discharging any s 8 order which is opposed. There is in fact nothing particularly new in the content of the checklist, but previously to the Children Act, the principles on which decisions were made were to be deduced only from case law if any applied, whereas now the matters in the list must be addressed in a structured manner.

The list does not express or imply any order of importance amongst the following:

- the ascertainable wishes and feelings of the child concerned;
- the child's physical, emotional and educational needs;
- the likely effect on the of any change in his circumstances;
- the child's age, sex, background and any characteristics of his which the court considers relevant;
- any harm which the child has suffered or is at risk of suffering;
- how capable each of the child's parents, and any other person in relation to whom the court;
- considers the question to be relevant, are of meeting the child's needs;
- the range of powers available to the court under the Children Act 1989 in the proceedings in question.

So far the checklist seems to be a useful innovation, and in particular although there is no precise definition of 'welfare' in the Act, it provides a formula whereby it may be decided *whether* a particular action is or is not for the child's welfare, which in practical terms is probably more useful than an express definition of the term.

The old case law is thus still of guiding importance, although it has to be read in the light of modern conditions, eg children of every class now in fact appear to mature earlier, beside which our contemporary attitudes to children are less paternalistic than before.

Thus children's views generally tend to be taken into consideration more than they used to be in the more traditional past where children were expected to be seen and not heard and above all to do what their parents told them. This greater amenability to the consideration of the child's point of view has manifested itself not only in a semi-formal channel in the first head of the checklist under s 1(3)(a), where their ascertainable wishes and feelings are to be considered, but also in the recognition in s 10(8) of the capability of children of sufficient age and understanding to make their own s 8 applications.

6.7.1   The ascertainable wishes and feelings of the child concerned in the light of his age and understanding: s 1(3)(a)

Obviously the *wishes* of a very young child will not be a serious consideration, especially if contrary to the child's long-term interests, but the *feelings* of such a child, in the sense of profound attachment to the parent to whom the child is used and with whom the child feels loved, secure and comfortable, must always be relevant: see further 6.7.2.

Note

The child's prime communication channel in this respect is the *welfare officer*, since in a contested s 8 application a welfare report will have been ordered. The welfare officer will have seen the child alone as well as with the parent with whom the child lives, and possibly with the other parent as well, so will be in a position both to ask expressly if a child of suitable age to say so has views, and to judge independently from the child's body language and demeanour, alone and in the company of one or other or both of the parents, whether one of them has coached the child in rehearsed responses.

Alternatively, or in addition, the judge (but not the magistrates if the case is in the Family Proceedings Court) may interview a child over the age of about seven, in order to find out at first hand about the child's views or feelings. Obviously, the older the child the more likely the judge is to want to know the child's view and then if appropriate to take expressed wishes into account.

There are some milestone cases which should be noted along the way to this result

Gillick v West Norfolk and Wisbech Area Health Authority [1985] 3 All ER 402 established the right of the teenage girl approaching 16 to obtain contraceptive advice from a doctor without her mother's knowledge or consent, while it was in the case of *Hewer v Bryant* [1969] 3 WLR 425, [1969] 3 All ER 402 that it was realised that the parental duty to care for and control the child will ultimately end in nothing more than a right to give advice as soon as the child matures.

Age is always important and although there is some room for degrees of maturity to be considered, an older child will obviously have more influence on the court's decision than a younger one, as is illustrated by the cases of *Stewart v Stewart* (1973) 3 Fam Law 107, where a 15 year old girl wanted to live with her mother and the court took her wishes into account, considering that she was old enough to express a wish sensibly in her long-term interest rather than making a decision for childish reasons. Conversely *M v M* (1977) 7 Fam Law 17, where a six year old girl wanted to stay with her father and her wishes were treated with caution, and *B(M) v B(R)* [1981] 1 WLR 1182 (where the girl was seven and a half and her wishes were similarly cautiously treated) show the likely position in the case of younger children.

Marsh v Marsh (1978) 8 Fam Law 103 is particularly interesting since that was a case of two girls who wanted to live with their mother and when they were eight and five the court took *no* account of their views: however when they were 12 and nine, and the mother reapplied, the court *did* listen to them and although there was nothing wrong with their father's care agreed to a move. This seems to suggest that children from about 10 to 12 may be able to dictate their future.

The case of *M v M* [1987] 1 WLR 404 shows that the court may even split children if their views differ widely on where they should live. In that case there was a girl of 12 and a boy of nine, where the girl wanted to stay with her father and refused to return with her nine year old brother to their mother, and the court upheld her wish to remain with the father.

Note

The child's *own* wishes are what matters. In the case of *Re S (Infants)* [1967] 1 WLR 396, [1967] 1 All ER 202, a 13 year old boy who had been coached by one of the parents expressed his 'view' which was ignored, because it was not genuinely his and was in any case contrary to his long-term interests.

It is now regarded as the duty of the court to have regard to the wishes and views of older children, especially if they are sensible, mature and intelligent: see *Re P (A Minor) (Education: Child's Views)* and *Re W (Minors) (Residence Order)* [1992] *Times*, 3 March, CA where it was held that it was correct to take account of the views of children aged 10 and 12.

6.7.2   **The child's physical, emotional and educational needs: s 1 (3)(b)**

There are six sub-points to consider here:

- do mothers obtain care of young children and/or girls?
- do fathers obtain the care of older boys?
- do living conditions count?
- will the court separate siblings?
- does education play a significant part?
- will religious and/or cultural differences be a significant factor?

Do mothers obtain care of young children and/or girls?

It was once thought that this was a *presumption*, and in the case of *Re W (A Minor) (Residence Order)* [1992] 2 FLR 332, CA, the court held that there was a rebuttable presumption that a tiny baby should be in the care of its mother, but except in such an extreme case it is generally now regarded rather as a *practice*, for obvious reasons, although there is no general rule of any sort that mothers have children of any age or sex living with them: *Re A (A Minor) (Custody)* [1991] 1 FLR 394 and *Re S (A Minor) (Custody)* [1991] 2 FLR 388. However, especially now custody and residence are distinct concepts, obviously the good mother in the right circumstances will always have a better chance of obtaining a residence order for babies and young children: *Re W (A Minor) (Residence Order)* [1992] 2 FLR 332.

Indeed, there is a long line of cases showing the court's apparent preference for the mother's care in such cases, for example *Greer v Greer* (1974) 4 Fam Law 187 where two girls aged eight and five were returned to the mother after they had been separated from her for some time subsequent to her departure from the matrimonial home, and it was even said that she had never taken much interest in them while the marriage had subsisted, preferring her career to either home or children. However, after she left she had kept in touch with them and was later successful in her custody application. In the case of *Ives v Ives* [1973] 3 Fam Law 16 there was a similar or perhaps even stronger situation in favour of the father, where he had looked after the two daughters for four years, and even the welfare officer was in favour of their remaining with him, but the court still returned them to the mother for the traditional reason. There was the same result in *Re W* (1983) 4 FLR 492, (1983) 13 Fam Law 47, where the father again lost to the mother a girl whom he had looked after for the whole of the first two

years of her life. In *Allington v Allington* [1985] FLR 586
there were even doubts about the mother whose new
relationship was unstable, but the daughter was still
taken away from the father and sent to live with her.

In *C v C* [1988] 2 FLR 291 the mother succeeded in
taking a four year old boy away from the father.

However, such traditional results are not always a
foregone conclusion, and if in a particular case it is felt
that a father has the merits on his side it is worth press-
ing on in the hope of demonstrating to the court that he
should retain a child with him whatever its age and sex,
especially since what used to be thought the *presumption*
of the mother's better right seems to have been dis-
lodged and is more precisely regarded nowadays as no
more than a *practice*.

In *B v B* [1985] Fam Law 29 just such a positive result
was achieved on the particular facts even though the
case did not look promising to start with in the light of
the decisions mentioned above. In that case the father
was left with an 11 month old child whom he assidu-
ously looked after for two years before the mother
sought custody by which time the child was strongly
attached to him and it was felt that the change might
harm her. This fact obviously had something to do with
the decision (see the checklist *status quo* at s 1(3)(c)
below) but what *really* tipped the balance it seems was
that the father was unemployed and could stay with the
child all day – although the court was very unhappy
about a man being out of work on a long-term basis and
barely stopped short of staying that he really ought to get
back into regular employment! However, this was 1985
since when the unemployment situation has meant that
many men now cannot find work whereas women, particularly middle aged women *can*, and the role of the
house husband and male child carer at the PTA and
Toddler Group has perforce had to be accepted! Thus,
while clearly it is *desirable* that a man should be working
and supporting his family rather than remaining at home
unemployed caring for house and children, there is actually no reason in *law* why a man should not do so if he
wishes and it suits the family situation.

Re H [1990] 1 FLR, CA, shows that a mother who
leaves her child for a prolonged period may definitely
now be regarded as at risk of the *status quo* operating
against her. In that case a boy came to England from
India to reside with an aunt and uncle, who neglected to
send home any news of him, as did the father, while the

mother it seems did not get around to asking for any. By the time the mother arrived in England to divorce the father the boy had settled with his relatives with whom he had thrived and the mother lost custody to them. It seems that if mothers behave in this way only some extraneous circumstance will now save them from losing the child, as in the case of *Re W* [1990] Fam Law 261 where the mother was young (18) and the father (47) was not of an age to relate as well to the child.

Do fathers obtain the care of older boys?

This has never been a *presumption* in the way that mothers having girls and younger children was thought to be, and as a *practice* was never as strongly established. The cases of *W v W and C* [1968] 1 WLR 1310, [1968] 3 All ER 408 and *Re C, C v A* [1970] 1 WLR 288, [1970] 1 All ER 309 seem to show a *principle* that fathers should have older boys with them (ie boys older than about eight when upper and middle class English boys traditionally went away to preparatory school as boarders) but it is far more shadowy than the mother principle in respect of girls and younger children. Probably another factor as well will need to be introduced into the equation for this point to be conclusive in favour of the father. Moreover, contemporary trends should always be borne in mind and it should be remembered that there is currently a significant and continuing statistical drop in boarding school numbers which may partly be due to the cost which can no longer be met by many families, but is also undoubtedly driven by the recent social trend of preferring to keep children, even male children, at home during their formative years so that they may be in touch with their families and not isolated in a single sex environment away from home.

Do living conditions count7

Obviously good living conditions will be superior to bad ones, but there is no argument for materialism as such. All other things being *equal* good accommodation will always have the edge as in the case of *Re F* [1969] 3 WLR 162, [1969] 2 All ER 276, but *not* where this is not so, as in the case of *D v M* [1982] 3 WLR 891, [1982] 3 All ER 897 where the father's relative affluence did not score in contrast to the mother's somewhat more basic but nevertheless adequate living conditions, on the basis that she was in fact the *best* person to bring up the particular child. Indeed in the case of *Stephenson v Stephenson* [1985] FLR 1140, where the court was anxious about other negative aspects of the mother's case, any disadvantage in less good *accommodation* was thought to be of relatively little importance, and this was also the view in *B v T* [1989] 2 FLR 31 (where a semi-detached house with a garden had to be compared with a tower block flat with a play area some distance away).

The standard of *day to day care* rather than the accommodation itself is likely to be more important to the court in forming a view about the best environment for the child. The court is not interested in acrimonious squabbles between the parents about minor matters, since incompatibility between the parents and their approaches to many things is likely to have been a factor in the divorce in the first place, but they will begin to take notice if one parent regularly allows the children to be dirty, ragged, ill mannered and undisciplined.

Obviously a parent who is undertaking the child's care personally will always have an edge over the parent who is not able to be at home full time, but if there has to be substitute care, the quality of that provision will obviously also be part of the overall environment provided by the one home as opposed to the other, and here the age of the child will be crucial – older children have their own pursuits and married parents may not see much of them, so this where the divorced working parent need be no worse off. A common sense approach is what is required here.

Note

If accommodation is positively and unarguably *sub-standard* then the parent in question should make strenuous and preferably successful efforts to change it.

If a move is proposed (obviously involving a child in moving schools, making new friends, settling in a new area etc) then the parent who is in the awkward position of having to disclose these plans to the court (which is *not* the ideal of most advocates conducting s 8 applications) should at least have clear and demonstrably workable plans for the children's future. At the least an attempt should be made to supply particulars of the sort of house that the parent could in afford in the new area, particulars of schools and if possible some plans for continuity of care,preferably from a relative rather than from paid help so that something will remain unchanged in the children's lives.

If council accommodation is depended on, a letter should be sought from the local authority specifying what will be available and when. The better advice is however *not* to go in for moves at this precise stage, but either to have done it already before an application is initiated, or else not to propose it until the s 8 order is safely made, as it merely creates handicaps in presenting the case.

Will the court separate siblings?

The court does not like to do this: *Re P (Custody of Children: Split Custody Order)* [1991] 1 FLR 337, for the obvious reason that a divorce is upsetting enough for children without disrupting their ties with siblings as well as with their parents as a married couple, but it is sometimes necessary for one reason or another.

There has been something of an argument as to whether if the children in a family are split between the parents, this can be compensated for by generous and frequent contact. At first the answer was thought to be in the affirmative: *Re P* [1967] 1 WLR 818, [1967] 2 All ER 229, where the problem was thought to be completely solved by the children meeting in the holidays, but in *C v C* [1988] 2 FLR 291 this idea was strenuously attacked on the basis that meeting frequently was *not* the same for the children as being brought up together, and the four year old son was sent to live with his mother along with the seven year old daughter as the court said the children would be a mutual support to each other. However, this result could be equally explained by the fact that the boy was only four, so it might not be a strong guideline after all.

Nevertheless, in the case of *B v T* above, while the tower block flat versus the semi detached home with a garden did *not* prove decisive, the court of Appeal could not apparently themselves solve the problem of whether or not to separate a boy of three and a girl of 15 months where the magistrates had initially given both children to the father and on appeal the High Court gave both to the mother! They sent the case back to the magistrates with instructions that the whole matter was to be gone into in depth and that they should consider the only solution so far not tried of giving the parents one child each! The answer to this sort of situation must be that other factors in the checklist must be used to flesh out the picture so as to indicate the right solution.

Does education play a significant part?

Education is now unlikely to be as important as it once was, other than applying the *status quo* under s 1(3)(c) so as to keep a child at the same school if possible, especially if the current stage of education is a crucial one such as the during GCSE or A level course or examination years.

Where educational preferences of the parents might play a part is in the classic situation where one of the parents considers academic achievement to be important and the other does not, as in the case of *May v May* [1985] Fam Law 106 where the father was insistent on a good education, and the mother and her cohabitee were not concerned about such matters. The father got the children, though this will often be the result where the father is willing to pay school fees. If the parties cannot ultimately agree on education however, and are otherwise not *genuinely* disputing where the child shall live, the solution is a specific issue order to decide where the child should go to school rather than a contested residence order application, because now that custody as such has been replaced by 'parental responsibility' and residence and contact orders, it is usually possible to contain the dispute within limited bounds by using the specific issue order machinery to look at the area of dispute in isolation from the broader basis of the child's upbringing in a home from which regular contact with the non-residential parent may be arranged.

Will religion, and/or racial and cultural differences, be a significant factor?

Any one of these factors can be of importance since despite the apparent decline of Christian religion in the United Kingdom, feelings can still run high within the minority for whom religion still matters. In fact in the non-Christian denominations religion is still very much a live issue, especially where culture and lifestyle is really part and parcel of the religion, eg both Islamic and Jewish families will almost certainly feel this. Alternatively religion may be a significant factor where the religion is regarded by some as belonging to the 'lunatic fringe', such as in the case of Scientologists, the Exclusive Brethren, the Mormons, Jehovah's Witnesses and similar sects.

The case of *Re L* [1974] 1 All ER 913 focused on the psychological damage done to a child who is uprooted from a familiar culture and language with further consequential damage to the child's identity and education. Such problems were considered by the House of Lords in the case of *J v C* [1969] 12 WLR 540, [1969] 2 All ER 788 where they concluded that the young Spanish boy who has spent 10 years in England with a middle class family, learning English and going to an English school with his English foster brothers and sisters, could not be returned to his desperately poor urban background where his working class natural parents would have no points of contact with him. However, the House could do one thing for the Spanish natural parents – his English Church of England foster parents were required to bring him up as a Catholic, and this is not an uncommon direction in cases where the child's religion differs from that of the carers: in *Re E* [1964] 1 WLR 51, [1963] 3 All ER 874 a Jewish couple had to undertake to bring a child up as a Catholic.

Negative influence of religion on decisions about where and with whom a child should live may be seen in some other cases, eg *Re B and G* [1985] FLR 493 where the father and stepmother who were Scientologists lost them although they had had the children for five years. While it is true that the courts much detest this cult, which has been called 'immoral' and 'obnoxious', what judges are apparently *really* afraid of in allowing children to remain under the influence of Scientologist carers is its dire influence on young people due to actual incidents which have shown how dangerous this can be: these have ranged from mere isolation from other people (which militates against any balance which might otherwise counteract the sect's extremism) to actual psychological damage and disturbance. The court is also anxious about young people losing their property through being enticed into giving it away to the movement.

Absence of normal social contact is also a negative aspect of the Exclusive Brethren, whose beliefs expressly limit such contact, which is not thought to be good for children, as was shown in the decision in *Hewison v Hewison* (1977) 7 Fam Law 207, whereas the problem with Jehovah's Witnesses is that in addition to not permitting house to house visiting (which is again thought to endanger children's social development) they also believe that medical treatment is wrong, so a Jehovah's Witness with care of a child would not be able to consent to any life saving emergency procedure such as a blood transfusion. Where the negative social aspect can be dealt with by ensuring regular contact with the child's other parent who does not belong to the sect, it was always possible under the old orders for custody, care and control and access to get round the medical treatment embargo by giving custody to the father and care and control to the mother, so that the former could if necessary, consent to any urgent treatment such as a blood transfusion or other surgical intervention as in the case of *Jane v Jane* (1983) 13 Fam Law 209. The same result could now be achieved either by a split or shared residence order or generous contact for the non-residential parent, provided of course the parent who is not a Jehovah's Witness genuinely keeps in regular contact, is likely to be told of an emergency and is therefore able to intervene.

The likely effect on the child of any change in his circumstances: s 1(3)(c)

There are two separate points here, the *status quo*, which it will clearly be desirable to maintain if at all possible, and whether there will be continuity of care which really concerns the child's quality of life, already considered under s 1(3)(a) at 6.7.1, and which after divorce is the most likely to suffer necessary logistical changes anyway, eg the mother goes out to work even if that were not formerly the case and has to employ childcare help, so that if the father, who will presumably *continue* to work in the occupation which he followed prior to the divorce, wants to make a bid for the children he might at that point succeed if it is a straight contest between working mother and working father. However he probably would *not* get the children if his arrangements involve a more complex chain of carers, however worthy, rather than the mother with some help. Obviously, in this situation, the mother who is at home and able to offer satisfactory full time care or who works only part time, has the edge over the father and even a highly trained nanny. However, each case has to be taken on its particular facts as the cases show.

The *status quo*

The *status quo* as such has always been important as the tragic result of the case of *J v C* showed, even though it was the very adherence to the *status quo* principle which had produced the unjust result due to the delay in proceeding with that case. This belatedly inspired the express statutory 'no delay' principle now in s 1(2) of the CA 1989. Where *existing* care is *satisfactory*, it is difficult to get the court to change arrangements because of some *potential* but *untried* alternative. The better remedy in this sort of case will be generous contact, not a residence order in favour of the parent seeking a change of basic living arrangements for the child, as is shown by the case of *S (BD) v S (BD)* [1977] 3 WLR 44, [1977] 1 All ER 656 where a father had remarried and wanted to obtain custody of two children a boy aged eight and a girl aged six, but the court did not think it was a good idea to move them from the mother and into a strange home and a strange area. *D v M* [1981] 3 WLR 891, [1982] 3 All ER 897, already considered under s 1(3)(b) above (where the father's relatively affluent living conditions did not triumph over the mother's more basic but adequate lifestyle) was similar case, where the attempt was to move a one and a half year old illegitimate boy from the mother, with whom he had lived all his life, to the father's home, following the father's marriage as a result of which he felt he could offer the child a better life: the court felt it inadvisable to disturb the *status quo*, as was also the decision in *B v T* (the case of the tower block flat versus the suburban semi-detached house with garden already considered at 6.7.2, which concerned a 15 month old girl who had lived all her life with her mother) and in *Re H* the case of the Indian boy left for an extended period by his mother with an aunt and uncle in England, also considered at 6.7.2. In the latter case the mother *did* obtain generous access.

The moral to be extracted from these cases is that where a mother is going to leave children in the care of a father or even of other relatives it is absolutely essential to keep in touch with the children or a *status quo* will develop which it will be hard to reverse.

However, where lines of communication have been established and kept open, it is possible to convince the court that what looks like a new *status quo* which has perforce developed for good reasons, and which should therefore in theory be valued as such, is really only a temporary arrangement from which such a mother is able to retrieve her children when she is able.

Nevertheless, the ongoing relationship is the key and if the children have really lost touch with the mother this approach will not work, as was shown by the case of *Stephenson v Stephenson* [1985] FLR 1140, CA, where the mother would have succeeded in obtaining custody of the seven month old daughter she had left with the father and his cohabitee for two years, during which she had set up house with a new cohabitee herself and had seen the child only six times. In fact the only hurdle to her success was that she had had the misfortune (or ill judgment) to pick as her new cohabitee a violent man with a criminal record, and the court made no secret of the fact that it was hanging its decision on the alternative peg of the *status quo* due to its dislike of the home circumstances into which it was invited to send the child owing to the mother's association with such an unsuitable surrogate parent.

However, in the cases of *Re DW* (1984) 14 Fam Law 17 and *Allington v Allington* (1986) 15 Fam Law keeping in touch with the children during her absence did enable both mothers to retrieve the children from the fathers, in the first case when a 10 year old boy was moved from a stepmother's care after five years and in the second where a girl was removed from her father despite some doubts about the mother's new relationship.

Continuity of care

The cases unfalteringly go in favour of the parent who can provide personal care, as in *Re K* [1988] 1 All ER 214, where the father was a clergyman who (due possibly more to a sense of outrage at his wife's adultery than to a desire to have the children himself) had assembled a team of worthy people to take care of them while he worked: however the court lost no time in deciding that a child would prefer its own mother who was available for full time care. Similarly the full time mother succeeded in *D v M* and *S (BD) v S (DJ)* already considered, where in both cases the mother was unemployed and the father and his new wife were both working, and so offered a similar chain of helpers to the clergyman's, and indeed in the latter case the father's new wife would clearly have been overstretched in trying to take in extra children on top of what she already had to do.

Sometimes the help of relatives in the extended family rates highly in the equation (as in the case of the Indian boy who settled happily and thrived with his paternal aunt and uncle) but this will not usually work where the contest is mother's full time care against father's care helped even by his mother, who as the child's grandmother clearly has something to contribute to the general family picture which is usually for the child's actual benefit, since grandmothers are well known to compensate for being a bit slow by often having the precious gift of *time* for children. Again the mother obtained care in competition with such an arrangement in the case of *S v S* [1990] 2 FLR 341, where the father was a builder who worked very long hours and although he had a willing and suitable mother, they could not compete with a mother offering full time care. Where the mother *works*, the balance of power is of course immediately evened up.

Sometimes the court will solve such a competition by giving care (ie now a residence order) to the person offering continuity of care and generous contact to the other, as in the case of *Riley v Riley* [1986] 2 FLR 429 where one parent was always on the move and the other led a settled life, the latter obviously being preferable to the court.

6.7.4 The child's age, sex, background and any characteristics of his which the court considers relevant

This is really an extension of earlier categories and the cases mentioned in relation to them give sufficient illustration of the problems which arise and the principles involved in resolving them, eg traditionally, if parents are really going to quarrel about contact, Christmas is often the catalyst because of the religious and/or cultural importance of that time of year and the key role in family life that it is supposed to assume in childhood, and certainly applications to the court escalate at that time of year: thus, here background and religion *may* occasionally be more important than usual and due to the prevalence of inter-cultural marriages and divorces, arrangements may have to be made, whatever the normal residence situation, for a Christian child to spend that period with the Christian relatives rather than with those from whom he has obtained the other half of his genetic and cultural heritage.

6.7.5 Any harm that the child has suffered or is at risk of suffering

This means harm in its widest sense, ie psychological as well as physical harm. Basically the court wants to keep the child from influences that a good parent would keep children from, ie violence, overt sex, crime and drugs, and any parent with a cohabitee who might bring such influences into the child's life will be a handicap to the parent seeking the s 8 order, especially if it is a residence order, as has already been seen in the case of *Stephenson v Stephenson*. The case of *Scott v Scott* [1986] Fam Law 301 was a similar one where the new partner had a record of violence and indecency which did not at all help the mother's case and in fact lost her the claim to custody she might otherwise have had.

Where a child is not able to see both parents, as where one parent opposes contact with the other, this may be considered to be harm: *Re S* [1990] 2 FLR 166 and see under s 1(3)(f) at 6.7.6.

How capable each of the child's parents, and any other person in relation to whom the court considers the question to be relevant, is of meeting the child's needs

There are four points to consider here: the parent's conduct, the parent's new partner, attitudes to contact of both the parents and homosexual relationships.

Parents' conduct

The court is not concerned with moral judgments and while it may regret the apparent injustice of having to decide against 'good' parents, will always consider the interest of the child first and the parent *qua* parent rather than *qua* conduct (although where the parent's new partner is an inherent disaster, such as in the cases of the new relationships of Mrs Scott and Mrs Stephenson above, these adverse factors inevitably enter the equation *despite* the parent's ill choice not precisely being 'conduct' within the meaning of the term).

Conversely the 'good' parent who loses the children to a 'bad' spouse because of care arrangements being inferior to full time mothering does not do so *regardless* of her conduct as such, but because the *interests of the children demand her good parenting*, irrespective of her personal shortcomings in relation to the marriage. The Rev K already considered above had perseveringly attempted a reconciliation with the children's adulterous mother, who had left him, no doubt thought he had done his best to provide a Christian home for the children and had taken pains to provide what in other circumstances might have been totally adequate childcare, so it must have been particularly galling that Mrs K was nevertheless given the children. Mrs S in *S (BD) v S (DJ)* was also definitely not an unimpeachable parent, as she had had three affairs, and still got the children, but these results are inevitable if it is only the availability of full time parenting as against carers which is in issue.

The parent's new partner

The *Scott* and *Stephenson* cases have already provided a sufficient illustration of this point.

Attitudes to contact

The case of *D v M* (the unemployed mother of an illegitimate one and a half year old who lived in a tower block versus the remarried father with a working wife in a suburban semi-detached with a garden) was further influenced by the father's attitude to contact, which he was reluctant to allow, and the court regarded this as a very serious matter and did not want to give him the child as a result. Similarly, in Re S [1990] 2 FLR 166, where lack of contact with one parent was considered to be potential *harm*, within the meaning of s 1(3)(f), there were two boys where one went to live with each parent and the wife would not allow the husband any access to the one in her care. This also deprived that child of the society of his brother as well as of contact with the father. The court felt that the wife might have to lose the boy she had living with her unless she proved less recalcitrant.

Homosexual relationships

This is not a matter to which the court has become much accustomed despite the general change in attitudes of the public. Recent cases on the subject still seem to suggest that the court does not want to allow a child to live in a homosexual household if that can possibly be avoided. This is because of problems as the child grows up, at school and with friends etc. Where it is the *only* alternative this leaves the court in some difficulty. It seems that where it can the court will hang the decision to remove the child on some other peg as in *Re C* [1991] Fam Law 175 where the wife's homosexual cohabitee had a criminal record, but in at least one case a child has been allowed to live in a lesbian household due to the role the father would play in the child's upbringing: in *B v B (Minors) (Custody, Care and Control)* [1991] 1 FLR 402, [1991] Fam Law 174 the youngest child was left with his mother, with whom it was preferable that he should not, due to his age, since the consultant psychiatrist in the case felt that the influence of the father, who himself had a heterosexual cohabitee whom he hoped to marry, and the existence of two other older children would be sufficient to counteract any adverse effects, besides which the mother was not a militant lesbian and was able to provide continuous childcare while the father would have had to use a childminder.

Note

Obviously a parent's health is relevant to ability to care for a child, but if physical health is poor this will not affect such ability provided there is both adequate domestic help and the parent will be present and not, for example, absent for prolonged periods in hospital. As far as *mental* health goes, this will be relevant only in so far as it may affect the child adversely. A little instability, especially if drug controlled, may not matter, whereas full blow schizophrenia obviously would. In either case, comprehensive medical reports would be advisable if a s 8 application is to be made or defended.

The range of powers available to the court: s 1(3)(g)

The court always has power to make any suitable s 8 order(s) in a case before it, irrespective of whether any application has in fact been made for those orders. The court can, for example, by s 10(1)(b) make a residence order in favour of some non party, such as a grandparent or other relative, if it becomes obvious that that would be preferable and the non-party is willing. The court can also bring an end to any particular saga by prohibiting any further CA 1989 applications without leave: s 91(14). The court's powers also include the power to order investigation by the local authority: s 37(1) which in itself may lead to any of the public law orders contained in Sections III–V inclusive of the CA 1989 being made in respect of the child or children, and clients seeking s 8 orders should be aware of the potential impact of these public law orders: see 6.7.7.

Power of the court to order investigation by the local authority: s 37(1)

6.7.7

Such an order may be made in any 'family proceedings' as defined by s 8(3) and where the court decides to give such a direction the local authority must carry out the appropriate enquiries and consider whether it should:
- apply for a care or supervision order;
- provide any services or assistance for the child or the family;
- take any other action in respect of the child: s 37(2).

Where the local authority decides not to take any action it must within eight weeks inform the court of the decision and of why that decision has been made, together with information as to any other action they have taken or propose to take in respect of that child: s 37(3) and must also consider whether they should:
- review the decision at a later date; and
- if so, when: s 37(6).

The public law orders: CA 1989 Parts III–V inclusive

6.7.8

This is an area where the Children Act 1989 has effected major changes. Instead of simply taking into care every child who is not being properly looked after (and usually resisting the return of that child to its inadequate parents) the local authority is now statutorily compelled to safeguard and promote the welfare of children within its area who are in need, and so far as it is consistent with that duty to promote the upbringing of children by their families, by providing a range and level of services appropriate to those children's needs: s 17(1). This range of services includes a duty under s 20 of the Act to provide temporary accommodation, as an alternative to the former duty of provision of care under a formal care order. This significant shift of emphasis underlines the change in the character of the local authority, which is thus transformed by the CA 1989, in theory at least, from ogre to fairy godmother at a stroke.

Note

A child is 'in need' if the child is unlikely to achieve or maintain, or to have the opportunity to achieve or maintain, a reasonable standard of health or development 'without the provision for that child of services by the local authority: s 17(10). 'Development' includes physical, intellectual, emotional, social or behavioural development: s 17(22) and 'health' includes both mental and physical health: s 17(11).

This is obviously a big shift of emphasis. However, if all the authority's help and assistance does not work, and it does not look as though there will be any improvement before the child suffers actual *harm*, inadequate parents can still expect to lose the child through formal care proceedings under s 31, or possibly initially through an emergency protection order under s 43. To facilitate decisions in this respect there is a new child assessment order available under s 43 which enables the local authority to obtain possession of the child for assessment purposes where the parents will not cooperate. However the philosophy of the Act is that these stages should only be reached after other methods have failed and parents whose families excite the interest of the local authority should probably *always* cooperate, since the authority's powers are in theory subject to its obligations and if the parents can demonstrate that any inadequacies in their childcare are not deliberate but as an result of ignorance or poor resources (and above all that they were unaware of the actual or potential harm caused) care orders should be able to be avoided and the onus thrown on to the local authority to carry out its obligations and *help*!

The local authority's duty to accommodate: s 20

This new duty is significantly different from formal 'care' and arises where:

- there is no person with formal parental responsibility for a child;
- the child is lost or abandoned;
- the person who has been caring for the child is prevented (whether or not permanently and for whatever reason) from providing the child with suitable accommodation or care.

A child so accommodated can be removed by any person with parental responsibility at any time without formality: s 20(8).

There are two exceptions:
- where a person with a residence order or with an old style care and control order made in the exercise of the High Court's inherent jurisdiction (ie what is technically called in the Act 'an existing order') agrees to the child being looked after by the local authority: s 20(9) though if there is more than one such person all must agree: s 20(10);
- where a child over 16 agrees personally: s 20(11).

If the local authority wants to object it has two choices, and must apply to the court for:
- a formal care order (it must then satisfy the statutory grounds under s 31); or
- an emergency protection order, which is for where the case is urgent: s 44(1).

The local authority must consider the child's wishes (or such wishes as they are able to ascertain, having regard to the child's age and understanding) wherever possible before providing that child with accommodation: s 20(6).

Note

If the child is over 16 any decision as to accepting accommodation from the local authority lies with the child:
- regardless of the child's parents' wishes: s 20(11);

- regardless of whether the local authority can accommodate the child: s 20(4).

There are thus now two distinct categories of children:
- those with a formal care order;
- those voluntarily in local authority accommodation for more than 24 hours.

The local authority must act as a good parent, by s 22 taking account of the child's wishes, as well as those of the child's parents and anyone else with parental responsibility, *before* taking any decisions about the child, and as well as taking account of the child's religion, racial origin and cultural and linguistic background; by s 24(1) they also have a duty to 'advise, assist and befriend' the child, with a view to promoting that child's welfare when the child ceases to be looked after by them. There is a statutory presumption that they must make arrangements to enable the child to live with one of the following:

- a parent;
- any person with parental responsibility, or who had it immediately before a formal care order was made;
- a relative, friend or person connected with the child

unless none of these solutions would be reasonably practical or consistent with the child's welfare: s 23(6).

Note

By s 22(3) there is a general duty on the authority to safeguard and promote the child's welfare and to make such use of services available for children cared for by their own parents as appears to the authority reasonable in any particular child's case.

Moreover, the Act requires the authority to conduct a general review at regular intervals of the progress of each child, so that the whole emphasis is on keeping children in their own families wherever possible.

If this is impossible there is a duty to promote contact, so far as is practicable and consistent with the child's welfare, between the child and the child's parents or those with parental responsibility in respect of that child or person with whom the child is connected: s 34 and Schedule 2. By s 34(1) there is a *presumption* that the child should have contact with such persons, though other person, eg grandparents, brothers and sisters, must obtain leave to apply to be named in a contact order, which if a formal care order is made can be made at the same time or later: s 34(10).

Obviously sometimes contact will be inadvisable, eg in cases of sexual abuse, in which case either contact can be on conditions: s 34(7) or the authority *only* can apply for such contact to be prohibited: s 34(4). Contact can also be refused altogether as a matter of urgency and for no more than seven days: s 34(1). All such orders would of course be discharged when the formal care order was discharged whereupon an ordinary s 8 order might be made instead: s 10.

A formal care order: s 31

Where a formal care order is applied for, the local authority must satisfy the statutory criteria in s 31 and the court must be satisfied that *both*:

- the child is suffering, or is likely to suffer, significant harm; *and*

- the harm, or likelihood of harm, is attributable to
  - the care being given to the child, or likely to be given to the child if the order is not made;
  - not being what it would be reasonable to expect a parent to give the child); or
  - the child's being beyond parental control.

Note

These criteria are cumulative and must both be satisfied.

'Harm' means ill treatment or impairment of health and development and 'ill treatment' includes sexual abuse and non-physical ill-treatment.

The court must then consider:
- s 1(1) welfare;
- s 1(3) the checklist;
- s 1(2) delay;
- s 1(5) the non-interventionist policy.

It will thus be seen that obtaining a new style care order is a demanding task for the local authority, although if the basis for an order is there, hairs will not be split, eg over whether a truanting child is beyond parental control or the victim of parents who did not give it reasonable care: *Re O* (1992) *Times* 6 March. The standard of proof of the threshold criteria is not as high as on a balance of probabilities because the court is dealing with predictions, ie a significant likelihood or 'real possibility' and not mere suspicion is the suggested yardstick since the court is dealing with the protection of a child: *Re H (Minors) (Child Abuse: Threshold Conditions)* (1995) *Times*, 15 December, HL.

Nevertheless, satisfying the threshold criteria is not enough. Once s 31(2) is satisfied, the local authority must also satisfy the other four sections listed above, ie particularly the welfare principle and the checklist (which includes as the final head 'the range of the court's powers': see 6.7.6). If necessary an interim order will be made.

An alternative to a care order is a supervision order under s 35, which requires the same statutory grounds to be made out and will usually last for a year, unless extended, which can be for up to three years before a fresh application will need to be made if such an order is to continue. The supervising officer does not acquire parental responsibility and the purpose of the order is to provide a degree of supervision, including specifying living arrangements and activities to be engaged in, and some positive help in the form of the requirement to 'advise, assist and befriend' s 35(1).

Emergency orders: ss 43 and 44

The principal orders in this category are the Child Assessment Order under s 43 and the Emergency Protection order under s 44.

Child assessment order: s 43 (CAO)

The former is to enable the authority to obtain physical custody of a child which it suspects is being abused or neglected, in order to establish what protection steps are necessary, and is used where the parents refuse to cooperate, eg by taking the child for a medical assessment.

Application has to be on full notice and the court must be satisfied that:

- the applicant has reasonable cause to suspect that the child is suffering, or is likely to suffer, significant harm;
- an assessment of the state of the child's health or development, or of the way in which the child is being treated is required to enable the applicant to establish whether or not the child is suffering, or is likely to suffer, significant harm;
- it is unlikely that the assessment will be made, or be satisfactory, without a child assessment order.

As usual the court must have regard to ss 1(1), 1(2), 1(3) and 1(5).

The maximum time for assessment is seven days: s 43(5) and the order has no effect on parental responsibility. It merely requires production of the child for assessment and requires the person in a position to produce the child to comply with any other terms of the order. The order makes provision for contact between the child and the persons connected with the child: ss 43(9) and (10).

Note

If the child is of an age to do so, he or she personally may refuse to consent! Both the child and the parents or those with parental responsibility may always apply for the order to be varied or discharged.

Emergency protection order: s 44 (EPO)

This is for really serious urgent circumstances where the local authority and/or the NSPCC is investigating a child's seriously worrying circumstances, their enquiries are being frustrated and they believe that access to the child is needed as a matter of urgency. The court can direct any person in a position to do so to comply with any request to *produce* the child to the applicant: s 44(4)(a), can authorise *removal* of the child to accommodation provided by the applicant and *prevention of removal* of the child from any hospital or other place where the child is being accommodated immediately prior to the order: s 44(4)(b). Anyone having this order has parental responsibility but contact can be directed by the court and the applicant is under the usual duty to allow contact with the usual person or persons acting on their behalf. The maximum duration of the order is eight days: s 45(1). However, this order can be challenged by the child or the child's parents or those with parental responsibility: s 45(8) but not before the expiry of 72 hours from the time the order was made, nor if the challenger had notice of the hearing and was present at it: s 45(11).

Other than this, there is no appeal against the grant or refusal of an EPO: s 45(10) and if the applicant returns the child because it appears to be safe to do so and then suffers a change of mind, the child may be removed again as long as the original order is still running (ie within the initial eight days or the permissible seven days of extension): ss 44(10) and (12) and ss 45(1) and (6).

Note _____

This account is of necessity brief and outline only, and there are other orders such as the police protection order under s 46 or the recovery order under s 50 which may be of use to the child practitioner but of which space does not permit more than a mention. Such an outline account of the impact of the public law provisions of the Act which sometimes affect private law clients is offered merely to make trainees aware of the possibilities such clients may face if they do *not* cooperate with the local authority in appropriate circumstances.

In general terms, especially if the client was *not aware* of any ill treatment, eg by a relative acting as childminder who *appeared* to be treating the child well, it is highly unlikely that any steps would be taken other than gentle informal supervision, *provided that* the client then cooperated fully and took swift and decisive action to prevent the situation continuing once it had been brought to the client's notice.

Children Act procedure   6.8

This is so different from that prior to the Children Act 1989 that it is worth detailing.

The Act has brought about a unified structure of High Court, county court and magistrates' courts for children cases. Not every judge in each tier is able to deal with such cases, which are assigned:

- in the High Court to the Family Division judges;
- in the county court to selected circuit judges sitting at designated trial centres;
- in the magistrates' courts, formerly the Domestic Court, and now called the Family Proceedings Court, to those magistrates who are designated for the work.

Note

There are three classes of county court:

- divorce county courts (not all county courts qualify);

- family hearing centres (not all divorce county courts qualify);

- care centres.

Where a s 8 order is to be obtained in divorce proceedings, clearly the petition should be filed in a divorce county court which is a family hearing centre (FHC), or it will have to be transferred.

The Children (Allocation of Proceedings) Order 1991 contains decisive criteria on the choice of venue and allocation of business between the courts. The principle that delay is prejudicial dictates the factors to be taken into account. Relevant factors will be the:

- length, importance and complexity of the case;
- urgency of the case;
- need to consolidate the case with other pending proceedings.

Example

A case that would otherwise go to the magistrates for several days, which is logistically difficult to arrange as all magistrates do not sit on consecutive days, can be transferred to a district judge.

Private law proceedings are usually self-allocating, therefore, eg:

- to the divorce county court where the proceedings have been started, provided it is a FHC; or
- another court where existing child proceedings are on foot with which such s 8 proceedings can be consolidated; or
- where the application is 'free standing' to whichever court the applicant prefers; or
- where the applicant is on legal aid, to the magistrates' court as this is cheapest venue and will therefore usually be the court specified in the certificate.

Note
_____

If divorce proceedings are dismissed a s 8 order can still be
made, unless the court determines that the matter would
better be dealt with outside England and Wales: FLA 1986
s 2(4).
_____

Proceedings begin on prescribed forms, and irrespective
of their type or the person applying are now made on
form C1 in all cases: Family Proceedings (Amendment)
(No 4) Rules 1994.

In *divorce proceedings*, if an application has been or is
definitely to be made for a s 8 order at the time of filing the
petition, this will have been stated on the Statement of
Arrangements and the district judge will have been
relieved of the obligation to consider the arrangements for
the children and to issue the s 41 certificate, and the s 8
application will go straight to the FHC judge for hearing.

Where the application is *outside divorce proceedings*,
the applicant has a choice, but if on legal aid is likely to
be restricted to the Family Proceedings court for the
reason given above.

Parties to be made respondents to the application are
set out in FPR 1991 Appendix 1 and FPC(CA 1989) 1991,
Schedule 2, and they are:

- every person with parental responsibility for the
  child;
- every person with parental responsibility prior to
  a care order, if such an order is in place;
- where the application is to extend, vary or discharge an order, the parties to the order in respect
  of which the application is made. You will need
  to consult the FPR 1991 r 4.7 and Appendix 3 and
  the FPC(CA 1989)R 1991, r 7 and Schedule 2 for
  detailed rules about parties and notice to be given.

Note
_____

However any person may make a written request to be
joined as a party or that that person cease to be a party, and
anyone with parental responsibility is entitled as of right to
be joined: FPR 1991, r 47(4) and FPC(CA)R 1991, r 9.
_____

The form then needs to be served. This is achieved by
serving a copy with Form C6, setting out the date, time
and place for the hearing or directions appointment, on
each respondent at least 14 days before the hearing or
directions appointment: Family Proceedings Courts
(Amendment No 2) Rules 1992 and FPC (Miscellaneous
Amendments) Rules 1992 rr 8 and 9, and to the rules of

service FPR 1991 r 4.8 and FPC(CA 1989)R 1991, r 8. After effective service the applicant must lodge the Form C9 statement of service at court.

The respondent must lodge an acknowledgment Form C7 within 14 days: FPR 1991 r 4.9 and FPC(CA 1989)R 1991, r 9.

Unlike in former custody proceedings, Children Act 1989 applications cannot be 'settled' by a consent order or even withdrawn without leave: FPR 1991 r 4.5(1) and FPC(CA 1989)R 1991, r 5.(1), although court conciliation may attempt to persuade the parents or other parties to agree on the child's future and to observe the spirit and philosophy of the Act by having no order in which case the application may be withdrawn with leave.

6.8.1 Directions

The no delay principle will require a directions appointment to be held forthwith, and either this may be the only one or the first of several: FPR 1991 r 4.14 FPA(CA 1989)R 1991. Two days notice is normally required for a directions hearing, which may be on request of the parties or one of them or of the court's own motion, though there is provision for oral application without notice to be made with leave: FPR 1991 r 4.14.(4) FPC(CA 1989)R 1991 r 4(6).

At the directions hearing there will be a thorough stocktaking of the case:

- a timetable will be drawn up, and adhered to, for the proceedings: CA 1989 s 11(1).

The following will also be considered:

- variation of time limits, which is only permitted by direction of the court or justices clerk: FPR 1991 r 4.15, FPC(CA 1989)R 1991 r 15(4);
- service of documents (only those served may be relied on and none may be served without leave of the court, a provision designed to prevent written statements potentially inflaming the situation;
- joinder of parties;
- preparation of welfare reports and attendance of the court welfare officer preparing them to give evidence;
- service of written evidence, in advance, including any experts' reports (no experts' or assessors' reports are allowed without written leave of the court: FPR 1991 r 4.18 FPC(CA 1989)R 1991 r 18);
- attendance of the child, unless excused;

- transfer of the case to another court either hori-
  zontally or vertically;
- consolidation of the case with other proceedings.

Note

All persons who have notice of a directions appointment
must attend, *including* the child if of appropriate age, unless
the court directs otherwise: FPR 1991 r 4.16 and FPC(CA
1989)R 1991 r 16, though the court can decide that the proceedings can take place in the child's absence if that is in the
child's interests, eg due to the nature of the evidence to be
given, or if the child is represented by a solicitor.

The respondent who does not appear *may* find that the
court has proceeded despite his absence. However it is
more likely to refuse the application in such a situation
unless it has sufficient evidence to dispense with the
respondent's presence.

Obviously if neither party appears the court will refuse
the application! Any adjournment of such directions
appointments must include a new date for resumption of
the appointment: FPR 1991 r 4.15(2) FPC(CA 1989)R 1991
r 15(5). Thus is the legacy of the 1969 case of *J v C*!

Proceedings can be and commonly are transferred hori-
zontally or vertically, eg not only to avoid delay but if
there is complex evidence and a higher court is needed.
Some applications have to go to the High Court (eg an
application made by the child personally).

Technically a s 8 order can only be made in 'Family
Proceedings' as defined in ss 8(3) and (4) but this covers
all the types of proceedings one would expect, and the
court may also make an order of its own motion despite
no application actually having been made for that order:
s 10 (1)(b). Directions appointments are in Chambers in
the High Court and county court and in private in the
Family Proceedings Court (FPC).

Evidence   6.8.2

A major change brought about by the Children Act 1989
is the restriction on evidence that can be given and how
it should be presented. Affidavits have largely disappeared, though a judge can order them (and some older
judges do, since they feel affidavits 'tell the story' in a
way in which the form based procedure does not).
However, the statements which have supplanted the traditional affidavit, although not sworn, must contain a
statement that the maker believes in their truth and
understands that the statement will be placed before the
court.

Evidence generally

Advance disclosure is the other principal innovation, as without leave of the court *nothing* may be adduced in evidence, not even orally, which has not been written down and served on the other side: FPR 1991 r 4.17 FPC 1989)R 1991 r 17. By the same rules *nothing* but the *prescribed* documents, ie as required or authorised by the rules, is allowed to be served without leave of the court. For the careful drafting required of statements, especially the parties' witness statements, see 6.8.3.

Evidence will be needed from any persons who will have much to do with the care of the child, eg nannies, childminders, grandparents and other relatives. If no advance notice has been given in the case of someone new or who has been missed out in the advance disclosure stage, such evidence can always be the subject of an oral application with leave of the court at the hearing. However, solicitors should beware of the witness who is reluctant as their evidence may be more damaging than helpful.

Note

Limited hearsay evidence is permitted: Children (Admissibility of Hearsay Evidence) Order 1990.

Welfare reports

These are normally prepared by the court welfare offices. By CA 1989 s 7 the court has an extended power to call for such reports, and these may be provided by the local authority: s 7(5) or by someone delegated to do so by them: s 7(1). Normally a welfare report is ordered automatically at the directions hearing, either requested by one of the parties or ordered of the court's own motion, as it is quite impossible to deal satisfactorily with s 8 applications without. Clients should therefore be warned of the necessity to make a good impression on the welfare officer, since although the court is not *bound* by their recommendations, it is unusual that their very experienced views are not taken significantly into account and in practice they are generally followed. The report should be filed at least 14 days before the hearing unless a different time limit has been prescribed and of course all parties will have a copy so as to be able to deal with the contents: FP (Amendment No 2) R 1992 r 12 and FPC (Miscellaneous Amendments) R 1992 paragraph 3.

Welfare officers' reports are therefore incredibly tactful since the welfare officer is too professional to 'take sides' if this can be avoided and will not want to be seen as biased by any party, but yet will manage to convey the recommendation in the most palatable terms for the party whose aspirations and hopes are to be dashed!

Expert evidence

Any expert reports obtained without leave of the court in the first place will need leave of the court to be used. This embargo covers *every type* of such reports, even educational psychologists' reports, although a routine ISCO type test done automatically at secondary school level, eg at most public schools in the 5th form, or Year 11, is probably all right if not prepared *specifically* for the proceedings.

Drafting a statement in support of a s 8 application   6.8.3

In the absence of affidavits and with the new constraints on evidence to be given at s 8 hearings, drafting of the witness statements, particularly those of the parties, is skilled work. Just as counsel used to draft old style custody, care and control and access affidavits, often counsel will now draft these witness statements, if counsel is to conduct the hearing, since they are as much an exercise in advocacy, in which counsel is a recognised specialist, as notice to the other side and to the court of what is to be given orally in evidence. They also afford an opportunity to get the court's attention and sympathy for the client's side of the story and this opportunity should not be thrown away in the hope that the position can be recovered at the actual hearing: it often cannot, and at the very least will give the advocate at the hearing a more uphill task than necessary. For this reason anything complex should ideally go straight to counsel, but some firms like to do all their own family work so it is quite likely that the trainee might have to tackle this task and should at least possess a working knowledge of how to do so.

Moreover, while leave will be required to withdraw a CA 1989 application once made, obviously there will usually be attempts to settle the matter without a hearing, if necessary with the aid of the court conciliation process: see 6.3, or that of other mediators, such as in London the Family Mediation Service. In this connection the sight of strong witness statements which are not in one side's favour may be instrumental in reducing that party's recalcitrance, which is often all that has stood between one side and the other, and this may quickly crumble once the relative hopelessness of a particular approach is spelled out in the opponent's formal statement and a trained mediator is involved who might be able to halt what is obviously going to be a painful disaster for the loser.

Effective drafting in this respect will usually depend, as far as you are concerned, on the *use of reliable precedents*, of which there are several collections, but a good contemporary loose leaf collection will be likely to be best since the precedents contained therein are likely to be up to date and well drafted by top practitioners. It is easy to take a suitable precedent and adapt it to one's own case, using at least the general framework, which usually includes well thought out headings to break the document up, and possibly some of the more apt phrases and sentences can be incorporated verbatim.

Note

All statements must begin with the formula 'I AB of   will say' and should contain as a first paragraph the words 'I make this statement in support of my application that I be granted a [residence/contact or other order, as appropriate] in respect of the children of the family CD and EF'.

As a general rule where the statement to be drafted is that of one of the parties, usually the parents of the child in respect of whom the order is sought, a framework such as the following will be suitable.

Background information

(No more than 2 or 3 paragraphs giving a *brief* history of the marriage, beginning with the date of the ceremony and detailing the births of the children, with dates, and some indication of when and how the marriage went wrong. A blow by blow account is not required or advisable, however aggrieved the applicant feels.)

The present dispute

(Further short paragraphs setting out how the dispute has arisen, eg the applicant's desire to remarry and, if, eg she is the mother, who has left the matrimonial home, to take the children back to live with her. Brief factual unemotional prose is what is required here, tactfully skating over any defects in the story, such as that the applicant deserted the children at a moment's notice to run off with a man she met at her evening class in assertiveness and has only just remembered them some time later. This is just the sort of case that counsel's specialist skills are *for*, since this particular scenario is not a promising one and good written advocacy will be required if the applicant is not to arrive at the hearing to find an atmosphere of polite incredulity, and less than sympathy, on the face of the judge hearing the case. However if counsel are not to be employed, and if you have a sound grasp of the law and a fluent command of persuasive prose you will find that you are in fact more than capable of producing something suitable.)

Present living arrangements

(This might be further subdivided into the applicant's present living arrangements, those proposed for the child, the educational arrangements for the child, and details of any new relationship into which the applicant has entered. Again factual informative paragraphs are required, somewhat fuller in both style and content than for the Statement of Arrangements which is filed with a divorce petition, and they should convey the same sort of inviting stability as the ideal Statement of Arrangements should provide, leaving the judge in no doubt that everything has been well thought out for the child's welfare. If there are any health matters to be noted in connection with the child, they should be included here and any reports mentioned and filed. If there are any such reports which have not been mentioned or filed, the court can order their disclosure if such reports come to its notice, despite legal professional privilege and despite any unwillingness on the part of the commissioning party to agree: *Oxfordshire County Council v M* (1994) 1 FLR 175. This is because in theory child proceedings are not seen as adversarial and it is the best result for the child which is being sought.)

Note

A parent with sub-standard accommodation is even more at risk in a s 8 application than at the Statement of Arrangements stage, and strenuous efforts should be made to remedy any such problem *before* filing the s 8 statement. If this cannot be done for some reason, clear arrangements for the foreseeable future should be detailed and supported by evidence, eg a council letter indicating when suitable accommodation will be available. Ideally accommodation should be in place (and perhaps already being used by the child for regular contact) so that the court welfare officer may visit and report on it, preferably with the child *in situ*.

Applicant's concerns

(Here the applicant may detail any *genuine, non-trivial* worries about the other party's care of the child or children. It is *not* an opportunity to enter again into the history of the unhappy marriage or a lengthy disquisition on the other party's manifold sins and wickedness. Such an approach is categorised by the court as *mud slinging*, is deprecated and discouraged and usually invites worse in return. It is *not recommended* therefore!)

Proposals

(This may further be subdivided into paragraphs on the child's wishes, if they have actually been expressed, attitudes to contact and comments on the other party's statement if it has already been served, and should include a suitable form of words to indicate the applicant's desire to provide the child or children with the opportunity to settle down to a period of stability, which at this stage of the case the court is usually fervently hoping that someone is going to take time off from domestic squabbles to provide).

The statement should end with the final paragraph: 'I declare this statement to be true and that I understand that it may be placed before the court.'

Note

Precedents for such statements may be found in the practitioners loose leaf works, such as Clark Parker & Blair.

6.8.4   **The hearing**

Procedure at Children Act hearings is governed by FPR 1991 r 4. 21 and FPC(C 1989)R 1991 and is deliberately on the informal side. Unless the court directs otherwise the applicant's evidence will be first, then the main respondent, and any other party with parental responsibility for the child, then other respondents, and finally the guardian *ad litem* if there is one and the child, if the child is a party and there is no guardian *ad litem*.

A note is kept of oral evidence by the clerk: FPR 1991 r 4.20 and FPC(CA 1989)R r 20. While hearsay evidence is admissible, the weight to be given to it will be in the discretion of the judge.

The no delay principle requires that the decision must be made 'as soon as practicable': FPR 1991 r 4.21(3) and FPC(CA 1989)R 1991 r 21.4 and any finding of fact and the reasons for the court's decision must be stated: FPR r 4.21.(4) and FPC(CA 1989)R r 21.6. If a s 8 order is made it must be entered on the appropriate form for the purpose and a copy served as soon as possible on the parties and any person with whom the child is living: FPR 1991 r 4.21(5) and FPC(CA 1989)R r 21(7).

Note

A hearing may be only for an interim application, since by s 11(3) the court is empowered to grant such an order at any time when it is not yet in a position to dispose of the matter finally. This may be a tactical move, since the operation of the *status quo* rule means that the longer the client is out of touch with the child or children the worse the client's chances are of retrieving the situation, provided of course that the other parent does not make any mistakes and invoke the operation of some other rule against that parent's interests. It is therefore advisable for any parent seeking, eg a residence order to obtain an interim contact order and to make the fullest possible use of it in the time it takes to set up the substantive hearing for the residence order which is really desired.

Appeals are possible against all such orders from:
*   the FPC to the High Court: CA 1989 s 94(1) heard by a High Court judge usually sitting in open court: *President's Direction* 31 January 1991 [1992] 2 FLR 140;
*   a district judge of the FHC county court to the judge of the FHC county court in question: FPR 1991 r 8.1 (this is not by way of rehearing);
*   a judge of the FHC county court or High Court to the Court of Appeal.

Note

The procedure for appeals is set out in the FPR 1991 r 4.22, and the time limit is normally 14 days or such other period as the court may direct.

Wardship   6.9

Wardships are family proceedings within the meaning of the CA 1989 and are part of the inherent jurisdiction of the High Court. This valuable High Court remedy was expressly preserved, alongside the new range of s 8 orders, although it is fair to say that in taking that decision it was anticipated that the flexibility of the orders which the court can now grant under the Children Act, and in particular specific issue and prohibited steps orders, would mean that s 8 orders would be applied for in preference to wardship, and this has mostly proved to be the case. However you should be aware of the existence of wardship and of what it can add to the range of s 8 orders, as there are occasionally reasons for the preference of wardship which have justified its separate existence, ie where:

- it is convenient to by pass the CA 1989;
- there is need for the court's continuing supervision (which, once s 8 orders have been granted the court cannot achieve under the CA 1989, and which is the special feature of wardship which makes it so expensive a remedy).

There are some essential restrictions, eg local authorities cannot use wardship either to take children into care or to determine questions of parental responsibility, nor can parents use it to take children out of local authority care: s 100(2).

Moreover, wardship cannot be used to stop abortions because a child *in utero* cannot be made a ward of court: *Re F (in utero)* [1988] Fam U2, [1988] 2 WLR 1297.

However wardship can be used to deal with:

- kidnapping;
- medical treatment cases;
- adoptions;
- undesirable associations.

Note

Thus a liberal construction of s 100 *does* permit a local authority to use wardship where a care order would not be appropriate and where a supervision order would not achieve the desired end, as in the case of *Devon County Council v S* [1995] 1 All ER 243, where the object was to protect the younger children in a family where the eldest was married to a person convicted of sexual offences. Wardship permitted supervision of his visits to the family without interfering in the mother's otherwise unobjectionable care of the younger children.

Kidnapping

The use of wardship to prevent kidnapping has to some extent been reduced in importance because of the Child Abduction Act 1984 and the Port Alert System. Section 1(1) of the Act makes it an offence for a 'connected person', ie a child's parent, guardian or person with a residence order or custody of the child, to take or send a child out of the country without the appropriate consent (which correspondingly means the other parent, guardian or person having custody or parental responsibility or the court). However, s 1(5) the offence is not committed if it is believed:

- that the child was at least 16; or
- it was done technically without consent if that is in the belief that the consent has been given or would have been if all the relevant circumstances had been known; or
- all reasonable attempts to communicate to obtain it have been unsuccessful; or
- consent has been unreasonably withheld;

unless *inter alia* the departure is in breach of a court order.

The Port Alert System is the subject of a *Practice Direction* [1986] 1 All ER 983, [1986] 1 WLR 475 and is a 24 hour service operated in conjunction with immigration officers at all ports including airports. To use it you must show that there is real and imminent danger of removal of a child. Help cannot be sought as 'insurance' so 'real' means there must be some evidence and 'imminent' is interpreted as meaning within the next 24–48 hours. Strictly there is no need to have any order in force, but in practice this will usually assist in engaging the police's attention in order to invoke the system, and a wardship order in particular commands respect.

Application should be made to the *local police station*, but in emergency to any police station. This will result in the child's name being entered on the 'stop' list at all ports for four weeks, after which it will be removed, unless fresh application is made.

Details will be required for effective help:

- a photograph of the child or at least a very good description, including of any accompanying person(s) who will probably be more easily recognised than the child, especially if the child is young;
- the likely port of departure and destination;
- details of the proposed route as departures of this type are seldom direct.

Medical treatment cases

This is subject to a *Practice Note*: [1990] Fam Law 375. Sterilisation and other disputed surgical procedure cases are particularly well dealt with by wardship as in the case of *Re D* [1976] Fam 185, [1976] 1 All ER 326, concerning a mentally and physically handicapped girl where the parents wanted her sterilised at the age of 11, as they were worried about the likelihood of her getting pregnant and being unable to look after either herself or a child in view of her obvious disabilities, but where the local authority's child psychologist opposed the operation and applied to the court for wardship; in that particular case the wardship was continued and the operation, *not* carried out, although in a similar case a 17 year old *was* sterilised. In the case of *Re B* [1981] 1 WLR 1421 the local authority wanted a life saving operation for a Downs syndrome child which the parents did not want as they wanted the child left to die; in that case the court *authorised* the operation.

Adoption

The court can investigate fully in such cases, eg where there is an issue as to whether the natural mother will continue to see or care for the child as in *Re O* [1978] Fam 196, [1978] 2 All ER 27 where this was initially agreed and then the adopter tried to put a stop to it. The court held the matter must be fully investigated within the wardship procedure. In *Re E* [1963] 3 All ER 874 the adopters whose application to adopt had failed tried to retain care of the child in its best interests. In this type of case, the court will follow only the child's best interests so if the application is a last ditch attempt to prevent a page turning in the child's life, the application will be dismissed immediately, but if there is an issue which requires investigation the court can look into it fully.

Undesirable associations

The court can prevent unsuitable marriages, homosexual associations, or joining an undesirable religious sect.

Procedure

No particular relationship is required to take out an application, which is one of the beauties of wardship as a remedy. The child can apply by a next friend. However this flexibility must not be abused, as it was in the case of *Re Dunhill* (1967) 111 SJ 113 where a night club owner warded a 20 year old model for publicity purposes, and the application was struck out as frivolous, vexatious, and an abuse of the process of the court, on top of which the applicant had to pay all the costs!

The application is made by originating summons in the High Court. Legal aid is available in appropriate cases. Applications can be made *ex parte*.

Wardship is immediately effective (which is why it is so useful in kidnapping cases) but lapses if not pursued, by obtaining a hearing date, within 21 days. The defendant must acknowledge service and furnish an address and also the address of the minor, noting any changes

The first appointment will be before the district judge for directions. The full hearing will not be for many months, and will be before a High Court judge in chambers. There is power to adjourn applications to open court, eg where the ward is missing and publicity is desired. The court will then confirm or discharge the wardship. If confirmed, 'care and control', ie similar to a residence order, will be entrusted to an individual, and a wardship application can if desired be coupled with any s 8 applications and the court can then make those orders instead if the wardship is not granted.

Once a wardship order is made, no important step can be taken in the child's life without the consent of the court, eg leave will be needed even for a short holiday outside the jurisdiction, ie even to go to Scotland which is not within the jurisdiction of England and Wales, but a certificate can be issued to show to immigration officials to obviate the need to apply every time. Leave will also be required to marry or to emigrate, in which case the wardship is likely to be discontinued as the court may not want to supervise the ward at a distance. Alternatively the applicant can be required to give an undertaking to return the ward to the jurisdiction if ever asked to do so. What the court considers here is *whether* the ward will in fact be returned if return is ever asked for and therefore whether it is in the ward's interests to go at all: *Re F* [1988] 2 FLR 116.

Both long-term and interlocutory injunctions are available to protect the ward.

Instructions to counsel in family cases   6.10

These follow in broad outline the format for Instructions in all civil cases and reference should be made to the books on civil litigation for suitable precedents.

However, because of the supposedly non-adversarial nature child proceedings of good instructions in child matters will aim to provide counsel with as complete a picture as possible of the situation which needs to be resolved and any available information which may assist counsel to do so should be included. It is not however generally a good idea to send counsel every scrap of paper in the case, neither all bundled up in plastic rubbish sacks nor beautifully organised in numerous ring binders, for which a large box van might have to be hired, or counsel's bill, either for sorting the wheat from the chaff or perusing needless papers, might be excessive. Some selection must therefore be made bearing in mind the overall purpose for which counsel is instructed.

You will recall that in instructing counsel the *aim* is not to get counsel to do work the solicitor does not *want* to do or to do *again* work that the solicitor has already done. The object of instructing counsel is to obtain counsel's *specialist advice*, either where the *solicitor is not sure how to proceed* or *cannot accurately estimate what a client's chances are* of obtaining a desired order, and this does *not* mean that counsel should be given the right papers to enable counsel to *redo the solicitor's work*: counsel should receive precisely what is needed to enable counsel to do counsel's work, which as everybody, except the under-informed general public, well knows does *not* in any way duplicate what the solicitor has done already. Solicitor and counsel are a team, each member of which has a separate and distinct function.

To get the best out of counsel in child matters, if you are left to prepare Instructions you should select from the divorce suit and ancillary relief files the following:

- copies of all the divorce documents, beginning with the client's initial statement, and including petition, statement of arrangements for children, respondent's acknowledgment of service, petitioner's affidavit in support of the petition, decree nisi if pronounced, and decree absolute if granted;
- copies of relevant ancillary relief documents, beginning with any further statement from the client, any opinion of counsel now being instructed or other counsel if applicable, affidavits of means, notes of any court attendances and of any financial orders made;
- copies of correspondence between instructing solicitors and client, but *if voluminous only where relevant*;
- copies of correspondence between instructing solicitors and the other side, but again if voluminous *only where relevant*;
- bundle of documents relating to client's means as per schedule on page 1 of the bundle;
- bundles of documents relating to the child or children in respect of whom orders are or may be sought, as per schedule on page 1 of (each) bundle (if more than one) including where available school and medical reports where relevant;
- client's legal aid certificate if applicable.

You should then compose the covering Instructions, in numbered paragraphs, divided up under suitable headings. These will obviously vary from case to case.

In a contested s 8 order case these should include:

- introduction (or background);
  (Here should be set out whether the client is on legal aid or not, brief details of the client (age, whether working etc) a short history of the marriage and the composition and ages of the family of children.)
- details of the childhood history, plans for education and upbringing and of the present dispute over the children;
  (Here should be set out what was agreed about the children's education and upbringing, if anything, when the parties were living together, and how matters have changed and why, together with any particular problems which have arisen.)
- details of the client's present living arrangements and proposals for the children;
  (Include here details of the client's means and financial arrangements if in place following ancillary relief proceedings which have been disposed of, or what is proposed if ancillary relief is still pending.)
- details if known of the other side's living arrangements and alternative proposals for the children;
- the solicitors view of the client's case.
  (This is the most difficult part, since you will need to have a sound working knowledge of the relevant law, ie principally ss 1(1), 1(2), 1(3) and 1(5) of the Children Act 1989, and have researched the latest position in respect of contested orders of the type sought, eg residence and contact, or if it be the case some specific problem which is to be resolved by application for a specific issue or prohibited steps order.)

You should take care in composing a list of the:

- questions which counsel is to be asked to express a view on;
- matters on which you can offer a preliminary view;

before attempting to draft this section, or the next which should contain the actual questions counsel is to answer.

Solicitors sometimes think that their views are either (i) not welcome to counsel,who wants to do everything from scratch or (ii) actually expected, so counsel can merely rubber stamp an approach that has already been taken. Neither is in fact true. Only very arrogant counsel *never* want to hear what the solicitor has already done in preparing the case, but *no* conscientious counsel would take a cursory look and confirm the solicitor's view without more.

It actually helps counsel to know how to pitch the opinion that will be written (or advice in conference that will be given) if counsel has an accurate idea of how much of a specialist the solicitor is. If the Instructions expressly state that 'instructing solicitors have no great knowledge of family law since their practice is almost entirely in the field of marine insurance and reinsurance and they habitually advise the client on these matters'. counsel will know exactly where to start (ie that it will be necessary to dispense a short crash course on the content and operation of the Children Act 1989 which would be equally suitable for any group of professionals as a continuing education seminar).

If on the other hand the Instructions set out knowledgeably the solicitor's hesitation in knowing which of recent authorities where the application of certain principles in the s 1(3) checklist has been restated might be relevant to the instant case, counsel will know that the Instructions come from a near expert who probably has not recently been to court much or at all and wants to check up on what the judges are currently doing in certain situations, in particular because that particular solicitor has no intention of going to court as advocate in the case if it comes to a contested hearing and wants to be sure that the advocate who will is in on the decisions at an early stage.

The great beauty of instructing counsel is that if a solicitor is *not* an expert in the field, it is perfectly proper to take the case notwithstanding and to instruct specialist counsel, since the preparatory stages will still be perfectly within the solicitor's capabilities, being much the same in any class of case. Guided by specialist counsel the generalist solicitor (or specialist in another field) can conduct more or less any case, usually no matter how complex.

The specific Instructions to counsel

Here the solicitor must ask the questions to which an answer is desired. It is usual to begin:

'Counsel is accordingly instructed (or requested) to advise on the following matters' and then to list in numbered headings the legal questions including questions of evidence on which the solicitor would like counsel's opinion, eg:

(i) On the basis of the limited information available is counsel of the opinion that the petitioner's suggestion that she should have a residence order for the girl, with a corresponding contact order for the respondent, and that the respondent should have a residence order for the boy, with a corresponding contact order for the petitioner, a realistic assessment of what the court might order if the matter were contested?

(ii) If so ...

(iii) If not ...

and finally, after all the specific questions are asked:

(iv) Generally.

This last head is somewhat cowardly, but is always put in as a catch all in case something has been forgotten!

Counsel is then further requested to settle any documents required, eg a draft s 8 statement for the client where appropriate.

Finally a suitable paragraph should be added inviting counsel to contact instructing solicitors if a conference with the client is desired or if any further information is required.

Self-assessment questions

1 Who has parental responsibility for a child?
2 How is parental responsibility obtained? Can it be lost and if so how?
3 What is the non-intervention principle and what is its source?
4 What is the no delay principle and how does the court meet its obligation to observe this principle?
5 What are the s 8 orders?
6 Can a child's surname be changed by a parent and if so how?
7 May a child be removed from the jurisdiction of the court by a parent and if so for how long?
8 What is wardship and what is its use?
9 Is there any definition of 'welfare' in relation to a child and how may whether any matter is for a child's welfare be decided in any particular case?
10 What are the duties of the local authority in relation to children living in its area?

Section 3

Financial relief on marriage breakdown – legal options, workable solutions, legal aid, tax and welfare benefits

Chapter 7

Ancillary relief:
the basic law

Orders which the court may make   7.1

Ancillary relief (ie a financial order dealing with the
spouses' money and property) is available following
decrees of divorce, nullity, judicial separation and presumption of death and dissolution of the marriage. The
court's power, which is contained in ss 23 and 24 of the
MCA 1973, arises in the case of orders for spouses 'on
granting a decree ...' and is subject to the court's consideration of the matters contained in s 25 of the Act, which
details the matters which the court must take into
account when exercising its powers under ss 23 and 24.

Note

Orders made in favour of spouses to take effect before
decree absolute are called *interim* orders, but become *final*
on DA.

Orders for *children* are always called *interim orders*,
because technically no order can ever be *final* in relation to
a child whose maintenance may always come back before
the court whenever appropriate. These orders can be made
at any time if either agreed between the spouses or, if the
children are *children of the family* who are *not* within the
jurisdiction of the Child Support Agency ('CSA') which
now deals with maintenance for all children whose biological absent parent the Agency can trace, if an application is
made to the court by the parent with care even if the other
spouse does not agree. If the child's parents save the CSA
the task of assessment by agreeing maintenance for the
child between themselves informally, at the moment the
intervention of the Agency can be avoided as the agreement may still be embodied in an order of the court which
is made *by consent*. The CSA must however assess the
child's maintenance and enforce payment against the
absent parent if the child and/or the child's custodial
parent are on welfare benefits: see 7.5.

Subject to the constraints of these three sections of the
Act, the court has a complete discretion as to how its

powers to make financial orders should be exercised (including whether they should be exercised at all) since there is no regime of matrimonial property under the law of England and Wales. This is criticized by some jurists overseas who are constrained by an inflexible code of automatic matrimonial joint ownership. They claim that the English law of ancillary relief is defective in that it is inappropriate to the modern concept of matrimony as a partnership since it is 'a law of separation of assets' and that it is illogical in a marriage partnership in which in theory there should be 'community of property' unless there are special reasons for contracting out of such a position.

The distinct approach of English law is often the reason for multi-millionaire divorces, where the parties have international connections, being conducted in England rather than in the community property jurisdictions which exist in much of the rest of the world. The reason for the selection of an English forum for divorce in these cases is that these community property jurisdictions are unfriendly to the rich husband, since the law of those states usually considers that the spouses already actually or notionally own the matrimonial assets jointly whatever the spouses themselves want, whereas English law more usually proceeds on the basis of what provision is actually reasonably needed for the financially weaker spouse (who is generally the wife) rather than that spouse should receive any particular proportion of the assets available for distribution.

This rejection of the purely 'arithmetical approach' was confirmed by the court of Appeal in the recent case of *Dart v Dart* [1996], CA, (unreported) where from assets of £400,000,000 the wife received only £10,000,000. The husband had carefully planned the family's 'habitual residence' in London so as to avoid the USA jurisdiction of Michigan.

The English scheme is thus one where the *actual ownership* in law of any asset which the court considers is available as a resource at its disposal is *irrelevant*, since by s 24, and subject only to s 25, the court has the power to rearrange ownership of the spouses' assets on divorce as they see fit. Moreover, since the s 24 jurisdiction is a discretionary one, the court is not bound by precedent, a point stressed by the *Dart* decision.

Ancillary relief is therefore an area which may still be commercially attractive to solicitors' practices despite chronic change in the law of divorce, and that is equally true both of the big City firm with a private client department at one end of the operational scale and the small general high street practice at the other, and also the medium size practice or the linked groups in the middle. Moreover, it is probably still a fruitful area for market growth following the likely reduction in solicitors' involvement in the actual divorce suit which The Family Law Act 1996 will turn over largely to mediators (and worse perhaps largely to non-lawyer mediators whose deals may be brokered in accordance with perfect methodology as far as the mediators are concerned, but which could pose endless problems for lawyers subsequently having to process them in a legal framework).

As a trainee specialising in family law you should therefore both prepare yourselves with energy and enthusiasm for this potential expansion in high value work, which might point you in the direction of an opportunity as lucrative as actual divorce suit work is ill paid. Prior to commencing the training contract you should also take every opportunity to work part time in firms of any size which have a busy matrimonial practice, since the high divorce rate has meant that there is usually scope in all such firms to obtain sound routine experience of handling ancillary relief. This can later be recycled as valuable 'experience' in order to obtain paid unqualified work if an immediate training contract is not available to complete the solicitor's qualification. The availability of this valuable short-term work is simply due to the volume of matrimonial work generated, with the result that the volume becomes unmanageable for the permanent staff.

You will first need to acquire a good working grasp of the provisions of ss 23, 24 and 24A of the Act as to the *types* of orders that may be made, of 25 as to the guidance the court must give itself in making those orders, of s 25A as to the policy of spousal self-sufficiency and the 'clean break' and also of ss 28 and 29 in relation to the duration of all orders that may be made. Note should also be taken of the power to award *maintenance pending suit* under s 22, often abbreviated to 'MPS', though this section is not much used because there are other methods of obtaining temporary maintenance until the long-term orders are finally in place. These alternative sources of temporary funding will usually have been considered at the first interview with the client and found more useful: see 5.2.

You will also need to be familiar with the relevant procedure whereby pursuant to FPR r 2.53(1) all claims for any species of ancillary relief order must be made by a petitioner in the prayer of the petition, or by a respondent in the Answer if the respondent files one. These claims should always be made at the outset of the suit (or if this has not been done the petition amended accordingly: see 5.8). Alternatively, there is provision in the FPR for respondents to make such applications *without* filing an Answer. The ancillary relief application is then *activated* and *pursued* within the relevant FPR constraints and this may be done at any time *after decree nisi has been obtained*, prior to which the ancillary relief aspects of the case cannot be progressed. This is because the power of the court to make orders *for spouses* arises 'on granting a decree ... or at any time thereafter'.

Thus all the long-term orders in ss 23 and 24 are restricted to taking effect upon *decree absolute* and not before and the application for them made in the prayer of the petition may not be activated until *decree nisi* has been pronounced.

Note

Although the power of the court arises on making a decree of divorce, it is not unknown for applications to be made many years later for which leave would be required and would only be granted if there is some reason for the delay and such delayed application would not cause injustice.

7.1.1   Income orders: MCA 1973 s 23 (and s 22 for MPS)

Basic maintenance in most cases – weekly, monthly or annually – will be provided by *periodical payments*, either for the spouse or the children or both – and will be awarded in the long-term under s 23(1)(a) for spouses and s 23(1)(d) for children. The duration of such orders will depend on what the court orders as suitable for the particular case.

Periodical payments

For a spouse periodical payments (unless they are *secured* as to which see below) usually last during joint lives of the payer and payee or until remarriage: MCA 1973 s 28, or for a limited period if intended to be part of a clean break arrangement: MCA 1973 s 25A (see below at 7.3.1). If no duration is specified at all, payments continue until further order of the court, which usually means until the payer or the payee applies to vary them under MCA 1973 s 31 (see below Chapter 10).

Obviously a *payer* is likely to apply to vary the order *downwards* (because, eg of job loss so that the payments are no longer affordable, or an increase in the payee's resources so that they are no longer necessary) and a *payee* is likely to apply to vary the order *upwards* because, eg the payments are no longer enough. This might be due to a combination of a rise in the cost of living generally and also an extension of the items of routine expenditure which the payee is called upon to fund. This commonly occurs where children grow up and become more expensive and their requirements for more space at home (or just being at home more, when home study is a common 6th form occurrence before A level or other public examinations) increase the regular outgoings, such as the ordinary utility bills. Either of these situations would produce a *further order of the court* whether that order reduced, increased or entirely discharged the original order.

Secured periodical payments

Where periodical payments are secured in favour of a spouse pursuant to s 23(1)(b), they can be made to last beyond the death of the payer. Secured periodical payments are not usual, since they require to be secured on assets, which are not generally available in most divorces in sufficient quantity to fund such security, and such an order would not be made without good reason, eg that the payer had a bad payment track record, or might leave the jurisdiction to work elsewhere, taking assets out of the jurisdiction at the same time. Secured periodical payments are therefore only likely to be applicable where the payer is particularly rich or particularly impecunious and it is necessary to protect the position of the payee by making a secured order.

Secured periodical payments for a child, which are possible pursuant to s 23(1)(e), are extremely uncommon although there are sometimes good reasons, eg to secure continued payment out of a payer's estate after his death without the necessity of taking further proceedings. For the court to make such an order a father would generally have to be an extremely unreliable and persistently bad payer, and since the court only retains jurisdiction in cases where the CSA would assess contested orders, secured periodical payments for children will be restricted to consent orders where the payer agrees to the security or to cases where the payment is sought in contested proceedings for children of the family who are not within the CSA's remit, ie stepchildren whose absent natural parent the CSA cannot trace, either because of the parent's death or disappearance or in some cases where the father of a stepchild is not actually known.

Children's periodical payments

The normal form of routine maintenance for a *child* who is within the court's jurisdiction will therefore be unsecured periodical payments and by s 29(2) these will last in the first instance until the child's seventeenth birthday, or by s 29(3) until the child finishes full-time education or training. The same section permits a child who is over 18 to continue to receive periodical payments if the child's welfare permits it, eg if the child is handicapped. All child orders terminate of the death of the payer in the same way as those for spouses, unless secured: s 29(4).

Note

Prior to the grant of the decree nisi no order may be made under s 23 *for a spouse* (though this restriction obviously does not apply to periodical payments for children for whom an *interim order* may be made at any time) because the court's power to do so has not yet arisen, so if periodical payments are desired at this stage, it will be necessary to apply for MPS as soon as the petition is filed. These payments can be backdated to the date of the presentation of the petition and will automatically terminate at the end of the suit on grant of decree absolute. The amount of MPS will not be generous since it is regarded as a subsistence allowance and is granted *separately* from the main application for long-term periodical payments and at a more basic rate payments precisely because it will not be possible until the ancillary relief proceedings are further advanced to determine what the terms and quantum of the final order should be.

7.1.2   Capital payment orders: MCA 1973 s 23

Instead of or in addition to the basic maintenance of periodical payments, in some but not all cases a cash *lump sum* order may be made, either for a spouse or for a child or children, or all of them and this also may be done under s 23(1)(c) for spouses and s 23(1)(f) for children.

The reasons for lump sums are many and various, although it was established as long ago as the case of *Wachtel v Wachtel* [1973] Fam 2, [1973] 2 WLR 366, [1973] 1 All ER 829, a case also famous for more than one other reason, that no particular purpose or justification is required before such an order may be made, and a lump sum order may in fact be particularly appropriate in a variety of cases, eg where the payee is likely to remarry, so that periodical payments would cease under s 28, a solicitor might seek a lump sum payment which would not be affected by the remarriage, since any lump sum will be outright. In some cases, where the degree of bitterness has been such that periodical payments would be undesirable, a lump sum may also be a tactful way of ending the war between the spouses.

However, in such cases care would have to be taken that the lump sum order was not *specifically* made as a form of capitalised maintenance, as it could then be attacked and possibly set aside if there had been any deliberate misrepresentation as to whether the payee was planning to remarry, as in the case of *Livesey v Jenkins* [1985] AC 424, [1985] 2 WLR 47, [1985] 1 All ER 105, where the wife omitted to mention that she was already engaged to be married shortly after the order was made.

Established cases particularly suitable for a lump sum include:

- where there is available capital of which the wife should have a share, as in *Trippas v Trippas* [1973] 2 WLR 585, [1973] 2 All ER 1 where the wife had been promised a share of the proceeds of the business because of her moral support in setting up and establishing it;
- set up a business, as *Nicholas v Nicholas* [1984] FLR 285 and *Gojkovic v Gojkovic* [1990] Fam Law 100, in which money was needed to set up respectively a guest house and a hotel where the payee spouse would thus be able to become self-supporting;
- reduce or replace periodical payments, as in *Gojkovic* above where the degree of bitterness and the capability of the payee spouse were both such that this was desirable, and in *Duxbury v Duxbury* [1987] FLR 7, CA, the case in which the now famous *Duxbury* calculation was first used to identify a sum which could be invested in a planned and cost effective manner so as to provide a particular applicant with lifelong maintenance by living at various times off both the income and the capital and at others a combination of the two;
- achieve a clean break as in *Duxbury*;
- compensate for loss of a matrimonial home, as in *P v P* above;
- replace maintenance where enforcement is likely to be difficult or as a punishment for concealing assets as in the cases of *Martin* and also *Nicholas*,

where the husbands were both potential bad payers and/or had tried to conceal their wealth, so that a clean break was clearly a better alternative to periodical payments.

Note

Where a lump sum payment is made to a spouse, only one such lump sum may be ordered, though the lump sum may be *paid* in instalments and expressed in the order to be so payable: s 23(3)(c) and such payment secured to the satisfaction of the court.

Where a lump sum order is made in favour of a *child*, this restriction does not apply and therefore successive lump sum orders may be made.

In both cases interest can be ordered if payment is deferred: s 23(6) provided provision is made in the order for such interest when the interest will be payable from whatever date on which such interest is specified in the order to be payable: see *per* Ewbank J in *L v L (Lump sum: Interest)* [1994] 2 FLR 324, and this is obviously a very useful provision to include in case of default when drafting an order.

It used to be thought that lump sums were only appropriate where the parties were wealthy and there was substantial capital, but it is now established that the exercise of this power is not restricted to cases where there are substantial assets, provided the payer can reasonably raise the sum required: *Davis v Davis* [1967] 1 All ER 123, [1966] 3 WLR 1157. A more recent instance of this is to be found in the case of *P v P (Financial Provision: Lump Sum)* [1978] 1 WLR 483, [1978] 3 All ER 70, which is clear authority for the proposition that no more than is really needed by the payee and can realistically be raised will be ordered to be paid where it has to come from a business, or home and business, which is needed for the family to live on. In that case the wife owned the property, a farm on which she and the three children of the family lived and on which the parties had worked. It was accepted that the husband owned £8,000 of the stock and contents of the farm (the total value of which was £102,000) and he appealed against an order of only £15,000 payable in three instalments over a year, having asked for a lump sum and also a transfer of property order. It was held that the wife could not realistically pay more, since she would need the property to remain unencumbered by more than the £15,000 that would suffice for an alternative home for the husband, in order to maintain herself and the children (having accepted only a nominal periodical payments order in favour of the children and nothing for herself).

Restriction or the grant of lump sums

The court will not cripple a spouse's earning power, nor a business off which the family has to live, nor put a home at risk, as was shown in the case of *Martin v Martin* [1976] 2 WLR 901, [1976] 3 All ER 625, where an order was reduced from £5,000 to £2,000 to avoid a husband's having to sell his hotel and thus lose his home as well as his business, and also in the similar cases of *Smith v Smith* (1983) 4 FLR 154 where the lump sum of £40,000 awarded was cancelled altogether because to raise it the husband would have had to sell shares in his company which was his only income producing asset, which would have benefited nobody, and *Kiely v Kiely* [1988] 1 FLR 248, [1988] 18 Fam Law 51 where the order was again cancelled since to raise a £4,000 lump sum each for the children of the family would have meant selling the former matrimonial home, which moreover was not necessarily certain to raise enough to pay the lump sum, leaving the husband in contempt of court through no fault of his own as well as unable to pay the order.

Otherwise if there are assets the court will not hesitate to make use of them for this purpose and does not much mind where the assets originated if they are required to do justice in the case and can reasonably be raised without violating the principles stated above.

Note

It should however be noted that where a business is *not* to be sold, because the family lives off it, it is pointless to spend large sums of money on valuations, sometimes obsessively indulged in by spouses keen to get compensation elsewhere in the agreement for the value of the asset which cannot be sold but of which they reckon they are entitled to a share, to be achieved by sale of some other asset!

A wife in these circumstances came in for some hard words from the court in the case of *P v P* [1989] 2 FLR 248 where the argument was about the value of shares in a haulage company which on any view could not be sold. It was held that it was pointless to spend money on a precise valuation since the court only wanted a broad view of the value of matrimonial assets which were not being sold, and secondly that as there was another source of a lump sum for her – the proceeds of the matrimonial home, which was to be sold anyway – they could take the approximate value of the shares into account when making orders from those liquid funds. As a result Mrs P received £240,000 out of the £260,000 sale proceeds of the matrimonial home and Mr P kept the shares since it would be reckless to put the business at risk by raising money from his fixed assets.

Adjournment until funds become available

Sometimes lump sum orders cannot be made because there are not, at the moment when the case is before the court, sufficient assets from which the court could order a lump sum, though it is anticipated that there will be in the foreseeable future. The solution here may be to adjourn the case, which may be done for up to a period of about five years (a period suggested in the case of *Roberts v Roberts* [1986] 2 FLR 152) if this is the only means of achieving justice between the parties. In the same year the case of *Davies v Davies* [1986] 1 FLR 497 considered the general desirability of this type of adjournment and held that ideally the matter should be dealt with as soon as possible but if there was a real possibility of capital becoming available in the foreseeable future, adjournment was permissible to achieve justice.

Adjournment, rather than making some sort of percentage order, is more appropriate where the future quantum of the anticipated asset is uncertain, such as the amount of a pension as in *Morris v Morris* (1977) 7 Fam Law 244, which concerned the likely amount of the husband's gratuity when he left the Army. He was a warrant officer and it was uncertain how much longer he would serve in the Army, which was directly relevant to the amount of the gratuity. The husband was ordered to notify the wife of the receipt of the money so that the application might be revived at that date. The principles applying to such adjournments were more recently reviewed in the case of *MT v MT* [1992] 1 FLR 362 a case dealing with the husband's prospects of inheriting from his 83 year old father on his reasonably foreseeably anticipated death. It was held that the court has a discretion to adjourn in any case where it would be suitable to do so because of the foreseeability of capital becoming available.

7.1.3   Property transfer orders: MCA 1973 s 24(1)(a)

The court may transfer freeholds, leaseholds, protected and statutory tenancies within the meaning of the Rent Act 1977, secure tenancies within the meaning of the Housing Act 1985, and council houses and flats. The consent of the local authority is not required but they have a right to be heard. The consent of a building society or bank may not be required but they should be given a chance by the court to be heard: *Practice Direction* [1971] 1 All ER 896. This 'chance' may not make much difference as is shown by cases such as *Lee v Lee* [1984] FLR 243 where the authority opposed the transfer because it disrupted its housing policy; the court did not consider that that merited the hardship that the wife would suffer and ordered the transfer. The case of *Buckingham v Buckingham* (1979) 129 *NLJ* 52 was similarly rather hard on a private landlord when a transfer was ordered despite his objections, although a landlord's objection to a particular tenant is regarded as of significant importance in the law of landlord and tenant because of the close proprietorial relationship which they must have. The case of *Tebbut v Haynes* [1981] 2 All ER 239 also indicates that the interests of third parties who live in the home (in this case the husband's mother and aunt) will be considered if the order will turn them out.

The most common use of the transfer of property power is to transfer the matrimonial home, especially if it is to effect a clean break: see 7.3, but it may also be used to transfer ownership of chattels such as cars, furniture, works of art and indeed anything which needs to be transferred to achieve the necessary reorganisation of the parties' financial affairs.

Settlement of property: MCA 1973 s 24 (1)(b)   7.1.4

This enables the court to set up settlement orders in relation to the matrimonial home, such as the *Mesher, Martin, Harvey* and similar occupation orders which enable a spouse to remain in the home with the children until the latter are grown up or even in some cases for longer: see 8.5. It can also be used to enable a spouse to establish a settlement of capital to provide for the other spouse and children, usually with reversion to the settling spouse or possibly ultimate remainder to the children.

Variation of settlements: MCA 1973 s 24(1)(c) and (d)   7.1.5

This is the power which allows variation of an ante- or post-nuptial settlement in favour of the parties or their children, including any settlement made by will or codicil. This provision, which permits the interest of a spouse to be reduced or extinguished, also sometimes permits variation of pension funds as in the case of *Brooks v Brooks* [1995] 3 All ER 257, HL although there are very few cases where this possibility applies. In *Brooks* it was possible to vary the provisions applicable to the pension fund so as to give the wife an immediate annuity and a deferred index-linked pension payable from the date of the husband's death, going on to direct that these two pensions for the wife were to be provided in priority to the pension for the husband, so that if necessary he would take less. However, this could only be done as the pension scheme was the parties own small company scheme whereas most pensions which would ideally be split on divorce are subject to the wife discretion of the trustees of the pension schemes in question which are not subject to the orders of the court.

This problem will to some extent be addressed by the Pensions Act 1995, s 166, which inserts new ss 25B–D into the MCA 1973. These provisions will directly affect the resources to be taken into account by the court under s 25(2)(a): see below at 7.2, and enable the court to require pension fund trustees, whether of an occupational or personal pension scheme, to pay part of the pension or lump sum available to one spouse under the scheme to the other according to the court's direction.

7.1.6   Order for sale: MCA 1973, s 24A

Whenever the court makes any of the above orders other than one which is simply for unsecured periodical payments, it may also order a sale of any property in which either of the parties has a legal beneficial interest. This power, not originally included in the MCA 1973, was introduced to provide the opportunity for the court not only to order a sale so as to facilitate payment of its orders – an obviously useful consequential benefit for the payee – but to make desirable facilitating arrangements, such as that the court's order be paid out of the proceeds of sale: s 24A(2)(a), that the property be offered for sale to specified persons or classes of persons: s 24A(2)(b) and to add any other condition of a practical nature that it thinks fit, eg as to which party's solicitor should have the conduct of the sale. This can be very important since clearly the applicant's solicitors would ideally prefer to be in the driving seat in such a transaction, rather than having to keep contacting the respondents to try to push the matter along, whereas some respondents, especially the more pernickety, would (sometimes rightly) be anxious about not being in control of the disposal of major asset.

Like other orders, those under s 24A cannot take effect until *decree absolute*.

The s 25 factors, s 25A and the ideal of spousal self-sufficiency

A detailed knowledge of this section is required in order to put together a suitable ancillary relief package in each individual case on which you is called upon to work. The method is to look at the orders available under ss 23 and 24 (for which see 7.1) then to apply the s 25 considerations systematically to the facts and finally to propose the combination of orders which most suits the family's circumstances, and is fairest in relation to the relevant s 25 factors. Obviously any such scheme will give priority to the *client's* interests where possible, but also, will bear in mind that what suits the family as a *whole* is also likely to *be* in the client's interests and to facilitate life after divorce, especially where there are children and an ongoing relationship is likely to be essential. It is sometimes necessary to tell clients that what they think they want is not necessarily going to secure the best deal with the best chance of producing a happy solution for the client, whatever the client thinks! However, as always, the client instructs and the solicitor advises, but must ultimately carry out the client's instructions, so good advice here as elsewhere may fall on deaf ears, in which case there is not much the solicitor can do but comply - or in an extreme case encourage the client to remove the case elsewhere.

An inexperienced practitioner, or one whose regular work is outside family law, will need to work through the range of orders and the s 25 factors on the checklist principle, but after a while this will become second nature so that` such a structured approach will usually not be necessary because the practitioner will be able to spot instantly the one or two points which will particularly favour the client and build the client's case around those.

The considerations themselves are contained in s 25, which is conveniently broken into two sub-sections, s 25(1) which sets out the court's 'general duty' in applying the whole of the section, and s 25(2), which itself may rationally be broken into two sub-parts, s 25(2)(a) which deals with the resources out of which the court will make its orders, and ss 25(2)(b) to (h) which set out the checklist through which the court will work in deciding whether and to what extent it should make orders.

Additionally s 25A has since 1984 given the court the power to *order* a 'clean break', if necessary regardless of the parties' wishes, a power which in the absence of *agreement* of the parties to that course no court had prior to the 1984 amendment to the statute. The clean break is in accordance with the relatively new policy of spousal self-sufficiency by which, if a clean break is not possible immediately, the court at least likes to see even untrained wives working towards a clean break in the future, if necessary taking part time work, acquiring a skill or, if older and out of the workplace for many years, perhaps retraining.

7.2.1   Welfare of children: s 25(1) ('The General Duty' of the court)

This section, while requiring the court to have regard to all the circumstances of the case, makes the welfare of the children the first consideration in every case where there are children of the family. It is important to understand the interaction of this principle with that of the clean break. The existence of children does not necessarily make a clean break impossible between their parents (though not of course between either of their parents and them) though it may make it inappropriate, or inappropriate for the time being: *Suter v Suter and Jones* [1987] 2 FLR 232 (where the wife with young children received nominal periodical payments as the future was insufficiently clear to impose a clean break immediately, despite the fact that she was cohabiting with a lover who could make a substantial contribution to the household as long as he remained with her).

The welfare of the children in the context of s 25(1) is usually interpreted as meaning that during their minority they must have a secure home and a sufficient income must be provided for them to live on: *Harman v Glencross* [1986] 2 FLR 241 (where the occupation of the former matrimonial home had to be given to the wife who had the children living with her, as otherwise they would have had no proper home).

Note

Children in the context of s 25(1) means 'children of the family' within the meaning of s 52, ie a child of both parties, or a child of one who has been *treated* by the other as a child of the family. Step parents can therefore successfully evade liability for their partner's children but this would need to be done expressly as the court is slow to recognise any such situation: *Day v Day* [1988] 1 FLR 278 (This was a case where the actual marriage lasted only six weeks, as Mr Day quickly decided that he preferred the bachelor life, although there had been lengthy pre-marital

cohabitation. When he sought to get out of paying maintenance for the two children of the wife, neither of whom
apparently had a father available to maintain them, the
court decided that he had fully understood his commitment and obligations towards the children for who he had
accepted responsibility and that he must therefore pay
maintenance for them both despite the brevity of the actual
marriage).

Evidence of the parties' means: s 25(2)(a)   7.2.2

This section requires that all the parties' means must be
taken into account so as to establish the nature and
extent of the resources out of which the court will be able
to make its orders. Clearly the size of the pie is the first
relevant point before it can be divided, and the ingredi-
ents will be of the first importance in establishing both
the precise make up of the dish and the size of the por-
tions available. The reality of the situation is that the
court must consider more than the surface of the parties'
respective financial positions. In order to do this,
whether the case is to be contested or the subject of a
negotiated settlement in the region of what the court
might *order*, it is usual for both parties either formally to
file affidavits of means (if it is certain that the case will be
contested or at least that it must be started on that basis)
or (where a negotiated settlement is the aim from the
start) to make disclosure in some other convenient
manner, eg they may choose to exchange affidavits informally in draft or exchange information by letter or in
person at a meeting, supported by such bundles of documents as are necessary to verify the position. Where
such negotiations are successful, the court may be
invited to make an order by consent upon lodgement of
a draft, thus making a considerable saving in both time
and costs.

The section requires the court to take into account
'the income, earning capacity, property and other financial resources which each of the parties to the marriage
has or is likely to have in the foreseeable future, including in the case of earning capacity any increase in that
capacity which it would in the opinion of the court be
reasonable to expect a party to the marriage to take steps
to acquire'.

Looking below the surface the court will therefore
need to be alert not merely to what the parties have but
what they might have, such as:

- both parties' *future* earning capacity as well as present earnings, including any *potential improvement* in earning capacity which might be acquired by retraining or other reorganisation of a party's lifestyle;
- family money, such as from wealthy parents or a private company on which the family habitually draws, as in the recent case of *Thomas v Thomas* (1995) 4 May 1995, *Independent*, CA where a husband's appeal against some fairly onerous orders, including for school fees, was dismissed because the judge said the husband had no real complaint if his wealthy family came to his aid to pay some school fees as before the divorce it had been understood that it would!
- The principle of financial independence in so far as consistent with the welfare of the children.

Besides family money, the variety of sources of means to be taken into account for this purpose will often include damages or compensation, anticipated interests under a will or settlement, the earnings of a new spouse or cohabitee, and property acquired since the separation and or divorce, besides the spouse's *true* income or earning capacity where that is different from what is being claimed in affidavits of means.

Damages or compensation

The general rule is that damages for pain and suffering and loss of amenity are not taken into account: *Jones v Jones* [1975] 2 WLR 606, [1975] 2 All ER 12 (where any alternative to the rule would have been particularly unsuitable, since the damages in question in that case were an award of only £1,800 for injuries following a knife attack actually perpetrated on the wife by the husband, which had severed the tendons in her hands and made it impossible for her to continue to earn her own living as a nurse). However, general damages *are* normally regarded as a resource as in the case of *Daubney v Daubney* [1976] 2 WLR 959, [1976] 2 All ER 453 where the wife had used the general damages in question to buy a flat which necessarily counted as a resource of hers in the ancillary relief proceedings.

Nevertheless, where damages have been calculated to provide continuing care for a projected lifespan then these will not be counted (as for example in the case of *Jones v Jones* [1983] 1 WLR 901, [1983] 2 All ER 1039 where the husband did not have to bring into account damages of £167,000 to provide care for the rest of his life after a motor cycle accident, and the case of *C v C (Financial Provision)* [1995] 2 FLR 171, where the wife and child were on state benefits but a settlement was refused because all the damages were needed to provide for the husband's needs). This contrasts with a case where the sum actually received was in excess of that party's needs and some of that excess was needed to do justice between the parties by righting a disparity which would otherwise exist between their respective financial positions: *Wagstaff v Wagstaff* [1992] 1 All ER 275, [1992] 1 FLR 333 (where the husband had received £418,000, also after a motor cycle accident, of which £32,000, was awarded to the wife, who had no particular need for the money except as an emergency fund, on the basis that she had contributed to a 12 year marriage, and had a child to support, and the husband did not need all the money).

In this latter case the court specifically took the opportunity to differentiate between smaller awards of damages specifically for pain and suffering (or any awards where the disabled spouse's needs used up all the money awarded) and those cases, like *Wagstaff* where the amount of the damages, even if some of them were for pain and suffering, clearly indicated that they should be considered a resource.

Interests under a will or settlement

Here policy varies, and the proximity of the availability of the money, together with the likelihood of its actually being received in due course will influence the decision as to whether the money will be considered a resource for the purposes of s 25(2)(a).

The alternative, especially if justice cannot otherwise be done, is to adjourn a decision on the ancillary relief application until the money becomes available, which may be done for four or five years as in *Roberts v Roberts* [1986] 2 All ER 483, and *Hardy v Hardy* (1981) 11 Fam Law 153 or perhaps to make the order on the basis that the money will eventually come in, if that is fairly certain, but that payment pursuant to the order should not be made until the funds have actually been received as in *Calder v Calder* (1976) *Times* 29 June 1976. See above at 7.1.2.

However, the availability of the assets in due course must be reasonably certain: it is not possible to subpoena aged and ailing parents to state their testamentary intentions as was discovered in the case of *Morgan v Morgan* [1977] Fam 122, and cases do arise where while it is by no means certain when and if such an inheritance will be

received, some account nevertheless has to be taken of
the expectations and in this situation the wealth, degree
of relationship age and health of the testator or testatrix
will all be relevant, how relevant depending on the circumstances of the individual case: *B v B* [1988] 2 FLR 490
where there was a quantifiable interest under the will of
a wealthy mother which the court could not ignore. A
second case called *B v B* (1982) 12 Fam Law makes it clear
that where the spouse is a beneficiary under a settlement
the court can treat the case as one of settled assets and
make an order on the basis that the payee spouse can
borrow against the expectations. In a further case entitled *B v B* [1990] 1 FLR 20 advanced age enabled the court
to take account of an expected inheritance without
adjournment (the mother from whom one of the parties
was to inherit was in that case 84 and the inheritance was
held not to be too remote). However, in *K v K* [1990] Fam
Law 19, [1990] 2 FLR 225 the testatrix was only 79 and in
good health and the court ignored the inheritance as a
resource as being too remote!

Note

Interests under offshore trusts are not safe from being
counted as a s 25(2)(a) resource: *Browne v Browne* [1989] 1
FLR 291, CA, where the wife was eventually committed for
contempt for not paying under an order which had been
quantified on the basis that she had access at will to two
offshore trusts where the trustees (who had previously
handed over whatever money she had requested) refused
to meet her request for funds for the purposes of the order.

While the court knows that no order is directly enforceable against offshore trusts outside the jurisdiction, judges
do not hesitate to make orders taking into account offshore
assets if they are satisfied that the money is normally at the
disposal of the beneficiary.

Thus trustees cannot in fact help such a beneficiary by
suddenly refusing to carry out requests to pay over money
if they have been in the habit of doing so in the past (as is
usually the case where offshore trusts are of the type
designed to be of financial benefit both to the beneficiaries
who obtain fiscal advantages by the money technically
being owned by the trustees off shore and to the holding
trust company which charges a large fee for the service).

Earnings of a new spouse or cohabitee

This is always a problematical area. No order can be
made which actually has to be *paid* out of the new spouse

or cohabitee's pocket as such, but there are two ways in which the new spouse or cohabitee can indirectly make money or assets available to the first family by:

- making over capital or property to the spouse as in *Ibbetson v Ibbetson* [1984] FLR 545 where the former wife's new cohabitee placed their new house into joint names, thus giving her a half share which had to be counted as an asset of hers in the ancillary relief settlement;
- paying some or all of the spouse's living expenses, thus releasing more of the spouse's income for the maintenance of the first family, as in *Macey v Macey* (1981) 11 Fam Law 248.

On the other hand, if the former spouse simply gives up work and elects to be kept by the new spouse or cohabitee, no order will be able to be made at all against either the former spouse or the new partner, as in *Wynne v Wynne* [1981] 1 WLR 69, [1980] 3 All ER 659 where the former husband was supported in great style in a luxurious flat in Knightsbridge but being a 'kept man' could pay no order himself, nor could the new partner be asked to pay that particular expense for him had an order been made against him despite her willingness to pay for anything else he might desire!

Note

It is impossible to compel a new partner to file an affidavit of means, even to establish what the ex-spouse might reasonably have access to financially. The only way to obtain such detail is to compel the respondent to the ancillary relief application, ie the ex-spouse personally, to give such detail as he or she knows of the new partner's means in the respondent's own affidavit (or in response to a r 2.63 questionnaire: see below at 11.6.2). Even a production appointment under FPR r 2.62(7) will not help unless the information is forthcoming through the respondent since this only enables an order to be made to compel a person who could have been compelled to produce a document in the course of the proceedings to do so at an earlier stage than the actual hearing: see below at 11.6 and the case of *Frary v Frary* [1993] 2 FLR 696.

Assets acquired after separation or divorce

These are *not* excluded as a resource especially if needed to do justice between the parties: *Schuller v Schuller* [1990] 2 FLR 193 where the wife inherited a valuable flat from a wealthy friend after the marriage had ended.

The spouse's true earning capacity

The court is not deceived by affidavits alleging a tiny income where the lifestyle does not match, as happened in the case of *J v J* [1955] P215, [1955] 3 WLR 72 where the husband was a property developer living far beyond his apparent means, but actually declared a tiny taxable income: the order was based on his lifestyle and not on his apparent income. The court is even quicker to do this where they realise that they are being deliberately deceived, as in the case of *Newton v Newton* [1990] 1 FLR 33 where they eventually decided that nothing the husband said could be relied on and based their order on his lifestyle. Sometimes respondents positively insult the court's intelligence as in the well known case of *Wachtel v Wachtel* [1973] 2 WLR 366, [1973] 1 All ER 829 where the husband's income was supposed to be £4,000 pa, but he actually spent £5,000 and was in fact accumulating savings! He came from a wealthy family and the court took the obviously sensible step in the circumstances of treating his income as at least £6,000!

Note

Where the respondent is from a wealthy family, it is not necessary for there to be actual deceit of this kind before the court will take the view that family money is likely to be available and that the respondent could reasonably expect to tap into those funds even to make a lump sum payment to his wife as happened in the case of *O'Donnell v O'Donnell* [1975] 3 WLR 308, [1975] 2 All ER 993 and the 1995 case of *Thomas* to pay school fees.

The court adopts the same sceptical approach when measuring *actual* earnings, even if the level of actual earnings is demonstrably true, where the spouse in question could and should be earning more, so it is no good such a spouse taking a low paid or *pro bono* job with a charity or working from choice for a friend at subsistence level if a more suitable level of earnings is genuinely realisable, as is shown by the cases of *Hardy v Hardy* above (where the husband went to work for his father, a wealthy racehorse trainer on a stable hand's wage of £70 per week and the court had no hesitation in making an order of £50 in favour of his wife and children on the basis of what he could really earn) and *McEwan v McEwan* [1972] 1 WLR 1217, [1972] 2 All ER 708 where the husband was actually already retired at the age of 59 on a police pension of £6 per week, but the court still made an order of that amount on the basis that he could still earn something as well.

This attitude is not confined to immediate decisions on current earnings. In *Mitchell v Mitchell* [1984] FLR 387, CA the court also took the view that the mother of a 13 year old daughter could return to work and raise a small mortgage when the girl left school so as to give the husband a bigger share of the matrimonial home when the house was sold on completion of the daughter's education. However where a spouse has genuine difficulty finding work and is obviously not simply workshy, an order will *not* be made on the basis of earning capacity: *Williams v Williams* [1974] 3 WLR 379, [1974] 3 All ER 377 where the husband was made redundant and while the judge at first instance took the view that he must be wilfully on welfare benefits and so made a maintenance order based on what he should have been earning, this was reversed on appeal when the court was satisfied of the true position.

Pensions

The new s 25B inserted into the MCA 1973 by s 166 of the Pensions Act 1995 requires the court to examine the parties' pension position for the purposes of s 25(2). Resources now include both existing and likely future pension benefits, so as to enable the court to consider wether an order should be made under ss 25B–D to require payment of part of the pension to the applicant spouse.

Other matters which the court must take into account: s 25(2)(b) to (h)   7.2.3

Once the s 25(2)(a) resources are identified, and the parties know on what figures their negotiations will be based, suitable orders will be worked out in accordance with the remaining s 25 considerations. This means looking at s 25(2)(b) as qualified by ss 25(2)(c) to (h).

The parties' needs, obligations and responsibilities: s 25(2)(b)   7.2.4

Under this head the court looks at the parties' needs and obligations, ie all the basic categories such as food, clothes, housing, and expenses in connection with the upbringing of the children, whose welfare will be the first consideration. Obviously common sense is helpful here – some regard will have to be had to a suitable lifestyle for each of the parties, and some sort of budget in keeping with that, in order to assess what *needs* actually means in each case. In deciding what the needs are, the court usually has two (sometimes inconsistent) aims in view, namely both to maintain a residence for the custodial spouse and children and to divide the family assets fairly (especially the matrimonial home, which is usually the largest asset).

The prime *need* will usually be for a home for each party, but while the court does operate on a rule of thumb of 'homes for both', because of s 25(1) that will be especially important for the party who has care of the children: *Mesher v Mesher* [1980] 1 All ER 126 (decided in 1975, although not reported till 1980, the first case in which the need of the wife and children to be housed, which precluded the sale which might otherwise have been ordered, led to a settlement of the matrimonial home to enable them to occupy it for as long as necessary and then for the proceeds to be divided later on the deferred sale).

This case, the origin of the term *Mesher* order as a generic description for occupational settlement orders in relation to the matrimonial home, has led to many variations on the theme, such as the *Harvey* order (where instead of leaving at the end of the occupation period, the spouse in occupation pays to the other an occupational rent assessed at a fair market rate), and the *Martin* order (where the spouse in occupation, usually the wife, controls the date at which the home is ultimately sold since the trigger event is that of her remarriage, cohabitation, voluntary removal or even death).

Note

Husbands can benefit from the court's policy of requiring that each party should have a home, as in *Calderbank v Calderbank* [1975] 3 WLR 586, [1975] 3 All ER 721, where the husband was held to need a house in keeping with the lifestyle he had enjoyed during the marriage to a wealthy woman, in which to receive access visits by the children, and *Browne v Pritchard* [1975] 1 WLR 1366, [1975] 3 All ER 721, where the husband and children remained in the matrimonial home since the wife had a council house and the unemployed husband could not afford to buy out her share of the former home. These occupational orders have therefore established a principle that ownership of the matrimonial home is relatively unimportant: what matters is where everyone is going to live.

Special situations

The court will also have to take into account any factors which increase needs or reduce ability to pay because of other obligations: the two most obvious and frequently occurring of these are *special needs* and *second families*.

Special needs

Needs will obviously take account of *special needs* in a health or education sense, especially where this affects the children, as in the case of *Smith v Smith* [1975] 2 All ER 19 where the wife had to do part time work as she had to look after a daughter with a kidney complaint. As a result she had no job security and clearly would not be able to rehouse herself if the matrimonial home were sold and the proceeds divided, even if the daughter were to leave home. In the circumstances the court transferred the home to her absolutely.

Second families

However, it is now established that the needs of second families are just as valid as those of the first family – there is no 'pecking order' as such: *Barnes v Barnes* [1972] 1 WLR 1381, [1972] 3 All ER 872. This was the case which both established that no one is entitled to throw the burden of maintaining a spouse and family onto the State, but is expected to work to support them if at all possible. This is sometimes called 'the rule in *Barnes v Barnes*'; the case also settled the principle that the obligation to a second wife and family does not rank second after that to a first wife and family, so that the subsequent obligations must be given the same weight as any other responsibilities. The cases of *Stockford v Stockford* (1982) 3 FLR 52 and *Furniss v Furniss* (1982) 3 FLR 46 were both decided on the basis of this principle and resulted in the first wife coming off worse in her claim for what money there was since she, being alone and without a waged partner, could rely on welfare benefits if unable to work, while the new wife, having both a partner in work and younger children, was unable either to fall back on social security or to work herself.

These decisions have been followed more recently in the case of *Delaney v Delaney* [1990] 2 FLR 457 where the judge, in justifying a similar decision, expressly invoked the principle that it is now recognised that '... there is life after divorce'.

The standard of living prior to the marriage breakdown: s 25(2)(c)

7.2.5

This requires the court to consider how the parties lived during the marriage and is responsible for some of the apparently very generous orders in recent high value divorces.

Obviously, wealthier families may suffer no drop as in the case of *Calderbank v Calderbank*, above, where the husband was able to hold on to his previous lifestyle on the basis that the children would expect it when they visited him, and *Foley v Foley* [1981] 3 WLR 284, [1981] 2 All ER 857, where the wife had to be financed to maintain her lifestyle on a par with that to which she had become accustomed, including buying a house with a bit of land so as not to lower her usual standard of living!

The very wealthy husband usually benefits from this principle by invoking it in the form usually known as the 'millionaire's defence', in which it is claimed that a detailed account of such a husband's assets is not required to be sworn in an affidavit of means because the husband in question is so wealthy that he can easily meet any order the court might reasonably make based on the parties' marital lifestyle, as happened in the case of *Thyssen-Bornemisza v Thyssen-Bornemisza (No 2)* [1985] FLR 1069. In that case, the wife's request for full details of her husband's assets (so she could be sure she was getting a large enough settlement) was refused by the court since the standard of living criteria in s 25(2)(c) meant that they only had to provide for her needs in preserving her usual lifestyle, for which it was not necessary to put the husband to more expense in preparing financial detail than was actually required to satisfy the court that he had the means to pay the order made.

Note

Section 25(2)(c) will *not* be relevant where the marriage has been *short and childless*: *Attar v Attar (No 2)* [1985] FLR 653 where an air hostess who had been married to a wealthy Saudi Arabian with disclosed assets of £2m received only a lump sum equivalent to two years' pay at the rate of her former salary to enable her to readjust to the end of her marriage and dependence on the husband.

Low and middle income families tend, however, to have difficulty in sustaining the former lifestyle, although the court tries to leave the parties on similar standards of living so the drop is share equally as in the case of *Scott v Scott* [1982] 1 WLR 723, [1978] 3 All ER 65.

Note

Where there is a dispute as to the appropriate standard of living, as in the case of *Preston v Preston* [1982] 1 All ER 41, [1981] 3 WLR 619 where the wife had managed on a very small amount of money at one time when the husband was building up the business on which they lived, the payee spouse is not expected to settle for the minimum level but can insist on a less frugal amount reflecting how the parties lived once their life had become more prosperous.

Age of the parties and duration of the marriage: s 25(2)(d)

This is a clear recognition of the relevance of a spouse's non-financial contributions as well as of the realities of life in that, eg a *wife's age* will clearly be relevant to her earning capacity (and therefore also to the clean break potential) and a *husband's* will be relevant to his retirement and ability to pay an order, whereas the *duration of the marriage* (which normally excludes any period of prior *cohabitation*) will be some guide to the contribution which the parties have both made to the relationship and which should be recognised in distributing the assets. It will thus be seen that the ages of the parties and the duration of the marriage in putting together a suitable ancillary relief package has nothing to do with the *merits* of the case and everything to do with the capability of the financially weaker spouse (usually the wife) to work and be self-sufficient following the divorce.

Note

An older wife who married in the tradition of non-working wives and mothers is less likely to be expected to work (and retrain if her skills are outdated or she has never had commercial skills) than a younger one who has grown up used to the culture of working wives and mothers. Moreover, a younger wife who can work can raise a mortgage, whereas an older one with less earning capacity may not be able to.

Cohabitation before marriage is not normally relevant in calculating the length of a marriage although in an exceptional case it may be, because of the difference recognised between formal commitment to marriage and the more flexible state of cohabitation, a difference emphasised in the case of *Campbell v Campbell* [1977] 1 All ER 1, [1976] 3 WLR 572 where it was expressly noted that the obligations of marriage begin only after the ceremony, despite the fact that the marriage in that case was of only two years duration, while it followed cohabitation of three and a half.

This case has, with one notable exception, set the tone for subsequent decisions such as *H v H* (1981) 2 FLR 392, where the same approach was taken in respect of a marriage of seven weeks following on and off cohabitation of six years and the wife received only a small lump sum to enable her to adjust to the change in her circumstances. Similar principles were applied in *Foley v Foley* [1981] 3 WLR 284, [1981] 2 All ER 857, where the marriage was five years and the cohabitation seven – although as there were three children some small weight was given to the cohabitation by considering this to be part of 'all the circumstances of the case' under the general duty pursuant to s 25(1) – and *Day v Day* [1988] 1 FLR 278, already considered in other contexts, where the marriage was six weeks and the cohabitation four years. Moreover, in *Leadbeater v Leadbeater* [1985] FLR 789 Balcombe LJ in restating the principle defined a short marriage as anything less than about four and a half to five years.

The notable exception was the case of *Kokosinski v Kokosinski* [1980] 3 WLR 55, [1980] 1 All ER 1106, where the marriage was extremely short but the period of cohabitation 22 years, and the wife, unable to marry the husband throughout almost the entire 22 year period because he was not free to do so, changed her name by deed poll, helped the husband in his business, bore him a son and, as the court specifically noted, gave him the best years of her life. Exceptionally, she received a large lump sum to enable her to buy a flat near her work.

However, more recently there has been a detectable tendency at least to look carefully at any period of cohabitation before deciding not to take it into account, and in the case of *B v B* [1995] 1 FLR 9, Thorpe J specifically recognised the reality of the increase in pre-marriage cohabitation as a relevant factor. Were this approach to be adopted more generally it might effect a significant change in the law on this point.

Note

Care should be taken to obtain compensation, whatever the length of the marriage, where a spouse has given up a lot to marry in the first place and has lost out as a result – eg a good job, a business opportunity or a residential tenancy.

7.2.7   Physical or mental disability of either party: s 25(2)(e)

This is clearly relevant to earning capacity and capabilities generally. Such considerations will usually immediately identify themselves as in the cases of *Jones v Jones* [1975] 2 WLR 606, [1975] 2 All ER 12, the case already considered in another context of the wife injured by the husband's knife attack who could not continue to work as a nurse; *B v B* (1982) 12 Fam Law 92, where the wife needed extra money for her expenses since she had MS; and *Newton v Newton* [1990] 1 FLR 33, where the wife had serious physical and psychological difficulties which required a regular companion and help with transport. *Sakkass v Sakkass* [1987] 2 FLR 398 was a similar case where the husband had MS, and the court felt that there had to be a *Mesher* order to enable the wife and children to remain in the home, but in that case could not decide on the eventual shares of the proceeds on sale till there was up to date information on the husband's condition because his future needs could not be properly determined at the time the house fell to be sold. This type of case may require an adjournment while the true position is ascertained.

The past, present and future contributions (financial and other) made or to be made to the welfare of the family by each of the parties: s 25(2)(f)   7.2.8

Contribution to be considered here may be either positive or negative, and this paragraph has been the most significant of any provision in securing adequate recognition of the contribution of unwaged spouses who remain at home to care for the home and family, immortalised in such cases as *Vicary v Vicary* [1992] Fam Law 429 in judicial comments such as '... the wife had supplied the infrastructure and support in the context of which the husband was able to prosper and accumulate wealth'.

The case of *Wachtel v Wachtel* [1973] 2 WLR 366, [1873] 1 All ER 829 is still good law on the value of the wife's unpaid work in homemaking and childcare as being every bit as deserving of recognition in money terms as the husband's in going out to work to earn a living for the family as a whole. As Lord Denning said in that case, the wife contributes in kind to enable the husband to acquire assets for both parties, and the value of the wife's work in this area is clearly demonstrated merely by costing the price of hiring help to do the domestic work which she undertakes for the benefit of both spouses and the children. The value of this contribution as an item in itself which earns the right to compensation is similar to a golden handshake on termination of employment after a lengthy period of service, and is quite independent of the need to maintain the spouse who has made that contribution. This is demonstrated by cases like *Smith v Smith* [1991] 2 All ER 306, [1991] 2 FLR 432, where the wife committed suicide six months after an order was made giving her a substantial capital sum, and although the court rescinded the part of the order which represented capitalised maintenance payments, for which being dead she no longer had either a need or a right, it did not disturb that part of the order which represented recognition of her contribution over a 30 year marriage, and that sum survived for her estate.

Note

A husband is equal before the court in this respect: *B v B* (1982) 12 Fam Law 92, already considered above, where the wife came from a wealthy family but the husband had worked hard to achieve success independently, had kept the family together despite the demands of his work, and on divorce obtained custody of one of the children. It was held that he was in the same position as a wife in similar circumstances who did not legally own the bulk of the family assets.

Contributions to the success of a business also count under this head, such as in the cases of *O'Donnell v O'Donnell* and *Gojkovic v Gojkovic*, already discussed above in other contexts, and this is especially so where a business in which the wives' hard work and willingness to turn their hands to everything has paid off so as to make the business profitable just at the time that the divorce occurred. Both the above cases involved hotels where initially the wives had given unfailing support, undertaking long hours of menial work to get the business off to a good start. There will usually be a similar approach where the spouses have endured some financial hardship in order to help initially struggling businesses as in the cases of *Kokosinski* and *Preston*. Moreover, the case of *Trippas v Trippas* [1973] 2 WLR 585 [1973] 2 All ER 1 shows that in appropriate circumstances mere moral support without actual work will be enough to establish a spouse's right to share in the proceeds if there has been a promise to that effect that the court can oblige the other spouse to honour.

Negative contribution under this head can be a way of recording due debit for less than supportive behaviour which does not amount to conduct under s 25(2)(g) as in the case of *West v West* [1977] 2 WLR 933, [1977] 2 All ER 705 where the wife would not even set up house with the husband, but insisted on remaining with her parents, where she stayed with the children, for which fact of ordinary marital commitment she not surprisingly received a reduced maintenance order. However, as always the spouse who can show that any such reduction will not be in the interests of the children, whose welfare is required by s 25(1) to be given first consideration, can probably wriggle out of any adverse result that might otherwise be meted out under this section, as in the case of the appalling wife in *E v E* [1990] 2 FLR 233 where her extravagance and adultery, neglect of the children and walking out on the husband not only amazingly did not amount to conduct within the meaning of s 25(2)(g): see 7.2.9, but also failed to attract any reduction in maintenance despite the negative contribution this portfolio of shortcomings undoubtedly constituted, on the basis that the court, while entirely agreeing about the negative aspect of such a contribution to the misfortunes of the family, had to conclude that leaving her in financial difficulties or even in severely reduced circumstances would not be in the children's interests, so she ended up with a large lump on a clean break! (Neither life nor the law of divorce purports always to be *fair*!)

Note

Contributions should usually be made over at least an average length marriage, ie one that has last at least the four and a half to five years envisaged by Balcombe LJ in *Leadbeater* mentioned above, but the case of *Cumbers v Cumbers* [1975] 1 all ER 1, [1974] 1 WLR 1331 makes clear that such contributions if sufficiently significant will still be counted even in a short marriage as it is the *quality* of the contribution *per se* which is relevant. Nevertheless, *Kokosinski* type cases apart, contributions usually need to be made during *marriage* and not during periods of cohabitation.

Conduct: s 25(2)(g)   7.2.9

The wording of this paragraph of the section requires the court to take in to account any conduct of either of the parties which in their opinion it would be 'inequitable to disregard'. This means exactly what it says and no other extraneous descriptions or terminology need to be imported into the definition. Moreover, the trend in modern divorce law is to *disregard* conduct *unless* it is shown that it is or may be inequitable (unfair overall) not to take it into account because, as was stated in the case of *Duxbury v Duxbury*, already mentioned in another context, the application of s 25 is a financial and not a moral exercise. In any case, as was expressly recognised in the case of *Vasey v Vasey* [1985] FLR 596, it is very difficult to discern what goes on in other peoples' marriages, an approach which has led to the essentially non-judgmental approach that is now felt appropriate, a distinct shift in both the general emphasis and the burden of proof in the matter which you should note – this can initially be traced back to the decision in the case of Wachtel, already mentioned above in another context, where the general non-relevance of conduct was first established, further to be refined in subsequent cases.

The overall result is that if conduct is going to be relevant at all it will have no relation to any ordinary considerations of morality, so you should abandon all 'normal' preconceptions in this regard, since in practice the conduct in question will need to be so appalling that it simply cannot be ignored. The following (non-exhaustive) are examples:

- *murder and conspiracy to murder* will always qualify, as in *Evans v Evans* [1989] 1 FLR 351 (where the husband having regularly paid maintenance for 32 years was the victim of a plot by his wife and another to kill him – her maintenance order was discharged). Encouragement of suicide is in the same category as was held in the case of *Kyte v Kyte* [1987] 3 All ER 1041 where the wife deceitfully set about ridding herself of the husband in order to set up house with another man, divorcing him for his behaviour as an unpredictable suicidal manic depressive, and obtaining an injunction to get him out of the house, and in the process lied to the court about her relationship with the other man. As she had done everything she could to facilitate his demise so she could benefit from his estate, not even by taking his own conduct into account could the court possibly consider hers anything but inequitable to disregard;

- *some violence* will be sufficient, depending on the frequency, nature and/or degree, especially if a weapon is used, such as in the cases of *Armstrong v Armstrong* (1974) 118 SJ 579 where the wife fired a gun at the husband, and *Bateman v Bateman* [1979] 2 WLR 377 where she stabbed the husband twice, and also especially if such conduct has financial consequences (as in the knife injuries to the wife which put an end to her nursing career and got the husband three years in jail in the 1975 case of *Jones*);

- *financial irresponsibility* will generally be sufficient because it is directly relevant to financial orders (especially where assets have been dissipated as in the cases of *Martin v Martin* [1976] 2 WLR 901, [1976] 3 All ER 625 where the whole £33,000 lost by the husband in a string of unsuccessful business ventures set up with his mistress was counted as his share of the assets that he had therefore already had, leaving the rest for his wife subject only to paying off his mortgage and giving him a small lump sum). Similarly, in the 1988 case of *Day v Day*, where the husband encouraged the wife to build up rent arrears so that money could be spend on other things this qualified as conduct: even less serious financial irresponsibility as in *Suter v Suter and Jones* (another case already mentioned elsewhere, where the court looked askance on the young wife inviting her lover to live in her home without asking him to contribute to the household budget) was capable of amounting to conduct within the meaning of the section;
- *misleading the court in financial matters*, especially deliberately, as in the cases of *Kyte* above, and *B v B* [1988] 2 FLR 490; this is always sufficient conduct, as well as separately qualifying as contempt of court;
- *alcoholism and laziness* if severe will in theory be relevant, again because of the direct effect on financial matters, but as in the case of *Martin* tend not to deprive the culprit entirely of financial relief for the simple reason that a home will still have to be provided for such a loser as happened in the case of *K v K* [1990] Fam Law 19, [1990] 2 FLR 225 where despite the husband's behaviour after being made redundant, as a result of which the matrimonial home had had to be sold, and which contrasted sharply with the wife's energy and industry which had resulted in a well paid job and a flat of her own, the court had to award him 60% of the proceeds of the home as this was the minimum he needed to rehouse himself; they did however, turn down his cheeky claim for maintenance from the wife!
- *leaving the blameless spouse/being the sole cause of the breakdown* may carry some weight but this will still tend to be reflected in the court's making an

order at the lower end of a scale instead of one which might have been at the higher end of a range rather than in distinctly downrating the award, and/or in the court's taking some care to try to see that the blameless spouse whose life has been disrupted is left as comfortable as possible. Nevertheless, in the relatively recent cases of *Robinson v Robinson* [1983] 2 WLR 146, [1983] 1 All ER 391 and *Ibbetson v Ibbetson* [1984] FLR 545 where the respondent wives could give no explanation for their actions their orders were reduced accordingly.

Note

Deliberately committing bigamy is conduct, and will preclude ancillary relief: *Whiston v Whiston* [1995] 3 WLR 405, [1995] 2 FLR 268, CA. Knowingly contracting an invalid marriage as a transsexual is in the same category: *J v S-T (formerly J)* (1996) *Times*, 25 November, CA.

Adultery alone is *never* sufficient although really repugnant sexual behaviour (as in the cases of *Bailey v Tolliday* (1983) 4 FLR 542 (where the wife had an affair with her father in law) and *Dixon v Dixon* [1974] 6 Fam Law 58 (where the husband committed adultery with his daughter in law in the matrimonial home) will be.

Moreover if the adultery is coupled with some other generally gratuitous and anti-social behaviour it will count as conduct, as happened in the case of *Cuzner v Underdown* [1974] 1 WLR 641, [1974] 2 All ER 357 where the wife conducted an adulterous affair during the marriage, said nothing about it when the husband generously transferred their home (to which she had contributed nothing) into joint names and then applied for an order for sale so as to raise money to set up house with her lover, of which the court took a poor view.

Moreover what used to be called 'living in sin' – cohabitation with a new partner after separation from the spouse – is certainly not conduct within the meaning of s 25(2)(g) even if as in the *Duxbury* case both parties had had affairs during the marriage as well, and even though in the case of *Atkinson v Atkinson* [1987] 3 All ER 849 such cohabitation following a decree absolute, but without remarriage, was found to be financially motivated. The most effect which such cohabitation will therefore have in financial terms is that the live-in lover will be expected to contribute to the ex-spouse's budget *if he can afford to do so* but in the case of Mrs Atkinson the court was not even able to make an order on the basis that some such contribution would be made, because Mrs Atkinson's new man was so financially ineffectual that the court had to decide she needed her continuing maintenance even more because she was cohabitation! Besides the fact that cohabitation created none of the ongoing obligations that a marriage would have, the cohabitee in question was a broken reed financially.

Good conduct is of course as relevant under s 25(2)(g) as bad conduct as the case of *Kokosinski* shows.

Note

Where there are allegations of conduct, transfer for hearing by a High court judge may be ordered: *Practice Direction* [1992] 3 All ER 151.

7.2.10

The value of any benefit lost on the dissolution of the marriage: s 25(2)(h)

This paragraph requires the court to consider the value of any such benefit lost – in the past this was usually, but not exclusively, pension rights – and to award compensation. If such compensation was impossible there might have a successful s 5 defence: see 3.1.2 or the applicant (if a respondent to a fact D petition) may be able to use s 10 to hold up decree absolute until financial provision is satisfactory: see 3.1.2.

This section can still cover any benefit which is lost on dissolution of the marriage, although pension rights, which can now also be dealt with under s 166 of the Pension Act 1995, have always been the most likely losses for consideration under this head. However, despite the 'earmarking' provisions of the Pensions Act, there may still be financial benefits lost if the husband retires early or dies as in the case of *Milne v Milne* [1981] 2 FLR 286 where the husband therefore had to pay the wife the anticipated sum involved immediately. Except in the few cases where pension rights can already be split, as in the case of company schemes (like that in *Brooks v Brooks* at 3.2.2) which can be varied under s 24, it is still incumbent on the solicitor to obtain an actuarial valuation of the pension and to seek a lump sum in compensation if earmarking pursuant to the new provisions is not suitable, since in such a case it may still be possible to achieve some compensation under this section. In any event the value of the pension rights must be considered under s 25B and the best recompense obtained for their value as well as for any other loss quantifiable under s 25(2)(h), such as in the case of *Trippas* where the court compelled the husband to pay the wife the share of the profits of the business in which she had been supportive, simply because he had promised she would eventually receive such a share.

Note

Until the sketchy provisions of the Family Law Act 1996 provide further assistance in securing for all divorced wives a proper share of pensions before they become payable on a former husband's retirement, the solicitor's duty in relation to obtaining actuarial valuation of pension rights and then seeking a substantial sum to represent their value (which may then be used to buy provision for the wife) will be the only way of realising the value of this potentially large matrimonial asset which may be more valuable these days than the matrimonial home. Otherwise, unless *Brooks v Brooks* applies, all that is available is 'earmarking' under s 25B–D which presupposes that the husband will have to live to draw the pension, before which the 'earmarked' share is not available to the ex-wife.

7.2.11 Suitable provision – open ended or nominal periodical payments versus the clean break: s 25A

Making use of the range of orders available under ss 23 and 24 of the MCA 1973 must always be subject to the provisions of s 25A, only formally inserted into the MCA by the Matrimonial and Family Proceedings Act 1984 but prior to that statute already a way of life in putting together ancillary relief packages. The only difference made by the statute was that prior to the insertion of s 25A the court could not actually *impose* a clean break unless the parties themselves were willing to have one: now, whenever they are making s 23 or s 24 orders, the court can and does, such power being given by ss 25A(1), (2) and (3) in the following manner:

- By s 25A(1) when exercising its powers under ss 23 or 24 '... it shall be the duty of the court to consider whether it would be appropriate so to exercise those powers that the financial obligations of each party towards the other should be terminated as soon after the grant of the decree as the court considers just and reasonable'.

This is the general duty of the court to *consider* a clean break in general terms in every case but *not* to impose one regardless unless that is suitable.

The importance of this point was emphasised in the case of *Clutton v Clutton* [1991] 1 All ER 340, CA, where a wife's clean break order was cancelled on appeal because it transferred the matrimonial home absolutely to her in return for cancelling her maintenance order, which the court thought unnecessary. First, it unjustly deprived the husband of his share of the matrimonial home acquired by their joint efforts and secondly that was in itself not even necessary since all that was required was an occupation order for the wife and the one child remaining at home, until she either remarried, cohabited or died. The court went on to say that if it was desired to achieve a clean break that could still be done, and much more fairly, by a *Martin* order, which would enable the house to be sold and the proceeds divided in the proportion of one third to the husband and two thirds to the wife, with the sale postponed until one of the triggering events occurred. As Lloyd LJ said, this solution, providing in effect 'a charge which does not take effect until death or remarriage which could only be said to offend against the principle of the clean break in the most extended sense of the term' is often an acceptable practical solution where a clean break is possible.

- By s 25A(2) when making any periodical payments orders under s 23 '... the court shall in particular consider whether it would be appropriate to require those payments to be made or secured only for such term as would in the opinion of the court be sufficient to enable the party in whose favour the order is made to adjust without undue hardship to the termination of his or her financial dependence on the other party'.

This is the section which requires the court to consider *limited term periodical payments*, though again to impose them only if appropriate, as part of an ancillary relief package.

- By s 25A(3) again when hearing any application for a periodical payments order under s 23 '... if the court considers that no continuing obligation should be imposed on either party to make or secure periodical payments in favour of the other, the court may dismiss the application with a direction that the applicant shall not be entitled to make any further application in relation to that marriage for an order under s 23(1)(a) or (b) above'.

This is the section which empowers the court not only either to dismiss an application for periodical payments outright instead of setting a limit on the period for which they should be paid under s 25A(2) but also to direct that no further application should be made, either at all, or to extend a limited term imposed under s 25A(2), and also to exclude future applications under the Inheritance (Provision for Families and Dependants) Act 1975.

Thus the three sub-sections give the court wide and flexible powers either to approve what the parties have agreed themselves or to impose suitable terms if the parties cannot agree.

Circumstances will dictate whether s 25A will be applicable at all and if so which precise type of order it will be most suitable to make. Orders may be made in the following forms:

- *open ended periodical payments orders* (ie an order for the amount of maintenance assessed as required by the payee, payable by periodical payments where the payee must apply to decrease or terminate the payments, or they continue indefinitely, at the rate originally ordered, unless or until the payer applies because of a change of circumstances to increase the amount originally ordered; this is sometimes called a *substantive*, as opposed to a *nominal* order, as to which see below);

- *nominal periodical payments orders* (ie an open ended order for a nominal *amount* of maintenance, usually 5p or £1 pa, which is meant only to indicate the payee's *continuing right* to maintenance, providing a long stop in case of future need for a substantive order, eg to protect the children if their mother loses her job, rather than actually to be needed as financial support at the time that the order is made, and which will continue in the same way as an ordinary open ended order unless terminated by the court);

Note

Nominal periodical payments must be distinguished from 'small' periodical payments, which used to have a technical meaning, being paid (when maintenance was not tax free in the hand of the recipient) gross and without deduction of tax. Nowadays if anyone mentions 'small' periodical payments (although they will manifestly be for a small amount, probably for the good reason that the payee is cash restricted for the time being, but it is thought right to collect some contribution on principle) they will be for something other than 'nominal', ie perhaps £10 per week, but not 5p a year. However 'small', these periodical payments are only a sub-species of open ended periodical payments if not specifically expressed in the accepted nominal format.

However *neither* open ended nor nominal periodical payments are compatible with a clean break because they continue the dependent financial link between the parties.

- *fixed term periodical payments* (ie the payer must apply to the court for variation under s 31 to extend the period of payment, *before* expiry, unless there has been a direction that this is not permitted, otherwise the payments end at the end of the fixed term originally ordered).

Note

This is the *only* type of periodical payments order which can co-exist with a clean break, because it only preserves the dependent financial links between the parties for a strictly limited period. This will remain the case even if that period is subsequently extended by the court, since if limited term periodical payments were thought suitable in the first place, such extension will not be granted lightly. Where limited term periodical payments are used there will be what is called a *deferred clean break*.

It will depend on all the circumstances of the case whether there should be open ended or nominal periodical payments (ie no clean break) or a clean break (ie no periodical payments at all for the weaker spouse, since periodical payments may still of course be paid to the *children* without affecting a clean break between the *parties*), but the important point for you to appreciate is which orders are *compatible* with a clean break and which are not, and then to decide whether or not a clean break is even feasible, which in turn will depend on whether the spouse who is financially weaker is capable of an independent financial existence without receiving regular maintenance from the other. Such independence may be achieved in a variety of ways: see 7.3.

Note

Lump sum order under s 23 can be made freely whether or not there is to be a clean break, since this a once for all payment, the only restriction being that only *one* lump sum order can be made per spouse, so if lump sums are required for various different purposes they must all be totted up and *one* global figure inserted into the order: see 7.1.2

7.3   Clean break options

As has already been seen in the case of *Suter v Suter* and Jones the existence of children does not necessarily preclude a clean break between the spouses, though a nominal order may be more suitable, as in the 1988 case of *Day v Day* already mentioned in another context. Generally there will be no clean break where there are children and the wife is unable or otherwise ill equipped to work, unless there is capital which could provide an alternative method of effecting a clean break, as in cases such as *Duxbury* where a sufficient sum of capital can be invested to provide an annual income that would otherwise have to be provided by the periodical payments which would preclude the desired clean break. There may be the same problem with older couples, where the wife's health and job prospects may be uncertain as in the case of *Scallon v Scallon* [1990] 1 FLR 193.

The clean break is therefore likely to be more suitable for short childless marriage cases or those where there is sufficient money to provide the wife with capital: see 7.3.3.

If however there is to be a clean break what is the most suitable way of dealing with a spouse's periodical payments orders? The two possibilities are:
- limited term periodical payments; or
- outright dismissal.

7.3.1   Fixed term periodical payments

Periodical payments on a temporary basis, but for a fixed term rather than an indefinite period, will be suitable where a spouse has or will have a recognisable earning capacity, and although unable to realise it immediately, eg because of domestic responsibilities, can reasonably certainly be expected to be able to do so within the foreseeable future. The type of case where this might apply would include that of the wife in *Mitchell v Mitchell* already mentioned (where the trained secretary could be expected to earn a good salary once her daughter, who was 13 at the time of the divorce, had left school), also any wife able to go back to work as soon as she has found a job using existing and recently used training and/or experience, such as the air hostess in *Attar v Attar* (although in her particular case as she had no children she received her two years' maintenance all at once in the capitalised form of a lump sum which will always be preferable to limited term maintenance if there are no children). Fixed term periodical payments would also suit any wife who embarks on a retraining course, or could be re-employed if she did (as in the case of Mrs Leadbeater, already mentioned above, who although 47 and out of touch with modern methods had been a secretary before the marriage) since in all such retraining cases there are reasonable prospects of obtaining a job without difficulty either at the end of the course or within a reasonable period afterwards.

Note

Sometimes the court expects the limited term to end as soon as children are at boarding school as in the cases of *Evans v Evans* [1990] 2 All ER 147 where the wife was already a trained secretary and *CB v CB* [1988] Fam Law 471 where the wife had capital of her own but no income and the court awarded limited term periodical payments only until the youngest child was 18 while she sorted out some other source of income. In both cases the order was made because the acrimony and bitterness with which the divorce was conducted obviously influenced the court in reaching a decision that a clean break was desirable as soon as possible! Sometimes the limited term will be staged as in *C v C* [1989] 1 FLR 11 where there was an order for £10,000 for two years, then £5000 for two years, then ending with dismissal of the payee spouse's claim.

The key to the use of limited term periodical payments is therefore *reasonable certainty*, about the payee's future plans and prospects of employment. Limited term periodical payments are thus *not* suitable for older wives who cannot be employed or re-employed and who cannot therefore be expected to adjust to the absence of maintenance even after a generous term to allow for gradual change. Examples of such cases are those of *Morris v Morris* [1985] FLR 1176 where the wife was already 56 and *M v M* [1987] 2 FLR 1 where the 47 year old wife had only worked part time during the marriage and having lost her husband's pension rights on divorce would have been too much at risk at the end of the limited term, while the husband remained secure on his pension, so it was accepted that no s 25A(2) order could be made.

Other cases where limited term maintenance under s 25A(2) will be no more suitable than an immediate clean break under s 25A(1) is where there are young children, as in *Suter v Suter and Jones*, or where there are children, an older wife *and* uncertainty about job prospects, which all came together in the case of *Barrett v Barrett* [1988] 2 FLR 516 where the wife was 44, without work experience and therefore of course also without a pension, and there were three children, including one still at home, after a 20 year marriage. In these case the right approach is that the husband should pay ordinary open ended periodical payments (and apply later to vary them if and when the wife gets work) or if she is willing to have a go at earning her own living that there should be a nominal order (which can then either be dismissed if she becomes independent or varied upwards to a substantive order if her attempts at financial independence fail).

Note

The court is cautious about limiting the right to apply for an extension of a limited term maintenance order and do not like to do it if there is any chance that an extension will be needed, as is shown by the case of *Waterman v Waterman* [1989] 1 FLR 380 where a wife with one young child appealed both against a five year limited term order following a short marriage of one year and against the restriction on applying to extend the five year term in appropriate circumstances. The court did in fact confirm the five year limited term but said there was no justification to exclude the wife's application to extend the limited term after the initial five years which she might need to do if circumstances changed. Thus it will only be in the clearest of cases that such a final cut off as excluding the right to apply to extend the limited term for good reason would be ordered.

7.3.2   Outright dismissal

This will only be suitable if the weaker spouse has a sufficient alternative source of income and does not need the transitional assistance of limited term maintenance. It will thus be suitable for wives who are going to remarry within a short period, wives who already earn a good income themselves, and wives who are to receive a capital settlement in lieu of any income orders, such as Mrs Duxbury, and will be especially suitable where there is plenty of capital such as in the case of *Gojkovic*.

Alternatively, outright dismissal may be suitable where the parties are on welfare benefits and nothing is to be gained by trying to work out (and regularly vary) what sums should be paid by one to the other when neither could really afford any lifestyle outside social security as in *Ashley v Blackman* [1988] 3 WLR 562, a courageous decision of Waite J who said that outright dismissal was the only solution 'to prevent a couple of acutely limited means from remaining manacled together indefinitely by the necessity of returning to court at regular intervals to thresh out at public expense the precise figure one should pay to the other, not for the benefit of either, but solely for the benefit of the tax paying section of the community to which neither of them had sufficient means to belong'. As the wife was mentally ill and living entirely off welfare benefits and the husband had remarried and had a wife and child to support, although he earned so little his income even fell below the lowest tax threshold, and the only reason for the application was to see if the DSS could recover some of the money they paid to the wife when her mainte-nance order was unpaid, this decision can only be classed as a victory for common sense over bureaucracy.

Such orders will also be suitable in any case where the court is dividing the assets fully and finally on divorce and is at the same time minded to make an order under s 25A(3) also, as in cases such as *Seaton v Seaton* [1986] 2 FLR 398 already mentioned above in connection with s 25(2)(e). In *Seaton* the quality of life of the severely disabled husband meant that there was no point in pre-serving his right to apply for maintenance from the wife because nothing she could pay him could improve it or improve on the existing financial security sufficient for his tiny needs which were already provided for by his living with his parents on a disability pension.

For the sake of completeness all possible applications for ancillary relief in all its forms should be made or be deemed to be made and be formally dismissed, includ-ing where appropriate an order made under s 25A(3) prohibiting a future application by either party against the estate of the other under the Inheritance (Provision for Family and Dependants) Act 1975.

When is a clean break likely?   7.3.3

Traditionally clean breaks are for short *childless marriages* and *older couples where the family has left home* and there are sufficient resources to provide each party with a home and to divide everything else without leaving the wife on social security in retirement.

However, a clean break must now be *considered* on every divorce although not necessarily *imposed* regardless if the circumstances are not suitable. Nevertheless, in every case the court likes to see the parties *working towards* a clean break even if that must be deferred. Wives of whatever social class, and of all ages except those nearing ordinary retirement age anyway, are therefore expected in principle either to work or if they come from a wealthy background where they have never been expected to work that there will be a clean break provided by the available capital. The policy is now *spousal self-sufficiency* and *not* the 'meal ticket for life'.

7.3.4   **Welfare hazards of the clean break**

A word of warning should be said about clean breaks, following the little noticed amendment to the social security legislation by the Social Security Act 1990 s 8 which amended the Social Security Act 1986 to make a spouse liable for the support of an ex-spouse even after decree absolute *if the ex-spouse is in receipt of welfare benefits*.

The effect of this is that if a clean break is achieved by an order for outright transfer of the matrimonial home to the wife in return for surrender of her right to periodical payments under whichever limb of s 25A, then there will be nothing to stop the Benefits Agency attempting to recover any benefits paid to the ex-spouse if that ex-spouse gets into financial difficulties and is obliged to claim them. This is a direct reversal of the previous position, where spouses could be *advised* to make such transfers as if the other spouse got into financial difficulties without periodical payments an application could always be made for social security payments. Now it will be unwise to achieve clean breaks by capital payment or property transfer unless the payee spouse is thought to be responsible and likely to be able to achieve financial independence without difficulties which might involve an application for welfare benefits. This is subject, of course, to the qualification that at no time will the Benefits Agency will be able to recover any money from a spouse who has not got any! Thus if such a husband were *himself* on benefits, or of very limited means, the Benefits Agency trying to recover money it has lent out will be out of luck!

The liability to pay maintenance to children under the Child Support Acts 1991 and 1995 must also be remembered, since whatever the parties agree between themselves, this ongoing liability will remain. Again if a wife applies to the CSA the husband will have to pay again subject to small relief introduced for capital payments in 1995.

Note

A clean break is possible *only* between spouses but *not* between parent and child, even if a lump sum is paid to the custodial parent on the understanding that that is in consideration of the payee parent assuming responsibility for maintenance of a child: *Crozier v Crozier* [1994] 1 FLR 126. While there are now rules which permit capital settlements to be taken into consideration by the CSA in computing the non-custodial parent's obligation to pay maintenance to a child, they are not particularly generous, and the only way of achieving the former situation where a custodial parent got the lion's share of the assets in return for assuming full responsibility for the children would be by means of an express trust. See further below at 7.5.2.

Calculating spouse maintenance   7.4

Quantum is always the most difficult part of assembling any ancillary relief package, whether in a capital or income context.

Maintenance for the spouse and maintenance for the children are two completely different and separate calculations which must be made independently of each other. However they will naturally have a knock on effect each on the other, except in cases where the parties' means are not limited.

The old method used to be to work out maintenance for the spouse, including what might be called the 'roof element' of the general household expenses and then to tack on something for each child according to their ages, finally making an order for £x p.a. for the spouse (which would be the larger of the two figures) and £y (which would often be a miniature amount for food and clothes) for each of the children. The advent of the Child Support Agency has meant that this can no longer be done if the family is cash limited, as the Agency's calculation allows for no discretion and will provide a computer generated figure when the carer spouse applies for an assessment (out of which eventuality it is not possible to contract) so that the amount which will have to be paid to the children now needs to be calculated *first* so it is ascertained what will be left to give to the spouse. You will find that most firms (and many counsel at the Family Law Bar) now use specialist software to produce these calculations swiftly and painlessly so it is worth finding out this extremely relevant figure as soon as possible before trying to calculate fair spouse maintenance. This exercise is often an incentive to a clean break where the spouse will not receive maintenance at all!

Spouses from wealthy families will have their maintenance based on *reasonable needs* so a budget will need to be prepared for the spouse to ascertain what those are and the order tailored accordingly.

Spouses from middle and low income families will need to have their maintenance measured against the yardstick of one of the long accepted guidelines namely the:

- net effect calculation; or
- one-third rule.

7.4.1   The net effect calculation

Irrespective of which guideline is used a net effect calculation is good practice to check the feasibility of the orders to be made and most district judges will want one so they can see how the proposed orders will work out for each party. However this will be essential for the poor family where every penny counts, as for such a family the so called one third rule (which is only a starting point anyway: see below at 7.4.2) will be hopelessly in appropriate.

The net effect calculation is achieved by taking either an existing order or an offer by either party, establishing the *net effect* of the proposal by calculating the parties' *respective spendable incomes* net of:

- tax, national insurance, pension contributions` and work expenses (ie travel);
- reasonable mortgage rent and council tax;
- proposed maintenance;

which will give the parties' net resources and then calculating each party's actual needs, ie reasonable expenses for:

- food, clothing etc;
- gas, electricity, telephone, TV etc.

This will show whether the proposed maintenance is the correct figure and if it fails to meet either of the party's actual needs then it must be adjusted accordingly until it produces a fair result.

These methods were pioneered as long ago as the cases of *Furniss v Furniss* (1982) 3 FLR 46 and *Stockford v Stockford* (1982) 3 FLR 52 which attacked the then favoured one-third rule on the basis that the net effect calculation suited low income families better because it enabled the court to see precisely what each side would have to spend.

Note

In *low income* cases welfare benefits may have to be a resource as in the case of *Delaney* already mentioned in the context of resources for the purposes of s 25(2)(a) at 7.2.2 above, and it is in many low income cases that the CSA's prior claims may mean that the paying spouse cannot afford to pay any spouse maintenance at all and the clean break or nominal payments, whichever is appropriate to the particular case, will beckon as the only alternative.

The court has a *subsistence level approach* to orders in low income families. It will obviously not make an order which depresses the payer below subsistence level as this would be pointless: see the case of *Allen v Allen* [1986] 2 FLR 265, although the relevant level which may be that which the Benefits Agency permits before requiring a contribution from a liable relative: see Chapter 13, is in fact slightly more generous since it preserves 15% of the liable relative's earnings above income support and allied benefit rates before contribution is required.

The one-third rule   7.4.2

This 'rule' had its origins in the idea that one third was the right proportion of assets to give to the wife since the husband would usually also maintain the children separately, pay school fees where incurred and also build up a pension out of which the wife, in the days of the 'meal ticket for life' philosophy of ongoing maintenance would continue to be maintained when he had retired In fact it is, especially nowadays, a so called rule which has always been regarded as a *guide* rather than a rule as such: this is because, having no law of matrimonial property as such, English law has always proceeded on the basis of the *wife's reasonable needs balanced against the husband's ability to pay* rather than on any proportional share of assets being awarded on divorce. Thus the 'rule' has now probably passed its heyday, increasingly so since the net effect calculation has proved in practice so much more useful for rich and poor alike. Occasionally cases crop up however in which the judge says that it is still a useful starting point, particularly in middle income cases where it may be a fair guide as to what is right to order as in the case of *Slater v Slater* (1982) 3 FLR 58 and

Bullock v Bullock [1986] 1 FLR 372 where one-third of the husband's assets was ordered and the judge noted that although had not always recently been followed it had never actually be disapproved, and was still a useful starting point, even if quantum was subsequently adjusted for other matters which had to be taken into account.

The cases mentioned at 7.4.1 indicate how it does not suit the poor. The case of *Preston* already mentioned shows how it may not suit a wealthy family either because of the principle of *needs*: Mrs Preston wanted £770,000 out of her husband's net assets of £2.3m, but only got £600,000, enough to buy a suitable house and to give her the right income to maintain herself in it.

The case of *B v B* [1988] 2 FLR 490, already mentioned in the context of failing to make adequate disclosure to the court, which tends to be regarded as obstructing a spouse in the pursuit of just remedies as well as contempt, also shows that a one-third approach will not be regarded as appropriate where the marriage is short.

Even if the rule still exists, as it may do, for income calculations, cases like *Preston* which emphasised the principle of the wife's reasonable needs and *Potter v Potter* [1982] 4 FLR 331, [1982} 3 All ER 321, where the husband had a small one man photographic business worth only £60,000 and the wife's capital award was reduced on appeal from £23,000 to £10,000, show that it is not appropriate for capital calculations, especially where any capital order must take into account the principle of not threatening the viability of a business. This was underlined in the case of *Dew v Dew* [1986] 2 FLR 341 where considerations of preserving the husband's business and focus on the wife's reasonable needs resulted in an order of only £135,000 where the wife's notional entitlement if the one third rule was applied was £350,000.

Note

To make a one-third calculation, add together the parties' joint incomes less the expenses of earning them, divide by three, subtract the applicant's existing income from the one third figure arrived at, and the resultant figure is the amount which the spouse with the lesser income can claim from the better resourced spouse. Of course if the potential applicant already has more than one third of the joint incomes, an application is ruled out unless it can be justified on the completely separate basis of *reasonable needs balanced against the other spouse's ability to pay.*

Child maintenance   7.5

Maintenance for children has to some extent been taken out of the hands of the courts by the Child Support Act 1991 (CSA 1991) which set up the Child Support Agency (CSA), a new system designed progressively to take over the assessment and enforcement of child maintenance except in the few cases where the court still has jurisdiction. The Agency started work in 1993 immediately after the Act came into force on 5 April of that year, and has at first dealt with new cases only, but it was intended ultimately that it would also deal with variations of existing orders after 1997. However, it looks as though this is not indefinitely postponed, although the 1991 Act has already been refined by the Child Support Act 1995 and by a steady stream of regulations.

The court has therefore in most non-exceptional cases lost its jurisdiction to make orders for children in contested proceedings: CSA 1991 ss 8(1) and 8(3) though it retains a power to revoke a maintenance order: s 8(4) and can vary a pre-1993 maintenance order under s 31 of the MCA 1973 or a pre-1993 maintenance agreement under s 35 of the MCA. Children whose maintenance orders may still be assessed by the court are all children of the family:

- up to the age of 16 (or 19 if remaining in full time non-advanced education after the school leaving age) whose custodial parent (called the 'carer' in CSA parlance) already receives the maximum amount assessable by the CSA but require further periodical payments sometimes called 'topping up' cases: CSA 1991 s 8(6). This may be specifically for school fees see s 8(7) or where extra expenses are caused by a disability s 8(8).

Where the order sought is to be made against the carer parent and not the absent parent all children of the family: s 8(10):

- over the age of 19;
- for whom lump sum or property transfer or settlement orders are sought;
- one or both of whose parents is not habitually resident in the United Kingdom;
- where an application for their maintenance was pending before 5 April 1993; and
- those children of the family whose absent natural parent cannot be assessed by the CSA to pay maintenance for whatever reasons, eg that parent has died or disappeared, so that an application is necessary against a *step parent*.

Such orders can either be made for children under ss 23 and 24 of the MCA 1973 (though transfer of property orders for children are rare) or under ss 2, 6 or 7 of the Domestic Proceedings and Magistrates' Courts Act 1978, although if the child orders are sought in ancillary relief proceedings MCA orders are most likely.

However, *agreed orders* can still be made in the transitional period (up to 1997 or later, when and if variations are taken over by the CSA) and this can be done by the court in relation to *all* children of the family, even those in respect of whom an assessment could be made by the CSA, if the order is incorporated into a consent order and is pursuant to an agreement in writing made between the parents. BUT this will not preclude an application being made at any time to the CSA for a CSA assessment to be made as any such attempted restriction is void: CSA 1991 s 9(4). In particular, if a party goes on to benefits, it will be mandatory for the CSA to make an assessment even if a there is a court order in force at the time. For this reason when drafting consent orders it is usual to include a recital to the effect that if such an assessment is made, the amount payable under the consent order shall be reduced by the amount of the CSA assessment, so that the payer is not legally obliged to pay twice or to incur the expense of applying to the court to have the consent order varied.

Should you need to work on a CSA case requiring an extensive knowledge of the detailed provisions of the Acts of 1991 and 1995 and the numerous Statutory Instruments making regulations under them, it will be necessary to refer to a specialist text, but the following may be found particularly helpful:

- Child Support Act 1991 (Commencement No 3 and Transitional Provisions) Order 1992 SI 1992 No 2644;
- Child Support Act (Commencement No 3 and Transitional Provisions) Amendment Order (SI 1992 No 966);
- Child Maintenance (Written Agreements) Order 1993 (SI 1993 No 620).

Note

As will be seen below at 7.5.4 the CSA assessment is not usually as advantageous to the payer as an agreed order which is part of a package embodied in a consent order, and the negotiated package will probably also be more advantageous overall to the payee than relying on strict CSA rights in respect of the children, so the trend is for both parties still to attempt to negotiate the ancillary relief package as a whole and only to have recourse to the CSA where essential.

However, some carers have wanted to obtain a CSA assessment in lieu of existing orders in which case it is necessary up to 1997 (unless the carer is on state benefits) to apply under CSA 1991 s 8(4) to revoke the order (because by s 8(5) and the transitional provisions the CSA cannot make an assessment if there is in force an existing order or maintenance agreement, either of which could be varied) although the court might not in fact agree to revoke such an order to facilitate a CSA assessment, because (since the CSA assessments are notoriously higher than the court's usual orders and are also completely no-discretionary and inflexible) the judge might feel that if the payer had to meet a CSA assessment it would make continued contact with the child less affordable (a consequence which has resulted in many such cases).

The court therefore weighs up all the relevant facts in the interests of the child, and may insist on varying the order itself rather than revoking it to facilitate a CSA application. In the case of *B v M* [1994] 1 FLR 342 such a revocation order was made at first instance and overturned on appeal, because the judge said that the proper course was an application for an upward variation of the order and not a revocation to permit a CSA assessment to take place.

Calculating child maintenance   7.5.1

In any case where the court is to make a consent order based on the parents' agreement and excluding the CSA's involvement, the order is still likely to be for periodical payments in the ball park area of what the CSA would have assessed, less the extra element added in by the CSA for child care which is the element which payers tend to dislike, since it amounts to indirect maintenance for the custodial parent.

Where the court is to *assess the quantum* of the order (rather than merely to embody the parents' agreement into a consent order) which of course will only be in any case where they still have jurisdiction, they must look at s 25(3) of the MCA 1973 which requires those s 25 considerations which are relevant to children to be taken into account in exactly the same way as when working out financial provision for spouses. This means they must take into account, or example, a child's:

- earning capacity (eg of child models, actors and film stars);

- property (including any income derived from it);
- needs; and
- any physical or mental disability.

By s 25(3)(d) the court must take into account how it was envisaged by the parents that the child was to be educated or trained, as in the case of *O'Donnell* already mentioned where the children already went to boarding school so the husband was ordered to continue to pay the fees, and the case of *Sibley v Sibley* (1979) 10 Fam Law 49 where the parties had envisaged a fee paying school so the husband was also ordered to pay the fees because that was what the parties had planned.

By s 25(4) the court must consider whether, in the case of an application for a step child, the step parent against whom the order is sought had assumed responsibility for the child's maintenance and if so to what extent and for how long, whether that stepparent did so knowing that the child was another person's and also the liability of any other person to maintain that child. The 1988 case of *Day v Day*, is a classic example of this situation as the court had no difficulty in deciding that the step father had clearly understood his commitment to the wife and her two children and as their natural fathers made no contribution, on the breakdown of the marriage he was obliged to support them as well as the wife, even though the marriage had been short.

Note
___

Financial provision orders under s 23 (though not transfer or settlement of property orders under s 24) can be made for children even though the *petition itself is dismissed*: s 23(2).

___

7.5.2   The Child Support Act 1991

You will first need to learn the language of the statute. The *dramatis personae* goes as follows:
- the *qualifying child* (the child who needs the maintenance) who is a child one or both of whose parents is in relation to him *absent*: s 3(1);

Note
___

An adopted child or a child born by artificial insemination by a donor is included as a qualifying child unless in the latter case the husband is proved not to have consented to the treatment: Human Fertilisation and Embryology act 1990, s 28(2). But a child who is or ever has been married is excluded from the operation of the CSA 1991: s 55(2).

___

- the *absent parent* (any parent who is not living with the child where the child has a home with someone else who has care of that child) and for the pursuit of whom the CSA was created: s 3(2);
- the *person with care* (the person with whom the child has a home who provides day to day care for that child, whether exclusively or in conjunction with any other person) sometimes also called the *carer parents*: s 3(3).

Note

The local authority does not appear anywhere in this cast of actors as the Children Act 1989 provides alternative means of their recovering the cost of caring for children when appropriate.

The CSA operates on the basis of the statutory duty to maintain a qualifying child which is set out in the CSA 1991 s 1(1) and makes each parent equally responsible, but by s 1(3) it is the absent parent who has the duty of making the payments under a CSA assessment. They then use a computer based formula to make assessments as to the operation of which see 7.5.4.

The CSA and benefit cases

Where a carer parent is in receipt of state benefits it is a requirement that the Secretary of State be authorised to take action to recover the amount paid out to the child in maintenance from the absent parent: CSA 1991 s 6(1) and by s 46 benefit may be reduced if cooperation is not forthcoming from the carer parent either in refusing authorisation or in refusing essential information, ie the identity of the natural father to pursue. However, in an appropriate case the carer parent can decline to do this without losing benefit, being given first an opportunity to explain her views and secondly possibly the benefit of the child support officer's discretion in deciding not to reduce her benefit if it can be shown that there would be adverse consequences of some kind or another since the officer must have regard to 'the welfare of any child likely to be affected by his decision': CSA 1991 s 2.

Review of assessments

There is provision for review of assessments every two years: CSA 1991 s 16 as amended and either absent parent or carer can apply at any time for a review if there has been a change of circumstances: s 17.

Note

Although there is no room for discretion in making assessments and if the figures fed in are right the result should also be correct, any assessment which is thought to be *wrong* should be appealed within 28 days, and further appeal is possible to the Child Support Appeal Tribunal, then to the Child Support Appeal Commissioner on point of law, and subsequently to the court of Appeal and House of Lords in the normal way: Child Support Appeal Tribunals (Procedure) Regulations 1992 (SI 1992/2641).

Collection and enforcement are also provided for by the Act and ultimately the CSA will take over the assessment, enforcement and collection of all child maintenance. The usual methods of enforcement can be used, but additionally including the administrative procedure of a deduction of earnings order for which no court order is needed and liability orders obtainable from the magistrates. Interest is available on arrears in excess of 28 days old.

The effect of clean break settlements

The Child Support and Income Support (Amendment) Regulations (SI 1995/1045) have since April 1995 enabled past capital settlements to be taken into account but, although these provide some relief where before there was none, the effect is hardly dramatic. The maximum deduction is £60 per week if the value of the transfer made under the capital settlement exceeds £25,000, and if it was less than £5000 it does not count at all! Up to £10,000 the absent parent gets £20 per week off maintenance and up to £25,000 it is £40 per week.

The capital settlement must have been made by court order or written agreement prior to 5 April 1993 (ie when the Act came into force), and must otherwise have satisfied the normal conditions of a clean break capital settlement, ie while the parties were separated (though divorce is not necessary) an outright transfer of property or payment of capital must have been made by the absent parent to the carer in circumstances other than to buy out the carer parent's share of an asset.

While this may be some help for people caught up in the maelstrom behind earlier settlements before the CSA was even a twinkle in the government's eye, this is a further incentive to contemporary parties to clean break settlements to take warning and attempt to deal with matters in a manner which benefits the family overall by agreement while they still can.

The parties affected by the legislation   7.5.3

The Child Support Acts affect all absent natural parents of qualifying children, whether they were ever married to the mother of the child or not.

The assessment formula – how maintenance is assessed   7.5.4

Both parents complete detailed forms to give the agency full information about their financial position. Maintenance is then assessed, not on the basis of any discretion, but by applying a rigid computer based formula which is aimed to achieve consistency in assessments and to provide a realistic sum which recognises the true costs of child caring and rearing, which the old court assessed orders, usually tacked on to a substantive order for the custodial parent, did not particularly in cases where the custodial parent was no longer being maintained, eg because of remarriage, under the former system the child would be left with an uneconomic order frequently too low actually to provide food and clothing let alone contribute to the cost of keeping a roof over its head. If the CSA assessments have done anything, they have thus helped remarried parents and step parents since the natural father will usually have to pay something closer to the true cost of bringing up the child, which should remove some financial strain from step parents and also from step parents' first families who often suffered under the former system.

The formula for calculating the child's maintenance is complicated. and is related to other social security benefits, mainly income support (for a general explanation of which see Chapter 13 below). The formula has four parts:

- *the maintenance requirement*: the income support level for the child + an allowance for the carer – child benefit (but not minus one parent benefit);

Note _____

This is the element of CSA assessments which annoys some absent parents as they then indirectly have to maintain the child's carer, usually the mother, through the carer's personal allowance, which is annoying where the father does not want to maintain the mother anyway, because, eg there is a clean break, but as it applies even where the parties were not married and there was never any obligation to maintain the mother as such, that category of absent father gets even crosser at having to pay through the CSA! (Moral: an agreed solution usually *is* better.)

- *the assessable income of each parent*: this is the net income of each parent after deducting income tax, national insurance, travel expenses to work and half pension contributions, *less* the parent's *exempt income* for basic living expenses at income support rates, though anyone on income support is treated as having no assessable income: CSA 1991 Schedule 1;

Note

The *actual* living expenses are irrelevant as those taken into account will be based on the income support formula and this is another item which makes absent parents crosser than the average hornet as even if they are, eg buying a car or a TV on hire purchase for the ex-spouse and child the regular payments do not count! If the mother and child *want* such a car or a TV this will therefore be another incentive to contract out of the CSA assessment.

- *the basic deduction rate*: this means the two parents' total assessable income is divided by two and if the resulting figure is equal to or less than the maintenance requirement above then each parent is liable to pay half their assessable income for the children;

Note

Where the absent parent is on income support that parent will still have to pay a minimum amount per week out of the income support received unless that absent parent is living with other children and already receiving family premium or comes into other specified exceptional categories. Thus even absent parents on income support have to pay *something nominal* which is probably a good thing and perhaps generates some awareness of responsibility towards children.

- *the additional element*: this is where the assessable income is more than the amount needed to satisfy the maintenance requirement above and enables those absent parents with more money to pay more maintenance, the maximum amount of which was halved in April 1995 due to complaints from absent parents that this took away further sums from their incomes which they could not spare! There is also a protected income level which is applied to prevent the absent parent from falling below subsistence level.

The timetable to 1997

The CSA was scheduled to take over all assessment, variation, collection and enforcement of child maintenance for qualifying children by 1997 but this appears to have been indefinitely postponed.

Self-assessment questions

1 What is the ideal of spousal self-sufficiency?
2 What are nominal periodical payments for? How do they differ from small maintenance payments?
3 What income orders are compatible with a clean break?
4 What capital orders are compatible with a clean break?
5 What is quantum in relation to ancillary relief and how is it calculated for income and capital payments respectively?
6 What is the so called one third rule and when may it still be useful?
7 What welfare hazards are there in a clean break?
8 What children can still have their maintenance assessed by a court?
9 Are there any advantages of avoiding assessment of child maintenance by the CSA?
10 What is an ancillary relief package and how do you put it together?

Chapter 8

The matrimonial home

The policy of homes for all   8.1

The fate of the matrimonial home will usually be the linchpin of any ancillary relief package: whether it is to be sold, transferred outright to one party or made the subject of a deferred settlement will have a profound effect on the remainder of the package.

The fate of the matrimonial home may well be decided at the outset by the court's duty under s 25(1) to give first consideration to the welfare of the minor children of the family or there may be considerable choice as to the precise manner in which the parties' assets should be distributed, but whichever is the case you will usually find it easier to put the package together if a decision is reached *first* about the home, especially as, with the possible exception of the husband's pension rights, the home will usually be the parties' most valuable asset.

Thus the home is probably the most important ingredient of whatever financial mix is to be proposed since it will usually be not only the most valuable asset but also potentially either a roof for one of the parties or the source of two new post-divorce homes. Only rarely is there so much money available that the destination of the home is completely irrelevant.

Quite apart from its duty to the children under s 25(1), the court operates a policy of 'homes for all' and any order will be driven by the principle that each party must have a home, so that an order that leaves one of the parties potentially homeless is unacceptable.

Nevertheless, the requirement of s 25(1) that while giving first priority to the welfare of the children, the court must consider 'all the circumstances of the case' does create a potentially insoluble problem for the court, in that it is usually trying to achieve at least three often inconsistent and mutually exclusive aims, namely to:

- maintain a residence for the minor children and the custodial parent;
- provide a home for each party;
- divide the family assets fairly, especially the matrimonial home.

Thus, in addition to looking for guidance in the detail of the various s 25 factors in order to obtain a general picture of each party's overall claims on what resources there are, recourse must also be had to the various well tried home disposal packages which have been put together in cases which have come before the court for consideration in the past. These packages tend to go by the name of the case in which that particular method of dealing with the matter was first used, such as the well known *Mesher* and *Martin* orders, but if you are unsure which precise variety to select you should remember that these precedents are meant to be a *useful tool* and *not* a shackle: none of the orders necessarily has to be adopted in total and unchanged, since the case on which you are working, whether in class, in the examination room or ultimately in practice, is *not* the same case as that of the *Mesher* or *Martin* family. Whatever order is ultimately drafted for your case will only be *generically a Mesher* etc order, but will in fact be *individually drafted* for the case in question. Thus if the name of the family in the case is Smith, and the trainee's ingenuity produces a useful variant of a *Mesher* order, that particular precedent may be filed away in the firm's library as a precedent for a *Smith* order (and if it is ingenious enough may even become more widely known in the profession under that tag).

You should not therefore be afraid to innovate where nothing suitable has yet been used for a particular situation: providing the components of the order proposed are not mutually exclusive (eg you will not be using any form of ongoing periodical payments for a spouse where a clean break is desired, but in that case must choose limited term periodical payments) good drafting will be able to effect any sensible package they care to propose.

8.2   Order of priorities and alternatives

Because of the welfare of the minor children which by s 25(1) must be given first consideration, the first priority will be to see how they and the parent with care of them can best be housed, then to see how the other parent can be housed and only then to check on the fairest way to divide actual *ownership* of such assets as there are.

Thus, the *first* priority will be to arrange matters on an *occupational* basis, for the moment disregarding questions of ownership. The *second* will be to consider ownership and property rights quite separately, and by s 24 whatever changes of ownership need to be made can be effected by the court at will, so who owns the various assets (including the matrimonial home) is of less importance than what the court wants to do with that asset. Unlike in strict property law, the approach here is not *whose is this?* but *to whom should this be given?*

Priorities are therefore likely to be approached in the same order as the court's competing aims, namely:
- where are the children and the custodial spouse going to *live*?
- where is the other spouse going to *live*?
- what is to be done about *ownership* of the home?

This leaves three possible alternative fates for the matrimonial home:
- immediate sale and division of the proceeds;
- outright transfer to one party;
- a trust for sale.

Each needs to be looked at in more detail.

Immediate sale and division of the net proceeds (often, but not necessarily, in equal proportions): s 24A

8.2.1

Obviously, the parties can always agree to sell the house, but sometimes the court will order it even if the parties are not agreed. This is suitable for three situations, where there is:
- sufficient equity in the home;
- enough equity to make a sale worthwhile but one party already has alternative accommodation;
- no significant equity in the home and neither party, nor even really both of them together, can afford the home at all.

Thus the court may *order* a sale in three typical cases:

(1) Where there is sufficient equity in the home (with or without the aid of a mortgage) to buy two new homes, one for each party, including *suitable* accommodation for the parent who will have the children to house, but as this does have a disruptive effective on the children and possibly on their schooling if a move of area and school is also involved as it sometimes may have to be, the court might be dissuaded from *ordering* a such a sale if the carer parent does not want it.

(2) Where there is enough equity to make a sale worthwhile but one party already has alternative accommodation, eg where one spouse has already moved in with a new partner who has secure accommodation. Immediate sale can then raise some essential capital for both parties, which can be used by the spouse without accommodation to buy a new property and by the one who already

has accommodation either to upgrade that accommodation or for some completely unrelated purpose – eg if a new family is to be started but this has not yet happened the funds realised can be simply taken as that party's share of the assets and invested until they are required, the point being that that spouse will have had some proper share of the housing capital. In these circumstances the court is likely to *order* sale, unless there are children to be housed, as in (1) above.

Note

If in the end this share of the housing capital money is never needed for housing there is nothing to stop that spouse from using it to go on a world cruise – the money is the spouse's share of the sale proceeds of the matrimonial home and no obligation to use it in any way, nor any form of trust express or implied, is to be imposed on the award.

(3) Where there is *no significant equity* in the home and neither party, nor even really both of them together, can afford the home at all. This is the type of marriage which breaks up over financial pressures and the best course will usually be to sell the home and divide the tiny proceeds, putting both parties into rented accommodation. Sometimes one or both parties can return to live with parents, even the custodial parent where there is a child or children, if a contribution is made by that parent to the household expenses and in the recent bout of unemployment and mortgage problems this has often been the solution. In these circumstances the court is practically certain to order a sale.

8.2.2   Outright transfer to one party: s 24

This is suitable as part of a clean break or where one spouse must receive a transfer as the only means of security which the court can award, as in the case of *Bryant v Bryant* (1976) 6 Fam Law 108, (1976) 120 SJ 165, where the husband was a disaster: he had paid neither maintenance nor the mortgage on time, had assaulted the wife and been found guilty of persistent cruelty and had three times been to prison for contempt for disobeying court orders. The court said they could never see him supporting the wife and children and the only way to protect them was to give the wife his half share of the house.

An outright transfer can be effected in three ways:
• on immediate payment of a cash sum by the transferee to compensate the other spouse for losing their interest in the home, or in other words

a 'buy out' as in the case of *Wachtel* already mentioned in other contexts, although the mania for
dubbing the various orders with the names of the
cases in which they were first noted has not for
some reason extended to this being habitually
known as a *Wachtel* order!

• in return for a charge over the home either for a
fixed sum or for a percentage of the sale proceeds
either at a fixed date or upon a certain event or
when the transferee chooses to sell (and since in
the latter case this choice may *never* be made it
may mean that the charge is not enforceable until
the transferee's death);

• with *no* cash payment and *no* charge, but in return
for some other benefit which will accrue to the
spouse losing their interest in the property, such
as the transferee foregoing periodical payments:
this is a *Hanlon* order.

Any *Hanlon* order must be effected *at the time that the
order is first made*, since property adjustment orders
under s 24 *cannot be varied* later under s 31: see Chapter
10. This caused a problem in the case of *Carson v Carson*
[1983] 1 WLR 285, [1983] 1 All ER 478 where the wife had
a *Mesher* order incorporating periodical payments for
herself. Later she ran into financial difficulties and
wanted the order changed to an outright transfer of the
husband's share of the home in return for surrender of
her periodical payments. Of course the court could not
accede to her request (although an ingenious way has
since been found round the difficulty: see 10.3).

A *Mesher* order cannot even be changed into a *Martin*
order as the wife tried to get the court to do in *Dinch v
Dinch* [1987] 1 WLR 252, [1987] 1 All ER 818 where she
applied to the court when the youngest child reached 17
because the husband had become voluntarily redundant,
had stopped paying periodical payments or his share of
the mortgage and as a result she had got into financial
difficulties. She wanted a postponement of the sale, a
lump sum and a further transfer of property order. The
Court of Appeal tried to help by changing the *Mesher* to
a *Martin* order so she at least need not sell the house till
she chose but the husband appealed to the House of
Lords who agreed with him that the Court of Appeal had
not power to change the format of the order, although
they realised that this left the wife in a very difficult position. In the earlier case of *Dunford v Dunford* [1980] 1 All

ER 122 the court saw the problem coming and immediately changed the initial *Mesher* on appeal to an outright transfer.

Note

It always used to be recommended that any deferred charge should be for a *proportion* of the sale proceeds, in order, when house prices rose dramatically from year to year, to protect the value of the share which the spouse out of occupation would ultimately receive, as in the case of *Browne v Pritchard* [1975] 1 WLR 1366.

However, now that inflation is so low and if houses must be sold they even sometimes sell at a loss, it may be better to arrange for a *fixed sum* to be paid, as in the case of *Hector v Hector* [1973] 1 WLR 1122, rather than that a proportion of the proceeds should be payable, especially as for tax purposes this will count as a debt and not as a share of the sale proceeds on which CGT might be levied if the sale takes place (as it usually will) outside the period during which an owner out of occupation must sell in order even to claim the main residence exemption even under the extra statutory concession D6 (see Chapter 12 at 12.4).

When a deferred charge is the right solution, a *Browne v Pritchard* (proportionate proceeds) or *Hector v Hector* (fixed sum) order can conveniently also be combined with *limited term periodical payments* to produce a deferred clean break under s 25A(2).

8.2.3   A trust for sale: s 24

This is the method of effecting a *Mesher* order and also all the variants, including the *Martin* and *Harvey* orders, with which the catalogue of name-tagged orders which the trainee is likely to meet in most training contracts may finally be regarded as complete, although it is fair to say that a *Harvey* order may sometimes also be referred to as a *Brown* order after the case of *Brown v Brown* (1982) 3 FLR 161 in which a somewhat similar order was made!

Where any of these settlement orders are made, the order may also provide for the payment of the outgoings, whether of the mortgage only or also of others such as repairs, insurance, utilities etc precisely as it seems fair to the parties and their advisers that these should be paid by one party or the other or both equally or unequally.

Note

When the Trusts of Land and Appointment of Trustees Act 1996 comes into force the 'trust for sale' as such will no longer exist as a separate institution, as all trusts will be 'trusts of land'. You should consult a specialist book on trusts for the changes made by the Act. Basically, 'trusts for sale' becomes 'trusts of land' and the range of deferred sale orders remains available for settlement of the home where appropriate.

Mesher orders

The *Mesher* is suitable where children and the custodial parent need to be housed until the children are independent and the order vests the matrimonial home in both spouses on trust for sale, giving a right of occupation to the custodial parent *either* until the children reach independence (which will in some cases be when the youngest child is 17 *or* where appropriate when the youngest finishes full time education or training), upon which event the house is to be sold and the proceeds divided in an appropriate ratio, such division of the proceeds being decided by the court at the time the order for settlement is made.

Note

The parties may *already* be trustees for sale of the matrimonial home, as joint tenants in law and in equity (since joint ownership of their home is now the norm rather than the exception in the case of most couples) so it will only be necessary for the order to vest the home in the parties as trustees for sale if one was formerly the sole legal owner. However, if the parties are already trustees for sale, the order will then direct that the home *remain vested* in the joint names of the parties, and then go on to declare new trusts (since of course the standard trusts under the former joint ownership would usually merely have been that the parties should hold the property on trust for themselves beneficially, which is no longer appropriate once a Mesher is to be imposed giving sole occupation to one spouse for a period and then declaring the ultimate interests in the proceeds of sale).

However, the order is only suitable where the proceeds of sale will be sufficient to rehouse the occupying spouse on sale and the spouse out of occupation has somewhere else to live.

Note

A *Mesher* order is final and cannot be varied so as, eg to postpone the date of sale. For this reason the circumstances need to be thought through very carefully, and while the order was first greeted with great enthusiasm as a solution to the problem of otherwise having to sell the house and disrupt the children's lives, it was quickly realised that it only stored up trouble for the future in a number of cases. This was because in the late seventies and early eighties house prices were unstable and many victims of the *Mesher* found that when they came to sell there was not enough money to rehouse the occupying spouse and yet the order could not be varied, so other methods had to be found to deal with the situation: see below Chapter 10.

Further, following the introduction of s 25A in 1984, the then latest fashion was for the clean break, with which the *Mesher* is incompatible. However, following the property market collapse at the end of the eighties *Meshers* came back into fashion, more or less by default since houses which were not actually repossessed for negative equity were often actually *unsaleable* so that a *Mesher* was the *only* solution. At the present time, with inflation at its lowest for many years, *Meshers* are not only favoured but values (especially of older houses) so stable that consideration may be given to awarding the spouse out of occupation a fixed sum rather than a proportion of the sale proceeds. However, in the event that a Labour government comes to power this last point may have to be reviewed since fixed mortgage rates currently on offer obviously contemplate a return to inflation which will of course be reflected in house prices. These practical considerations are of course at the very heart of a solicitor's advice on property division following marriage breakdown and every trainee intending to practise in family law therefore needs to be fully abreast of current economic affairs as they will affect the ordinary family.

Martin orders

A *Martin* order differs from a *Mesher* in that while the settlement is the same the period of occupation is *not* linked to the children in any way, and indeed there may be a *Martin* order where there are *no* children, as in the original case, provided the only other essential requirement (that the other spouse has secure alternative accommodation) is met: Mr Martin had a council flat, and although the Martins had no children, Mrs Martin needed somewhere to live, there had been a 15 year marriage and the court was of the opinion that but for the divorce the house would not have been sold for another 20 years. Thus instead of the children reaching adulthood, the triggering event will be either the occupying spouse's death, or earlier remarriage, sometimes cohabitation or becoming dependent on another partner, or voluntary removal.

Obviously this order is less attractive to the spouse out of occupation than a *Mesher*, since the non-occupying spouse may never see the proceeds of sale which may ultimately only accrue to that spouse's estate many years later, but it does preserve the capital of the spouse out of occupation, rather than giving it up completely as would be the result if there were an outright transfer for no value. This was the entire rationale of the case of *Clutton v Clutton*, and since the sale is postponed for so long and is under the occupying spouse's control (and the order is therefore in effect virtually indistinguishable from an outright transfer with a deferred charge) it does not fall foul of the clean break rules as was confirmed in *Clutton*. Nevertheless an outright transfer with a deferred charge payable on any of the usual *Martin* triggering events will usually be preferred by the occupying spouse and really makes no significant difference to the spouse out of occupation.

The *Harvey* order

This order, sometimes also called a *Brown* order, is a variant of the *Martin* order where the occupying spouse still has the right to remain indefinitely in the property but upon the children becoming independent or the mortgage being paid off, usually whichever is the later, the occupying spouse is required to pay a market rent to the spouse out of occupation for that spouse's share of the property, so as to provide some return on the capital tied up in the house for that spouse. Such rent is usually to be determined by the district judge in accordance with market rates at the date at which the triggering event occurs.

Another feature of the *Harvey* order is that it may specify a greater share of the ultimate sale proceeds for the occupying spouse who is paying the mortgage and the outgoings to recognised that whoever is in occupation will probably end up paying more of the mortgage than the spouse who is out of occupation. However, this provision may always be written into any order drafted, since as explained at the outset you should always remember that the order being drafted is the *your own order* for *your own case* and all clauses of all these well known orders may be swapped about to produce something totally original provided the resulting package does not put incompatible clauses together.

Note

When deciding upon a suitable order, you will of course remember the hazards of any form of outright transfer, unless in 'buy out' form, in relation to potential future claims for welfare benefits by the transferee and also the very limited account taken of such capital transfers by the CSA: see 7.3.4. Thus a *Hanlon* order would pose potential risks for the husband today unless the wife were thought to be a responsible sort of person who would use the opportunity of receiving the house outright to make secure overall provision for herself for the future by working hard to guarantee her income.

8.3   Legal Aid statutory charge: Legal Aid Act 1988 s 16

You will recall that the Legal Aid Act (LAA) 1988 s 16 requires the Legal Aid Board if it can to recover its costs of the ancillary relief suit (and also of any other proceedings financed on behalf of the assisted person, such as for an order under the Children Act) and that the impact of this is normally felt in relation to property recovered or preserved in the ancillary relief package obtained, in particular usually in the form of a statutory charge taken over the home to avoid the property having to be sold in order to finance the very proceedings in which it was recently awarded to the assisted person: see above at 5.1.5 and 5.1.6. It will therefore always be necessary to bear legal aid in mind if it applies when deciding on which particular ancillary relief package to go for.

8.3.1   Drawbacks for the client

As has already been explained legal aid is a loan not a gift, and also a somewhat ungenerous loan in that the interest charged on the unpaid bill of costs which has to become the subject of a statutory charge over the client's property which is preserved in the ancillary relief proceedings will not be cheap, since it is at the rate of money in court for the time being. Thus the legal aid client not only has a charge over the home that has just been recovered but will also be paying a high rate of interest for the privilege. Sometimes it will be possible for the client to refinance this bill by taking a mortgage or second mortgage over the home and paying the Legal Aid Board off as soon as possible, but this will only be feasible where the client's status permits such a loan to be raised – sometimes a client will have insufficient status to do this, which will leave the Legal Aid Board's finance through the statutory charge as the only possibility. It must therefore always be remembered that the costs will have a profound impact on the net effect of an order, whether made by consent or after a hearing, since there are more hidden costs to the statutory charge than meet the eye!

You will have to be sure to bear this drawback of the statutory charge in mind throughout the ancillary relief proceedings and particularly in relation to the settlement. Not only must you be sure to see that it is recorded on the face of the order made that the home was recovered or preserved as a home for the assisted person (including the assisted person's dependants if applicable but it is not essential that there should be dependent children) or it will not be possible to make use of the statutory charge at all, but the rising bill for costs must be constantly drawn to the client's attention and every effort made at every stage both to keep costs down and to settle at the earliest possible moment and for the least cost possible so as to avoid decimating the value of the client's victory (and provision for the client's future) by running up a disproportionate bill of costs.

It should also be remembered that pursuant to LAA 1988 s 16(7) compromises of all kinds are caught as much as bills in cases which have been contested. Thus a balance must be struck between persevering in the hope of getting a better deal for the client and persisting in a weak case in such a manner that good money is thrown after bad!

Mitigation of the statutory charge   8.3.2

Obviously you will already have used the most obvious already mentioned above at 5.1.6 – obtaining periodical payments for the spouse and/or the children wherever appropriate since these are exempt from the charge regardless of amount, and the first £2,500 of any money or property recovered or preserved will be exempt from the charge anyway – but the next step must be to try to obtain costs from the other side since this will be the *first* source of recovery of the money they have spent for the Legal Aid Board to tap.

In some cases this will be impossible – eg where the other spouse is also legally aided – but in every case where costs *are* potentially recoverable this possibility must be rigorously pursued. Nevertheless, it sometimes has to be recognised that while they *may* ultimately concede money or the home, especially to a spouse who has to look after the children, some respondents have a congenital dislike of paying costs! In this case it may be better to try to get a bit more the better to enable the assisted person to pay the costs or support the burden of the statutory charge over the home that has been recovered or preserved.

The one thing that you absolutely must grasp is that *if* energetic steps are not taken at the outset and throughout the case to keep costs down, the court will *not* be sympathetic to parties who want to litigate at public expense and then expect the court to wave some kind of magic wand to manufacture some kind of added value out of the order made!

The court is not moved by pitiful tales, such as of Mrs Hanlon who won £10,000 from Mr Hanlon only to see it nearly all swallowed up in costs of £8,025. The court also gets very cross indeed at wastefulness in conducting the case, as in *Evans v Evans* [1990] 2 All ER 147 where the Court of Appeal said it despaired – the costs of both parties were £60,000 (£35,000 the husband's and £25,000 the legally aided wife's) and the total assets only £110,000, two mortgaged houses where the parties respectively lived, and a small company belonging to the husband, the wife having no independent means. The court suggested the most obvious of economies would have been to use shared valuers or at worst agreeing valuations where such expense as had been incurred really could not be justified and would have such serious consequences for the parties.

Appeals *are* possible if the costs destroy the whole scheme of distributing the assets between the parties, as was established in the case of *Simmons v Simmons* [1984] 1 FLR 226 and followed in *Anthony v Anthony* [1986] 2 FLR 353. The latter was a particularly badly run case where both parties were legally aided and initially the husband got the home and the wife £9,000, nominal maintenance for herself and maintenance for the two children. However, she and the children were going to be homeless as her costs left her only with the initial £2,500 which is exempt from the charge – so the court started again, remaking the order to use all the available exemptions by abandoning the lump sum, which was otherwise going to be swallowed up by the costs bill, giving her a *Mesher* so she could stay in the home and the husband still got some capital out of it at a later date, and making a more generous periodical payments package, an altogether different result.

A similar case was that of *Stewart v Law Society* [1987] 1 FLR 223 where the costs were £4,600 and someone had been sufficiently daft to allow the court to make an order of £7,000 for capitalised maintenance leaving her with very little left of the money which had been meant to provide for her – this is precisely the sort of case in which to use the exemptions, and if necessary go for limited term periodical payments, which like all periodical payments will be exempt from the charge.

However, the court much prefers to make orders which give the parties the benefit of exemptions in the first place than to be asked to make some last minute alteration. Even if an appeal is entertained at all, it is unlikely to be heard without some extremely sharp things being said on the Bench about such a situation being allowed to develop in the first place. Moreover, the court is much less likely to intervene on appeal now the principles of running ancillary relief cases on legal aid without spending all the gains on costs are well established, particularly as if cash is awarded in the form of a lump sum, provided it is earmarked for the purchase of a house it will not be necessary to pay the costs bill immediately out of that, as was previously the situation. Now the statutory charge may operate against the new home once bought, which was the outcome in the case of *Scallon v Scallon* [1990] 1 FLR 193 there is less need for the court to intervene. In that case the wife appealed against an order for sale of the matrimonial home of which she was to receive a proportion, relying on the decision in *Simmons*, because the effect of the legal aid bill meant she had too little money to buy a house with. The court refused to help her since the revised operation of the statutory charge meant she could postpone the bill by means of a charge on the new home, which they took the view the Legal Aid Board would be unlikely to refuse to entertain if it frustrated the court's order.

The saddest cases are where the bulk of the bill has been substantially run up in child proceedings (in which no property is recovered and often little is achieved except the guarantee of constant future expense on the children concerned!) and the costs of both child proceedings and the ancillary relief proceedings have to be set against the property recovered in the latter, as in the case of *Mason v Mason* [1986] 2 FLR 212. In that case the parties ran up a huge bill by energetic litigation against each other in an acrimonious case involving both adultery and behaviour, which ultimately had to be compromised so that there was a decree under Fact D, followed by a long drawn out custody suit which also ultimately had to be settled. The costs were £23,000 and the home was only worth £53,000 so that little was eventually left. This is the sort of case which should be an awful warning to legally aided parties and the court usually comments on this sort of situation when they realise that what has happened has been entirely due to the parties' recalcitrance.

8.4   Drafting of orders

Whatever ancillary relief package is finally agreed on, it must be formally incorporated into an accurate and comprehensive draft order to be placed before the court, so that subject to such amendments (usually of style rather than substance) which the district judge wishes to make the court can actually make the order sought in that form.

8.4.1   Preparing to draft the order

Knowing what to put into the order is obviously an essential pre-requisite of actually drafting it, so the trainee is well advised to start by making a *list* of all the terms which it is desired to incorporate into the order, and then actually to *draft* from that list. Such a practice is a good insurance against inadvertently forgetting to include some essential provision, and also against putting any particular item into the wrong part of the order, especially since the order can be quite complex since it must usually contain separate paragraphs dealing with:

- periodical payments for the payee spouse (or dismissal of such claims);
- periodical payments for children, often both for general maintenance and for school fees;
- transfer, settlement or sale of the home;
- transfer of other items, whether of real or personal property or chattels;
- payment of a lump sum to a spouse;
- possibly payment of lump sums to children;
- restrictions on future application to the court, in life and on death of each of the parties;
- costs, including legal aid taxation where appropriate;
- certificate for the purposes of the statutory charge.

Note

There should *never, ever,* be any paragraphs in ancillary relief orders dealing with the residence of or contact with children (whatever books the trainee may have consulted which appear to indicate that such paragraphs *are* possible). Such *orders* can only be made under the Children Act 1989 and due to the non-interventionist philosophy of the Act are now most commonly *not made* at all: see Chapter 6. The confusion experienced by some students in this respect stems from the fact that prior to 1991 when the Children Act came into force, such orders for custody, care and control and access were routinely inserted into orders primarily dealing with ancillary relief but this practice then *ceased and has never since been appropriate.*

The above advice is initially intended to help the inexperienced but it is actually also good methodology even when you have progressed into practice as a family lawyer. At that stage, when settling a case with the other side, it will actually usually be useful to incorporate the agreement made into written Heads of Agreement so that both sides know what is supposed to be in the order, prior usually to one of them drafting it for submission to and agreement by the other, although sometimes both parties lawyers will prepare the draft together.

However, there are tactical advantages both in preparing the draft oneself for submission to the other side (you get it in the form that you want, and if you leave something obvious for the other side to fix on and insist on amending they will often leave the rest as you want it!) and in allowing them to prepare it and offering your own amendments which may even be able to make the way the order works even more favourable to you (they may prepare something more favourable to you than you hoped to which you can agree with a big smile and take the benefit, at the same time acquiring a reputation as being very reasonable to deal with!) Either of these approaches is called 'getting back on the drafting what you lost on the negotiation' and is an art form in itself which you will acquire with experience.

The format of the order   8.4.2

In actually drafting the order, you must take care to make the draft clear, comprehensive and accurate, as emphasised in the disastrous case of *Dinch v Dinch* [1987] 1 WLR 252 where the (combined) awful drafting of several lawyers produced such a result that Lord Oliver of

Aylmerton felt obliged to criticise it at length, not least because it seems that the draughtsmen in question, having failed to give effect to what was apparently agreed about the disposal of the petitioner's claims for ancillary relief, then tried to blame the court for not picking up and correcting their mistakes! Lord Oliver said:

> 'I feel impelled once again to stress in the most emphatic terms that it is in all cases the imperative professional duty of those invested with the task of advising the parties to these unfortunate disputes to consider with due care the impact which any terms that they agree on behalf of clients have ... and to ensure that such appropriate provision is inserted in any consent order ... as will leave no room for any future doubt or misunderstanding or saddle the parties with the wasteful burden of wholly unnecessary costs. It is of course also the duty of any court called upon to make such a consent order to consider ... the jurisdiction it is being called upon to exercise ... I would however like to emphasise that the *primary* duty (author's italics) in this regard must lie upon those concerned with the negotiation and drafting of the terms of the order and that any failure to fulfil such duty ... cannot be excused simply by reference to some inadvertent lack of vigilance on the part of the court or its officers in passing the order in a form which the parties have approved.'

This means the buck stops with you, and although as a trainee you are supervised and suffer no burden of ultimate responsibility, for example in negligence if the order made results in the client suing, the sooner you learn to take *practical* responsibility on to your shoulders for a successful outcome to cases, the better for your career prospects.

Note

Lord Oliver was talking about consent orders (the power to make) which, after they have been agreed between the parties, is by MCA 1973 s 33A expressly given to the court *without* conducting a full hearing as would happen where the orders were made after a contested application, but what he has to say in principle applies to all forms of order, which should always be checked by the parties' advisers, including those drafted after a *decision of the court* following contested proceedings so as to see that the order accords with what was asked for and that it contains what the judge actually ordered after the hearing. Moral: THINK AHEAD to how your order will actually work out in practice and try

> to envisage any difficulties or ambiguities and cater for them. If the *judge* has made a mistake, most judges would rather hear that sooner, before the order has been drawn up let alone sealed, rather than later when making amendments under the slip rule or setting aside an order that has somehow got mangled at the drawing up stage.

You will of course consult the usual volumes of precedents for the proper format for consent orders of the various types mentioned above, and should with practice very soon be able to master a repertoire of orders including the *Mesher, Martin, Harvey* and *Hanlon* types which are the most common, together with the *Browne v Pritchard* and *Hector v Hector* variants for giving the spouse out of occupation of the home either a proportion of ultimate sale proceeds or a fixed sum out of them. Samples of some of these common orders will be found in Appendix 6.

In mastering the art of simple drafting you should not try to be too ambitious. the ability to put together a portfolio of clauses and paragraph so as to draft a handful of *simple straightforward* orders is what is expected of a trainee entering the training contract, not the expertise of a specialist who has been in practice some years. You should be able to produce something respectable in draft which the principle will amend rather than put straight into the waste paper basket, at the same time wondering why you were ever taken on.

The layout of the order   8.4.3

Every order has at least two and possibly three or four parts:
- the heading (essential);
- recitals and/or undertakings (but neither of these is essential);
- the body of the order (essential).

An examination of the usual precedents will indicate to you that the *heading* is copied directly from that of the suit, showing the court, identifying number and parties.

Recitals and/or undertakings come next, before the body of the order, and are not essential. They exist to record any term which it is desired to incorporate into the order, but which cannot be comprised in the body of it because that item does not fall within the scope of what the court can order under ss 23 and 24 of the MCA 1973.

Recitals

Recitals which may be appropriate include:

Whereas it is agreed that in the event of an assessment being made under the Child Support Act 1991 in respect of the children of the family or any one of them the periodical payments hereinafter ordered for the said children and the petitioner shall be reduced by the amount of the assessment. (So the payer does not pay double if a CSA assessment is made: see Chapter 7 at 7.5.2)

Whereas it is agreed between the parties that the following order is in full and final settlement of all financial claims made by each against the other for themselves under the Matrimonial Causes Act 1973 and s 17 of the Married Women's Property Act as amended. (For a completely comprehensive clean break, though it is probably not absolutely essential to include this provided some other form is used in the body of the order which makes it clear that all other claims by one spouse against the other are deemed to be dismissed, whether or not they have actually be made.)

Undertakings

These immediately follow the recitals, have the same *force* as an order of the court as the undertaking is given to the *court, making breach contempt,* and are preceded by the format

'Upon the Petitioner/Respondent undertaking': any of the following undertakings may be appropriate

To invest the net proceeds of sale of the property at [address] in the purchase of a freehold dwelling house for the sole use and occupation of the Petitioner [to a Respondent who is to provide a house for the Petitioner – cannot be *ordered* because it involves payment of money to a third party, not contemplated by s 23 or s 24 which envisages orders payable between the *parties*]

To permit the Petitioner to reside in the said property free of rent during her lifetime until remarriage [to a Respondent who is to permit the Petitioner to remain in a house rent free – cannot otherwise be *ordered* for same reason as above]

Not to sell, charge or otherwise dispose of the said property without the prior consent of the Petitioner in writing [otherwise cannot be *ordered* under ss 23 or 24]

To attend a one year full time course of training in word processing [to a payee spouse who is receiving limited term maintenance or open ended periodical payments on the basis that employment will be sought and retraining undertaken to secure such employment – something not contemplated at all by ss 23 and 24 so could not be *ordered*]

To sign and deliver within 7 days of this order an irrevocable instruction to the trustees of the pension fund to pay to the Respondent a full widow's pension in the event he predecease her, provided at such time she has not remarried [to a husband whose pension cannot be varied by the court under s 24 but where the ancillary relief package contemplates some voluntary provision for the former wife from his pension]

To use her best endeavours to secure the release of the Respondent from his covenants under the mortgage account No. 1234XYZ with the Blankshire Building Society on [address of property] and in default of such release to indemnify him thereunder {typical undertaking in an order transferring the home to one spouse who will take over the mortgage – cannot be *ordered* but really essential if there is to be a new sole owner; *not* necessary for settlement of the home where the parties will both be trustees for sale, in which case the occupying spouse can undertake to meet all mortgage repayments, and other outgoings including repairs, or these can be shared in which case *each* party can undertake separately to pay whatever is agreed as in the next example]

To pay or cause to be paid as from the date of settlement of the property known as [address] as hereinafter provided all moneys which shall become payable in respect of the mortgage of the said property and insurance premiums, water rates and all other outgoings on the property

Note
_____

In all cases, you should consult a reliable precedent book rather than making up undertakings where the precise wording and effect may be a matter of debate. Apart from the fact that there is no sense in reinventing the wheel, there is no point in ignoring the benefit of years of drafting expertise. The *real skill* is in selecting the *appropriate* clause from the precedent book, according to the end it is desired to achieve, and this aim should drive all good drafting, especially of ancillary relief orders.

The *body of the order* contains the paragraphs which will effect the provisions which have been won from the other side and which the court can order, in the same way that the *recitals and undertakings* embody those provisions of the parties' agreement which the court cannot order.

Sample paragraphs which the trainee may find helpful are as follows (in all cases Petitioner may be swapped for Respondent and vice versa):

For periodical payments

The Respondent do pay to the Petitioner for herself during their joint lives or until the Petitioner shall remarry or until further order periodical payments at the rate of £50 per week, the first payment to be made on the   day of   199 .

The Respondent do pay to the Petitioner for the benefit of the children of the family John Smith and Jane Smith until they shall attain the age of 17 years or cease full time education or training or until further order periodical payments at the rate of £25 per week each. [Payment to the spouse for the children secures a small amount of tax relief: see Chapter 12].

The Respondent do pay to the Petitioner for the benefit of the children of the family John Smith and Jane Smith

(i) until they shall respectively attain the age of 17 years or cease full time education or until further order periodical payment at the rate of £50 per week each [ie this is for basic maintenance for food and clothes etc]

(ii) in addition for the benefit of John Smith such sum as shall be equal to the annual fees of the school that the said child attends, such sum to be payable in 3 equal parts on the first day of each term of the said school [this covers his school fees, whatever they are when raised each year as the practice of such schools, without the need to return to the court for upward variation]

The Respondent do pay periodical payments to the Petitioner at the rate of £50 per week for a period of two years commencing on the first day of June 199 [and the Petitioner be not entitled to apply for any extension of the said period] [This provides limited term periodical payments, plus restriction of the right to apply to extend the term, which may be included or not as appropriate.]

The Respondent do pay maintenance to the Petitioner at the rate of 5p per annum until further order. [Nominal maintenance.]

Lump sum orders

The Respondent do pay to the Petitioner a lump sum of £50,000. [An ordinary uncomplicated lump sum order.]

The Respondent do pay to the Petitioner a lump sum of £50,000 payable by 10 equal instalments of £5,000 on 1 January and 1 July in each year commencing on 1 July 199   . [Lump sum by instalments, which may be as complex or as simple as the trainee drafting the order likes, provided this has been agreed by the parties.]

Orders disposing of the matrimonial home

The Petitioner do transfer to the Respondent all her interest in the property known as [address]. [Outright transfer. Where there is to be an outright transfer *in return for a cash payment* this paragraph will need to be accompanied by another giving the transferor a lump sum and the two paragraphs may be linked, making the lump sum payment *first* in one paragraph and the transfer second in another one, and if liked expressed to take place *upon receipt of the lump sum.* Alternatively if a *Hanlon* order is desired, the outright transfer may simply be followed by a separate paragraph in which the transferee's claims for periodical payments and indeed all other forms of ancillary relief are dismissed. The precedent books contain plenty of examples of how such dependent paragraphs may be drafted, possibly including a penalty if the cash payment is later than desired.]

The Petitioner do transfer to the Respondent all his interest in the property known as [address] and the said property be charged with payment to the Petitioner of 25% of the net proceeds of sale [alternatively £   ] when sold or on the death of the Petitioner, such sum to be calculated without regard to any future mortgage to be taken out by the Respondent. [Outright transfer with charge for a proportion of the ultimate sale proceeds in favour of the transferor.]

The Respondent do sell the property known as [address] the net proceeds of sale to be divided between the Petitioner and the Respondent in the proportion one quarter and three quarters. [Order for sale under s 24 and division of the proceeds.]

The Respondent do forthwith transfer into the joint names of himself and the Petitioner the property known as [address] to be held on trust for sale, not to be sold until further order, or until the Petitioner shall die or remarry, or the said children of the family John Smith and Jane Smith shall have attained 18 years which ever shall be the soonest, and thereafter to be sold and the net proceeds of sale to be divided between the Petitioner and the

Respondent in equal shares. [*Mesher* order where the husband was previously the sole owner of the home.]

The property known as [address] do stand vested in the joint names of the Petitioner and the Respondent on trust for sale in equal shares, not to be sold until the Petitioner shall die or remarry or voluntarily cease to occupy the said property or become dependent on a man other than the Respondent, whichever shall be the soonest, provided that when the said children John Smith and Jane Smith shall have attained the age of 18 years, [or when the mortgage is paid off whichever shall be the later] the Petitioner shall pay the Respondent an occupation rent to be assessed at such time by the district judge. [*Martin* order with option to include a *Harvey* clause.]

Dismissal of all future claims

The Petitioner's claim for periodical payments for herself do stand dismissed [and that the Petitioner be not entitled to make any further application for periodical payments or secured periodical payments for herself]. [Suitable dismissal of claims for a Hanlon order.]

The Petitioner's claim for a property adjustment order do stand dismissed. [Suitable dismissal of s 24 application where the applicant's claims have been settled in cash under s 23.]

Save as aforesaid all the Petitioner's [and the Respondent's] applications for ancillary relief do stand dismissed and it is directed that neither party shall be entitled to apply to the court thereafter for an order under s 23(1)(a) or (b) of the Matrimonial Causes Act 1973 as amended. [Comprehensive dismissal of all claims other than those specifically met by paragraphs earlier in the order – very useful and less long winded than dismissing them all individually – and in particular no further claim allowed for periodical payments secured or unsecured.]

Neither the Petitioner nor the Respondent shall on the death of the other be entitled to apply for an order under s 2 of the Inheritance [Provision for Family and Dependants] Act 1975. [Barring all claims by either spouse against the other out of their respective estates.]

Self-assessment questions

1 What competing aims is the court trying to satisfy in dealing with the matrimonial home?
2 What is the order of priorities?

3 What orders in respect of the home are compatible with a clean break?

4 What are the following orders: *Mesher*? *Martin*? *Harvey*? *Hanlon*? *Hector v Hector*? *Browne v Pritchard*?

5 What hazards are posed to the clean break by the Benefits Agency and the CSA?

6 What problem is associated with the statutory charge?

7 What can be done to mitigate its impact?

8 What are Heads of Agreement for?

9 Whose fault is it if an order turns out eventually not to suit the client's circumstances after it has actually been made by the court?

10 How will you set about drafting a suitable consent order?

Chapter 9

Preventing evasion of liability or enforcement of orders

Preserving the assets against which orders are made

9.1

Some respondents never intend that ancillary relief orders will be made against them, or, even if they are, that such orders will ever be successfully enforced. However, the powers of the court would be empty if respondents to financial applications could get away with such schemes. If the trainee suspects such a situation to exist or that it might arise, urgent steps should be taken to prevent assets being moved out of the jurisdiction (or in any way put beyond the applicant's reach, for example by their being transferred into the names of third parties).

Especially in cases where there is an international element, this matter should routinely be considered at the first interview when it is usual in any event to establish whether any action needs to be taken to register the client's rights of occupation under the Matrimonial Homes Act 1983. If protection *is* required for other assets not within the MHA, there is special provision in s 37 of the MCA 1973 which will usually meet the client's needs, but in an appropriate case a *Mareva* or *Anton Piller* order, with which you will be familiar in civil litigation, is also of course available, although due to the expense and strict requirements for such orders the use of s 37, which does not have such disadvantages, will generally be sufficient unless the respondent is very rich and the assets very widely spread around the world.

Section 37, MCA 1973

9.1.1

The section can achieve two distinct results:
- *preventing* a suspected disposal: s 37(2)(a);
- *setting aside* a disposal which has already taken place: s 37(2)(b) and (c).

By s 37(1)(b) a disposition made before the court has had time to make a financial order may be set aside, and by s 37(1)(c) a disposition made *after* the court's financial order, and with the intention of preventing enforcement, will be similarly caught.

Note

In all cases the actual or intended disposition must be for the purposes of *defeating the applicant's claim*, that is to say:

- *preventing* financial relief being granted at all, either to the applicant or any child of the family; or

- *reducing the amount* which might be granted; or

- *frustrating or impeding enforcement* of an actual or antici-pated order: s 37(1).

Thus, if the respondent is wealthy and wishes to transfer property which is not in practice needed to meet any order that the court might make, the section cannot be used to prevent this, or commercial paralysis would follow!

In order to use any of these provisions the client will need to have started proceedings against the respondent for financial relief. That means that in divorce a petition must have been filed claiming ancillary relief in the usual way, or if the applicant is not the petitioner a Form M11 must have been filed, in a variation case an application must have been made under s 31 (or in the case of varia-tion of a qualifying maintenance agreement under s 35) and in the case of s 27 proceedings, an application must have been made for provision. Once this has been done an application can be made under s 37 immediately, sometimes with quite dramatic results, as in *Hamlin v Hamlin* [1985] 2 All ER 1037 where the husband was stopped from selling a house in Spain, which happened to be the only matrimonial asset.

Note

There is a *presumption* that the disposition was in fact *designed to defeat the claim* if made within the past three years and if it would in fact defeat the claim if not set aside: s 37(5). Such a disposal is called a *reviewable disposition*, and by s 37(4) includes *any disposition* made otherwise than for valuable consideration, other than marriage, to a person who at the time of the disposition acted in good faith and without notice of any intention on the part of the respon-dent to defeat the applicant's claim for ancillary relief.

By s 37(6) a *disposition* includes a conveyance, assur-ance or gift of property of any description, by instrument or otherwise, except any provision contained in a will or codicil, for example mortgaging a house, giving away assets or even dissipating money (although in the latter case some assistance might be required from the law of trusts under the doctrines of knowing receipt and dealing).

In theory, ss 37(4) and 37(6) leave very little room for the respondent to make off with assets, but since dispositions caught by s 37 are voidable and not void, a principle which has essential commercial importance, sometimes a technically *bona fide* transaction escapes, even though the respondent had every intention of defeating the section, as happened in the case of *National Provincial Bank v Hastings Car Mart* [1964] 3 All ER 93, [1964] Ch 665 where the husband conveyed the matrimonial home to a company which he had formed for the purpose and then the company mortgaged it to the bank. The court held the conveyance to the company to be a sham and set it aside as it was clearly intended to defeat the wife's claim, but the mortgage to the bank was a *bona fide* commercial transaction and had to be upheld.

In particular, although transfers to a controlled company or a relative will be caught, dispositions for valuable consideration (other than marriage) cannot be set aside if a third party acted in good faith and without notice of any intention to defeat the spouse's claim, the section may be insufficient protection without backing it up with registration of a spouse's claim as a pending land action, a situation which came to light in the case of *Kemmis v Kemmis* [1988] 2 FLR 223 where a bank was lending on mortgage to a husband: it was held that such a bank might have notice of the husband's intention if they knew of the wife's occupation of the home and that she might be making a financial application.

The difficulty in such a situation is that the bank might have no reason to know of the husband's personal circumstances, so there may be no constructive notice on the part of the bank: this problem is obviated by registering the pending land action and thus giving notice to any such third party who may need to have it. Obviously if the mortgagee already has constructive notice such registration will not be necessary, as in the case of *Perez-Adamson v Perez Rivas* [1987] 3 All ER 20 where the Bank made a loan without bothering to search the register, where the wife *had* duly registered her pending land action under the Land Charges Act 1972, so when the husband left the country with the money she took priority over the bank as mortgagee, although in fact it turned out that they had constructive notice of her occupation anyway. If there is any doubt about constructive notice, it is better to register and be safe rather than not and be sorry!

In all cases evidence will be required, and fanciful imagining will not be sufficient, since the court must be *satisfied* that the respondent is about to deal with the property in question in the manner feared, or that such a disposition has been made. It can then make such order as it thinks fit to restrain such a disposition or to set it aside if it has already been made.

9.1.2   *Mareva* and *Anton Piller* orders and the writ *ne exeat regno*

A *Mareva* may be used to freeze assets or an *Anton Piller* to gather information from relevant documents, and finally the writ *ne exeat regno* to prevent the respondent personally leaving the country but obviously these will be used sparingly in matrimonial proceedings because of their expense and complexity. Usually such extreme measures are reserved for cases where the respondent has a history of flouting orders as in *Emanual v Emanual* [1982] 2 All ER 342 where the husband fell into this category and *K v K* (1982) *Times* 25 October, where the husband had failed to make full disclosure and it was necessary to obtain details of his stock in trade.

9.2   Enforcement

Normally, payments under money orders will be left to the parties to make as they see fit, and this will usually be by direct payment by monthly cheque, or standing order, unless the order is payable through the Family Proceedings Court, where different arrangements may apply: see below at 9.3. You should in any event tell the client as soon as the order is made not to delay in bringing to the firm's attention any problems that arise, preferably straight away when they first occur, as pursuant to MCA 1973 s 32 leave is required to enforce arrears more than 12 months old, and in the Family Proceedings Court arrears more than 12 months old will not be enforced at all (on the basis that if the applicant has managed that long without the money, it cannot be essentially required).

Where the client is the payer, advice should be given to keep records of payment, of both lump sums and periodical payments, such as by paying through a bank by cheque or standing order.

All the same methods of enforcement of orders with which the trainee will be familiar in civil litigation are equally available to enforce matrimonial financial orders, ie a:

- warrant of execution;
- attachment of earnings order;
- charging order and order for sale;
- garnishee order.

There are also some extra possibilities more particularly tailored to typical matrimonial orders:

- a judgment summons: FPR 1991 r 7.4;
- s 24A MCA 1973 sale order;
- enforcement of property adjustment orders: SCA 1981 s 39, CCA 1984 s 38, MCA 1973 s 30;
- registration of periodical payments orders in the Family Proceedings Court.

Note

Before any process is issued to enforce an order made in matrimonial proceedings, it will be necessary, pursuant to FPR 1991 r 7.1(1) as amended, to file a certificate specifying the amount due under the order, ie the amount of arrears of periodical payments or the unpaid portion of a lump sum. It may also be advisable to make an application for an oral examination in order to ascertain the nature and extent of the defaulter's means and therefore the best way of proceeding to enforce the order. Application is to the district judge who can compel the production of any necessary documents.

Judgment summons: FPR 1991 r 7.4   9.2.1

This requires the defaulting payer to attend before a judge to be examined as to his (or her) means, and the judge will then make such order as is though fit in relation to the unpaid sums, whether they be arrears of periodical payments or an outstanding lump sum or both. The judge does have power to commit the defaulter to prison for non-payment though this is unlikely actually to happen if the money is paid within a specified period as the more usual course is to suspend any committal order on condition that the payments are made.

Section 24A, MCA 1973 order for sale   9.2.2

This is a useful provision since where it has not been thought necessary to use this section to include a specific order for sale in the original order made, it still permits the unpaid payee to seek an order for sale at a later date with a consequential direction that the proceeds of sale or part of them should be paid over to the payee in satisfaction of the existing unpaid order.

Note

Vacant possession can be ordered to facilitate such a sale: FPR 1991 r 2.64.

9.2.3 Enforcing property adjustment orders

Drafting of any necessary documents can be undertaken if necessary by one of the conveyancing counsel to the court who can settle the proper instrument for execution by all those who must be a party to them.

Execution can be effected by an order that unless the defaulter does this within a specified time the district judge shall execute the document: SCA 1981 s 39, CCA 1984 s 38.

Note

Where the order has been made in divorce, nullity or judicial separation proceedings, ie where there is a decree which can be withheld, pressure can be put on to the defaulter by the court's providing that the decree shall be deferred until the instrument has been duly executed!

9.3 Registration of periodical payments orders in the Family Proceedings Court

This is by far the most effective way of getting a periodical payments order observed if there is likely to be any difficulty in enforcing it. It is not therefore unusual to obtain a legal aid certificate for ancillary relief proceedings which extends to registration of one substantive order in the Family Proceedings Court.

The magistrates have a long history of effective collection of maintenance payments. This is because their somewhat parochial methods have always enabled payment to be made *through* the court, thus putting the Clerk on immediate notice when the money was not paid, and enabling swift enforcement to follow. However, the introduction of new powers under the Maintenance Enforcement Act 1991 has made them even more effective.

This Act came into force on 1 April 1992 and for the first time enabled the magistrates to specify how an order should be paid, whether by standing order or attachment of earnings or otherwise, and also to require the opening of a bank account to provide payment by standing order where that was appropriate: Maintenance Enforcement Act 1991 s 2. The result has obviously been to provide an even more efficient system, making

registration of other courts' orders even more worthwhile since the new methods in respect of their own
order free time to enforce those of other less effective
courts also. Combined with the removal of much child
support business to the Child Support Agency, the resulting streamlining of magistrates' courts systems makes it
more than worthwhile to register even overseas orders
(in respect of which there are many long-standing and
sometimes little known reciprocal enforcement provisions which may be found in *Rayden*).

Note

While it has for many years been similarly possible to register Family Proceedings Courts orders (made under the
DPMCA 1978: see Chapter 14) in the High Court under the
Maintenance Order Act 1958, this is only worthwhile for a
large amount of money (eg accumulated arrears). The
traffic is very much the other way around.

Pursuant to the DPMCA 1978 s 32(1), all magistrates'
courts orders can be enforced in the following ways:
- attachment of earnings: AEA 1971;
- committal to prison: Magistrates' Courts' Act
  1980 s 76;
- distress, *ibid*.

There is also the Diversion Procedure, whereby the
Benefits Agency will take over the order and enforce it,
meanwhile paying the applicant social security benefits
in lieu (see Chapter 13 and para 14.4).

Note

An additional advantage of registration of orders in the
FPC is that that court can then *vary* as well as enforce them,
which may sometimes be useful rather than the parties
being obliged to return to the court granting the original
order.

High Court and county court methods   9.4

If registration in the Family Proceedings Court is not for
some reason the complete solution in the particular case,
the trainee will have to weigh up the alternative methods
available in the High Court and county court – for
example the High Court affords the possibilities of the
writs of *fi fa* and sequestration, though the latter is
hugely expensive and a solicitor should obviously
beware of incurring costs which might not even meet the
order defaulted on, and there is also the possibility of

appointment of a receiver by way of equitable execution to compel sale under an LPA 1925 s 30 order – and pick the one most suitable to the circumstances of the defaulter.

Self-assessment questions

1 How can s 37 MCA 1973 help to stop assets being made unavailable for ancillary relief orders?
2 When can s 37 be invoked?
3 What is a reviewable disposition?
4 Can s 37 freeze all a respondent's assets?
5 Can s 37 set aside all a respondent's commercial transactions within the reviewable period?
6 What alternative remedies exist to locate and freeze assets other than by use of s 37?
7 Can s 37 prevent a respondent from escaping enforcement of ancillary relief orders?
8 What methods exist to enforce payment of periodical payments orders?
9 What methods exist to enforce orders for sale and property transfer?
10 What is the effect of registration in the Family Proceedings Court?

Chapter 10

Variation

Principles of variation

10.1

Variation of ancillary relief orders is governed by s 31 of the MCA 1973 and the general principles will be found in this section. Not *all* orders can be varied, however, and it is important to understand precisely what can be done on an application for *variation* under s 31, and what requires some other approach – in some cases where *variation* as such is technically not possible because of the provisions of s 31, there may be another way of achieving what is wanted: for the ingenuity of matrimonial lawyers in this respect, see 10.3.

Routine variation

10.1.1

Generally, only *continuing* money orders may be varied, ie periodical payments (whether secured or unsecured) including maintenance pending suit and interim maintenance orders, and instalments of lump sums: s 31(2). There is no power to vary:

- *fixed term periodical payments* where a prohibition on extension of the fixed term has been attached pursuant to MCA s 28(1A);
- the *amount* of a lump sum order (although if it is directed to be paid in instalments, the *instalments* may be varied) nor the time within which the lump sum is to be paid *unless* the order itself provides that, by expressly giving 'liberty to apply for extension of the time for payment' in an appropriate case;
- a property adjustment order under s 24(1)(a);
- a settlement of property order under s 24(1)(b) or a variation of settlement order under s 24 (1)(c) or (d) unless the order was made after a decree of judicial separation.

The last two prohibitions are often unexpectedly found very inconvenient, such as in the case of *Carson v Carson* [1983] 1 WLR 285, [1983] 1 All ER 478 where the wife wanted her property adjustment order varied to give her the husband's share of the matrimonial home in return for her giving up her periodical payments, a reasonable enough exchange often incorporated into clean break orders following divorce. The object of her proposal was so that she had enough money to buy a new home on the sale at the end of the *Mesher* period to which her existing home was subject, but the court could not help her because of the prohibition on varying property adjustment orders. Moral: the practitioner should think of this at the time that the *original* order is made if the wife might want to make such a swap, because it *can* be done at that stage (such an arrangement commonly being called a *Hanlon* order), but *not* later on *variation* – but see 10.3 for the practitioners' ingenious extra-statutory solution to this problem.

Note

A strange exception: an order for sale under s 24A, which certainly does not logically fall into the category of continuing money orders, may be varied by changing the date of the sale: s 31(2)(f). Students (rightly perhaps!) therefore wonder why the date of sale in a *Mesher* or similar order cannot similarly be changed – but unless the order has been specially drawn to cover that eventuality, it cannot. The words 'liberty to apply', which students are always enjoined to add to consent orders to facilitate implementation, cannot be interpreted so liberally as to permit this – they apply only to *implementation* of the order, so as to clarify the terms and to facilitate payment under it without there being unnecessary enforcement problems: such words do not permit actual changes in the order which once the order is made is a variation and is governed by s 31.

Moreover, when any of the continuing money orders *are* varied, this can only be done by increasing or decreasing the amounts to be paid under those orders, or discharging them completely. It is *not* possible to vary such orders by discharging them and substituting a different *type* of order, eg a periodical payments order cannot be varied by making a *lump sum* order on the variation application, even though the applicant may have received no lump sum in the original order which the application seeks to vary, and even though it would be convenient to order a lump sum as capitalised maintenance and this *could* have been done when the order was originally made: s 31(5).

Note

Notwithstanding s 31(5) it is possible to vary a child's periodical payments by ordering a lump sum. This is because it may be convenient to give a child a lump sum, eg for an older child who needs the money for higher education, and the approach to child orders has always been somewhat more flexible (eg there is no need to wait for decree nisi to make orders for children and they can have more than one lump sum).

The most common occasions of variation applications are when there is a change of circumstances in the lives of either the payer or the payee.

In the case of the *payer* it will usually be because (s)he:

- has been promoted, dismissed or made redundant or has lost opportunities for overtime (and therefore can afford more or less than the original order), ie a change in the s 25(2)(a) considerations; or
- has remarried, started to cohabit or acquired a new family (and therefore has new obligations), ie a change in the s 25(2)(b) considerations.

In the case of the payee it will usually be because of:

- inflation;
- the children being older and more expensive

(in both of which cases an increase is likely to be sought by the payee).

Or because of:

- cohabitation or receipt of financial support from a third party, but where there is no remarriage;
- children leaving home, thus increasing the payee's earning capacity

(in both of which cases a decrease is likely to be sought by the payer).

When the court does vary orders in any of these circumstances it may:

- increase;
- reduce;
- discharge;
- suspend; or
- revive

such orders: s 31(1).

The court also has the power to remit arrears, completely or only in part: s 31(2A).

What the court considers when deciding whether to vary an order   10.1.2

On variation, the court is still expressly locked on by s 31 to the same s 25 considerations which had to be checked off before making the decision when the *original* order was granted, but this time it will focus on any *change* in those matters, in accordance with s 25(1) *still* observing the general duty to consider all the circumstances of the case, but *first consideration* still being given to the welfare while a minor of any child in accordance: s 31(7).

Sometimes, changes will be *non-monetary* such as in the case of *Evans v Evans* [1989] 1 FLR 351, already mentioned in connection with conduct, where the husband had paid maintenance regularly and uncomplainingly for 32 years, for which he was rewarded by the wife entering into a conspiracy to murder him. The court took the view that this was a sufficient change of circumstances to justify discharging the order.

10.1.3   The impact of s 25A clean break principle on variation

Even if there has been no clean break at the time of the original order, by s 31(7) any court dealing with an application for variation must consider whether the order should be varied so as to impose a fixed limited term for periodical payments, after which the payee should have been able to adjust without undue hardship to their terminating altogether. However, marked reluctance has been displayed to make use of this section, and a payer is often left indefinitely vulnerable to a nominal order as the payee's 'longstop'.

The case of *Atkinson v Atkinson* [1987] 3 All ER 849 was one where one might have thought the court would take the s 31(7) duty somewhat seriously, but instead this case produced the rather curious result that while finding that Mrs Atkinson's reason for cohabiting rather than remarrying was financially motivated, nevertheless would not end her maintenance order, because (as they commented) a wife who cohabits might need the money more than one who was not cohabiting, because cohabitation is a relationship which by definition is even less permanent and committed a relationship than marriage, and in particular had none of the financial obligations which attend the dissolution of a marriage by divorce! This case was complicated by the fact that the co-habitee was not even in a position to *contribute* to Mrs Atkinson's support, let alone to assume responsibility for it instead of the husband.

Much the same happened in the case of *Hepburn v Hepburn* [1989] 3 All ER 786, another cohabitation case where the wife went, after dissolution of a 10 year marriage, to live with another man with whom she entered into business ventures which the husband claimed were financially irresponsible. When he was 45 and she 40 the husband succeeded in getting her order reduced to a nominal one, but not in getting it discharged altogether: the court again talked of the backstop safety factor, saying that cohabitation is not the same as marriage and that unlike cohabitees, husbands did have obligations and should discharge them! It probably did not help Mr Hepburn that he was himself wealthy and could afford to.

Sometimes, one finds a dissenting judgment in this type of case such as that of Lord Justice Balcombe in *Whiting v Whiting* [1988] 1 WLR 565, [1988] 2 FLR 189, who said in that case that it was absurd to keep a nominal maintenance order alive for purely safety net purposes, as it was clearly contrary to the clean break legislation which had been passed for good reasons of policy and which should not therefore be flouted unnecessarily.

In the case of the Whitings, it is hard to fault his view, since Mrs Whiting who had admittedly had to give up work in the early part of a 14 year marriage when the children were young, was by the time they were older a full time teacher with a good salary, whereas the husband, who had remarried, had been made redundant and had been forced to take a new job at a much lower salary than previously. He spent all his income on his second family and had therefore not illogically applied to end his first wife's nominal maintenance order once she was established in full time employment. However, the court refused to do this since they took the view that he was the wife's only longstop against ill heath or redundancy and that she could not be assumed to be independent of him indefinitely since she had limited capital resources. However, if there is not to be a clean break on variation in this type of case, it is difficult to see when that *would* be right.

It is not just the relative impermanence and commitment of marriage which prevents the court from imposing a clean break on variation applications where they otherwise might reasonably do so. The case of *Fisher v Fisher* [1989] 1 FLR 423 shows that even where the parties' own children have grown up and the wife who has been maintained while they were doing so might reasonably be expected to go out to work to realise an earning capacity which has had to lie fallow during the earlier years, this may to be possible, through no fault of the payer who may have been patiently awaiting such a day in order to gain a certain financial freedom on the termination of what may have been a long period of obligation to an ex-wife with care of children.

In that case the wife had care of a child who was 15 and applied for an upward variation of periodical payments due to inflation, which inspired the husband to cross apply for discharge of her order altogether – after all their child was 15 and she should at that stage have been able to go out to work. However, in the meantime she had had another younger child by another man as the result of an affair, and claimed she could not work due to her obligations to this younger child. The court agreed with her, holding that she had a limited earning capacity, but that due to her obligations to the younger child she was necessarily prevented from becoming independent of the husband and that it made no difference that the younger child who was the cause of this limitation on her availability for work was not the husband's. They examined the meaning and purpose of s 25A and s 31(7) and restated the principle that while their combined effect was to discharge the so called 'meal ticket for life', this did not extend to bringing about a clean break regardless in appropriate cases. They had regard to the meaning of the words 'undue hardship' in both sections and reiterated their wide discretion to do what was appropriate. They considered that it was much too soon because of the existence of the younger child to think about a limited term order.

Ashley v Blackman [1988] 2 FLR 278 was, however, an exceptional case where the judge *did* courageously terminate the order. The facts indicate just how exceptional the case was however. Both the parties were very badly off, the wife being mentally ill and living off welfare benefits. The husband had remarried and had to support his new wife, but his income was so low that he did not even pay tax at the lowest threshold. He therefore applied to discharge the wife's maintenance order, which seemed reasonable enough especially as she was living off benefits and was so close to the poverty trap if she received maintenance that it was obviously hardly worth having any.

However, there was the so called principle in *Barnes v Barnes* which apparently did not permit the husband to give up paying maintenance when he *could* do so. Fortunately the judge realised the absurdity of the situation. He said it was a case for a clean break as everything the husband paid to his former wife was swallowed up in her benefits and in his memorable words the clean break was available 'to prevent a couple of acutely limited means from remaining manacled together indefinitely by the necessity of returning to court at regular intervals for no other purpose than to thresh out at public expense the precise figure which one should pay to the other, not for the benefit of either, but solely for the benefit of the tax paying section of the community to which neither of them had sufficient means to belong'.

Variation after a clean break   10.2

Potential for variation after a clean break will necessarily be limited, since a clean break is supposed to be in full and final settlement. However, that does not necessarily mean that a *consent order* is not variable: it is, just like any other order, but the *scope* for variation is likely to be limited since clean breaks and consent orders *are* supposed to deal with the matter once and for all, which is the whole point of the clean break legislation.

Therefore if a consent order is to be variable that should be made clear when it is made, as otherwise the parties may be stuck with the terms of it without possibility of alteration as in the case of *Dinch v Dinch* [1987] 1 All ER 818. In that case where the Court of Appeal had thought they could vary a property adjustment order but the husband was able to have the purported variation set aside, Lord Oliver of Aylmerton in declining to confirm the variation to help the wife in unforeseen difficulties under the original order, had some hard things to say about practitioners who do not check the terms of orders sufficiently, to the detriment in such a case of their clients when there are new circumstances and nothing can be done to the consent order scheme to meet them. There are a number of different principles here which need close examination.

'Liberty to apply'   10.2.1

The most basic principle is that returning to the court which made the order, under the 'liberty to apply, will only permit working out of the existing order, not variation as such.

Where the welfare of a child is at stake   10.2.2

If it can be shown that the existing order does not make proper provision for a child, which may include not providing properly for the custodial parent, the court may reopen a consent order: *N v N (Consent Order: Variation)* [1993] 2 FLR 868.

10.2.3   **Making a late application for relief where claims have not actually been made or dismissed immediately after the decree**

Where comprehensive claims have been made at the time of a divorce and those not effectively pursued as far as obtaining an order of a particular type have actually been *dismissed*, then clearly no further application will be possible: *De Lasala v De Lasala* [1980] AC 546. However, if there has not been actual *dismissal*, whether because there has never been actual application (eg defective prayer in the petition of a petitioner or no Form M11 filed by a Respondent) or perhaps because neither the parties, nor their advisers nor the court addressed the matter, then in theory a late application could be made, since the power of the court to make orders arises *on or after the grant of a decree*.

Nevertheless, the court does not like this because it is felt that parties should be protected against unexpected and stale claims long after the decree. Thus what may be a technically permissible fresh financial application to get around s 31 may not be allowed, as was the case in *Pace v Doe* [1977] 1 All ER 176 where a wife whose second marriage had swiftly failed tried to apply for a further order against her first husband to help her out of her unexpected financial difficulties.

However, in an appropriate case, leave for such an application might be granted, as in the case of *Chatterjee v Chatterjee* [1976] Fam 199 where the post divorce situation had not yet settled and the wife was allowed to make an application for a property adjustment order and for a lump sum order.

Note

It is not surprisingly now usual to deal in advance with the possibility of late claims by including an actual *recital* in a consent order that the provision is made in 'full and final settlement, thus avoiding the tedious problem of whether a claim should be allowed.

10.2.4   **Appeals out of time**

The alternative may be to appeal out of time for which leave will be given in limited circumstances, on the principles set out in the case of *Barder v Barder* [1987] 2 All ER 440, [1987] 2 WLR 1350, HL, which had bizarre and tragic facts involving the death of both the wife and the two children of the family for whom provision had been carefully made, when the wife killed both children and then herself committed suicide. Four conditions need to be satisfied that:

- a new event or events have invalidated the basis of the order *and* that the appeal is likely to succeed (this includes fresh evidence which could not have been known at the time the order was made, but *not* any new or more correct interpretation of what was *then* known all along);
- the new event has occurred within a few months of the order;
- the application for leave is made reasonably promptly;
- no prejudice will occur to third parties who have acted in good faith and for valuable consideration on the basis of the order.

Similarly tragic situations arose in the case of *Smith v Smith (Smith intervening)* [1991] 2 FLR 432, CA and *Barber v Barber* [1992] Fam Law 436. In the former an appeal out of time was granted, but in the latter where the wife died three months after the order, recognition was given to the contribution a wife makes to the marriage and the building up of assets by distinguishing between the part of a capital order made by way of 'golden handshake' at the end of a marriage, and the part made actually to provide for a wife and children after divorce, eg by buying a home or providing a lump sum to do so. In the latter case the court felt that the wife's share of the home should pass to the children of the marriage when they were grown up and did not accede to the husband's request that the order be rescinded on the basis that its whole purpose was nullified.

The court will not vary orders where the alleged basis is not really new but relies on facts which could have been ascertained at the time the order was made as in *Barber v Barber* (1980) Fam Law 125 where the wife knew about the husband's pension rights at the time of the order. Thus it is no good saying that tax calculations have been erroneous and that overseas legal proceedings have turned out differently from what was expected as in *Penrose v Penrose* [1994] 2 FLR 621, nor that the payer's wealth has dramatically increased because of land values depending on planning permission if that could have been foreseen as in *Worlock v Worlock* [1994] 2 FLR 689.

The court does not like granting such leave, although they have done so, eg in *Hope-Smith v Hope-Smith* [1989] 2 FLR 56 where the husband wilfully delayed three years before paying a lump sum order calculated on the basis of the value of the matrimonial home, which meantime soared to £200,000, requiring a consequent upward adjustment of the wife's lump sum or injustice would be done. Equally, such leave has been refused where the value of the home has *fallen* as in *B v B (Financial Provision: Leave to Appeal)* [1994] 1 FLR 219 and where shares have shot up in value as in *Cornick v Cornick* [1994] 2 FLR 530 but where there is no complicating factor such as in *Hope-Smith*.

In order to succeed in cases like the last two it will be necessary to show that there has been some undermining factor such a fraud, mistake or incomplete disclosure which destroys the whole basis of the order. This is particularly the case where the order is a consent order, as in *Munks v Munks* [1985] FLR 576 where an appeal was allowed only because there was a procedural irregularity as the order had in fact been granted before decree nisi which it should not of course have been, and *Redmond v Redmond* [1986] 2 FLR 173 where the husband had agreed not to apply for redundancy and had then done so.

Cases of subsequent remarriage or cohabitation within a short time of the order's being granted are not usually sufficient to undermine the order, unless blatant, and did not have that effect in the cases of *Cook v Cook* [1988] 1 FLR 521 nor *Chaudhuri v Chaudhuri* [1992] 2 FLR 73, [1992] Fam Law 385 though such an order was overturned after early remarriage of the wife in *Wells v Wells* 1992] 2 FLR 66, [1992] Fam Law 386 (this case was in fact decided in 1980 despite not being reported till more recently). Wives' changes of mind about sale of the home fall into the same 'foreseeable' category as in *Edmonds v Edmonds* [1990] 2 FLR 202 where the husband failed to get the order overturned, despite a rise in the price of the home when it was sold.

Note

There seems to be some doubt as to whether the technically correct procedure in seeking to appeal against a consent order is to appeal to *vary* it or to have it *set aside*.

10.3   Variation in practice

Naturally practitioners sometimes have to get round all these rules where the alternative is deadlock which has disadvantages to both sides. The main problem has been to find a way of discharging a periodical payments order on a payer's application where the payee will not agree because of discontent with the amount of money that is going to emerge at the end of a *Mesher* type order, since a periodical payments order cannot officially be varied by making the lump sum order that would unlock this particular impasse.

Getting round s 31(5)   10.3.1

The creative way to fit s 31(5) and s 31(7) together was found in the case of *S v S* [1987] 1 FLR 71, [1987] 3 All ER 566, where both the husband and the court wanted to terminate the wife's periodical payments order, and to give her a once for all lump sum, as she was a spendthrift who was always needing extra money over and above the actual order in her favour. They could not do so because of s 31(7), but the court decided it was possible to interpret s 31(5) sufficiently widely to enable them to *allow* the husband to *offer* a lump sum payment and when that was done to discharge her periodical payments order under s 31(7).

In *Boylan v Boylan* [1988] 1 FLR 282 they were happy to do this, but not happy with the husband's offer which was £40,000, despite his having just sold his business for £1.2m, and especially as the court calculated that she needed £16,000 pa for which the sum offered was insufficient compensation. The court could not itself fix the correct lump sum but if he wanted the scheme to work the husband clearly had to do better!

In *Peacock v Peacock* [1991] 1 FLR 324 the court in formalising the system a little further, while confirming that it could not itself either fix the amount of a suitable lump sum if the parties could not agree, nor *order* it, since this would be to fall foul of s 31(5), did concede that it can order that, once a lump sum payment (or a transfer of property) has been made by the paying party, the payee's periodical payments are to be discontinued, and if the lump sum or transfer of property never happens, can then reinstate the payee's periodical payments or grant any other application made by the payee such as for an increase.

The last resort   10.3.2

The ultimate remedy is to sue the solicitors responsible for the client's being restricted by an invariable or unappealable order for negligence, entitlement being to damages for what would have been received if the matter had been properly handled, as in the case of *Dickinson v Jones Alexander* [1990] Fam Law 137 where the solicitors used a junior member of staff, who did not realise that the husband was a wealthy man, to run a case without adequate supervision: proper disclosure of the husband's means was not obtained. The wife received a tiny lump sum of £12,000 and a maintenance order for the children of under £2500. Eventually the husband did not pay even this and the wife had to go on to welfare benefits. Ten years later she sued and obtained a total of £330,000. Not surprisingly the solicitors admitted liability immediately!

Similarly in *Re Gorman* [1990] 2 FLR 284 the wife received no property adjustment order so when the husband went bankrupt the trustee in bankruptcy sought possession and there had to be a temporary suspension of the order while the wife sued her former solicitors for having let the situation develop by not dealing with the matter properly on divorce and protecting her position.

You will of course take care not get into any such situation!

Self-assessment questions

1 What orders can be varied?
2 What orders can not be varied?
3 What does 'liberty to apply' mean and what is the effect of its inclusion in an order?
4 What does the court take into account on a variation application?
5 What are the usual reasons for a variation being sought by the payer? and by the payee?
6 Can a clean break order be varied?
7 Can a fresh application be made following a consent order which neither gives a party all s(he) might have had on divorce nor expressly bars such a claim?
8 When can you appeal out of time?
9 How do you get round the restrictions of s 31(5)?
10 Can a lump sum order be varied?

Chapter 11

Ancillary relief procedure

Introduction   11.1

Together with the (usually straightforward) conduct of
the actual divorce suit and the resolution through
Children Act procedure of any problems in relation to
the children, the successful settlement of ancillary relief
claims comprises the main workload of the matrimonial
solicitor. This chapter should be read in the context of
recent changes in the conduct of ancillary relief which
were inaugurated in *some*, but not *all*, courts in October
1996. These changes are fundamental, in the adoption of
a Pilot Scheme, designed to improve the efficiency of
ancillary relief procedure, details of which may be found
in the *Ancillary Relief Pilot Scheme* (1996) Fam Law 612.
The Principal Registry is participating in the Scheme but
many other courts are not, so its relevance to you will
depend on where you practice.

While you will therefore need to be armed with a
sound knowledge of the existing law and practice of
ancillary relief, including a knowledge of procedure,
even that full procedure may infrequently or even never
be used, since settlement, and formalisation by the existing abbreviated consent order procedure, and not litigation at all, will be the aim. On the other hand if you are
working in a court using the Pilot Scheme you may never
come across the 'old system'.

The prime reason for this is financial, since contested
ancillary relief proceedings are so expensive that to litigate
merely reduces the value of the assets available to provide
for the family, but as all litigation is wearing for the client
and matrimonial litigation arguably the most wearing of
all, a secondary aim of such changes will usually be to
save prolonging the inevitable stress and strain.

Note

Sometimes a client will press for a quick solution, for either
or both of the above reasons, and this may be a legitimate
concern which will influence the conduct of the case.

However, you should be aware that unless there are
very clear instructions, eg that full disclosure of the other
party's means is specifically *rejected* in favour of an early
solution which produces *some* financial provision immediately, perhaps because the client has some distressing

outside pressure such a terminal illness in the family, it is unwise to believe all clients say in this respect!

Settling early, particularly on disadvantageous terms which amount to less than the court is likely to order after a contested hearing, is often likely to lead to a later negligence action, against the firm, since clients have notoriously short memories and are inclined to take the money and *then* try to come back for more, like the wife in the notorious case of *Edgar v Edgar* [1980] 1 WLR 1410: although Mrs Edgar's solicitors *told* her not to enter into a disadvantageous separation agreement because it would prejudice any later application to the court, she would not listen and was subsequently very cross when they were proved to be right.

Despite the aim to settle as soon and as cleanly as possible consistent with a fair solution, it is better always to advise the client accordingly where it is necessary to litigate or to hold out for a better settlement.

Furthermore, despite the valid concern of avoiding unnecessary emotional stress for the client, it is not a good idea to resort to settling cases by *bullying* your own client to accept less than the net figure you could probably get by litigating. This is called selling your client down the river and is not an acceptable practice! Both solicitor and client must sometimes suffer a little in order to achieve a suitable settlement, and that may include a good deal of telephone harassment by the agitated client, particularly in the final stages of reaching formal agreement, until the case settles. A matrimonial solicitor is paid, inter alia, to endure these irritations.

11.2   Terminology

Irrespective of who was petitioner and who respondent in the *divorce suit*, for ancillary relief purposes, the parties are called the *applicant* and the *respondent* (ie in the technically separate *application for ancillary relief*, ie financial relief *ancillary* to the divorce suit).

11.3   Tactics

Since contested ancillary relief actions are expensive and wearing, the aim in most cases will be not to litigate at all but to settle; such settlements will lead to a consent order made by the court under the abbreviated procedure for approving such orders which have been previously agreed by the parties. Thus not every ancillary relief application will follow the full procedure set out below, although every suit will have common initial and final stages.

Sometimes, the full ancillary relief package will be agreed before the divorce petition is even filed (and every detail of that suit will also have been previously agreed). For example, if the divorce is based on Fact D, consent may not be forthcoming from the respondent until every financial detail is to that respondent's satisfaction.

Thus, planning the case for ancillary relief may in fact begin at the first interview with the client, yet nothing may be processed through the court until much later; alternatively, at the first interview the client's statement may indicate that there is going to be a stand up fight over ancillary relief. Obviously (for reasons of costs) it would be unwise even in such circumstances to embark on a contested action before at least an exploratory approach to the other side, but it *may* be necessary to go through the full procedure, blow by blow, using every tactical weapon provided by the Rules. Sometimes, there will be a hybrid approach, when ancillary relief matters start out as in theory on a cooperative basis, and it then turns out to be necessary to make use of the court's powers to compel disclosure or locate and freeze assets.

When to start thinking ahead to the ancillary relief proceedings
11.4

Ancillary relief orders cannot be made before decree nisi and cannot *take effect* until decree absolute. Nevertheless it is essential to start thinking about ancillary relief matters as soon as instructions have been received from the client.

Indeed, in every case, although detailed planning may be left till later, some *brief* attention must be given to ancillary relief at the first interview, for three reasons, so as to:

- apply for Legal Aid where that will be necessary (and warn the client about the impact of the statutory charge on the relief obtained: see 5.1.3);
- claim appropriate relief in the petition: see 5.3;
- begin negotiations as soon as possible.

Note _____

Ancillary relief cannot realistically be conducted on the Green Form, so the client will be either a private client or on Legal Aid. The trainee will also remember at the first interview of all, or at the first interview in relation to ancillary relief, to consider the existing position in relation both to the client's assets and the other party's and remember that it may be necessary to:

- register rights of occupation under the MHA 1983;
- sever a joint tenancy;
- advise that a new will should be made: see 5.2.

11.4.1   The prayer of the petition

The initial application for all forms of ancillary relief (except an order for sale under s 24A) must be made in the prayer of the petition, or in the prayer of any Answer filed by the respondent to the divorce suit: FPR 1991 r 2. 53(1). If no Answer is filed, a respondent (ie to the divorce suit) claims ancillary relief by notice in Form M11: FPR r 2.53(3). Under the Pilot Scheme there is a new form, Form A, which takes the place of Forms M11 and M13.

Note

Once one of the parties has claimed ancillary relief there will be an *applicant* for ancillary relief purposes and a corresponding *respondent*, so the trainee should watch out carefully for the terminology, since the respondent in the divorce suit may *not* also be the *respondent* in the ancillary relief proceedings.

You will remember that in preparing the petition, *all* forms of ancillary relief should be included in the prayer, and even if some inappropriate at the time, *none* should be omitted. Thus if the petition has not been prepared by the firm, a first task in any ancillary relief case will be to examine the petition to *check* that it makes a comprehensive claim. In many cases a check will prove fruitful even where the petition *has* been prepared by the firm! People make mistakes, especially when in a hurry, so it is unwise to take other peoples' work for granted, especially where a mistake will matter, as it will here.

Moreover, while the petitioner's claims to ancillary relief are routinely made in the prayer of the petition, if the *respondent to the divorce suit* wishes to make any, it will be necessary to file the form M11 to give notice of that if there is no Answer. Thus you should be alert to the necessity of filing a form M11, claiming the full range of ancillary relief, as *routine* at some stage during the course of the divorce suit (and certainly before decree absolute) if ancillary relief is likely to need to be claimed by a respondent, and to do this promptly if acting for such a respondent who has not filed an Answer.

While in theory the court can make any order on or after granting any decree, and leave may be sought to claim ancillary relief at a later stage – perhaps a long time after the divorce provided the applicant has not remarried, since s 28(3) would then preclude such application – the court tends not to like to grant such leave which may result in a party being taken by surprise by a stale claim which had reasonably been thought unlikely ever to be made.

What to do if the petition (or Answer) does not make a comprehensive claim for ancillary relief (whether the fault is your firm's or not)

With luck, the other side might agree to the relevant party's making a claim without leave by notice in Form 11, and this will almost certainly be the case if the parties have agreed a settlement: FPR r 2.53(2)

If the other side will not agree, what must be done depends on whether a decree nisi has been pronounced or not:

- if a decree has not been pronounced, there is still time to amend the petition or Answer, with leave of course and there should be no difficulty in obtaining such leave: see 5.8.
- if a decree has been pronounced, then a Form M11 will have to be filed, again with leave: FPR 1991, r 2.53(2);
- If a decree absolute has been pronounced and your client has remarried (as is sometimes the case, and of course without mentioning it to you first!) see Chapter 16.

Starting the action

11.4.2

An ancillary relief action starts with filing of either Form M11 or of Form M13, or Form A in the case of the Pilot Scheme and accompanying documents. The difference in M Form used depends on whether it is a party who has made a claim in a petition or Answer who is applying, or one who has not made a comprehensive claim in one of these pleadings.

Where the necessary comprehensive claim is in place in a petition or Answer, the application for ancillary relief is activated by filing Form M13, which gives notice of the intention to proceed with the ancillary relief claimed in that petition or Answer: FPR r. 2.58(1).

Where Form M11 had to be used anyway, that is sufficient notice, and nothing further, neither M13 nor any other form, is required in addition to the M11.

Filing

The following must be filed:

- Form M11/M 13, plus copy for service;
- Affidavit of Means in support of the application*;
- legal aid documentation if appropriate,* ie
  - certificate;
  - copy notice of issue;
  - notice of acting* if not already on the record (ie where the client was formerly on Green Form or is a new client);
- copy of any current Family Proceedings Court maintenance order: FPR r 2.56;**
- time estimate;**
- fee, if payable (ie if the client is not on legal aid when no fee is payable).

* one copy of each of these for the court but extra copies should be prepared for service which is undertaken by the solicitor and not by the court, unlike in the case of the divorce suit: if there is a solicitor on the other side, service will usually be on that solicitor.

** These items can be supplied later if necessary.

The copy M form (or Form A) will be issued, ie stamped and handed back for service.

Note

1 Where there is an application for a property transfer order, the land must be identified in the M or A form, stating whether it is registered or unregistered, and identifying the Land Registry title number, and giving particulars of any mortgage or other third party interest: FPR r 2.59(2). The trainee may already have this information if there was an MHA registration.

2 There will probably be no hearing date fixed at this stage, but most courts now issue standard directions covering affidavits, valuation of property, discovery and inspection of documents etc. There may or may not then be a later preliminary hearing for giving further directions, since some courts leave it up to the parties to ask for them if they are required, others routinely fix a short directions hearing so that there can be a stocktaking before the hearing itself is reached. The district judge has a power to give directions about pleadings, affidavits, filing, serving, specific discovery, valuation etc at any stage anyway: r 2.62(5). The directions hearing can be used to make interim orders and costs of such hearings will usually be costs in the cause.

Service

The other party must be served within four days of issue: FPR rr 2.55 and 2.58(1) with:

- sealed Form M11/13;
- copy affidavit;
- notice of issue of legal aid certificate;
- copy notice of acting.

The respondent to the ancillary relief application should file and serve an affidavit in reply within 28 days.

Note

If there is an application for variation of settlement the trustees and the settlor if alive will need to be served with a copy of the Form M11/13 or Form A and in some cases the supporting affidavit: FPR r. 2.59(3) and (4).

If there is an application for a property adjustment order in relation to mortgaged land (ie generally the matrimonial home, which is usually mortgaged) the mortgagees must also be served, and the latter can apply to the court for a copy of the applicant's affidavit: FPR r 2.59(4) and may also file an affidavit in answer to the application: r 2.59(5), although this is rare in practice.

Affidavits of means   11.5

The spouses' affidavits of means are most important documents and call for the assembly of detailed information and some skill in drafting.

The *applicant* must, unless otherwise directed, file an affidavit with the M11 or M13 to support the application: r 2.58(2) ; if the applicant is asking for a property transfer or settlement of property order details must be given of that property together with details of the property to which the party against whom the application is made is entitled either in possession or reversion and if a variation of settlement is requested, details must be supplied of all settlements, whether ante- or post-nuptial, including details of all money brought into the settlement(s) by each of the spouses: r 2.59(1). In the Pilot Scheme there are usually no affidavits, the information is supplied on Form E instead. Affidavits may be directed *as well*.

The *respondent* to the application must similarly file an affidavit in reply to the applicant's within 28 days, and that affidavit in reply must give details of all the respondent's property and income: r 2.58(3). It is possible for this 28 days to be extended and it often is, due to the extensive enquiry which must be sometimes be made to supply the required information if the case is the least bit complicated. Indeed, the complexity and expense of such affidavits is the foundation of what has come to be known as the 'millionaire's defence', where a rich respondent (such as Baron Thyssen-Bornemisza in the case of the same name) successfully asks the court not to insist on filing of a detailed affidavit on the basis that the extent of his wealth is such that he can easily pay any order which the court might reasonably make for the support of his former wife, and that the expense and delay occasioned by compiling a detailed affidavit is therefore not justified.

11.5.1 Drafting affidavits

The precise form of each of the spouse's affidavits will therefore depend on which spouse you are drafting for, since the applicant's will be claiming relief and justifying the claims made, whereas the respondent will be resisting the claims and justifying that resistance. However, there is a printed form which is generally used in simple cases, although in any case other than the simplest where the parties are employed and have no complex financial affairs, an affidavit drafted from scratch will be best since it permits the solicitor to set out the client's case as attractively as possible. Nevertheless, where the printed form is not used, it is usual to follow the order of topics as dealt with in the printed form, since this is convenient for the court which, being used to the common use of the printed form, is half expecting at least routine matters to be dealt with in the same methodical order. Sample precedents for both types appear in Appendix 5. For greater variety, you should consult one of the practitioners' collections, such as Clark, Parker & Blair.

The following will need to be covered:

- *income* (all sources, ie employment, or self-employment, or more than one of each, even state benefits; investments, including bank, building society and other interest, dividends etc. and if the client is self-employed, accounts for the past three (or possibly five) years will be required, alternatively income tax returns for the same period);
- *benefits in kind* (company car, tied accommodation, low cost loans, discounts etc);
- *outgoings* (including NIC, expenses of travel to work, meals at work, union dues and professional subscriptions, mortgage/rent, council tax, water

rate, house and contents insurance, gas, electricity, TV, car and associated expenses, school fees and extras, recreation and clubs, loans and credit cards, legal fees or legal aid etc, etc).

Note

These two heads may be compiled from the budgets and schedules compiled for the purpose of advising on ancillary relief: see Chapter 7, and be double checked against the client's income tax returns:

- *assets* (everything owned by the client alone or jointly with the spouse or any other person or persons, all real property and bank and building society accounts should be included, plus shares, unit trusts, PEPS, TESSAS, cars, boats, antiques, works of art, jewellery, silver, etc, etc);

Note

The history of the acquisition of some assets may be relevant, where, eg one spouse has been a major contributor to the acquisition of that asset.

- *pension rights, insurance policies, and interests under settlements or trusts* should not be forgotten, and *expectations under wills or intestacies* may also be relevant;

Certain other matters will have to be dealt with in most cases:

- *actual or intended remarriage or cohabitation* (this will obviously be relevant to provision);
- *conduct* (the court is only interested in conduct which it is inequitable to disregard and all other conduct will be irrelevant to the ancillary relief decision: see MCA 1973 s 25(2)(g) at 7.3;

Note

Allegations of conduct in this context may necessitate transfer of the case to the High Court due to its difficulty or the complexity or gravity of the issues: *Practice Direction* [1988] 2 All ER 103, [1988] 1 FLR 540. Where adultery is alleged in an affidavit of means (or an allegation of an improper association with a named person) a copy of the whole or part of the affidavit must be served on that person together with a copy of Form M14 and the person in question will be entitled to intervene in the proceedings. The moral to be drawn from this is that only the most essential and material allegations of adultery should be indulged in at this stage, unless the clients have time to spend and money to burn!

- *argument in support of the party's case/Comments on the other party's affidavit* (it is usual under this head, whether the printed form is used, in which case the final paragraph invites such 'write in' comment, or whether the affidavit is drafted from scratch to wind up the affidavit with a request for or against the grant of such orders as are sought).

Note _____

Whoever is going to argue the case before the district judge if it is not settled should draft the affidavits. It is only fair that the advocate should have the final say as to how the case is to be put. Normally each party should file one affidavit only, although more than one is permissible if really required, and there may be further affidavits in support of the claim/resistance to it, in which case the advocate should draft these too.

11.5.2   Insufficient affidavits – what to do

Note _____

Under the Pilot Scheme these will be a first hearing by which time all information must have been supplied on the Form E within 10 weeks of commencing the ancillary relief suit so this section only applies if you are still using affidavits.

There are two categories of defective affidavits:
- those not filed at all; and
- those actually filed but which are inadequate.

In the former case, where no affidavit has been filed, the remedies are:
- *a formal request for the affidavit to be filed*, either by letter to the other side, giving a short period, eg seven, 14 or more days in which to comply, or if that is ignored, by application to the district judge for an order, if necessary with a penal notice attached: by r 2.62(5) the district judge can make such an order at any time, and if an order is made without penal notice attached, eg on standard directions, such a notice can also be added at any time;
- *an interim periodical payments order*, preferably at the high end of the possible scale, which normally flushes out the desired affidavit since the respondent will want to protest and exclaim at the iniquity of requiring an oppressive level of payments to be made.

Note

No affidavits of means, or other disclosure, can be obtained from lovers and mistresses, though the other spouse can be asked to depose to such persons' means so far as they know about them: *Wynne v Wynne and Jeffers* [1980] 3 All ER 659.

In the latter case, where the affidavit you have is so coy that it is hardly better than none at all, the remedies are:

- *a rule 2.63 questionnaire*, administered either informally by letter or more formally in a similar format to the Request for Further and Better Particulars with which the trainee will be familiar in civil litigation generally;

Note

All questions must be at directions under the new Pilot Scheme.

- *an application to the district judge for directions* (which is equally suitable for no reply at all to the rule 2.63 request or to replies as inadequate as before).

Note

Clearly this is a game that can go on for a long time. It is better *not* to deliver questionnaires in instalments, both because it saves costs, time and temper and because it is much more effective to hit the other side with a comprehensive shopping list of requirements. Instead you should go for one big sortie, preferably of intelligent questions based on a little careful sleuthing beforehand.

Ask the respondent for as much detail as possible and then threaten to use r 2.62(4) to obtain documents and/or personal attendance for cross-examination and r 2.62(7) for a production appointment, whereby any person can be compelled to attend to produce documents at an earlier stage provided those documents could have been compelled for the actual hearing: r 2.62(9).

Then examine the documents obtained carefully – credit card statements are usually very productive, since they often inadvertently reveal undisclosed accounts and certainly often bear witness to some very expensive habits and extremely costly non-essential consumption in parties who are resisting comparatively small maintenance for their former nearest and dearest, or even worse for their children who often come long after expensive club subscriptions and large regular payments to exclusive stores.

11.6   Discovery and inspection

Discovery is automatic, unless some other period or arrangement is agreed, 14 days after the last affidavit is filed, with inspection seven days later: *Practice Direction* [1981] 2 All ER 642, [1981] 1 WLR 1010. The basic system is no different from that pertaining in ordinary civil litigation. However, matrimonial cases are distinct in that again it will be usually be necessary to adopt an intelligent approach to what is produced and to look for clues as to what you are not being given. Obviously you will not wish to have a pitched battle over every gas bill, but an analytical approach to the documentation you are given is likely to yield reward. The obligation is to provide full disclosure to the court which cannot make orders properly without it: while this was always the practice, as was made clear in the case of *Livesey v Jenkins* [1985] 2 WLR 47, it is now also formally enshrined in a *Practice Direction* [1995] Fam Law 156 and the court does not take kindly to being misled, so you are more than entitled to probe. You can always ask the district judge for specific discovery of any document which you suspect you need and have not got. This can be *very* productive, since one document often leads to another, until it becomes absolutely clear why you did not get the one you first asked for at the beginning!

Note

At this stage, if it has not been considered before or even incorporated in an affidavit, it may be advisable to make an offer of settlement or one may be expected from the other side. This may be an open offer or a *Calderbank* offer.

The latter is an offer, called after the case of the same name, reported at [1976] Fam 93, which is expressed to be 'without prejudice, but reserving the right to refer to the offer on the issue of costs'. Obviously such an offer is better in writing and is usually in a letter. It is the matrimonial equivalent of a payment into court and is subject to the same rule of not being referred to at the hearing. If the district judge awards no more than was offered, the offer may then be referred to and should protect the party on whose behalf it was sent at least from having to pay the other side's costs from the date it was made, and may indeed enable the offeror's own costs to be recovered also.

There is a special system for disclosure of such offers under the Pilot Scheme.

The hearing   11.7

The hearing will usually be in Chambers before the district judge and will be private, although there is power to refer the application to a judge of the court: r 2.65. Such hearings are normally very informal though occasionally a particular judge will prefer more formality. The furniture is usually arranged in a T shape in front of the judge and the parties and their lawyers sit either side of a table along the leg of the T with the judge at the top and address the court seated.

The case will normally be opened for the applicant, witnesses called and cross examined, the same order followed for the respondent, and then the advocates for the respondent and the applicant respectively will address the court. However, some district judges are much more informal and will indicate from the start what they are considering by way of order and will adopt an inquisitorial approach based on their reading of the affidavits, inviting comment on specific matters before deciding on an appropriate order, which may be delivered in the form of a short judgment or alternatively may merely announce the decision. If possible a good note should be taken of the whole proceedings or at least the judgment, in case there is to be an appeal, and if counsel is instructed this will usually be the task of the solicitor.

Note

The President's Direction on Case Management, delivered in the *Practice Direction* referred to above, follows those handed down in the Queen's Bench and Chancery divisions, and now limits the length of opening and closing speeches, both of which are required to be 'succinct', and also the time allowed for examination and cross-examination of witnesses and reading aloud from documents and authorities; unless otherwise ordered, witness statements and affidavits are now treated as evidence in chief and these are themselves supposed to be confined to what is reasonably essential. Moreover, a bundle should be agreed and sufficient copies produced in A4 format for the use of the court and parties, and be duly lodged with the court, properly paginated and indexed, two clear days before the hearing. Such, obviously, has been the standard of previous preparation, that the Direction indicates that the President even finds it necessary to require that such bundles be 'wholly legible' and 'arranged chronologically'! A pre-trial review and skeleton argument is required in cases estimated to last five days or more.

However, it seems that the court retains a realistic view of the general standard of preparation which is likely to be achieved notwithstanding these instructions, since provision is made 'if there is no core bundle' for parties to furnish the court 'with a list of essential documents for a proper understanding of the case'.

The advocate with any experience at all will swiftly see how essential to the proper presentation of a case the requirements of the *Practice Direction* are and wonder why it was necessary to formalise those requirements in such a manner! Clearly such preparation makes all the difference between a case with which the advocate is familiar and which can be presented in a readily digestible manner which is likely to produce the desired order and one where the district judge has got to dig and delve to discover what it is all about, and as a result may well not be drawn to the inevitable conclusion that the order sought is the one that should be made!

11.7.1   The order

The following should be remembered:

- periodical payments can be backdated to the date of the application (though the court might not want to make them so if this produces large arrears which cannot conveniently be met);
- the order may be registered in the Family Proceedings Court: 9.3;
- costs must either be ordered or allowed for in the order, always a vexed question in ancillary relief where there may be no clear winner and where one or both parties may be on legal aid;
- legal aid taxation should be ordered (and must therefore be asked for) to enable costs to be recovered from the Legal Aid Board where appropriate;
- certificate for counsel will be required (and must therefore also be asked for) if counsel was instructed or this will not be recoverable either from the other side who is paying the costs or on legal aid;
- *liberty to apply* should be included to enable the parties to return to court if difficulties subsequently arise in the implementation of the order, though this means strictly for the purposes of implementation not variation: see Chapter 10.

The order will be drawn up and available for the parties usually within a few days of being made. Unless there is an appeal, or enforcement problems: see Chapter 9, that is the end of the ancillary relief matter.

Appeals

Either party may appeal from the district judge to the judge within 14 days of the order: r 8.1(4), setting out the grounds of the appeal. The judge will exercise a complete discretion in hearing the appeal, but will give such weight as is thought fit to matters determined by the district judge – the judge decides to what extent such matters are to be reopened and has a complete discretion as to what further evidence may be admitted: *Marsh v Marsh* [1993] 2 All ER 794.

Consent orders: see 11.7, can also be appealed, but it seems that the correct way to do this is to apply to set the order aside: FPR 1991 rr 1.3(1), 8.1 and 8.2, CCR 1981 Ord 37 r 6. Pursuant to Order 37 r 6 a rehearing will be ordered on application within 14 days, or later with leave to make the application out of time.

Consent orders: s 33A, MCA 1973

The full procedure described above is not necessary if the parties succeed in what is now usually the original aim of agreeing a consent order from the start. In that case, MCA 1973 s 33A gives the court power to make a consent order, r 2.61 of the FPR 1991 will apply and the abbreviated procedure may be followed:

- If agreement is reached before Form M11/13 is filed, application is simply made by one party or the other on Form M11/13 as appropriate for an order in the agreed terms, lodging with the application two copies of a draft order one of which must be endorsed with a statement signed by the respondent agreeing to the terms
- if agreement is reached at any time *after* Form M11/13 is filed, the same procedure may still be followed
- in either case, pursuant to r 2.61 the full procedure need not any longer be followed (ie if no Form M11/13 has been filed, no affidavits of means are even required) but the court will required a short statement of financial information on which it may base its order and there is a form, called a Rule 2.61 form, for this purpose, although it is not strictly necessary to use it and although it is usually convenient to use the form, the information required *may* be given in another manner, if desired in more than one document, so that those affidavits might satisfy the rule such as where affidavits of means have already been filed.

Note

> The purpose of this procedure is to avoid the court making a consent order on inadequate information as to whether each of the parties intends to remarry or cohabit (clearly relevant to the provision in the order), where each party is to live and, briefly, what capital and income is at the disposal of the each of those parties. without this the court is unable to have an opinion as to whether the order is broadly fair, and might make an order such as in the case of *Livesey v Jenkins* where the wife who was receiving a generous order suitable to her not remarrying immediately neglected to mention that she was engaged to be married and proposed to do so with indecent haste!

Where agreement is reached only long after the proceedings have been established, and perhaps at the door of the court, the court does have the power to dispense with the strict requirements of r 2.61 and can both manage without the draft order and direct that the r 2.61 information be given in any form that is convenient, thus enabling an order to be made before the parties change their minds: r 2.61(3).

Note

> It is the *practitioner's* responsibility, and *not* the court's, to see that the order is carefully drafted so as to reflect accurately and comprehensively what the parties have agreed: see *per* Lord Oliver of Aylmerton in *Dinch v Dinch* [1987] 1 WLR 252 at 8.4.2 above and *Sandford v Sandford* [1986] 1 FLR 412. It is for this reason that it is a good idea to take some time to settle the terms of the order, possibly have them approved by counsel, and then to bring a properly agreed draft to the court, as otherwise in the haste attending the order drawn up in the court corridor, far from protecting your clients from the results of the other side's aggressive negotiation, it may be they who are enabled to get back on the drafting what they have lost on the negotiation, a well established practice in the supposedly co-operative atmosphere of 'doing the best for the family as a whole'!

11.9   Good practice in ancillary relief

It must be stressed that the only good settlement is one which is made on the basis of full and frank disclosure, and the only good consent order is one which is fair in relation to all the matters that must be taken into account in arriving at a balanced result. The consent order should therefore be for relief in the ball park area of what the court would be likely to order after a contested hearing at which the parties had both been properly represented.

It may therefore be a good idea, in some cases even if the full ancillary relief procedure is not to be followed, to ask for affidavits to be exchanged in draft, or possibly even sworn, although disclosure may be made much more informally, either orally at meetings, supported by such documents and vouchers as are reasonably required to verify what is being said, or in correspondence. Acceptable documentary support would often be tax returns and such other more detailed documents as the other party's advisers might reasonably request. This achieves as full and frank disclosure as is really necessary and saves a lot of time and expense since the greatest part of a contested ancillary relief matter is not the hearing but the preparation.

The abbreviated procedure may then be used with some confidence to obtain the actual order once it is agreed. This approach usually does *tend* to produce the best result for the family as a whole, since the best use may be made of tax planning, and it may also generate a more cooperative attitude which may benefit everyone in other ways.

Note

The only situation in which full and frank disclosure on the approved model might *not* be insisted upon is where the parties are obviously co-operating well, and nothing is to be gained by turning down or querying good offers which are being made. Nothing is to be gained by putting either or both of the parties' backs up and if there are still small areas of disagreement in such a case, either small concessions can be made (it is unusual for a party to have to make no concessions at all) or a persuasive solicitor can often put the final touches to an agreement which has already been substantially made by the parties by coaxing the last items of detail out of a party who has already showed more than willing.

If a half way house is desired between an agreed order and a court hearing, there is available a service provided by the Family Law Bar Association Conciliation Board which provides an adjudicator from a panel of senior barristers to consider the papers and make a recommendation, which may or may not be binding on the parties as they wish themselves to provide before seeking the adjudicator's help. It is only available where both parties are represented by solicitors and is not a free service but can be useful in avoiding much more expensive proceedings.

11.10   Drafting consent orders

A good set of precedents and some practice is all that is required to produce good consent orders, and for basic advice reference should be made to Chapter 8 above.

Self-assessment questions

1 When should you first think about ancillary relief?
2 Is litigation or negotiation a better approach to ancillary relief matters?
3 When and how must ancillary relief claims be made?
4 What do you do if a comprehensive claim has not been made at the appropriate time?
5 What is full and frank disclosure?
6 What is an affidavit of means and what goes into it?
7 How is discovery effected?
8 What is a r 2.63 questionnaire?
9 What is the abbreviated procedure for consent orders?
10 Whose responsibility is it to see that consent orders reflect what the parties have agreed?

Chapter 12

Taxation

Introduction

As revenue law is a pervasive subject on the LPC, a working of knowledge is already presumed to have been achieved before family law is started. This chapter therefore concentrates on tax considerations likely to be useful to the general practitioner in family law, especially those practising principally in the field of divorce.

There is now little change in the tax position when a couple either *separates* or *divorces* because of:

- fundamental changes in the taxation of maintenance from 30 June 1988 whereby all orders made after this date are paid tax free into the hands of the recipient: Income and Corporation Taxes Act (ICTA) 1988 s 347A as inserted by the Finance Act (FA) 1988 s 36; and
- the fundamental change to separate taxation of spouses which took effect in 1990: see 12.2.

Prior to 30 June 1988 extensive tax relief was widely available on divorce, and this made the payment of maintenance much more attractive to divorced people who could afford to pay generous orders off the top of their income by utilising the personal allowances of their divorced spouses *and also* of each child payee. Divorces for tax purposes were not unheard of, especially as orders could be made by the court in favour of children *which were technically orders against the payer*, thus providing tax relief to divorced people for expenses, ranging from ordinary food, clothing and household bills to school fees, which had to be paid out of taxed income by people who remained married. Clearly, although it was originally thought to be right to help those who had suffered the misfortune of divorce in this way, the system was too good to last when numbers divorcing escalated and it was realised that such tax relief was not only unfair to those who managed to keep their marriages together, but was also morally indefensible. Militated not only against marriage and intact families, but also against the concept of spousal self-sufficiency, since a wife who already received maintenance using all her personal allowances had no incentive to go out to work when if she did so she would begin to be taxed at a much higher rate than other people earning the same.

It is in this context that the general rule is that pursuant to ICTA 1988 s 347A and FA 1988 s 36 maintenance is now tax free in the hands of the recipient, whether the payee is a spouse or former spouse or a child of the family, and this is the regime with which you should expect to be familiar during the training contract. However, some awareness of the previous system may be necessary should you be obliged to deal with a variation of a maintenance arrangement made under the old system, since the parties are be entitled to remain under the old regime if they wish.

Happily, there have been no transitional arrangements in switching to separate taxation of spouses: *all spouses* will now be subject to separate taxation, so if you are consulted by a client who is separating and/or wishes to obtain a divorce will only have to consider the few minor quirks of the system which have special application to married couples. This is relatively simple for the solicitor to master, even one not a specialist in revenue law, so it will not usually now be necessary, except in the most complex and high value cases, for reference to be made to an accountant.

The work lost to accountants when the fundamental change was made in 1988 has now, however, more than been replaced with forensic accounting work in ancillary relief cases, especially those involving creative application of the assets to make best use of what there is to provide for the family as a whole. A *working knowledge* of tax is therefore essential for the divorce solicitor, so that you are able to:

- identify cases where an accountant will be necessary; and
- understand what the accountant instructed is proposing;

but a *detailed knowledge* of revenue law is not.

Note

Where tax considerations *are* relevant in divorce, it will depend on the individual tax in question whether it is *separation* or *divorce* which triggers a change. In the case of Income Tax (IT) and Capital Gains Tax (CGT), any changes will take place at the end of the tax year in which the parties *separated*, but in the case of Inheritance Tax (IHT) the fundamental change will be when the decree absolute of divorce is obtained. The right to MIRAS is usually immediately affected when a party moves out of the matrimonial home though limited temporary arrangements are available for MIRAS purposes: see 12.3. Divorce practitioners will also need to be aware of the existence of Value Added Tax (VAT) and National Insurance Contributions (NIC) especially in relation to family businesses: see below at 12.5.

If you have a case involving a pre-1988 arrangement

12.1.1

Although the change to tax free maintenance took effect some eight years ago, because the radical nature of the changes made in 1988 could not be accommodated in existing ancillary relief packages, some maintenance is *still* being paid subject to the old taxation rules, under arrangements which were referred to in the Finance Act 1988 as 'existing obligations' which are defined by s 36(4) as:

- periodical payments orders made by the court before 15 March 1988;
- periodical payments orders made by the court before 30 June 1988 where application for the order was received on or before 15 March 1988;
- any maintenance agreement under a deed or set out in writing made before 15 March 1988 and sent to or received by an Inspector of Taxes on and before 30 June 1988;
- any oral maintenance agreement made before 15 March 1988 which is then confirmed in writing and those written particulars sent to and received by an Inspector of Taxes before 30 June 1988;
- any variation of any of these.

Tax relief still therefore benefits those paying under an 'existing obligation', and can continue when such arrangements are *varied*. However, tax relief is pegged at the 1988–89 tax year level. The parties can change to the contemporary system if they prefer.

Income tax

12.2

Each spouse is now taxed separately, each setting off an annual personal allowance against income tax, and the husband also receives a *married couple's allowance*, unless this is paid by choice to the wife or it is split between them: FA 1988 ss 32 and 35 and Schedule 3.

Where there is a child or children, a *single parent* left to manage alone, through death, divorce or the *wife's* total incapacity, can have an allowance equivalent to the married couple's allowance, *on top of* the ordinary personal allowance to which there would be routine entitlement as a single person: where the married couple's allowance is available in this way it is then called *single parent's allowance* (which is the term commonly used) or *additional personal allowance* which is the correct title for the allowance in ICTA 1988, ss 259 and 260. These allowances are often referred to in abbreviated form as 'SPA' and 'APA' which is clear enough, but 'MCA' in a taxation context means 'married couples allowance' and not the 1973 statute to which family lawyers make constant reference!

Note

Tax relief in respect of the married couple's allowance is pegged at 15% for 1996–97.

Each spouse is taxed at basic rate, only paying the higher rate over the annually fixed threshold. (When working out a divorce client's tax position, however, trainees should remember that below the basic rate there is also the lower rate of tax payable on the first small slice of income after the allowances are exhausted, designed to help the lower paid.) Each spouse is responsible for making their own tax return and paying their own tax on all income, a change which has reversed many years of wives' resentment of officially not existing separately from their husbands for tax purposes, which has also benefited the Family Law practitioner, since there will not be much tax impact of the parties' separation and/or divorce.

12.2.1   1996–97 tax rates and bands

For the tax year 1996–97 the rates and bands of tax are as follows (all applicable to taxable income after all allowances have been exhausted):

Lower rate (20% tax)   £0–3,900
Basic rate (24% tax)   £3,900–£25,500
Higher rate (40%)   Everything over £25,500

Allowances to be deducted from gross income before applying the applicable band to remaining income, which is the taxable figure

Personal allowance*   £3,765
Married couple's allowance* (MCA)   £1,790
Single parent's allowance (SPA)   £1,790

* These allowances are increased at age 65 and again at age 75.

The single person's/additional personal allowance   **12.2.2**

Either spouse who has one resident dependent child can claim this allowance after the parties are separated provided the:

- spouse is separated, whether or not also divorced, but if divorced is not remarried;
- the child is under 16 or if over 16 is in full time education or training.

Note

The allowance is the same irrespective of the numbers of dependent children who are officially living with the claimant (and even children at University or away elsewhere for educational purposes qualify as resident for this purpose) so if both parents claim it, the Inspector may split it between the two of them. On the other hand, if there at least two children, both parents can have the allowance if at least one qualifying child resides with each. No CA 1989 s 8 order is now required, although sometimes parents could not use this extra allowance because in the pre-Children Act regime one or the other of them had to have an order for custody, with or without care and control, and this sometimes cut across the tax considerations which would have benefited the family as a whole.

To claim the allowance, it is *crucial* that the claimant has n*ot remarried*. The allowance is *always lost* on remarriage, even though that parent is *still* a single parent in relation to that child and may have taken on onerous obligations on remarriage. The Inland Revenue thinks wicked stepmothers are confined to fairy stories.

Tax implications of separation and divorce   **12.2.3**

Where the parties *separate* the Inspector may not consider them to be separated for tax purposes immediately. By s 282 of ICTA 1988 they consider the separation to be a fact for Inland Revenue purposes if separated if they are separated in such circumstances that the separation is likely to prove permanent, but individual tax offices may operate different procedures and may be prepared to consider a couple separated in other circumstances. Separation is relevant in IT terms to whether a man is entitled to the married couple's allowance or whether either party is entitled to the single person's/additional personal allowance. The husband generally keeps the married couple's allowance until the end of the tax year in which the parties separated and the additional personal allowance will be available to either or both parties from the end of that tax year.

Divorce has no independent IT implications.

While pursuant to ICTA 1988 s 247A maintenance under all post 1988 arrangements is paid gross, the *payment of maintenance* is subject to one special IT rule contained in ICTA 1988 s 247B(1). Under this section, payments to a *spouse or ex-spouse* are classed as *qualifying maintenance payments*. Payments made to *children* are *not* however covered, although they can be brought within the definition by drafting the order or agreement to express the payments to be made to *the spouse or ex-spouse* but *for the benefit of* the children in question. When this is done, the payer will receive tax relief equivalent to the (presumably by that time lost) married couple's allowance of £1,790, although this £1,790 is only now allowed at the rate of 15%, ie £258. This tax relief is available to set against CSA maintenance assessments as well as against court orders.

Note _____

As the relief is only meant to replace the lost married allowance, it follows that the payer cannot claim it as well as the married allowance, so if the £1,790 married allowance is already being claimed that will be the total of the relief allowed!

Moreover, if the payee spouse remarries, it will no longer be possible to make qualifying maintenance payments to that spouse pursuant to ICTA 1988 s 347A because of MCA 1973 s 28(1)(b) which terminates periodical payments on remarriage, so it will not be possible to route periodical payments to the ex-spouse even for the children.

Although it is such a small sum, it is always worth drafting consent orders to take advantage of the small tax relief available as it seems to be important in principle to payers, regardless of the fact that *any* tax relief on maintenance, even this tiny amount directly linked to the married allowance, is now so small.

12.3   MIRAS: ICTA 1988 s 355(1)

Mortgage interest relief at source is the 'tax deductible' element of money paid in interest on mortgage loans, a routine element of the budget of most couples for whom the divorce practitioner will act. Interest on such loans is deductible in calculating the income of the payer for tax purposes: ICTA 1988 s 353(1) and the tax relief is given at source so that the payer need only pay to the mortgagee the net monthly amount which falls due. The scheme is restricted to loans of up to £30,000 only for the purpose of buying the payer's only or main residence, although the interest will not qualify unless it is on a loan to:

- buy an estate or interest in the home (whether that is the whole interest or a part share, including to buy another party's share); or
- pay off another loan on which interest would have been eligible for relief; or
- (for loans made before 6 April 1988 only) improve or develop land or buildings on it or in doing repairs the need for which had arisen before the purchase: ICTA 1988 s 355(2B) as inserted by the FA 1988 s 43.

Note

Since 6 April 1991 by FA 1991 s 27 and Schedule 6, MIRAS is not allowed against higher rate tax and has since also suffered the almost routine pegging to 15% which has hit other tax allowances, so out of every £100 due in mortgage interest £85 will now actually be paid. However, it does not matter for MIRAS purposes if the mortgagor does not pay tax, as in that case the payment is still made net as if tax were paid, although by ICTA 1988 s 369(4) relief may be given against unused personal allowance through the mortgagor's code.

Normally only one home may qualify for MIRAS at any one time, though if bridging finance is necessary, because a taxpayer cannot sell the existing home before buying another, tax relief will be available for both loans, but only up to a total value of £30,000 altogether, for a transitional period of a year from the date the second loan is taken out: ICTA 1988 s 354(5).

For the purposes of MIRAS relief, husband and wife living together count as one taxpayer despite the introduction of separate taxation! However, whereas this used to be unfair in relation to cohabitees, who could each have a separate allowance for the same property, since 1988 MIRAS relief is restricted to one claim per property (although where cohabitees were already each claiming under the prior system that has not been disturbed unless or until the property is sold or remortgaged, when the double entitlement to relief now goes).

When husband and wife *separate* they each qualify for MIRAS, and subject to the transitional arrangements the spouse out of occupation of the home will not qualify for

MIRAS, so it is then better for the spouse who remains in occupation to pay the mortgage, if necessary being given periodical payments to fund the mortgage, thus continuing to claim MIRAS for the property, although the spouse out of occupation will still be restricted to the current total tax relief on maintenance of £1,720 at 15% in respect of the periodical payments! Divorce is definitely not the bargain it used to be prior to 1988!

Note

Because MIRAS cannot be claimed by a spouse out of occupation of the home, it is not usually a good idea for that spouse to agree to pay the mortgage personally under a *Mesher* order.

12.4 Inheritance Tax: Inheritance Tax Act (IHTA) 1984

You will be familiar with the general operation of IHT. This is a tax which only impacts on spouses on *divorce*.

During the marriage, no IHT is payable on transfers of value between the spouses: IHTA 1984 s 18 and this position will continue, regardless of separation, until *decree absolute of divorce*. Even then IHT is unlikely to affect any dispositions which, having been ordered by the court following decree nisi, will take effect in accordance with the normal ancillary relief rules only on decree absolute. The reason for this is that either s 10 or s 11 of the IHTA 1984 will probably cover the situation where IHT might otherwise have been payable because either it:

- does not confer gratuitous benefit: IHTA 1984 s 10; or
- is a disposition for family maintenance: IHTA 1984 s 11.

The rationale behind the first exception is that husband and wife are no longer 'connected persons' for the purposes of the IHT and CGT legislation after decree absolute: IHTA 1984 s 270 and Taxation of Capital Gains Act (TCGA) 1992 s 286, and therefore transfers between them pursuant to an order of the court in ancillary relief proceedings will be transactions at arm's length and not intended to confer gratuitous benefit: IHTA 1984 s 10. For the avoidance of doubt, in 1975 the then Senior Registrar (now called the Senior district judge) issued a statement on the point with the agreement of the Inland Revenue which is reported at (1975) 119 SJ 596.

The rationale behind the second exception is that a disposition is not a transfer of value if made by one spouse in favour of the other or of the children for their maintenance or for a child's education or training, and by s 11(6) a disposition in favour of a spouse 'on dissolution of marriage' or *varying* such a disposition is specifically expressed to be within s 11. It would therefore appear that unless such a disposition were unduly delayed no IHT is likely to be payable on divorce, though if there were in any particular case the parties may use their annual exemptions (£3,000 pa in total under s 19 *plus* £250 per person in any number of small additional gifts under s 20 for the tax year 1996–97) and such gifts may include potentially exempt transfers under s 3A). No IHT will of course be payable if the disposition falls within the transferor's nil band which is £200,000 for the tax year 1996–97.

Note

While it is inadvisable to invite trouble from the Inland Revenue by abusing the rules, the opportunity may be taken in the ancillary relief proceedings to have the court order any disposition which can reasonably qualify as maintenance and this will enable wealthier payers to pass property on to the next generation and at the same time to provide for the family with a saving in IHT.

This should always be remembered when an ancillary relief package is being proposed: normally the practitioner will in any case look behind the actual assets available, eg trusts and trust property, and family companies, in order to ascertain their true nature and potential for providing for the family before making or agreeing to any proposals: see above at 7.2. However, when the parties are wealthy, and sometimes even when they are merely reasonably well off, the overall package can be designed to make the best use of the assets available in a tax efficient way which because of the potential tax saving costs the payer little (because of the tax saved) and yet brings disproportionate benefits to the payee. It is also surprising what some payers will do, when the tax saving is explained, which they would not consider at all in favour of spouse whom they are shedding, if they could not find some virtue in doing the Inland Revenue out of some tax!

Capital Gains Tax: TCGA 1992   12.5

You will be familiar with the general operation of CGT. This is a tax which impacts on spouses on *separation*, and can therefore be little more than a nuisance to divorcing spouses.

During the marriage, transfers between spouses which might otherwise give rise to a chargeable gain are treated as if neither a gain nor a loss accrues: s 58. This does not mean that the transferee will be able to dispose of it free of CGT, but that that transferee acquires the asset at the value at which the transferring spouse acquired it. This is a hangover from the days when the spouses were one person (and that one person was the husband!) for tax purposes. Even while they are married, the spouses now have an annual CGT allowance each to set against gains (£6,300 for the 1996–97 tax year) so there is no incentive to separate promptly for CGT as *separation* ends free inter-spouse transfers, although usually the Inland Revenue will regard the married rule as continuing, as in the case of Income Tax, until the end of the tax year in which they separated. There can therefore be CGT problems in relation to the division of their assets in ancillary relief proceedings:

- while there is no CGT on disposals of *cash*, so lump sum payments ordered under s 23 will be exempt, there is no CGT relief on disposals of assets which have to be paid to enable the payer to pay the lump sum to the payee;
- property transfer orders under s 24 (and any similar arrangement made between the spouses *without* a formal s 24 order) may give rise to a disposal for CGT purposes unless the Inland Revenue can be convinced that the transferee already owned that asset, eg a share in the home where *legal* ownership was in one spouse but both owned the property *beneficially*, ie in equity.

For this reason, despite the court's powers under s 24 to rearrange family assets how they choose, subject only to s 25, it may still be necessary to know which spouse owned what according to the ordinary rules of property law: see Chapter 16 below.

Note

Regardless of the annual exemption of £6,300, certain assets transferred on divorce will be outside the CGT rules anyway, eg cars and other household chattels, commonly transferred under s 24, and tangible moveable property which is a wasting asset (ie with a predictable useful life of 50 years or less). The only potential problem in most cases is likely to be the home, and that will only be if, because it has not been occupied as such by one of the spouses for the whole period of ownership, it does not completely qualify for exemption from a charge to CGT as the principal private residence of both spouses: TCGA 1992 ss 222 and 223. Even here CGT can usually be got round by one means or another as the gain will be apportioned and only part, for the period(s) out of occupation, charged to CGT, but as the home is deemed to be the principal residence for the last 36 months of ownership there will have to be some delay in selling the property, or transferring the share of the spouse out of occupation to the other spouse, or a *Mesher* type order for a CGT problem to arise at all.

Avoiding or reducing CGT on the matrimonial home

12.5.1

This will only be necessary if the home is sold or transferred more than three years after the transferor left.

The first line of defence is the *Extra-statutory concession D6*. This applies where the transferor spouse has moved out more than three years previously but has not elected any other property in lieu of it as the qualifying only/or main residence for tax purposes. The spouse out of occupation is simply deemed to have remained in occupation right up to disposal and no CGT is payable. The divorce practitioner should point this out to the client, but in practice there is more to life than saving *all* possible taxes, an effort which may not be cost effective in other respects. A particularly irritating facet of CGT is that it is a costly tax which is levied on money which has probably already suffered income tax, but there are various mitigations, not least of which is that the property market is now so slow and inflation so stable at a low figure that the great capital gains of the past are certainly to figure as a worry in most people's divorces, since clients are more likely to be grateful if an eventual disposal of the home is not at negative equity.

Where ESC D6 does *not* apply, because the non-occupying spouse has a new principal residence, that spouse will therefore have to bite on the bullet and take comfort from the following:

- only the gain attributable to the period of ownership over the ESC D6 36 months while the spouse was out of occupation will be taxed, not the whole period of ownership;
- the gain can be index linked from March 1982 (although since November 1993 this cannot create a loss as it previously could – now it can only cancel or reduce a gain);

- the non-occupying spouse's annual exemption of £6,000 can be used;
- the gain may be held over under FA 1980 s 79 so that it is not payable immediately.

Note

Certain orders create CGT settlements which bring special CGT rules into effect at the beginning and end of the settlement and while it is in force. All orders giving the wife a right to occupation for life, or until remarriage, or voluntary removal fall into this category, eg the *Martin* order, and if the trainee has to work on a case involving such an order it will be necessary to consult the firm's tax department or else an up to date specialist practitioner's book on matrimonial finance and taxation for the taxation consequences of the order. However a *Mesher* order is not in this category.

12.6   The importance of taxation in ancillary relief

You should not suppose that tax considerations should drive the ancillary relief package regardless of all other matters to be taken into account. The important point is to achieve a workable and acceptable overall package which suits the family as a whole, and only *then* to consider the tax implications, to see if added value may be extracted from the picture than at first appeared, eg in making use of the divorce to achieve some IHT planning, and also to see that the *net* effect when tax is taken into account is not radically different from what was envisaged when the package was proposed. The family's future is usually more important than saving a little tax, but it is foolish to throw away any benefits that may be available by arranging matters in one way rather than another, eg where a spouse is to retire from the husband's family company tax advantage may be taken of giving her (and possibly the husband as well) a tax free 'golden handshake' which will provide both cash for her and a means for the husband to pay it. You should get used to using knowledge gained in one part of the LPC (in this case Business Law and Practice) in another, since this is how practice as a solicitor works and how experience is built up over the years.

You should also be on the lookout for the *tax implications* of the client's instructions.

Example

The client wife has been working in the husband's business during the marriage. You will want to know whether she is a paid employee, a partner or working for nothing. If the latter it will usually increase her share of any assets obtainable for her. It will then be relevant whether the business is run by the husband as a sole trader, or if it is a partnership or a limited company, and what its profits – or debts! – are. Has the wife paid income tax and National Insurance Contributions? If it is a partnership, is it registered for VAT and has this been paid? Has the wife outstanding tax liability in respect of this business, either qua partner or director, or personally, and in particular any liability for which the husband should be required to indemnify her?

You are *not* expected to be a walking tax encyclopaedia but *are* expected to be able to hear alarm bells ringing, and call on the fire brigade (ie the firm's tax department or if there is no such department, the principal) where anything untoward appears to justify it.

Worked examples   12.7

Because of the net effect calculation: see 7.4.1, it will often be necessary for you to work out what is the net spendable income of each of the parties under the proposed order. This is not a complex calculation but a simple arithmetical task, and is much rewarded by the approval of district judges when it has been done, not only in a case where it is vitally necessary, but where it would be helpful to know the effect of the order, and the calculation should be prepared in advance without specifically having to be asked for.

Something which could be done on the back of an envelope is quite sufficient, although it looks better if it is well word-processed on one sheet of paper.

Example

If in a fairly typical 'net effect calculation' family where both parties are in work, the husband earns around £12,000 and the wife, working part time, earns £6,000. The husband is to pay £3,000 to the wife for the children of the family, the family's position will be as follows:

Husband's net spendable income:

Wages		£12,000.00
Less personal allowances		£3,765.00
Taxable income		£ 8,235.00
Tax on £3,900 @ 20% lower rate	£ 780.00	
Tax on £4,335 @ 24% basic rate	£ 1040.40	
Total tax	£ 1,820.40	
Less QMP relief @ 15%	£ 268.50	
Tax payable		£ 1,551.90

The husband's net spendable income	£12,000.00	
Less maintenance @	£3,000.00	
Less tax payable @	£1,551.90	
Total to spend		£7,448.10

which is a significantly different figure from the £12,000 started off with or the £12,000 started off with less the £3,000 maintenance for the children, and not a figure which anybody would have been likely to guess accurately without doing the calculation.

Note

NIC and pension contributions have been ignored for the sake of simplicity in demonstrating the method.

Wife's net spendable income:		
Wages		£ 6,000.00
Less personal allowances		£ 3,765.00
Taxable income		£ 2,235.00
Tax on £2,235 @ 20% lower rate	£ 447.00	
Less £1,790 SPA @ 24% basic rate	£ 268.50	
Tax payable		£ 178.50
The wife's net spendable income	£ 6,000.00	
Less tax	£ 178.50	
	£ 5,821.50	
Plus maintenance (entirely tax free)	£ 3,000 .00	
Total to spend		£ 8,821.50

Self-assessment questions

1 In what ways does taxation of married persons differ from that of single persons?
2 What are 'existing obligations'?
3 Is there any tax relief available when maintenance is paid?
4 What is Additional Personal Allowance?
5 Is it separation or divorce of married persons which is relevant to IT/IHT/CGT?
6 What is MIRAS?
7 Is it worth a husband out of occupation of the home paying the mortgage?
8 Are there usually any IHT problems in relation to divorce?
9 Are there usually any CGT problems in relation to divorce?
10 How important is taxation in ancillary relief proceedings?

Chapter 13

Welfare benefits

Introduction

You will need to be aware of the availability of welfare benefits for separated and/or divorced clients. Benefits may be needed either short-term on marriage break-down or permanently following divorce: in some cases where the parties are of acutely limited means, welfare benefits will be needed in both situations. You will need to be able to recognise implications for welfare benefit entitlement of any ancillary relief orders obtained, and vice versa, since it is of course essential that if mainte-nance is to be received which disentitles the client to ben-efits, the order should deliver a significantly better financial result than if reliance is placed solely on welfare benefits. If this matter is not addressed clients risk falling into the 'poverty trap'.

Benefits are obtainable either from the Benefits Agency or in some cases from the Local Authority. It will be for the client, not the solicitor, to make the actual application. This must be done on the appropriate form, which will be completed at the local office of the Agency. This is usually followed by an interview for new claimants, following which those not required to be available for work they will be given a book of orders to cash at a post office: if the claimant does have to be avail-able for and actively seeking work, the benefit will be paid by fortnightly giro cheque which will include their unemployment benefit if applicable.

However, you will find that a working knowledge of the system is still essential for the trainee so that appro-priate advice may be given to prompt the client to apply where appropriate and this will be a routine task when advising initially under the Green Form. The main sources of the law are the Social Security Contributions and Benefit Act (SSCBA) 1992, as amended, and the various regulations governing each benefit, ie for income support, the Income Support (General) Regulations 1987, for family credit the Family Credit (General Regulations) 1987, for housing benefit, the Housing Benefit (General)Regulations 1987 and for council tax the Council Tax Benefit (General) Regulations 1992 (SI

1992/1814). In social security law the regulations are at least as important as the statute.

As a trainee working in a practice where clients commonly use benefits, you will need to have regular access to a good up to date practitioner's book on the subject, such as the annual publication of the Child Poverty Action Group, established some years ago as the 'benefits bible', although there are now a number of other authoritative works. The CPAG is usually issued in paperback and regularly updated since annual changes in the rates and sometimes applicability of the various benefits are generally announced each autumn for implementation at the start of the next tax year in the following April.

The Benefits Agency also publishes regularly updated leaflet and booklets describing the individual benefits, including a useful booklet entitled 'Which Benefit?' which explains the range available, and these are available from Post Offices and Benefits Agency offices. A practice dealing regularly with clients using benefits will usually have a stock of such material to hand out to clients, since this saves taking up Green Form time going over the detail, as where appropriate the client can be advised in outline, given the booklets and advised to go straight to the Benefits Agency office to claim.

13.2   Two types of benefits

Benefits are either:
- means tested (most benefits); or
- not means tested (Child Benefit and One Parent Benefit) often abbreviated to CB and OPB.

13.3   Non-means tested benefits

The two non-means tested benefits, child benefit and one parent benefit, are also tax free, although they will count as income for the purposes of some other welfare benefits. The law is to be found in the SSCBA 1992 ss 141–147.

At present, all clients with children to care for are likely to be receiving child benefit, and some may also have one parent benefit: if the second benefit is not, received, one parent benefit should be applied for as soon as the client has been separated for 13 weeks. The client can do it, on a standard form obtainable from the Benefits Agency which is sent in by post for processing at the Child Benefit Centre in the provinces, and when processed the extra amount due will be added to the child benefit already received. However, some clients who already receive child benefit may not know about the extra money and will need to be advised to apply: if necessary the client should be pressed to do so, and to do so promptly as soon as 13 weeks are up since the separation, since there is no point in foregoing this useful extra money which is an uncomplicated automatic tax free entitlement to anyone on child benefit who becomes a single parent and which has no downside.

Child benefit, and where appropriate one parent benefit, is paid to every person, regardless of means, who is responsible for a child either up to the age of 16, or up to the age of 19 where a child is in full time non-advanced education or training (ie any course below University first degree level), but there is a current proposal to remove both for children aged 16–19 so as to provide further funds for youth training and similar schemes.

Note

These two benefits are the only non-means tested benefits. Every other benefit is means tested. Like child support from the Child Support Agency, child benefit, and one parent benefit if applicable, is only payable for children over the school leaving age (16) when they are in full time *non-advanced* education or training, ie A levels or even a secretarial course qualify, a University degree does not in any circumstances. Where a child leaves school at 16 or later, or stops further non-advanced education under the age of 19, either or both of these benefits usually continue to be paid until the child obtains a full time job or goes into some form of training which does not qualify for the Benefit, or ultimately when the child reaches 19, whatever that child is then doing.

Child benefit

Child benefit is claimed from the Benefits Agency for any child living with a client or to whose maintenance a client contributes at a rate not less than the weekly child benefit rate. This is a standard weekly amount, in 1995–96 £10.40 for the first child and £8.45 for each subsequent child). The benefit will usually be paid to a parent, but this is not necessarily always the case, if someone other than a child is living with or maintaining the child.

Sometimes when parents separate, there are arguments as to which parent is entitled to the child benefit

13.3.1

and one parent benefit which will then become available after 13 weeks of separation. While the parties are married and living together, child benefit is technically payable to either of the parents, and if it is paid by order book, both names will be on the cover of the book and either may draw the orders, but the mother usually has the prime claim to receive it. Historically, child benefit was introduced to provide mothers with the care of children with one reliable source of income to spend on the children. However, once the parties are separated either can qualify since in law a person is *responsible for a child* if:

- the child lives with that person; or
- that person contributes to the child's maintenance at a weekly rate not less than the rate of child benefit.

When the person receiving child benefit (usually the mother) separates from the other parent, she is obliged to inform the Child Benefit Centre of this change of circumstance, and thereafter child benefit will usually be paid to her if the child is living with her. If the other parent, usually the father, disputes this there are rules which enable the dispute to be solved by the Benefits Agency, which you need not be concerned with, as this is a matter which the client can properly sort out independently by going round in person to the local office of the Benefits Agency, irrespective of whether other benefits are being paid. Once claimed, child benefit is paid four weekly, usually direct into the recipient's bank account.

Note

Child benefit will continue to be paid where there is a claim to it regardless of whether the person responsible for the qualifying child or children is married, separated, divorced, remarried or living with a new partner, though this is not the case with one parent benefit: see 13.3.2.

13.3.2   One parent benefit

One parent benefit is a flat rate tax free extra sum added to the child benefit (£6.30 in 1995–96) for which the claimant already qualifies as soon as that person has been separated for 13 weeks. No formal separation is required, though the separation must be 'permanent'. However to qualify for one parent benefit, it is essential that the claimant does not remarry or cohabit with a new partner.

Means tested benefits   13.4

The means tested benefits are:
* income support;
* family credit;
* housing benefit;
* council tax benefit;
* the social fund.

As there are a number of them the various benefits are often abbreviated to IS, FC, HB, CTB and SF.

These benefits form a framework, the main beam of which will be *either* income support *or* family credit, as these benefits are mutually exclusive. Of the two it might be said that *income support* is the principle one, since that is the benefit for people with *no income* or *negligible income* (since, eg, there is a tiny earnings disregard which is increased, but not significantly, for single parents). Where a client cannot claim income support, because of earnings from working more than 16 hours a week, but is still low paid, and in need, and has at least one child, *family credit* will be available. In other words, while income support is the basic welfare benefit payment for the unwaged, family credit is a benefit targeted at low paid families who *are* in work, and for whom not being able to obtain income support because they are working is a hardship. Clients of most general practices working on legal aid will use family credit if not income support, and whether they are also entitled to any of the portfolio of other benefits will depend on the detailed working of income support or family credit respectively in relation to their particular circumstances.

Income support: SSCBA 1992: ss 124–27   13.4.1

Income support is paid to anyone whose income does not exceed the 'applicable amount' (see below) and who is:
* over 18 years of age;
* habitually resident in the UK;
* not in full time work, ie not working more than 16 hours a week, and whose partner is not in full time work;
* available for full time work and actively seeking work or excused (eg heavily pregnant women, the disabled, or a lone parent with a dependent child);
* not in 'relevant education' (full time non-advanced education) unless living away from home or responsible for a child.

Note

A child up to the age of 19 who is receiving child benefit cannot claim income support. One claim is payable per household, and a household is either a married couple, cohabitees living together as man and wife or a lone parent with a child or children, and the income of the unit will be taken into account in calculating how much income support should be paid. The amount payable will vary with the needs and circumstances, eg the numbers and ages of the dependent children.

Capital affects the claim. *No claim* is possible if the claimant has capital or savings over £8,000, and a reduced amount is paid if savings are between £3,000 and £8,000 (£1 is taken off for every £250 of capital). The capital value of the home is ignored.

Calculating income support

The means test works on the basis of how much a person needs to live on. This is called the 'applicable amount' and against it is set the total of any income. The second figure is taken from the first and the balance paid in income support.

A person's 'applicable amount' includes:
- a personal allowance for the claimant and any partner;
- a personal allowance for dependent children;
- a family premium (where there is at least one dependent child);
- a lone parent premium;
- various other premiums (eg for the disabled or pensioners);
- mortgage interest where applicable.

Note

Water rates, council tax and insurance are not included in the applicable amount.

A person's income includes:
- earnings of the claimant and any partner (net of tax and NIC and half any pension contributions);
- maintenance;
- child benefit and one parent benefit;
- 'tariff income', ie the £1 per £250 of capital over £3,000 mentioned above, since this is treated as producing income at that rate whether or not it in fact does so.

Note

Maintenance is counted as income, whether paid voluntarily or under formal agreement or court order, *including* lump sums whether paid by instalments or not, as are statutory sick pay, maternity benefits *and part time earnings* over £5, though this disregard is raised to £15 for lone parents.

Income support also entitles the successful claimant to a range of 'passport benefits':
- free school meals;
- free NHS prescriptions and dental treatment;
- free milk and vitamins for expectant and nursing mothers and pre-school children.

Note

Loss of passport benefits is one way in which a claimant can fall into the 'poverty trap' by working and losing income support instead of remaining on benefit, and careful calculations should be done before deciding that it is worth the claimant giving up income support.

However, the greatest benefit of all is that mortgage interest (though *not* the repayment of capital element of the monthly payments) can be included in the applicable amount, although there are now restrictions on the total amount of the mortgage on which interest can be paid, as well as a lengthy delay before the payments can commence. Claimants are expected to have mortgage protection insurance to cope with mortgage payments when they are out of work. This is a significant change in the former situation, where mortgages could always safely be taken over when the home was transferred outright to the occupational spouse on divorce since if the client fell on hard times the State would pay till matters improved. Where mortgage interest is paid through income support the interest will normally be sent direct to the lender.

Note

Once mortgage interest relief is qualified for, loss of it is another way in which the claimant may fall into the 'poverty trap' by losing income support on going back to work.

Appeal and review
Review by the adjudicating officer is the first step in any appeal against a benefit decision with which the claimant is dissatisfied. Appeal can then be made to the Social

Security Tribunal, which has a legal chairman and two lay members experienced in social security matters, and finally on point of law and with leave to the Social Security Commissioners, and again with leave to the Court of Appeal.

Note

The trainee working with clients using income support will need to become familiar with the Income Support (General) Regulations 1987 (SI 1987/1967) which are usually amended annually and with the latest benefit rates which are contained in the Social Security Benefits Uprating Order 1995 (SI 1995/559).

The diversion procedure

You will need to know what to do where payment of maintenance is erratic or insufficient to preclude income support. In this situation, a client may be able to claim income support one week and not the next, which is irritating and time consuming to say the least. The solution may be found in the *diversion procedure*, which puts the claimant permanently on benefit but enables the maintenance order to be assigned to the Benefits Agency who can then pursue the maintenance payments. To use this procedure, the maintenance order must be registered in the Family Proceedings Court, ie it must be one of their own or an order of another court, including a divorce county court: see Chapter 14.

13.4.2　Family credit: SSCBA 1992 ss 128 and 129

This is a tax free benefit designed to give help to low paid working *families with children* and is paid to anyone with at least one dependent child who is:
- habitually resident in Great Britain;
- in full time work (or whose partner is in full time work, or if both partners are in full time work, ie 16 or more hours per week).

The *family* can consist of a married or unmarried couple but it seems that any other 'couple' or family grouping is excluded.

The capital limit is again £8,000, with a reduced amount payable if savings are over £3,000, so that as with income support a tariff income will be presumed of £1 per £250 of such capital or savings.

The amount of family credit actually paid will depend on the claimant's circumstances but if a claimant has less than a fixed sum coming in, called the *threshold*, currently £73 per week, the maximum appropriate family credit will be payable. If it is over £73, then the family credit paid will be reduced by 70p in the £ (not £ for £ as with income support).

Income for family credit purposes includes earnings, all periodical payments either to the claimant or the child or children, however paid, over the first £15, most social security benefits and pensions, and any tariff income must also be added, but it excludes the child benefits and housing benefit which are ignored for family credit.

Note _____

The £15 *maintenance disregard* is exclusive to family credit, and does *not* apply to income support where there is a similar £15 *earnings disregard* for lone parents.

Family credit is claimed by post and once granted lasts for six months (26 weeks) regardless of all changes in the claimant's circumstances unless the claimant's job is lost, when it will be necessary to come off family credit and go onto income support instead. Family credit does not carry the complete range of passport benefits applicable to income support, but it does now entitle the claimant to free NHS prescriptions, dental treatment and eye tests, and help with the cost of spectacles.

There is a 'fast service' for processing applications from newly employed and self-employed people.

Housing benefit: SSCBA 1992 s 130   13.4.3

This is a useful benefit which is:
- paid to anyone liable to pay rent for a home;
- whether or not the recipient is in receipt of income support or family credit;
- who has capital not exceeding £16,000.

Note _____

The payment will be made either to the person who is *liable* to pay the rent or to a person who is *obliged* to pay the rent in order to remain in the home because a third party has not paid it, eg usually the partner of the person claiming.

It is claimed as a *rebate* on council rent or *direct to the claimant* to meet private sector rent payable to a landlord. Generally only one home is allowed.

It covers all eligible rent:
- 100% of rent where the claimant is on income support or with income not over the income support level;
- at a reduced level according to a formula for higher incomes.

'Eligible rent' does not include water rate and sewage charges, nor some service charges. Moreover, 'eligible rent' can be reduced by an 'appropriate amount' if the dwelling occupied is too large for the claimant or if the rent itself is unreasonably high for that accommodation. Rules about rent have recently been made more restrictive and housing benefit at the full rate will no longer be paid where the rent in question is above the level for the area where the home is situated.

For the purposes of housing benefit income is defined in the same way as for income support, and family credit if claimed is *included* as income.

13.4.4   Council tax benefit: SSCBA 1992 ss 131–33

This is a useful benefit usually automatically available to those on housing benefit and income support. The maximum benefit is 100% rebate of the tax and it is available to those:

- on low incomes;
- with less than £16,000 capital;
- whether or not they are on income support, family credit or housing benefit.

The scheme is a national one although it is administered by the local authorities collecting the tax, and the DSS makes the regulations which govern its operation. There is a reduced level for those on higher incomes. Income is defined in the same way as for income support, and there is a £15 *maintenance* disregard.

Note

Married and unmarried couples are both responsible for each other's council tax while they are cohabiting.

13.4.5   The social fund: SSCBA 1992 ss 138–40

The further source of benefit money was originally set up by the Social Security Act 1986, s 32 to replace the former system of single payments for special needs, such as furniture, which could not be met out of the ordinary weekly benefit income. Whereas single payments were outright, those made under the social fund are either grants or loans to those on low incomes for meeting exceptional expenses, and the new concept is that both loans and grants should be discretionary and cash limited.

There are two types of loans:

- budgeting loans; and
- crisis loans;

both interest free.

Budgeting loans

These are for persons on income support and are repayable, (out of the income support received), discretionary according to needs and limited to repayments affordable to the claimant. They are designed to spread the cost of larger items over a longer period, and besides furniture could include removal expenses.

Crisis loans

These are to meet immediate short-term expenses following disaster, or emergency where the health or safety of the family, discretionary according to needs and also limited to repayments affordable and in any case to £1000. This type of loan can even cover living expenses for up to 14 days or travel costs.

Alternatively, there are community care grants, which are not loans and therefore not repayable, but their availability is both discretionary and cash limited. These are designed to help people lead independent lives in the community, such as when they leave residential institutional care, but may also be made to relieve exceptional pressures on families, and could include minor house repairs, travel or removal costs and furniture.

Example

One or other of these payments may be available to deal with family crises such as smashed furniture or a fire following domestic violence, or travel or removal to be with a sick relative. Generosity depends on area and although there is extensive and complex guidance for social fund officers adjudicating on claims, inevitably some human element creeps in besides which the cash limiting system will mean that some particularly deprived areas will exhaust their funds earlier than others.

There are also funeral grants, available to applicants making funeral arrangements who are on income support, family credit, housing benefit, council tax benefit or the disability working allowance, and also maternity payments, designed to buy clothes and equipment for a new baby. The former are loans and are repayable out of the deceased's estate; the latter are not loans and are not repayable.

Marriage breakdown and welfare benefit planning   13.5

The basic principle is that welfare benefits are not a primary resource for s 25(2)(a) purposes, but that the facts of life are such that sometimes when there is not enough money to go round, particularly when a low paid man starts a new relationship or second family, somebody may have to go onto welfare benefits. This is most common where the man has left a first wife and children, caring for whom will prevent the first wife from working, and has set up house with a cohabitee or second wife, who is herself prevented from working, by caring for a young child or children. As the second woman will have a partner who is working, welfare benefits will be unavailable to *her*, but the first wife who is now without a partner will *not* be debarred from benefit, since her problem will be that her husband has left her for the other woman. It will thus usually be the *first* wife or partner who will have to go on to welfare benefits, or when the children become older, will have to go out to work.

The Child Support Act 1991, which has been in force since 1993, is having some success in enforcing the support of children by their liable parents, so that wherever possible neither the state nor the step parents are now paying for these children. However, the problem is still not entirely eradicated, as some such children have no liable parents (if those parents are dead or have disappeared) in which case there are various principles which are applied in attempting to resolve the matter of who shall be supported by the state as fairly as possible.

13.5.1   The principle in *Barnes v Barnes*

The first principle is that a husband or father cannot throw the burden of maintaining his family onto the State, but equally that there is no sense in making orders that reduce him below subsistence level. This was initially established in the case of *Barnes v Barnes* [1972] 1 WLR 1381, [1972] 3 All ER 872 and has been several times reiterated, including in the case of *Ashley v Blackman* [1988] 2 FLR 278 where the judge courageously decided to terminate a wife's periodical payments on a variation application because the parties were both of such acutely limited means that the public money spent in their returning to court for such purposes at public expense (since both were on legal aid) was simply not justified when the mentally ill wife living off welfare benefits merely lost some of her benefits whenever the husband (who earned so little that he paid no tax) could afford to pay maintenance. In that case the judge in expressly referring to the *Barnes* decision said that it was a 'salutary principle, protecting public funds from feckless or devious husbands who seek to escape their proper responsibilities' but also recognised that sometimes it was simply not possible for a man to pay for two families out of one wage.

The Child Support Act continues the recognition of the *Barnes* principle, but as tempered by the obvious sense of not exacting payments which reduce the payer below subsistence level, in requiring *all* liable parents, even those on income support, to contribute a nominal amount out of their benefit payments for the support of their children.

Previously judges had for years been recognising the pointlessness of making orders which took the payer below subsistence level so that in turn he would have to claim benefits, and this became enshrined in the cases of *Stockford v Stockford* and *Furniss v Furniss*, both already mentioned in earlier chapters, which are together credited with having produced the net effect calculation now widely used to assess the effect of potential orders in families of limited means, although there was an occasional backlash against the use of welfare benefits as in the notorious 1988 case of *Day v Day*. In that case Mr Day's cheeky assertion that he should not have to pay maintenance for his wife and step children because she would be in a better financial position on benefits, did *not* find favour with the court.

The case of *Reiterbund* already mentioned earlier, carried the *Barnes* principle into pensions when it was decided that where there were limited resources the availability of state benefits was in the particular circumstances a viable alternative to the husband's pension, the right to which the wife would lose on decree absolute if he died before she was 60 and entitled to her own pension.

The more recent case of *Delaney* also mentioned earlier, is a classic one of the first wife who had to be the one to go out to work or on to benefits because the husband could not afford to pay for both families even with his cohabitee's contributions, his second partner being unable to claim benefits due to living with him. In that case the judge, overturning an earlier order that the husband should pay substantial maintenance to the children of the first union, expressly said that the husband was entitled to balance his future aspirations for a new life against his earlier responsibilities, so that the proper course was to allow the wife, who was eligible for benefits to claim them, thus preserving the husband's income, such as it was, for his second family.

The second principle is that if a husband is truly out of work and unable to find employment he cannot be assumed to have an unrealised earning capacity and order to pay maintenance on the basis that he should be working. The CSA requirement of a minimum contribution of £2.33 per week out of such a father's income support is the only exception to this rule. The CSA was in fact not the originator of this principle, which was first established in the case of *Freeman v Swatridge* [1984] FLR 762 where the judge ordered an out of work father to pay 50p a week each to his children, thus making it clear that being on welfare benefits did not automatically have to preclude the imposition of a maintenance order as a matter of principle. The CSA seems to have recognised this view, on the basis that if the court makes an order that is fair and reasonable – such as a total of £1 per week in this case – it does not necessarily follow that the husband will be taken below subsistence level, so there is no need for a *rule of law* that maintenance cannot be ordered against a husband on welfare benefits.

However, if the husband is out of work, a *nominal* order, which can later be increased when work is obtained, is the right one as was made in the case of *Berry v Berry* [1986] 3 WLR 257, [1986] 2 All ER 948.

13.5.2   The liable relative formula

There is a statutory duty on a man to maintain both his wife and (since relatively recent but little noticed amendments to the law) his ex-wife; Social Security Administration Act 1992 ss 106, 107 and 108 and Income Support (Liable Relatives) Regulations 1990, and also his children, whether he is married or not, and similarly a woman is liable to maintain her husband and all her natural children. Thus if a liable relative fails to fulfil this statutory obligation to maintain, and a dependent claims benefits, the Benefits Agency will want to be reimbursed. It is usual practice to attempt a voluntary agreement with the liable relative first but failing this the Agency will take proceedings if they think they can recover the money expended on benefits. Obviously, this has created hazards for those contemplating a clean break involving transfer of property or capital in lieu of periodical payments for a wife, as has been mentioned above at 8.2.3, and to this is now added the right of the CSA to assess an absent parent for child support payments regardless of a carer parent's agreement (which cannot in law oust the Act or Agency involvement) not to ask for a child support assessment.

The only complete defence against liable relative claims following a clean break is for the liable relative to be without the means to satisfy any judgment so that the Agency in question is forced to the conclusion that the person in question is not worth their powder and shot! Otherwise some creative practitioners are apparently now abandoning clean breaks and returning to *Mesher* orders where the proceeds of sale that would otherwise be paid to the spouse who asks for CSA assessments are reduced by the amount of the assessment.

Note

The liable relative formula is widely used by courts to assess what subsistence level is for a potential payer before making orders that can on that basis be afforded.

Structuring the ancillary relief package to make the most of benefits

13.6

The practitioner with the type of practice where welfare benefits are widely relied on will obviously have a good grasp of the available benefits so as to advise clients whether it is or is not worth applying for a maintenance order.

It will also be necessary to beware of the capital limits on the various benefits, and the tariff income deemed to come from capital above the lower limit, in deciding whether clients should or should not receive lump sum orders. In particular, capitalised maintenance in the form of a lump sum may be a problem, since the client will be expected to use this up over a period before being entitled to benefits. Even where a lump sum is in fact for another purpose, unless it is the client's share of a capital asset, and is earmarked for the purchase of a new home, it can be treated by the Benefits Agency as disguised maintenance. The proceeds of sale of a former matrimonial home will be disregarded if it is used to buy a new one within six months. On the other hand the value of the home is ignored so it may be better to take a residential property which can be classed as a home in settlement rather than cash.

13.7 Relevance of the matrimonial home in welfare benefit planning

The value of the matrimonial home will be disregarded for welfare benefit entitlement, but there are other problems to watch out for.

13.7.1 The home and the CSA

Limited credit can now be given in CSA assessments for past capital settlements: see Chapter 7. However, this is not entirely satisfactory and prevention of the problems which have arisen in the past would now be better than relying on such imperfect cures.

Attention has already been drawn to the hazards of a clean break settlement where the transferee subsequently goes on to welfare benefits. This problem can also be particularly acute in relation to child support under the CSA 1991 where the former matrimonial home is transferred in return for the transferee agreeing to support the children as in the case of *Crozier v Crozier* [1994] 1 FLR 126. In that case Booth J refused to reopen such a clean break settlement when the wife applied for a CSA assessment for the child, holding that there can never be a clean break between parent and child. If a spouse wants to make such a deal, transferring either property or cash with the intention that this would effect proper provision for a child's maintenance, a trust would have to be set up and this would only be suitable in an appropriate case where transfer of a share of the home and/or of capital could generate sufficient income to provide for the child's needs, which would restrict its application to a minority of cases.

13.7.2 Income support and mortgage interest on the home loan

While the Benefits Agency will pay some of the interest element if the payer is on income support, they will not pay all of it (see 13.4.1) nor any capital repayments. The best way round this problem is to negotiate with the building society or other lender to restructure the mortgage, eg to suspend payments, to accept interest only, to extend the term and/or to capitalise arrears. The Benefits Agency does in fact have a discretion to ignore capital payments from the other party to the mortgage. See 15.1.

Self-assessment questions

1 Which benefits are means tested?
2 Which benefits are not means tested?

3 What are passport benefits?
4 What is the difference between income support and family credit?
5 What is the social fund and what does it provide?
6 What is the diversion procedure?
7 What is a 'liable relative'?
8 Is there any appeal against benefit decisions, and if so where to?
9 Who can have housing benefit and for what property?
10 Can benefits ever be regarded as a legitimate resource in ancillary relief?

Section 4

Matrimonial jurisdiction independent of the decrees: the DPMCA 1978, MCA 1973 s 27 and agreements outside court proceedings

Chapter 14

Financial provision without a decree of divorce, nullity or judicial separation

Introduction
14.1

Leaving aside the possibilities of either negotiating voluntary payments or going on to welfare benefits as a regular source of income for the separated client who does not wish to petition for one of the principal decrees, there are also three other possibilities for obtaining formal maintenance in such a situation:

- a maintenance order from the Family Proceedings Court under Part 1 of the DPMCA 1978;
- a maintenance order from the county court under the MCA s 27; or
- a separation and maintenance agreement.

DPMCA 1978 in the Family Proceedings Court (FPC)
14.1.1

If an order is to be sought at all, this is probably the quickest and easiest type to obtain. While the magistrates have lost to the Child Support Agency much of their former jurisdiction to make orders for children, they can still make orders for spouses and at the same time for children of the family not within the CSA jurisdiction. This includes:

- orders for stepchildren;
- child orders outside the CSA's powers, ie for lump sums, as opposed to periodical payments;
- for 'topping up' of periodical payments above the CSA's ceiling, eg for school or further or higher education fees; and
- orders for children over 19 who are then outside the CSA age limit.

The DPMCA is therefore a sort of magistrates' court equivalent of the MCA for these purposes, for use when a decree is *not*, or not yet, being sought. Only a spouse can apply, but child orders can be made at the same time when a spouse makes application: ss 1 and 6(1).

Note

The magistrates' court, which is called the Family Proceedings Court when exercising its matrimonial and family jurisdiction but is still only a species of magistrates' court, is based on a commission area for which the magistrates are appointed. A particular Family Proceedings Court will therefore have jurisdiction to hear an application under Part 1 of the DPMCA 1978 if either the applicant or the respondent ordinarily resides within the commission area in which the court is situated: DPMCA 1978 s 30. Domicile is irrelevant.

Three distinct orders are obtainable under:
- s 2, for which grounds set out in s 1 must be established;
- s 6, which may be made purely on agreement of the parties;
- s 7, where the parties have resided apart for at least three months and one has been making payments to the other for that party or for a child of the family.

Note

As only spouses can apply under the Act, divorced ie ex-spouses cannot use it, nor of course can cohabitees. A *child of the family* is defined in s 88 and is the same as the that of child of the family in s 52 of the MCA 1973. Children who are not children of the family cannot be included in any orders under the DPMCA, but they may be able to claim maintenance under the Children Act 1989: see Chapter 18 at 18.6.

14.1.2   The types of orders available

Both periodical payments and lump sums can be awarded but no property orders can be made.

Periodical payments can be made weekly or monthly, for whatever term the magistrates think fit, including for a limited period, as was made in the case of *Robinson v Robinson* [1983] Fam 42, [1983] 1 All ER 391, where the period was for five years. However, pursuant to s 4:
- no order can *begin* before the date of the application;
- all orders *end* on the *death* of either the payer or payee;
- an order will *end* on the remarriage of the payee, although any accrued arrears will remain payable provided they are claimed within one year: the Magistrates' Courts Act 1980 s 95 as inserted by the Maintenance Enforcement Act 1991 gives the

magistrates power to remit them in whole or part, they usually will remit all arrears over a year old and might do so faster in the case of remarriage so application for enforcement in this case should be prompt!

Note

Divorce has *no effect* on a Family Proceedings Court order. Cohabitation has very little effect. Both s 2 and s 6 orders can still be *made* if the parties are still living together, though s 7 orders *cannot* and a s 7 order will cease *immediately* if the parties resume cohabiting: s 25(3). However, even s 2 and s 6 orders will be *discharged* if the parties cohabit for more than six months at any time: s 25(1). Orders for *children* are totally unaffected by their parents' cohabitation: s 25(2).

Children's orders end at 17: s 5(2), unless s 5(3) applies which permits the court to make:
- an order for a child which will last beyond the child's 18th birthday;
- an order for a child already over 18.

In either case such an order can be made if:
- the child is in full time education or training (whether or not also in gainful employment); or
- there are special circumstances justifying the order.

Note

Such periodical payments will always end on the death of the payer.

Lump sums are subject to a limit of £1,000: s 2(3), though where there are children more than £1,000 may be awarded by giving lump sums to each of them as well as £1,000 to the applicant spouse: *Burridge v Burridge* [1982] 3 All ER 80. Moreover, the £1,000 limit does not apply if the order is made by agreement under s 6.

Note

1 Lump sums can be made payable by instalments or time can be given for payment: Magistrates' Courts Act 1980 s 75. There is no rule that lump sums cannot be ordered unless the payer has capital, since all that is necessary is that the payer should have capacity to pay, from income or otherwise: *Burridge v Burridge, supra*.

2 Where a lump sum order is payable by instalments, these can subsequently be varied, on application to the court, either as to amounts or numbers of instalments or dates on which they are payable: DPMCA 1978 s 22.

14.1.3   Orders under s 2

Periodical payments and lump sums can be ordered for a party to a marriage or to a child of the family if the other party to the marriage has:

- failed to provide reasonable maintenance for a spouse;
- failed to provide reasonable maintenance for any child of the family;
- behaved in such a way that the applicant cannot reasonably be expected to live with that other party;
- deserted the applicant.

The grounds can be relied on in the alternative. Brief details of any behaviour alleged must be given in the written application for a s 2 order, which must now be made on Form 1 specified under the current Rules which are the Family Proceedings Court (Matrimonial Proceedings) Rules 1991 as amended.

How reasonable maintenance is determined

There is no formula in the Act or elsewhere. The court simply:

- takes the figure which it would have ordered if making an order from scratch;
- compares it with what is being paid;
- if it is significantly less, the respondent is not making reasonable provision.

There is no need to prove that the respondent's failure is morally reprehensible, indeed the respondent need not even know that maintenance is required, so the ground can even be proved by a wife in desertion, as in the case of *Robinson v Robinson* mentioned above, which would clearly be illogical if any moral element were required in the failure to pay.

The respondent is *probably* still *failing to provide reasonable maintenance* even if a suitable amount has been hurriedly paid between the application and the hearing. There is no specific decision on the point, although by analogy the case of *Irvin v Irvin* [1968] 1 WLR 464, [1968] 1 All ER 27 decided that in the case of *desertion* that must continue up to the date of the hearing. However, it is thought that one or two payments cannot alter a well established pattern of chronic failure, since it would be ridiculous if a respondent could get out of paying regularly simply by making one or two payments just before coming to court.

Establishing behaviour and desertion

These are the same as under the MCA 1973.

The test for *behaviour* is exactly the same: *Bergin v Bergin* [1983] 1 WLR 274, [1983] 1 All ER 905, [1983] 4 FLR 344. Cohabitation after the last incident of behaviour is irrelevant, although application must be made to the Family Proceedings Court within six months of the last incident relied on, unless it is a continuing form of behaviour which is alleged: Magistrates' Courts Act 1980 s 127.

The elements of desertion are also exactly the same as under the MCA 1973, save that it is not necessary for a period of two years to have passed since the desertion – simple desertion with no particular minimum period is all that is required.

Matters to which the court must have regard when making s 2 orders: DPMCA 1978 s 3

This is the magistrates' equivalent of s 25 of the MCA 1973.

By s 3(1) there is the same general duty as under s 25(2) of the MCA, whereby the court must consider all the circumstances of the case, giving *first* consideration to the welfare while a minor of any child of the family who has not attained the age of 18.

The s 3 factors are virtually the same as those under s 25 of the MCA except for the following:

- s 3(2)(c) directs the court to have regard to the standard of living enjoyed by the parties to the marriage before the *occurrence of the conduct alleged* (compare s 25 where the standard is that before the breakdown of the marriage);
- there is no s 3 equivalent of s 25(2)(h) whereby the court considers the value to each of the parties of any benefit that might be lost by the dissolution of the marriage, eg a pension, as the magistrates do not dissolve marriages and thus do not trigger any such loss depending on status.

The clean break provisions do not apply in the Family Proceedings Court since the magistrates do not dissolve marriages.

The one third rule does if it is appropriate to the case, but often it is not because of the relatively limited means of those who normally apply to the FPC.

Note

The magistrates now take the same approach to conduct as is the case under the MCA in the higher courts. For a time between 1973 and 1978, when the magistrates got their new Act in the DPMCA, there was a difference, since the magistrates were then applying the law as it had universally been before the Divorce Reform Act 1969 changed the approach of the divorce courts.

14.1.4   **Agreed orders under s 6**

This is the magistrates' version of a consent order. The only grounds are that the parties have agreed the order: s 6(1). The type(s) of financial provision agreed, the amount and the term of any periodical payments must be specified in the written application which must be made on Form 2 specified for the purpose. Either party, payer or payee, may apply for the order to be made. However it is not a rubber stamping procedure since there is still a general duty to be satisfied that the provision is broadly right.

By s 6(3) the court has the right to approve financial provision for a child and will not do so unless it considers that the order makes a proper contribution towards the child's financial needs. Otherwise, the court will normally make s 6 orders if:

- it is satisfied that the applicant or the respondent as the case may be has *agreed* to make the provision; and
- it has no reason to think that it would contrary to the interests of justice to exercise its powers under s 6.

If it is *not* so satisfied, the court will refuse to make the order unless the parties agree to make any amendments which it wishes to make, including that *either* party makes any further provision that the court requires: s 6(5).

Note

The *advantages* of having a s 6 order include that the parties are more likely to observe one which they had had a hand in putting together, rather than one that is imposed on them from above, the terms of the parties' agreement are embodied in the order just as on a consent order after divorce, and neither party can repudiate the order unilaterally. On the other hand, once made, the order can only be varied by agreement of both parties or returning to court for a variation, which might put some parties off!

The court can treat a s 2 application as one for a s 2 order if the parties agree terms before the s 2 application is heard.

Orders under s 7 to continue voluntary payments made during separation

14.1.5

The use of this order is that it can be made where the parties are living apart but cannot:

- make out any one of the four grounds required for a s 2 order; and
- come to a sufficient agreement for a s 6 order.

The parties *must* have been living apart for a continuous period of three months, neither of course being in desertion since that would permit an order under s 2. One of the parties must have been paying maintenance for the benefit of the other or of a child of the family.

The payee party must specify in the application the aggregate amount of payments made by the other to that party and the children of the family in the three months: s 7(1). The respondent cannot be ordered to pay more under the order than the rate of payment during the three months: s 7(3)(a). The court must check that the order is in line with what they would have ordered under s 2: s 7(3)(b) and (c), ie:

- not too much;
- not to a child of the family who is not the respondent's child unless they would have ordered this.

The court will not make an order under this section if it thinks that it would not provide reasonable maintenance for a child: s 7(4).

The s 3 considerations apply to s 7 orders, including the standard of living enjoyed by the parties, prior in this case to their separation, rather than prior to the *conduct* relied on in s 2: s 3(2)(c).

Note

The court can treat a s 7 application as one for a s 2 order.

Procedure

14.2

The Green Form and ABWOR (Assistance by Way of Representation) is normally used in the FPC. Legal aid is technically available for FPC financial orders but is seldom used, unless by an applicant who would be outside the Green Form limits.

Proceedings are commenced by written application, governed by the Family Proceedings Courts (Matrimonial Proceedings) Rules 1991 as amended by the Family Proceedings Courts (CSA 1991) Rules 1993. The forms now give details of any assessment carried out by the CSA. (Specimen forms may be seen in the Rules.)

There are different forms for applications under the different sections. The forms contain a statement of means of the applicant, which must be completed when the application is prepared, a notice of hearing (or directions appointment) which the court completes, and a blank form for the respondent's answer and statement of means (which the respondent will complete in due course).

14.2.1   Application and service

The application is lodged at the court with a copy for service on the respondent: FPC(MP)R 1991 r 3(1)(a). The justices' clerk will fix the date, time and place for the hearing (or directions) and enter these details on to the copy for service: r 3(2)(a) and (b). The copy is then returned to the applicant for service: r 3(2)(d). The respondent must have 21 days notice of the hearing or directions appoint: r 3(1)(b).

Note

The justices' clerk must consider if there should be a directions appointment: r 6(1). Directions can assume some importance. The clerk may give, vary or revoke directions which will usually cover a timetable for the proceedings, service of documents and evidence generally, and may consider written or (with leave) oral representations: r 6(1) and (3). However, if a request is made in writing without the consent of the other party to the proceedings the clerk must fix a date for a hearing of the request on at least two days notice to both parties: r 6(4). Both parties will than have to attend the directions hearing: r 8(1). If the respondent does not, however, turn up the directions hearing can nevertheless proceed without the respondent, provided the court is satisfied that due notice was given: r 8(2).

Service can be in any of the usual ways, including personal service: r 4. A statement of service must be filed specifying the method of service used before the appointment mentioned on the papers: r 4(4).

The respondent has 14 days to file and serve an answer, including the statement of means, indicating whether he or she will defend: r 5.

14.2.2   The hearing

Written statements of evidence in the usual form must have been filed and served on each other by each party before the hearing takes place: r 9(1) Moreover, a chronology should be supplied, together with copy documents which each party intends to rely on, eg payslips, loan and hire purchase agreements, and details of each party's outgoings – these can be supplemented where necessary: r 9(2).

As in other courts, a party failing to comply with this rule will not be allowed to adduce the evidence in question without leave of the court: r 9(3).

In other words, the FPC has opted for full advance disclosure on the lines of superior courts, with a view to encouraging early settlement once the parties have each seen the strength of the opposition case and saving court time. For further saving of court time, before the hearing the justices are required to read the papers which have been filed: r 12(1).

Note

The justices' clerk is still nevertheless required by the rules to keep a note of any oral evidence at the directions appointment: r 11.

The hearing is then conducted in the usual manner.

Pursuant to s 65 of the Magistrates' Courts Act 1980 as amended, the hearings are domestic proceedings and are held in private with a restricted attendance, including only court officers, the parties, their legal representatives, witnesses and other person directly concerned with the case, the press and pursuant to the Magistrates' Court Act 1980, s 69(2) 'any other person whom the court may in its discretion permit'. By s 67(2) it must be before magistrates from the domestic panel and there should be a man and a woman amongst them: s 66. The respondent is supposed to attend and failing such attendance there is likely to be an adjournment although the court can proceed in the respondent's absence. a respondent to a s 6 application can send a statement of means and need not attend.

The allegation is put to the respondent, but such is the habit of centuries and the parochial manner of proceeding in the magistrates' court that the evidence is still heard anyway, even if the respondent admits everything!

The applicant opens the case, witnesses are called and examined, cross examined and re-examined, and then the respondent (or respondent's advocate) addresses the court. If there is a question of law the respondent's advocate (if any) will be given leave to address the court on that and then if there is a further speech for the respondent, the applicant will have a second speech also.

If either party is *not* represented the court is under a duty to help that party: Magistrates' Courts Act 1980 s 73 (when the case may take a long time since such help must be meticulous).

The magistrates will then consider whether the case is proved and a decision will then be given as soon as possible: r 12(4). By r 12(6) reasons must be given, stating any findings of fact. Costs may be ordered, in whole or in part: r 13(1).

Note

The court has power to make interim orders: DPMCA 1978 s 19, although this has been reduced by the CSA jurisdiction. Such orders can be backdated: s 19(3), but will expire when the case is finally determined, or after three months or some other date specified by the court. By s 19(7) only one interim order is supposed to be made, but that can be extended if time is running out, provided it does not last for longer than three months from the first extension, ie an interim order has a maximum life of six months: s 19(6).

14.3 Variation

All orders are variable, revocable or can be suspended. The format is to consider the case *de novo*. Some sort of change of circumstances will be required and the court can give effect to any agreement between the parties so far as it seems just to do so: s 20(1). On variation, the court will be able to specify the method of payment of the new order if it has not already done so in respect of the earlier one: Maintenance Enforcement Act 1991 s 4 amending the Magistrates' Courts Act 1980 s 60. Suspended provisions of an order can be revived under s 20(6) Curiously, periodical payments orders under ss 2 and 6 can be varied by making lump sum orders, but this power does not apply to those orders made under s 7.

14.4 Enforcement

The magistrates have always been well known for enforcement, since even before the Maintenance Enforcement Act of 1991 the clerk provided an excellent service in receiving and paying out maintenance and enforcing any order which was not paid, and for this legal aid certificates often extended to registration of one substantive order obtained elsewhere in the magistrates' court. Besides this, the diversion procedure described in Chapter 13, has always been extremely useful to those applicants who would otherwise be on welfare benefits one week and chasing maintenance payments the next.

The MEA 1991 was originally an interim measure pending the implementation of the Child Support Act in April 1993, but it has nevertheless made some useful permanent contributions to enforcement of maintenance payments generally. Pursuant to s 2, an amendment to s 59 of the Magistrates' Courts Act 1980 enabled magistrates for the first time to specify how payments should be made, for example by standing order or attachment of earnings, previously only possible if the debtor consented or was previously in default on payments, due to wilful refusal or culpable neglect. The court could even for the first time require that a bank account be opened to enable a standing order to be set up.

Now any DPMCA money orders may be enforced as an FPC maintenance order: DPMCA s 32(1) by:

- attachment of earnings: Attachment of Earnings Act 1971;
- committal to prison: Magistrates' Court Act 1980 s 76;
- distress: also s 76;
- registration in the High Court under the Maintenance Orders Act 1958 (not generally worth it except for high sums, eg accumulated arrears, but it does permit access to High Court methods of enforcement which may frighten the payer, eg sequestration which is notoriously expensive).

Note

Foreign orders are sometimes registered in the FPC for the area where a respondent resides when the clerk will enforce them in the same way as an English order. There are reciprocal enforcement provisions in respect of a number of foreign jurisdictions, which the trainee may sometimes have to research to enforce English orders overseas and vice versa. Rayden should always be consulted for full particulars if such a need arises in the solicitor's practice.

Committal   14.4.1

There are stringent conditions before this method can be used:

- the court must be of the opinion that the debtor has not paid due to wilful refusal or culpable neglect;

- attachment of earnings or some other method if available must be used first unless the court is of the opinion that that is inappropriate;
- the debtor must be present when imprisonment is imposed: Magistrates' Courts Act 1980 s 93(6).

The maximum is only six weeks: s 93(7). However, pursuant to s 76 and Schedule 4 a lesser maximum may apply, and payment of the debt will prevent imprisonment, or secure release if it has already been imposed, with reduction in the time to serve *pro rata* for part payment: s 79, and arrears do not accrue, unless the court otherwise directs, while the debtor is in prison: s 94.

It is however fairly easy to get out. Any debtor can apply for the order to be reviewed and the warrant of commitment cancelled: Maintenance Orders Act 1958 s 18(4) and although the debt is not cancelled by time served, it is not possible to be imprisoned more than once for the same debt: Magistrates' Courts Act 1980.

Most usually the court will suspend any committal order if the debtor pays the maintenance in future and also pays something off the arrears each week: Magistrates' Courts Act 1980 s 72(2). The debtor will be warned if he stops paying *before* the warrant is issued so as to have a chance to show cause why the committal order should not take effect, and only if that opportunity is not successfully seized will committal occur: Maintenance Orders Act 1958 s 18. Sometimes the court will merely adjourn the hearing to see what the debtor does. If no attempts have been made to pay by the time the adjourned hearing resumes, then committal may well follow.

14.4.2   Enforcement procedure

The clerk normally automatically brings proceedings for enforcement if requested in writing to do so by the payee: Magistrates' Courts Act 1980, s 59. This was the beauty of the clerk's service in the days before the MEA 1991 or CSA, and as the court kept the record of payment (or non-payment) proof of default was easy. The clerk now has a standing authority to take proceedings if payment is normally made through the court. The Magistrates' Courts Act 1980 was amended by the MEA 1991 to insert new ss 59A and 59B to facilitate this type of enforcement, and s 59B imposes financial sanctions if the debtor fails to make payments by the methods which can now be specified. By s 94A (inserted by the MEA 1991 s 8) interest can now be ordered on all or part of unpaid maintenance.

The debtor will normally receive a summons for proceedings but if necessary a warrant of arrest will be issued: s 93(5).

Matrimonial Causes Act 1973 s 27   14.5

This section allows a free standing application to the county court for financial relief *without* petitioning for any of the principal decrees, though a s 27 order can also be made after a decree of judicial separation.

By s 27(1) either party may apply if the other spouse has failed to:

- provide reasonable maintenance for the applicant; or
- provide or make reasonable contribution towards, reasonable maintenance for any child of the family.

An order is available upon proof of the fact; it is apparently no longer necessary that the respondent should actually know of the requirement for maintenance and of course, as in the case of the DPMCA, it is not necessary for the failure to pay to be morally reprehensible.

The possible orders available under this section are those for:

- periodical payments;
- secured periodical payments;
- Unlimited lump sums including by instalments.

Note

Lump sums orders can be made for any purpose, including to defray debts incurred in providing reasonable maintenance for the applicant and/or children prior to the application. No maintenance pending suit is possible since the application *is* the whole suit, unlike in the case of ancillary relief following a divorce suit.

Orders are available for both spouse and children irrespective of failure to maintain only one or the other of them.

The s 25 considerations must be taken into account as on ancillary relief, and the duration of orders is the same as after one of the principal decrees: MCA 1973 ss 28 and 29.

Separation and maintenance agreements   14.6

Solicitors often forget that a separation or maintenance agreement is a seriously viable alternative to a formal order from whichever court, and that if it is carefully drafted such an agreement can also actually be superior to an order where no proceedings for a principal decree are for the time being contemplated.

First, within reason an agreement can be designed to incorporate virtually whatever provisions the client desires to include, thus importing more flexibility than even the most advantageous consent or agreed order, which can only include either clauses which the court is able to order under ss 23 and 24 of the MCA 1973 or undertakings which the court is willing to accept. These categories exclude all orders which only the appropriate court (and not that granting financial orders) can make under the Children Act 1989, whereas an agreement is able to incorporate arrangements for the care of the children.

Secondly, agreements are cheaper and less trouble than obtaining an order from the court.

Thirdly, it provides evidence of the fact that the parties regarded the marriage as at an end, which is essential for proving separation when that this necessary in divorce and judicial separation, and of the *date* of such separation: *Santos v Santos* [1972] Fam 247.

Fourthly, an agreement which is observed will rebut any claim on the basis of failure to maintain under either the MCA or DPMCA.

Fifthly, any tax relief available for a court order is similarly available for an agreement.

Sixthly, human nature being what it is, the parties are more likely to observe an agreement they have forged themselves with the assistance of their lawyers and more likely to embark on such observance in a non-confrontational frame of mind conducive to a fresh start which will benefit themselves as well as the children, than if they have just been engaging in adversarial litigation, which often brings out the worst in the parties even if the case settles.

However, there are *disadvantages* in that such agreements can be:

- more difficult to enforce;
- not so final as the court's ultimate ancillary relief jurisdiction cannot be ousted;
- not so easily varied unless the parties agree; and
- unless the agreement is within MCA 1973 s 34 (see 14.6.2) consent of both parties *will be needed* to effect any variation. Care also needs to be taken with drafting as there are a few points to watch;

- an agreement for *immediate* separation is legal, as is a *resumption of cohabitation* agreement containing provisions for *possible future* separation if the reconciliation does not work out: the case of *Wilson v Wilson* (1848) 1 HLC 538 established that an agreement for future separation *per se* is *invalid* as being contrary to public policy because it prejudices the status of marriage, but such an agreement is *valid* if the parties are *already separated* or on the point of it since it may regulate their life following the *fact* of separation, and the case of *Re Meyrick's Settlement* [1921] 1 Ch 311 is a warning that even such agreements for *resumption of cohabitation* should be carefully drafted so that the overall effect of the agreement is to *promote reconciliation*;
- separation and maintenance agreements can be oral or written but are usually *written*, for obvious reasons, and are usually by *deed*.

Usual clauses

14.6.1

To live separate and apart

This clause terminates both the duty to cohabit and therefore also desertion whether it has begun or might otherwise begin: if such a clause is not included, the agreement is only a *maintenance* agreement so that desertion can *still* start or continue.

Not to take matrimonial proceedings

This must be expressly included and will not be implied. It is not contrary to public policy as ousting the jurisdiction of the court, because the effect is to *forgive past conduct* (none of which can then be used in proceedings in the future) rather than to *preclude filing a petition*.

The clause is sometimes called a *Rose v Rose* clause after the case of *Rose v Rose* (1883) 8 PD 98 which gave it its name.

Non-molestation clause

This is a clause which excludes any act that would annoy a reasonable spouse and excludes any act done *with the authority* of the spouse as well as personally by that spouse. It does *not* preclude starting divorce proceedings as was established in the case of *Fearon v Aylesford* (1884) 14 QBD 792.

A *dum casta* clause

This must also be *expressly* included. It is sometimes inserted for the protection of husbands whose liability to maintain a wife who is committing adultery can then be ended.

Maintenance for either party

This can take the form of periodical payments, secured or unsecured, or lump sums and should again ideally be limited by some phrase such as 'while the parties are married and living apart', which coupled with a *dum casta* clause prevents the husband from assuming an open ended obligation which might otherwise last not only beyond adultery or cohabitation with another man but possibly even after the death of the payer when it could still be enforced against his estate!

You should remember the impact of the CSA on such agreements – if anyone in the family is on benefits, the CSA assessment will take priority over anything agreed under such a clause, and such a clause would also not prevent the carer parent from asking the CSA for an assessment which again would take priority over the agreement: CSA 1991 s 9(2) and (3). It would however be possible to link any such assessment to a reduced share of the division of any family property, eg at the triggering event of a *Mesher* type order, which can be included in the property clause of the agreement.

Great care is required in drafting this clause – there should be no covenant not to claim maintenance from the court (as this void since it tends to oust the jurisdiction of the court).

Note

If such a covenant is included, the remainder of the agreement is valid: MCA 1973 s 34(1) including any other financial arrangements: s 34(1)(b), but this will *not* be the case if the *whole purpose of the agreement* can be interpreted as to oust the jurisdiction of the court, in which case the entire agreement, and not *just the objectionable covenant*, will be *void* and *of no effect*.

An agreement relating to property

This could be, for example, a *Mesher* or similar type trust regulating the occupation of the matrimonial home during the children's minority and providing for eventual sale and division of the proceeds.

Care and maintenance of children

This type of clause is only enforceable if for the benefit of the child or children.

Note

Stipulations encouraging the end of marriage will always be void.

Both parties should have *separate legal advice* so as to obviate any suggestion of *fraud, mistake* or *undue influence*.

Applying to the court to vary written financial arrangements: MCA 1973 s 34(2)

This *only* applies to certain *written* agreements, and *oral* agreements *cannot* be varied under s 34. The reason is that ss 35 and 36 of the MCA permit variation of written agreements which meet the definition in s 34(2) *by the court* if the parties cannot agree this themselves, so it is essential, first to know to *which* agreements this applies, and secondly, what are the precise *terms* of the agreement which is to be varied, which is hardly compatible with the variation of oral agreements of which the record, if any, may be dispute.

The agreements which are within the section are:
- *any* agreements containing *financial arrangements* whether made during the continuance or after the dissolution or annulment of the marriage;
- *separation* agreements which contain *no financial arrangements* in a case where *no other agreement between the same parties* contains such arrangements.

There is a wide interpretation of 'financial arrangements': the term includes periodical payments and any dispositions for both parties and *any* child, *not* necessarily a *child of the family*.

However, the case of *Sutton v Sutton* [1984] 2 WLR 146, [1984] 1 All ER 168 shows how careful it is necessary to be in observing *all* the rules applying to separation and maintenance agreements if one wants to apply to the court either for variation or enforcement. In that case the wife entered into an oral agreement which was not formalised as a deed or even put into writing even after the parties were divorced. The husband was supposed to transfer the home to the wife and she was supposed to pay the mortgage and not to apply for maintenance. He did not do it. The wife could not apply to the court to *vary* the agreement as it was oral and thus outside s 34. She could not apply to *enforce* it either as it purported to oust the jurisdiction of the court under ss 23 and 24 and therefore rendered the whole agreement void. She therefore had to fall back on applying under s 24 in the normal way for a transfer of property order ancillary to divorce as the only means of getting financial arrangements moving again.

It will be necessary to show that because of a change in circumstances (including a foreseen change) since the arrangements in the agreement were made, there should be an alteration to make different arrangements or that the agreement does not contain proper arrangements for a child of the family.

Variation by the court includes revocation or insertion of such arrangements as appear just, having regard to all the circumstances: s 35(2). The case of *Gorman v Gorman* [1964] 3 All ER 739 established that this will be considered from an objective point of view. Sometimes, the court *will* decide to vary an agreement because of subsequent change of circumstances, and sometimes the circumstances are adjudged not to be sufficiently changed. In the case of *D v D* (1974) 118 SJ 715, for example, the fact that the parties had taken legal advice when making the agreement made them decide against variation when the home, which the wife had agreed to transfer for only £1,500, suddenly shot up in value, part of their reasoning being that by the time of the application the husband had remarried and had spent a considerable sum on the house so it did not seem fair to change the agreement. In the case of *Simister v Simister (No 2)* [1987] 1 FLR 194, however, they did vary the agreement – in that case the husband had agreed to pay one third of his salary to the wife, and when that shot up he tried to argue that it was in excess of her needs – clearly a different situation, especially because of the importance of needs in deciding what a wife should receive in accordance with the established rules of quantum.

The court's powers are wider on variation under ss 34–36 than under s 31. For example, s 35 variation can include insertion of a lump sum order which the court could not do to vary a periodical payments order under s 31.

Agreements are variable after the *death of the payer* if:

- they *provide* for payment after death;
- the deceased died *domiciled* in England and Wales: MCA 1973 s 36.

Note

An alternative is always available in this case, namely to apply under the Inheritance (Provision for Family and Dependants) Act 1975.

14.6.3   Application to the court for variation

Application may be made either to the county court or the FPC.

The county court powers are *wider* and include inserting:

- unlimited lump sums;
- secured and unsecured periodical payments;
- property adjustment orders;
- variation of periodical payment orders.

The FPC can only:

- vary or terminate periodical payments orders;
- insert unsecured periodical payments: MCA 1973 s 35(3).

Transfer to the High Court is possible: Matrimonial and Family Proceedings Act 1984 s 37, *Practice Direction* [1987] 1 All ER 1087.

The effect on future financial applications of entering into an agreement   14.6.4

The *existence* of such agreements will always be *considered* as part of all the circumstances of the case under s 25 of the MCA 1973 in subsequent ancillary relief proceedings because the jurisdiction of the court can *never* be ousted. Whether the substance of the agreement will *influence* the court is another matter and depends on the individual circumstances. some principles emerge from the case law on the subject.

The basis principle is that *no* agreement will ever have the effect of preventing the court from exercising all its usual powers under ss 23 and 24 of the MCA because it is simply not possible to oust the jurisdiction of the court. However, the *fact* that it was entered into, whether that was done freely, whether advice was taken, and the extent to which it has been carried out by both parties, will all be relevant to the general duty under s 25: *Dean v Dean* [1978] 3 WLR 288, [1978] 3 All ER 758.

The case of *Edgar v Edgar* [1980] 1 WLR 1410 is an awful warning of what happens when advice is taken and then *ignored*. Mrs Edgar entered into a maintenance agreement with her husband including a term that she would not apply for maintenance, although her solicitors told her that if she applied to the court she would get better terms. When divorce proceedings were started, she did apply to the court, thus breaking the agreement. However, the court decided in its discretion that it would not go behind the agreement since they took that she was bound, especially as she had had legal advice.

Moral: If a client wants to do this sort of thing, it is better done behind the solicitor's back, since taking advice and ignoring it is fatal!

However, sometimes the court does intervene even in situations like this, as in the case of *Jessel v Jessel* [1979] 1 WLR 1148, [1979] 3 All ER 645 where they decided not to hold the wife to her agreement not to apply under s 331 of the MCA to increase an existing order.

14.7   Which remedy?

The choice of remedy will obviously depend on the individual client's circumstances. The solicitor should weigh up the pros and cons of each possibility and make a decision based on convenience to the client's case, but if the rules are *observed* to avoid the hazards which can arise, and the agreement is carefully drafted in the client's favour, there is much to be said for an agreement which can be varied under ss 34–36, since on balance that combines the best of all the remedies.

Self-assessment questions

1 What can s 27 of the MCA do which ss 2 and 7 of the DPMCA cannot?
2 What are the grounds for applying for a s 2 order under the DPMCA 1978?
3 Can orders be made under DPMCA ss 2, 6 and 7 if the parties are still cohabiting?
4 What effect does a decree of divorce have on a financial order under the DPMCA?
5 What effect does cohabitation of their parents have on DPMCA orders for children?
6 How are maintenance orders enforced in the Family Proceedings Court?
7 Can the FPC enforce foreign orders?
8 When can a spouse who is not paying a maintenance order be committed to prison and how is this done?
9 What are the advantages of a separation or maintenance agreement?
10 What are the disadvantages?

Section 5

The home and contents: occupation and owner- ship issues on marriage breakdown

Chapter 15

Practical issues in relation to the home

Introduction 15.1

Both during the marriage and on marriage breakdown, the home serves two linked but distinct functions: first it is a roof for the couple or family, and may remain so for one of the spouses and any family after separation and divorce, and secondly it is usually the couple's most valuable capital asset (although the value of pension rights may well come a close second to that).

It is therefore vital on separation that certain practical matters are addressed, possibly urgently, and the initial opportunity which the solicitor has to check whether the client has done that, and to give advice, is at the first interview, when an early question asked of the client will be to establish the precise ownership of the matrimonial home with a view to registering rights of occupation under the Matrimonial Homes Act 1983 if that should prove to be necessary: see 5.2. You will recall that MHA protection applies to both *owned* and *rented* homes, so should not assume that the client's position in relation to the home is entirely safe simply because there is a only a tenancy.

In an appropriate case, ie where the home is owned rather than rented but the other spouse normally pays the mortgage and it is not certain following a separation whether it is still being paid or not, it might be necessary to give urgent further consideration at that stage to how the mortgage is going to be paid and, if matters have already got out of hand, to whether it is going to be necessary to resist possession proceedings: and if the answer to that is in the negative, to what is going to happen to the client, especially if there are children, since they will obviously need to be rehoused in some way: see 15.2.

Note

The contents of the home will probably not be an urgent matter at this stage, and any problems can usually wait for solution at leisure: see Chapter 16.

15.2   Preventing a sale or mortgage of owned homes

Especially if there is not much equity in the home, the spouse out of occupation is all too likely to default on the mortgage, whereas if there is significant equity there will be a temptation to raise money, or further money, by mortgaging the home or taking out a second mortgage or loan for which the equity in the home is again given as security. You need to be on the watch for both of these situations.

15.2.1   Home in joint names

This is a relatively safe situation since if the client is a joint tenant the property cannot be conveyed, transferred, mortgaged or charged as security for a loan *without* the client's signature – unless, of course, that is forged, which is not, unfortunately, unknown! Although banks and finance houses have now become somewhat more alert about inspecting properties for signs of spousal occupation, and some now require charges to be signed by both spouses in the presence of the spouses' own solicitor, nevertheless occasional cases continue to occur where husbands fraudulently dispose of the home, if necessary hiring a third party to pose as the wife for the purpose of executing the charge! Obviously there is nothing that you can do to protect the client against such determined dishonesty, and it will be sufficient to obey the rules in those cases where swift pre-emptive action *can* preserve the priority of the client's interests.

Client already a party to a prejudicial transaction

More problematic is the situation where it turns out that the client is already a party to a transaction, such as a mortgage or sale, which has already taken place and which clearly prejudices the client's interests. Generally, where the client has apparently willingly and knowingly co-operated in the transaction, often a mortgage to secure the other spouse's business debts, or sometimes a mortgage for their mutual benefit, it will be too late to do anything to redeem the situation. However, if it can be said that there has been *undue influence* or *fraud* on the part of either the other spouse or of the third party, the mortgage or sale may *not* be binding on the client:

- where the client *relied on the other spouse* by placing trust and confidence in that spouse to manage their joint financial affairs, *undue influence will be presumed*, although the client will in that

case also have to show that the transaction was *disadvantageous* to the client;
- where, however, the client is not relying on such a *presumption*, but can *prove* that the other spouse did *exert undue influence* then it will not also be necessary to show that the transaction was disadvantageous to the client.

If you have a client in one of these situations it may be possible to have the transaction, often a mortgage to a bank, set aside. This will be possible where:
- the other spouse was technically acting in procuring the client's agreement to the transaction as *agent for the mortgagee*; or
- the mortgagee had *actual* or *constructive notice* of the facts.

Note

In the latter situation, the mortgagee will have to show that the client *entered freely into the obligation with knowledge of the relevant facts*. This will be quite hard for the mortgagee to show unless there has been a meeting with the client, where the other spouse was not present to exert influence, undue or otherwise, when the legal liability being taken on was explained to the client, together with all the risks involved, and the client was expressly advised to take independent legal advice: *Barclays Bank v O'Brien* [1994] 1 FLR 1.

You should be on the lookout for such a situation and report to the principal any indications that there might be a problem.

Joint tenancies: to sever or not to sever?

The other matter which the trainee should consider where the home is in joint names is whether the joint tenancy should be severed so as to avoid the other spouse succeeding to it on the client's unexpected death before the divorce is finalised, since even filing a petition making a comprehensive claim for ancillary relief does not automatically sever any joint tenancy which exists: *Harris v Goddard* [1983] 1 WLR 1203. The trainee should be aware that this is so despite the fact that issuing proceedings under the Married Women's Property Act 1882 does automatically operate to sever the joint tenancy. (However, if the *client* might succeed to the *other* spouse's half share, eg if the other spouse is unwell and has a poor life expectancy, then this matter might be better left, as severance would of course preclude the client's gaining the other half of the home on *the client's* succession by survivorship!)

> *Note*
>
> Any such notice should be carefully drafted so as not to *admit* that there is a joint tenancy in *equity* under which the other spouse would be entitled to a half share, as this would prejudice future proceedings under the Married Woman's Property Act 1882. The notice should sever any such joint tenancy if, which is not admitted, one exists.

How to recognise an existing tenancy in common (ie there is no need to sever)

A tenancy in common already exists if:

- the conveyance or transfer to the parties *expressly* states that they hold as tenants in common;
- there is a *separate* declaration of trusts to that effect;
- there is a *note or memorandum of severance endorsed or annexed* to the conveyance;
- there is a *restriction* to that effect on the proprietorship register.

However, as the building society usually has the deeds, the solicitor may have to issue a notice pursuant to the LPA 1925 s 36(2) without *knowing* for certain what the position is.

15.2.2   Home in sole name of the other spouse

This situation can give rise to different problems from those at 15.1.1. First, early *registration of MHA rights of occupation* would be prudent to avoid a sale of the property over the client's head, and secondly if that is done too late to effect the usual protection, some thought might have to be given to non-MHA rights which may protect the occupying spouse, ie whether the client has an *overriding interest in registered land* or a *beneficial interest in unregistered land*, and whether in any event the client's ancillary relief claims should be registered as a *pending land action*, which may be done by lodging a caution in the Proprietorship Register, and any supporting action taken under MCA 1973 s 37: see 9.1.1 above.

> *Note*
>
> While the MHA registration will only apply to the home, a pending land action can be registered against *all* property, including, eg a holiday home, and MCA 1973 s 37 applies to *any* assets which may be needed to satisfy the client's claim for ancillary relief: see 9.1.1 above for protection under s 37.

Non-MHA interests which may protect the occupying spouse where the home is in the sole name of the other

The trainee should always remember the *overriding interest* and the *beneficial interest* in *unregistered land.*

For *an overriding interest* the client must be in *actual occupation of registered land* (which means physically present, though not necessarily all the time) and must have a *beneficial interest* in the property as an equitable tenant in common by reason of contributing to the purchase price: LRA 1925 s 70(1)(g). This was established in the case of *Williams & Glyns Bank Ltd v Boland and Another* and *Williams & Glyns Bank Ltd v Brown and Another* [1981] AC 487, [1980] 2 All ER 408, HL, a pair of cases heard together where the two wives were held to be entitled to resist the Bank's application for possession as their husbands had mortgaged the homes without the wives' knowledge. As a result of these cases, however, banks now tend to ask everyone living in a home to sign a deed agreeing to postpone their interests to the bank's.

The same principles apply in the case of actual occupation of *unregistered land* in which the spouse has a beneficial interest, where knowledge of the spouse's occupation depends on the doctrine of notice, as was shown in the case of *Kingsnorth Finance Ltd v Tizard* [1986] 1 WLR 783, [1986] 2 All ER 54. Unless the mortgagees actually enquire properly about the position they will have constructive notice of the occupation of such a spouse and their rights will be postponed to the occupying spouse's beneficial interest. Mr Tizard actually pulled a fast one on the bank in this case as he told them he was single and although the wife was at the house some of the time (she slept away but came daily to look after the children) he arranged for them to visit when she was absent. He then went off to the USA with the cash! The court held that the wife's occupation would have been discovered if the mortgagee had made proper enquiries and that her occupation was no less effective because she did not sleep there.

Statutory right of occupation under the MHA 1983   15.3

Section 1(1) of the Act gives a spouse who is not the owner of the matrimonial home a statutory right of occupation. Section 1(11) gives the same right to a spouse who has an equitable interest, and by s 9 where *both* spouses have ownership rights, eg they are joint tenants, the Act gives them *both* the right to apply to the court to determine who shall occupy the home. The statutory right may be enforced either under s 1 or s 9 depending on whose name the legal title is vested in. The right of occupation is an equitable charge binding on third parties as well as the owning spouse and are registrable: s 2(1).

Note

This statutory right of occupation applies only to homes which are or have been the matrimonial home: s 1(1)) and do not apply, eg to holiday homes, though if there is more than one home which might qualify as the matrimonial home the spouse seeking to register rights of occupation must choose which one to register against.

When Part IV of the Family Law Act 1996 comes into force (which is expected to be in the autumn of 1997) the MHA and will be repealed in its entirety and the statutory right of occupation will be replaced by 'matrimonial home rights' which provide much the same protection. See FLA 1996 ss 30–32 and Schedule 4.

15.3.1   The rights conferred by the statute

What the precise rights are which may be enforced under the statute depends on whether the spouse applying is in occupation or not. The statutory right of occupation is defined in s 1(1) as:

- if *in* occupation, the right is not to be *evicted or excluded* from the home *or any part of it* by the other spouse *except with leave of the court*: s 1(1)(a);
- if *not* in occupation, the right is to *enter into and occupy* the home *with the leave of the court*: s 1(1)(b).

By s 1(2) the court may regulate these rights in each case by:

- declaring, enforcing, restricting or terminating those rights;
- prohibiting, suspending or restricting the exercise by either spouse of the right to occupy;
- requiring either spouse to permit the exercise by the other of the right: s 1(2).

The court's power is wide and allows *excluding the owning spouse*. The court must regulate the rights of occupation in the light of the criteria in s 1(3) of the Act, namely in relation to the:

- parties' conduct in relation to each other and otherwise;
- parties' needs and financial resources;

- needs of any children; and
- the circumstances of the case

and no one of these criteria is more important than any other.

For a discussion of how the criteria are applied in practice (usually, but not exclusively, in relation to domestic violence applications, see 17.2.1).

Termination of the statutory right   15.3.2

The statutory right is terminated by:
- the death of either spouse;
- the dissolution or annulment of the marriage (ie on DA);
- order of the court under its wide power to regulate the occupation of the home during the subsistence of the marriage.

Note _____

The court has power to direct that rights of occupation which would normally come to an end on DA should *continue* beyond that event: s 2(4). In this case it is essential that application is made for such an order *before* the marriage has actually ended.

The FLA 1996 preserves this position.

_____

Registration of occupation rights   15.3.3

This is effected by registration at the appropriate registry of the client's right of occupation by means of a:
- class F land charge in the case of *unregistered* land, which is effected against the *name* of the other spouse in the register of land charges: LCA 1972 s 2;
- notice in the case of registered land, which is effected against the *land* in the charges register: LRA 1925 – see MHA 1983 s 2(8)(a).

A spouse can register occupation rights whilst out of occupation, but in that case cannot enforce them without leave of the court: *Watts v Waller* [1972] 1 WLR 365, [1982] 3 All ER 257.

It is *essential* to register in the *correct form* at the correct place as otherwise the registration will be no use whatever, as happened in the case of *Miles v Bull (No 2)* [1969] 2 FLR 389 where the wife lost her protection even though she was not the one to register at the wrong place!

How to find out if the land is registered or unregistered so as to register correctly

In order to discover whether the land is registered or unregistered, the trainee should search the Index Map at the district Land Registry, and if it is registered obtain the title number for identification.

Once registered, the client's rights will be protected against third parties because the registration is *actual notice* to the purchaser. However, the court can still determine the client's rights of occupation under s 1(3) and can permit the other spouse to enter and occupy instead. In only one notorious reported case does the spouse's priority seem not to have been secured by registration of the occupation rights, and that was because of the way in which the court applied s 1(3), as to which the dissenting judgment of Sir Denys Buckley took the view that that decision was badly wrong. This was the case of *Kashmir Kaur v Gill* [1988] Fam 110, [1988] 2 All ER 288 where the wife, who was out of occupation but had registered her rights thus binding her husband and a purchaser to whom he had sold the home, applied to enter and occupy. Unbelievably, the court refused her application, considering the interests of the purchaser, a blind man who particularly wanted the house, and deciding that he had a higher degree of socio-economic need than she did! The court said it would be different if the husband and the purchaser had colluded to exclude the wife and to nullify her registered right of occupation but that this was not the case. Sir Denys Buckley, dissenting, obviously thought that this could hardly have been the result that was intended when the s 1(3) criteria were devised in a statute designed to regulate the rights of married people rather than to assist third parties.

However, further cases on this tack have been notable by their absence, so the moral is obviously to remember the registration in time and all should be well.

15.3.4   Regulation of the right

This normally takes place on applications in connection with domestic violence in which case the court may make an *ouster* or *exclusion order*: see below Chapter 17, although as has been seen above in the case of *Kashmir v Kaur Gill* applications may be made for reasons unconnected with violence.

Regulation of the right of occupation can extend to excluding a spouse from a certain *part* only of the home, for example a studio or separate office or study: s 1(3)(a). it may also include requiring a spouse to pay for outgoings or repairs to the home: s 1(3)(c).

Rights to pay the mortgage and in possession proceedings

A spouse entitled to occupy the matrimonial home may pay the mortgage and other outgoings and the money must be accepted: s 1(5).

A further advantage of registration is that a spouse with registered rights must be kept informed of mortgage enforcement proceedings: s 8(3) and may be entitled to be made a party: s 8(2). The client wishing to exercise this right must apply to the court and will be entitled to be joined if the court:

- does not see any special reason against allowing joinder; and
- is satisfied that the client is likely to be able to contribute sufficiently towards the payments to affect the outcome of possession proceedings.

Bankruptcy   15.3.5

The statutory right of occupation may not provide protection in bankruptcy.

The court has a duty to balance the interests of the creditors and the principle that a person should pay his debts against the interests of the other spouse, usually in these cases the wife and family, as it tends to be the husband in these situations who goes bankrupt. In such a case, while the husband's property vests in his trustee in bankruptcy, the wife's right of occupation is *binding* on the trustee and creditors once it is registered, as is any right she may have to a legal or beneficial interest. However her right of *occupation, even coupled with a beneficial interest*, may not be able to prevent an order for sale of the home being made to pay the husband's debts, since the trustee can apply for such an order under s 30 of the LPA 1925, the court will make whatever order is just and reasonable and s 336(4) which is similar to the MHA s 1(3) criteria will have to be applied, taking into account (in addition to the interests of the creditors):

- the wife's conduct (if any) in contributing to the bankruptcy;
- the wife's or former wife's needs and resources;
- the needs of any children; and
- all the circumstances of the case;

other, that is, than the needs of the bankrupt husband: Insolvency Act 1986 s 336(4). After one year from the trustee in bankruptcy taking office, in the absence of any special considerations to be taken into account in that particular case, the court presumes that the creditors' interests outweigh all others: s 336(5).

However, there are ways of dealing with this problem. Three separate situations need to be considered.

Where there is already charging order over the home and the creditor seeks an order under s 30 LPA 1925

Here the creditor's claim is likely to prevail though a sale may be postponed to mitigate immediate hardship to the family. Postponement tends not to be for long, eg in the case of *Re Turner* [1975] 1 All ER 5, where the court balanced the interests of the creditors and the family and ordered the sale of the home within two months. This may be regarded as fairly average. In *Re Bailey* [1977] 2 All ER 26 the sale was ordered immediately – obviously tough on the family. In *Re Lowrie* [1981] 3 All ER 353 the sale was ordered in three months – a sufficient delay to provide some breathing space. However, in *Re Holliday* [1980] 3 All ER 385 the sale was postponed for five years till the youngest child was 17. This is not at all the norm, especially in the light of more recent cases where the court appears to be getting tougher, initial longer periods being reduced drastically on appeal.

A prime example of this type of case is that of *Re Citro* [1990] 3 All ER 952, [1991] 1 FLR 71 where there were two brothers in business together, both married, both owning a half share in their homes and with young children who would not be 16 for four or five years. Both had gone bankrupt and initially won a postponement of sale till the children were 16. On appeal this was cancelled and only short postponements substituted on the basis that the interests of the creditors were superior to those of the children whose parents would have to find alternative accommodation and schooling for them, though there was a dissenting judgment indicating that this might be wrong at a critical stage of their education. Basically, the message is that bankruptcy is now so commonplace that it will be unusual to find the lengthy periods of postponement that were achieved in the previous recession in the early 80s.

The same year saw the case of *Re Gorman* [1990] 2 FLR 284 where there was originally a two year postponement, ordered for the wife out of sympathy because before he had become bankrupt she had divorced the husband and claimed his half of the home, already owning her own half herself; on appeal this was reduced to six months so that the husband's creditors were not prejudiced.

Moral: Start the divorce proceedings and have the ancillary relief orders made before the husband goes bankrupt. Failing that, look at the possibilities of the next situation.

Where the s 30 proceedings are transferred to the Family Division pursuant to the institution of divorce proceedings

This is not a complete cure all as sometimes it will not be allowed. However, if it is, there is a much better chance of obtaining a more lengthy postponement of the sale, because the divorce court has greater flexibility in considering the needs of the wife and children, as was evident in the case of *Austin-Fell v Austin-Fell* [1990] 2 All ER 455, [1989] 2 FLR 497. In that case the husband owed the bank £7,000 and they obtained a charging order over his half share of the home. On divorce the wife applied to set this aside and the registrar (now called the district judge) found that unless he did this and gave her the whole house she would not have enough money left after settling the mortgage and the legal aid bill to rehouse herself, especially as the bankrupt husband was obviously not going to be able to pay any maintenance, so she would only just be able to keep the household going on her own earnings. The registrar therefore granted her application. On appeal the bank instead obtained a 10-year postponement of the sale to when the youngest child would be 18, on the basis that it was not fair not to enforce the charge just because the creditor was an affluent bank and that sometimes debtors' families would have to accept less security in life than might be desirable! Nevertheless, the 10-year postponement was a significant advance on the fate of the Citros in the same year.

However, in *First National Savings v Hegarty* [1985] FLR 80 transfer to the Family Division was refused even though the husband had forged the wife's signature in order to obtain the loan! The court gave the creditor a charging order and said that the wife's position should be considered if and when he applied to enforce it, so application for transfer does not always work.

Where the debtor is bankrupt

As explained above there is little that can be done where the debtor is actually bankrupt as after one year s 336(5) will apply. Moreover, transactions designed to defeat the creditors will usually be set aside, as in the case of *Lloyds Bank v Marcan* [1973] 1 WLR 1381, [1973] 3 All ER 754 where the husband leased his business to his wife, well knowing the bank wanted possession to sell it when he became bankrupt. The lease was set aside. On the other hand, *Re Densham* was a case where the transfer to the wife of a one-ninth share of the home survived the trustee in bankruptcy's application to set it aside, so she got her one-ninth share of the sale proceeds.

Note

Usually the trustee in bankruptcy will be able to set aside any transactions designed to prejudice the interests of creditors or to put assets beyond their reach: Insolvency Act 1986 s 423. Transactions at an undervalue suffer the same fate within five years of the presentation of the bankruptcy petition: s 339. However, in the case of those more than two years before the bankruptcy it will be necessary to show that the debtor became insolvent as a result of the transaction, or that at that time the debtor could not pay debts as they became due: s 341.

In these circumstances the best advice that might be given to a client who is not a joint tenant of the home and who fears that the other spouse may dispose of the property and make off out of the jurisdiction with the proceeds would be to ask for a share of the money *in lieu of* registering the MHA rights of occupation! On the other hand for the client who is a joint tenant. There seems to be no solution the solicitor can offer but tea and sympathy and encouragement to do what can be done with whatever is the value of the client's share of the sale proceeds! Even energetic opposition to the trustee in bankruptcy's claim for an order for sale is likely, after the one year delay, to result in nothing but a large private or legal aid bill for the client, and the money could obviously be better spent.

Note

Cohabitees curiously often have a better chance. While unlike spouses they have no *registrable occupation rights* as such, and no rights under the Insolvency Act, if they have a beneficial interest in the property they can oppose the trustee in bankruptcy's s 30 LPA application and should be able to operate the year's delay in that the creditor's interests may not be presumed to outweigh all other considerations for that year at least if 'all the circumstances' in s 336(5) include the cohabitee's interests.

Rights where the home is rented   15.4

The same MHA rights of occupation apply even if the home is rented: MHA 1983 s 1(6).

The spouse's occupation will also be effective for security of tenure under the Rent Act 1977 and the Housing Acts 1985 and 1988.

By s 1(5) of the MHA rent paid by the occupying spouse must also be accepted by the landlord, just a the mortgagee must accept mortgage payments.

Alternatives where the home cannot be saved   15.5

Since those on Income Support are able to have mortgage *interest* paid for them, the first attempt to save the home for one spouse (and children) should be to negotiate with the mortgagee for *interest only* to be paid on the mortgage, on the basis that the DSS will pay the interest after the qualifying period appropriate to the date when the mortgage was taken out. The mortgagee may agree to this, especially if the reliance on welfare benefits is likely to be temporary and there is every likelihood that the spouse who has been paying the mortgage (or both the spouses) will soon be back in work. The arrears will have to be paid off, or sometimes the mortgage can be restructured so that the arrears can added to the capital element of the mortgage and the mortgage term extended, thus also lowering the monthly payment. Often the mortgagee would rather do this than repossess the home, and in the current cut-throat competition for mortgagors' business, many of them keep departments for working out schemes to retain mortgages of people who would otherwise leave them for other lenders. If the situation is not too bad an attempt to save the existing home and mortgage should always be made first.

Failing this, the possibilities are basically living with relatives, or friends, renting privately (housing benefit will be available: see Chapter 13 at 13.4.3 above) or trying the local authority. A council house or flat is unlikely to materialise immediately, however, and if the local authority is obliged to house the family it may be in bed and breakfast accommodation. Children can now in emergency be voluntarily accommodated pursuant to their duty by the local authority, *without* any danger of a care order: CA 1989 s 20, including where parents are unable to look after them temporarily: see Chapter 6 above at 6.7.8. This might be an option if there are no relatives and the spouses are both trying to find work, though it is obviously not to be recommended except in absolute emergency.

15.5.1   Local authority housing

Housing the homeless is now dealt with under the Housing Act 1985 Part III which imposes a duty to house the homeless. However this obligation is limited by various concepts, and what follows is only a very rough thumb nail sketch of the position. A trainee who has clients who need advice on local authority housing needs to research the up to date position in a specialist book. A specialist vocabulary also needs to be learned, including the appropriate definitions of the words and phrases in common use in local authority housing law, such as *homeless, intentionally homeless,* and *priority need.*

Someone is *homeless* who has no accommodation for themselves or their family or who has accommodation and must leave within 28 days, eg under a possession order from the court, or if the person has accommodation and cannot use it because of violence or threats of violence from someone else living there.

15.5.2   Priority need

Those with *priority need* include people with children old age pensioners, handicapped persons, pregnant women or other vulnerable people.

15.5.3   Intentional homelessness

People are *intentionally homeless* if they would not be homeless but for giving up accommodation.

Note
_____

For this reason it is usually better to wait for a mortgagee to obtain a repossession order in respect of the home rather than to hand in the keys.
_____

Moreover, any accommodation which may be classed as available does not have to be within the jurisdiction, as it could be anywhere within the European Union territory. However a battered wife leaving home is specifically excluded from the category of intentionally homeless.

15.5.4   Local authority duties

Depending on the interrelation of these key concepts, the local authority *may* have a duty to house a person either temporarily or permanently, or possibly not at all. For example, a homeless person who establishes a priority need must be housed temporarily while it is established whether their homelessness is intentional. If it is then decided that that person's homelessness is *not* intentional the authority must provide permanent housing. If the homeless person has no priority need, the only duty on the authority is to advise and assist. Where a person has become homeless intentionally, there is still a duty to provide temporary housing if that person has a priority need.

Note _____

A priority need is established even if the person in question could live elsewhere but might reasonably be expected to live with the person seeking accommodation.

There are also new 'local connection' rules to prevent people 'trading up' to better areas, so that an authority descended upon by other authorities' people can insist on transferring responsibility for those people back to their originating authority.

Self-assessment questions

1 Are there any dangers against which a client should be protected where the home is in joint names prior to separation with a view to divorce?
2 Should any immediate action be taken if the home is in the sole name of the other spouse?
3 What is the right of occupation under the MHA and to whom does it apply?
4 Can this right be lost and if so when?
5 In what way can the court regulate the right?
6 What should the client do if the other spouse is not paying the mortgage or rent of the home?
7 What will become of the client (and the children if any) if the other spouse goes bankrupt?
8 What can the client do if the mortgagee seeks possession of the home for non-payment?
9 What duties, if any, does the local authority have when a home is repossessed?
10 If the home is about to be repossessed by the mortgagee should the client wait for a possession order or hand in the keys without delay?

Chapter 16

The home and contents outside divorce proceedings

Introduction

16.1

Normally precise ownership of property belonging to a married couple, whether that property is the home itself, chattels used in their home or other property in the nature of an investment, is of no particular interest in divorce, since pursuant to MCA 1973 s 24 the court has a wide power to effect whatever adjustments it perceives to be necessary by making a property transfer order. However there are occasions when proprietary rights are important, eg because the parties are not *divorcing*, so that the s 24 jurisdiction is not being invoked. The jurisdiction which will then be that of the Married Women's Property Act (MWPA) 1882 s 17 as amended, which is confined to establishing *strict property rights*, allowing *no s 24 discretion*.

Applicants

16.1.1

The section *may* be used by the following:
- either party to a marriage *during* the marriage;
- either party to a marriage within three years after dissolution/annulment of the marriage: Matrimonial Proceedings and Property Act 1970;
- engaged couples within three years of termination of engagement: Law Reform (Miscellaneous Provisions) Act 1970.

Note

Cohabitees are not included unless they have been engaged. They will have to rely on the general jurisdiction of the court under the ordinary rules of property law for:

- an order declaring and enforcing a resulting or constructive trust;

- an order for sale under LPA 1925 s 30;

- an order for possession of real property;

- injunctions and damages for wrongful interference with chattels.

Thus, s 17 *is* in practice used by:

- *existing spouses* in a non-divorce situation, eg where for tax or bankruptcy purposes precise ownership of an asset must be established;
- *former* spouses who have remarried without remembering to apply under s 24 for a property adjustment order, or where one spouse has died and there is a title dispute;
- *formerly* engaged couples but not mere cohabitees whose property rights have become intertwined in anticipation of a marriage which has not after all taken place.

16.1.2   Orders: declaration or order for sale

The section is very widely framed. It enables the court to:

- consider any question 'as to the title to or possession of property' and make a declaration of the parties' property rights;
- make 'such order with respect to the property in dispute as it thinks fit', eg an order for sale.

This dual power to make both *declarations* and *consequential orders* provides very flexible remedies, and may be exercised over every type of property, both real and personal, and chattels.

Note

Whether an order for sale *will* in fact be made will of course depend on the court's discretion. While land held jointly is always automatically subject to a trust for sale so that application may be made under LPA 1925 s 30 for a sale: *Bull v Bull* [1955] 1 QB 234, whether a sale *will* in fact be ordered will depend on whether the underlying purpose of the trust for sale, ie the purpose for which the property was acquired (usually to provide a home for the parties and any children) is still subsisting: *Re Buchanan-Wollaston's Conveyance* [1939] Ch 738.

In deciding whether the underlying reason for the trust still subsists, it is usually only necessary to look at the facts since cases tend to fall clearly into one category or the other: for example, in the case of *Jones v Challenger* [1960] 1 WLR 1327, [1960] 1 All ER 785 where the husband was left alone in the matrimonial home, the underlying purpose had clearly come to an end. On the other hand, in *Bedson v Bedson* [1965] 3 All ER 307, the home in which the husband was again left alone was in fact a flat over a draper's shops where he conducted the business on which he depended for a living, and besides the fact that the wife had deserted him the property had been bought out of his life savings, so in that case the court did *not* order a sale. Nor did they do so in *Re Evers Trust* [1980] 1 WLR 1327, 3 All ER 399 where the property was a cottage in joint names bought by a couple as a home for themselves and their various children. The woman paid more than the man and when they separated he wanted it sold. However the property was still needed as a home and he had no need either of the money or of the accommodation as he was living with his mother.

You should look at any similar fact pattern encountered in practice and decide whether the underlying purpose does or does not subsist, and this will provide the correct signpost for further action.

However, in view of the wide application of the section, it is irrelevant if when the application is made the property has *already* been sold. Not only can a *declaration* still be made although the court will not be able to reinforce it with an order for sale, by s 7 of the Matrimonial Causes (Property and Maintenance) Act 1958 *payment of the proceeds of sale* can be ordered, or a sale can still be ordered of *another* property which represents the proceeds of sale of the property already sold.

Note

It is important to grasp the difference of approach under MWPA 1882 s 17 and MCA 1973 s 24. In s 17 proceedings the court will ask 'Whose is this?' In s 24 proceedings the question will be 'To whom should this be given?'. Thus only legal and equitable principles of property law will be relevant under s 17 and the old cases which attempted to buttress the weaker financial position of the wife by giving credit towards a property interest for the wife's contribution (which is *relevant* under s 24, but *irrelevant* under s 17) are no longer followed.

Section 17 is therefore *purely procedural and declaratory*: see *Pettitt v Pettitt* where the judgment refers to 'a purely procedural section' [1970] AC 777, [1969] 2 WLR 966, *Gissing v Gissing* [1971] AC 886, [1970] 3 WLR 255, [1970] 2 All ER 780 where it was said that 'the ... principles are those of the English law of trusts'. More recently the law has been augmented by the case of *Lloyds Bank v Rosset* [1990] 2 WLR 887, [1990] 1 All ER 111 which has reaffirmed strict property principles, in particular that where there is no express agreement only evidence of direct contributions to the purchase will be sufficient to confer an interest. It is this decision which some commentators have stigmatised as setting back the position of women as property owners by 50 years, when earlier it appeared that a more liberal approach had developed.

However, it seems that the strict direct contributions rule is already being eroded as in the case of *Midland Bank plc v Cooke* [1995] 4 All ER 562, [1995] 2 FLR 915, CA it was held that once the applicant had *established a beneficial interest*, the court was entitled to draw references as to the *proportions* in which the parties held the property. Thus, if on the basis of the complete financial history of the matter, it could be concluded that the parties had meant to share equally, the will not necessarily hold the property in shares directly proportional to their contributions. The court will *first* have to see if there is evidence of agreement as to the proportions in which the property is held, and if it discovers none, may then fall back on the maxim, 'equality is equity'.

16.1.3   How to establish ownership for s 17

In the case of *land* the first thing to do will be to check the deeds, and then to take appropriate action. In the case of *personalty* there are certain rules which may assist: see below at 16.1.8 *et seq*.

16.1.4   Checking the deeds

Any declaration of the legal or equitable title in the conveyance will be conclusive evidence of the shares unless:

* the conveyance can be set aside for fraud or mistake: *Goodman v Gallant* [1986] 1 All ER 311 where the wife had her former matrimonial home conveyed to herself and her new cohabitee as joint tenants, thus giving him the half share she had just obtained from her husband, since she already owned the other half share herself! However, when she and the cohabitee parted, she was not allowed to claim that she should have the whole house, since the *conveyance was conclusive* unless set aside or rectified; a similar situation arose in the case of *Re Gorman* [1990] 2 FLR 284 where a transfer was to a married couple in equal shares although the wife had contributed more of the money);

* s 37 Matrimonial Proceedings and Property Act 1970 (with regard to improvements to the property) operates to confer a share or bigger share;

- there is a separate trust deed dealing with the beneficial interest.

Any of these exceptions will override the provisions of the conveyance.

Thus, the first task is to *inspect the deeds* and, if the client does not like what is there, to see if there is any chance of fraud or mistake. If the deeds are not specific, then a resulting or constructive trust may apply, failing this proprietary estoppel or a contractual licence may help the client to establish the desired interest.

Resulting or constructive trusts   16.1.5

The ordinary rules applicable to these forms of non-express trusts will therefore apply when a declaration is sought under this jurisdiction.

Note

You will recall that there is a requirement that any equitable interest be *evidenced* in writing under s 53(1)(b) of the LPA 1925, and by s 53(1)(c) that any *disposition* of such an interest must be *in writing*. Since 1989 there is now a requirement that such an interest should also be *created* by contract in writing, containing all the terms expressly agreed, and signed by or on behalf of each party: Law of Property (Miscellaneous Provisions) Act 1989 s 2. However, since spouses and cohabitees, and other persons purchasing property together, do not always regulate their affairs as they should, such a person seeking to establish an equitable interest may ask the court to declare a resulting, implied or constructive trust where necessary since these three types of non-express trusts are specifically excepted from the strict rules of s 53: LPA 1925 s 53(2), LP(MP)A 1989 s 2(5).

Resulting trusts

Resulting trusts arise from the *action of the parties* plus *the court's giving effect to their presumed intentions*, and this is the first type of trust to look for, since it will exist wherever there has been a *direct financial contribution by one party* (by paying all of part of the deposit/legal costs/mortgage instalments) and the *property is in the name of the other*.

To establish a resulting trust it is necessary to prove:
- a common intention between the parties that although one has the legal title the other has a beneficial interest; and

- that the owner of the beneficial interest has acted to his or her detriment based on the common intention.

The common intention usually gives rise to the inference that the beneficial interest is in proportion to the financial contributions but the case of *Midland Bank v Cooke*, above, may now affect this conclusion. The case of *Re Rogers Question* [1948] 1 All ER 328 is the simplest example of the operation of the doctrine. There the house was in the husband's name and he paid the £900 mortgage while the wife had contributed £100. She did not work or make any other contribution and it was held that the property belonged to the couple in the proportions one tenth to the wife and nine tenths to the husband.

Subsequent case law has shown refinements of this doctrine, eg where the wife has worked in a business from the profits of which the home is bought, she may be entitled to a bigger share than her original contribution on the basis that her work in the business, as well as running the home for both parties, has a money value too, as in *Meutzel v Meutzel* [1970] 1 WLR 188, [1970] 1 All ER 443 (the wife in this case obtained a one third share having contributed £650, while the husband paid the mortgage of £3,150). Where there is a *joint venture* the share may be a half as in *Falconer v Falconer* [1970] 3 All ER 449 where the parties bought a building plot, built a house together and the wife paid the housekeeping and the wife the mortgage, and *Chapman v Chapman* [1969] 3 All ER 476 where the parties had each sunk all their resources into a similar project in a similar way and it was held that they must have acquired equal interests.

The recent case of *Midland Bank plc v Cooke*, enabled Waite LJ to throw further light on this sometimes tricky task of quantifying a beneficial interest under a resulting trust. He said that when determining '... (in the absence of express evidence of intention) what proportions the parties must be assumed to have intended for their beneficial ownership, the duty of the judge is to undertake a survey of the whole course of dealing between the parties relevant to the ownership and occupation of the property and their sharing of burdens and advantages. That scrutiny will not confine itself to the limited range of acts of direct contribution of the sort that are needed to found a beneficial interest in the first place. It will take into consideration all conduct which throws light on the question what shares were intended. Only if that search proves inconclusive does the court fall back on the maxim "equality is equity"'.

This is a broader interpretation than that of *Lloyds Bank v Rosset* but not necessarily inconsistent with that case.

Note

You should watch out for the *presumption of advancement*, whereby payments made to or in the name of a wife by a husband (or a child by a parent) are found to be a gift to the wife or child whereas the reverse, where the transfer is *from* the wife or child, does not apply. Cases (such as *Pettitt*) which have considered this rule have doubted its continued existence in modern times, although in the case of *Tinker v Tinker* [1970] 2 WLR 331, [1970] 1 All ER 540, where a husband conveyed a house into his wife's name to evade claims from creditors, it was held to belong to her absolutely.

There are very few modern cases on the point (probably because social change has meant that no one in practice regards it as a presumption any more) but the case of *McGrath v Wallis* [1995] 2 FLR 114, CA, has recently enabled the point to be considered and to confirm on how the presumption, if it still exists, may be rebutted by the facts. In that case a father and son bought a house, and 70% of the purchase price came from the sale of the father's previous house. The property was however conveyed into the son's sole name as the father was 63 and unemployed, and could not get a mortgage. The parties did have a declaration of trust prepared (indicating 80% of the interest in the property going to the father and 20% to the son) but it was never executed and when the father died intestate and his daughter claimed a share of the property the son claimed it outright. The judge at first instance said the presumption had not been rebutted. On appeal, the Court of Appeal referred to *Pettitt*, commented that the presumption was a judicial instrument of last resort and that it could be rebutted by comparatively slender evidence and reversed the decision.

This decision should be useful in any situation where there clearly has been such a practical arrangement as was adopted in this case, and it will probably be rare that if the presumption can be said still to exist in any case it cannot be rebutted by a simple explanation of what happened in the particular circumstances.

Constructive trusts

Constructive trusts arise from the same *pre-conditions* as for the resulting trust, ie:

- common intention; and
- acting to detriment.

However, by *operation of law* whereby a trust is implied because it would be *inequitable to allow the legal owner to claim the sole beneficial interest* rather than from the court giving effect to the presumed intention of the parties as in the case of resulting trusts.

Such a trust usually arises where the financial contributions are *indirect* rather than *direct*, as they would be in the case of the resulting trust, so this type of trust should be looked for where direct contribution sufficient to establish a resulting trust is absent. The constructive trust is the usual way to establish an interest or an increased interest where the contributions are in *money's worth* rather than in actual cash, or are by way of *purchases* made with money which has not been spent on *direct contributions to the acquisition of the property*.

It is much more difficult to establish the necessary *common intention*, when this is in doubt, where contributions, whether in money or money's worth, are *indirect*, especially where the parties are not married.

Note

However, where common intention is already established, and has been relied on by the non-owner to that person's detriment, such indirect contributions, whether in money or money's worth, will *not* be necessary and this principle is expressly not disturbed by *Lloyds Bank v Rosset, per* Lord Bridge.

The type of evidence showing common intention varies: the important thing is that it must show in one way or another that whether or not the parties were to share was *discussed at all*, and not necessarily the outcome of the discussion, since that may be deduced from the parties' subsequent actions. For example in the case of *Eves v Eves* [1975] 1 WLR 1338, [1975] 3 All ER 768 the fact that the man lied to the woman as to why her name was not on the title to the property (he said it was because she was under 21) showed that the matter had been addressed, and in a similar case the lie was that it might prejudice the woman's forthcoming divorce proceedings. In *Re Densham* [1975] 1 WLR 1519, [1975] 3 All ER 725 where the wife's name was omitted from the conveyance, a letter instructing the solicitors showed that this was due to a misunderstanding, and in *Grant v Edwards* [1986] 1 FLR 87, [1986] 3 WLR 114, [1986] 2 All ER 426 the parties acting as though they were joint owners was enough, in this case receiving a fire insurance payment into their joint account.

Note

The only relevance of marriage in the operation of these principles of strict property law is that it helps to show common intention where that is in issue, since marriage is regarded as a partnership.

There are three methods of making *acceptable indirect contributions*:

- payments enabling the other party to pay the mortgage: *Fribrance v Fribrance* [1957] 1 All ER 357 (where the wife worked and paid the day to day expenses, and the husband saved all his earnings and paid the mortgage – Lord Denning commented that the ownership of family assets could not depend on such a chance division of tasks and resources) and *Hargreave v Newton* [1971] 1 WLR 1611, [1971] 3 All ER 866 (where it was expressly noted that in such a situation the husband could never have afforded to pay the mortgage if he had also had to meet the household bills);

Note

The share will not necessarily be a *half* share in such circumstances however as it depends on what is fair in the circumstances: *Hazell v Hazell* [1972] 1 WLR 301, [1972] 1 All ER 923, where a wife got a one-fifth share as while she worked like the former two wives, the husband in this case had had help from his parents in buying the house on mortgage, and the wife's contribution had been limited to the housekeeping and the children's clothes.

- substantially improving the property: *Cooke v Head* [1972] 1 WLR 518, [1972] 2 All ER 38, where the man bought the plot, and arranged and paid the mortgage, and the woman did a lot of rough work including demolition and cement mixing, and acquired a one-third interest for the value of her work, and *Eves v Eves* where the woman got a quarter share for similar work; the Matrimonial Proceedings and Property Act 1970 s 37 gives a statutory right to a share for this type of work for *married parties only* – unmarried parties must continue to use the principle in *Cooke v Head*;

- helping in the other party's business where there will be entitlement to a share of both the profits of the business and whatever is: bought with them *Re Cummins decd* [1971] 3 WLR 580, [1971] 3 All ER 782, *Nixon v Nixon* [1969] 1 WLR 1676, [1969] 3 All ER 1133 (where in each case the wife got a half share, and in particular Mrs Nixon's unpaid work enabled the husband to buy the home).

The following are *not acceptable* as indirect contributions:
- marriage as such, especially where the property was acquired prior to the parties' even meeting, though this would not matter for MCA 1973 s 24: *Kowalczuk v Kowalczuk* [1973] 1 WLR 1 WLR 930, [1973] 2 All ER 1042;
- money or money's worth where there is *no common intention*: *Thomas v Fuller-Brown* [1988] 1 FLR 237 where the man who went to live with a woman who owned a house was held to be a mere licensee doing the work on his own initiative when he obtained an improvement grant, spent the money on materials and fixed up her house, especially as when the relationship ended the woman then had to obtain an exclusion order to remove him from the property so she could return to live there;
- insufficient contributions where there is also no common intention: *Allen v Allen* [1961] 3 All ER 385, which showed that the mere fact that the wife works and contributes her earnings to the house does not raise a presumption of a beneficial interest unless there is agreement or common intention (though social change may make this harder and harder to sustain in the case of married couples because of the inference that such conduct must raise that there was a common intention) and *Burns v Burns* [1984] 2 WLR 582,

[1984] 1 All ER 244, where the parties were not actually married, which made establishing common intention virtually impossible although the woman did as much as any fully committed wife but only bought furnishings rather than improving the actual property, since the man gave evidence that the woman had never actually raised the matter of a share of the property in return for the earnings she had used in the household, he had never thought of it as he did not in fact need her contributions in order to service the mortgage, and even had the effrontery to add that if she had asked rather than assumed he would have put her name on the title!

Note

In *Windeler v Windeler* [1990] 2 FLR 505 underlines the fact established in the *Burns* case where the relationship was 19 years and had produced two children, that where there is *no* common intention *nor* sufficient contribution, the *length of the relationship* is irrelevant, as that only counts under MCA 1973 s 24 where the parties are divorcing, and are therefore married in the first place. 'Mrs' Windeler (again unmarried, like 'Mrs' Burns) had done ordinary housework, looked after the decorators and entertained for Mr Windeler, and in the absence of common intention this was not enough. In the case of *Richards v Dove* [1974] 1 All ER 888, a loan of £150 and some trivial bills and no common intention were also not enough.

- no acting to detriment on the basis of common intention: *Midland Bank plc v Dobson* [1986] 1 FLR 171 where the wife could not show that she had used her earnings for household expenses other than for an utterly trivial amount, to which may be compared *Bernard v Josephs* [1983] 4 FLR 178, [1982] 2 WLR 1052, [1982] 3 All ER 162 where the unmarried couple contributed unequally to the deposit but pooled their earnings and worked together on the house, which led the court to decide that they own the property in equal shares.

Note

There is *no share nor increased share* available under strict property law from doing housework or looking after the family, as Mrs Burns (who was not a wife and had changed her name by deed poll) unhappily discovered, and this will *always* be the case whether the parties seeking to establish whether there is or is not a constructive trust are married or not, since credit for such domestic duties is only available under MCA 1873 s 24. Moreover, when establishing the precise *share* which a party should have, *some regard* will be paid to the proportions in which the parties contributed. Help may be obtained in this respect from cases involving joint purchases by members of the family other than mere husband and wife transactions, such as *Sekhon v Alissa* [1989] 2 FLR 94, a complex mother and daughter purchase, which the daughter variously tried to pass off the mother's contribution as a gift or loan, and the court worked identified the necessary common intention and out a fair division of the value of the property acquired, and *Passee v Passee* [1988] 1 FLR 263 where the purchase was made by a man, contributed to by his aunt and her daughter, and then supported by renting part of the property to other relatives. Again the court unravelled the *types* of transaction, ie which relatives were paying *rent* and which contributing to the acquisition of the property by making *direct capital contributions* (rejecting the man's claim that those were loans) and came up with a fair division of the equity interests.

You should however be aware that a loan can be sufficient to give a beneficial interest, if it is *interest free* and there are no *repayments* as in the case of the woman's loan in *Risch v McFee* [1991] 1 FLR 105 which eventually played a part in obtaining a beneficial interest for her.

Alternatives to a constructive trust

If it is impossible to establish even a constructive trust, the trainee should look for evidence of two alternative legal relationships, either of which may assist cohabitees and mistresses as well as wives to establish useful rights:

- a contractual licence; or
- proprietary estoppel.

A *contractual licence* is a contract like any other and requires:

- a legally binding relationship;
- consideration.

It will not usually confer property rights other than of *occupation* but will enable a wife, cohabitee or mistress to stay when the owner demands that they leave a property, as in the case of *Tanner v Tanner* [1975] 1 WLR 1346, [1975] 3 All ER 776 where there was only ever a 'visiting relationship' and no cohabitation, but a property was acquired for the woman to live in, whereupon she gave up her own rent controlled flat. When the man asked her to leave the house subsequently acquired for her and their twins to live in, she was held to have a contractual licence entitling her to damages for breach, and she was allowed to remain in the home until the children had finished their education or other suitable change of circumstances. Similarly in *Hardwick v Johnson* [1978] 1 WLR 683, [1978] 2 All ER 935 a wife was entitled when the marriage broke up to stay in a home rented from the husband's mother (but on which they had not been paying as they were short of money) as there was a contractual licence.

However, if there has never been a legal relationship this will not work, as in *Horrocks v Foray* [1976] 1 WLR 230, [1976] 1 All ER 737 where there was a relationship of 17 years, including the birth of a child, but when the man was killed in a road accident, the wife successfully sought possession from the mistress as the court could find no consideration and identified the man's generous provision for the woman as going beyond any possible contract. Similarly in *Coombes v Smith* [1987] 1 FLR 352 the woman was unable to show any consideration as she had left her previous marriage because it was unhappy (not for the benefit of the man) and left her job because she was pregnant (albeit by the man) so she had to leave the property he had provided when the relationship ended.

Note

Where there *is* a contractual licence there is no need to establish *detriment* (though if this exists it may be the required consideration) since the point of a contractual licence is that once existing it *cannot be revoked*.

Proprietary estoppel is a very useful remedy, especially as its very nature is that it is *flexible*, and requires that one party acts to his or her detriment in the belief, encouraged by the other party, that this will result in some right being given over a property belonging to that other party; this right sometimes affects only the promisor, but sometimes binds third parties as well. There is no need to establish common intention, but only that the claimant has been misled. It is similar to a constructive trust, but different in that if the conditions are satisfied the:

* legal owner will be *estopped* from relying on an owner's strict legal rights; and
* remedy will be flexible, in that it will be appropriate to the right which the person who was misled thought was being acquired.

Thus, there will not always be a conveyance of the freehold – some lesser remedy, such as a life interest, may be more suitable.

The most recent case in which the doctrine was exhaustively re-examined was that of *Re Basham* [1986] 1 WLR 1498 where the variety of situations in which it could apply was reviewed and the flexibility of the remedy was confirmed. Leading cases include that of *Pascoe v Turner* [1979] 2 All ER 945 where a conveyance was ordered when a housekeeper who had developed a relationship with her employer, but she had refused his proposal and they had not married, was settled in a house which he had given her for her life, together with its contents. Understandably did not want to leave when their relationship ended, as she had spent a substantial part of her life savings on it. He was not allowed to take the house back and the court said only a conveyance would protect her adequately.

However, in *Greaseley v Cooke* [1980] 1 WLR 1306, [1980] 3 All ER 710, mere occupation was all that was wanted by the maid who had been promised that in lieu of wages she could remain for life in her employers' home, and this she got, despite the fact that her occupation (living with the family) was not exclusive. Similarly, in *Maharaj v Chand* [1986] 3 All ER 107 where a man and a woman lived together and the man provided a house for her and her children which he assured her would be a permanent home, she was allowed to stay when their relationship broke up as she had given up her own flat in reliance on his promise, and also used her earnings for household expenses, and the children needed a home until they were grown up.

Sometimes, proprietary estoppel appears in family purchases of property across the generations and the fact that this will create rights can cause particular ill feeling where step relationships are concerned, as in *Jones v Jones* [1977] 2 All ER 232 where a man bought a house near his own for his son and invited his son to move there, which the son did, giving up his job and his own house to do so. He did pay the rates and did work on the house but he never paid rent, and when the father died his widow, the son's stepmother, failed in her attempt to take the house back as the father had represented that the son should have it for life.

Note

Coombes v Smith had no more success as a case of proprietary estoppel than as a constructive trust, because the man had made no *representations* nor *promised the woman she should stay.*

On the other hand, the promise that a woman may remain 'for life' sometimes has strange results as in the case of *Ungarian v Lesnoff* [1990] 2 FLR 299 where the woman was Polish and had given up her accommodation in Poland and come to England to live with a man whom she did not marry. When he bought a house in his name for her and her children to live in and she and her two sons did substantial work on it, with materials bought by him, he did not succeed in turning her out at the end of their relationship because of what he had said. She could not establish either an outright gift or a constructive trust, as a result of which the court said if she was to have a life interest it must be as a tenant for life under the Settled Land Act 1925 entitling her to a vesting deed and all the incidents of that status!

Personalty   16.1.6

Disputes over property other than the home tend to fall into four categories:
* chattels generally;
* housekeeping allowances;
* joint bank accounts; and
* wedding presents.

The general category of chattels may be anything from cars to kitchen tables, and encompass the whole range of utilitarian items which a family needs to cope with life, but might equally include valuable works of art, family jewellery or other heirlooms, and all sorts of property the ownership and use of which is taken completely for granted until the parties split up, whether or not they are divorcing, and for the first time it is therefore necessary to decide where that item shall be kept and used.

Chattels generally, whether in the utilitarian or luxury or investment categories, can always be transferred by MCA 1973 s 24 in a divorce situation, if their ownership is certain and it is desired to change it. Where their ownership is *not certain* and the argument must be resolved, for example because of bankruptcy, inheritance or one of the other reasons for which precise ownership may need to be known, MWPA 1882 s 17 is available for the purpose exactly as in the case of real property. If there is no other way of resolving the matter the court can order a sale.

Note

There are special rules in the case of engaged couples. Engagement rings are presumed to be an absolute gift: Law Reform (Miscellaneous Provisions) Act 1970, but engagement presents from *third parties* are presumed to be given conditionally on the marriage taking place. However, engagements presents *between the parties* may be *either* an absolute gift if not related to the actual or planned life together *or* conditional on the marriage taking place. It is irrelevant who terminates the engagement: Law Reform (Miscellaneous Provisions) Act 1970 s 3(1).

16.1.7 Housekeeping

The Married Women's Property Act 1964 s 1 provides that such allowances made by the husband to the wife for the expenses of housekeeping etc. belong to the parties equally, as does anything bought with them.

Note

In *Tymosczuck v Tymosczuk* (1964) 108 SJ 656 it was considered that mortgage repayments were not within the Act, since an allowance to pay them was not for 'the expenses of the matrimonial home or similar purposes' but a later case queried, *obiter*, whether this was in fact a logical interpretation of the Act.

16.1.8 Joint bank accounts

Ownership of funds in joint bank accounts depends on the intentions of the parties. As in other cases where *intention* is relevant, social trends may influence what the parties' intentions are thought to be likely to be. Probably now that marriage is considered an equal partnership, such accounts are generally regarded by spouses as 'our money' whereas in the past the man tended to buy investments and set up savings accounts in his sole name in order to provide for the two, just as until the early 1960s the matrimonial home tended to be in the name of the husband, regardless of whether the wife had contributed. It is difficult to say when this system, which had its roots in middle class life in leafy suburbs before World War II, came to an end and when it became more normal for married couples to own their home together, but the 1960s which is usually blamed for everything controversial, was probably the watershed, the era when we allegedly 'never had it so good' and young married couples began to be able to amass money and property.

There are therefore not many cases which help in deciding the ownership of money in bank accounts, since many of them are opened for pure convenience so that one party may pay certain bills and there is no intention to make a gift of the money in the account to he spouse who writes the cheques on it. However, if all else fails in deciding the intentions of the payer and payee, and the account is in joint names, the spouses will own both the money in the account and anything bought out of it jointly on the basis that equality is equity, unless perhaps where the account is regarded as a joint purse any items *bought* with the funds in that account are of a personal nature. The wife is not going to want Saville Row suits made to measure for the husband and the husband will probably not want to lay claim to Janet Reger knickers (though he might want to bid for half a Villeroy and Boch dinner service) and similarly in the case of any purchase which was in the nature of an investment, such as an antique or *objet d'art* or a monetary investment such as shares in a privatised industry.

These principles have to be applied to the facts of actual cases when they arise. In the case of *Jones v Maynard* [1951] 1 All ER 802, there was a joint account which was fed by the husband's earnings and various funds paid in by the wife. The husband paid in more than the wife. There was no evidence of their intentions but it did seem that they used it as a common savings account. The husband normally took out money and invested it, in his sole name, as did the wife in hers, but to a lesser extent. When they divorced it was held to be a joint account and the investments were joint investments, being an extension of the savings from which they were bought. On the other hand in *Re Bishop decd* [1965] 2 WLR 188, [1965] 1 All ER 249 the investments bought in this way with money from a joint account were each held to belong to the spouse who had bought them, on the basis that the withdrawals of cash had been made in each case with the *presumed authority of the other* and to spend as the parties chose. However, the remaining money in the account belong to the wife on the basis that she was the surviving joint tenant and so took by survivorship as is normal in such cases.

The presumption of advancement, whereby husband-to-wife gifts are the wife's and wife-to-husband gifts are still the wife's (on the basis that he intends to benefit her but she does not intend to benefit him) probably has no place in modern life. It was considered in *Re*

Figgis decd [1968] 2 WLR 1173, [1968] 1 All ER 999 where a husband paid his salary into a joint account and the money was presumed to belong to the spouses equally. However, in *Heseltine v Heseltine* [1971] 1 WLR 342, [1971] 1 All ER 952 the account was held to be for convenience only where the 'gift' was from the wife to the husband, and both the money in the account and the assets bought with it were held to belong to the wife alone.

You will therefore need to look carefully at the circumstances of each case. *If* there is still any presumption of advancement, which works in the case of parent-child gifts as well as in the case of those in a husband-wife direction, this can relatively easily be rebutted on the facts where there is a credible explanation for the property being in the 'donee's' name, as in the case of *McGrath v Wallis* [1995] 2 FLR 114, CA, where a property was shown to be in the son's name although the father put up much of the money because the father was in his 60s and unemployed and could not get a mortgage, whereas the son was a credible mortgagee. Social conditions have changed so much that whereas such an arrangement might once have been interpreted as conferring a gift, it is now a common situation that families buy property together and by no means the case that parents (or husbands) will necessarily be in a position to give their children (or wives) handouts, so that the facts will usually dictate some other transaction.

16.1.9 Wedding presents

Wedding presents are usually presumed to belong to the party whose relatives or friends gave them, *not* to *both* parties, although it can also depend on the intention of the donor, if that was specifically different.

The leading case is that of *Samson v Samson* [1960] 1 All ER 653 where it was established that wedding presents do not necessarily belong to both parties. On the other hand in *Kilner v Kilner* [1939] 3 All ER 957 where the gift was £1,000 from the bride's father, it was held to belong to both parties, although that may have been inevitable since the cheque was paid into a joint account the funds in which the couple had doubtless decided to use for joint purposes.

16.2   MWPA 1882 or MCA 1973 s 24?

The MCA 1973 will *always* apply on divorce, since it is not possible to oust the jurisdiction of the court under s 24. The object of s 24 is to give the court a wide discretion in regulating and reorganising all financial and property arrangements between the parties and their children where necessary. Thus the court will resist any attempt to evade their powers in this respect (such as by attempting to use the MWPA or s 30 of the LPA 1925: *Williams v Williams* [1977] 1 All ER 28, [1976] 3 WLR 494 where an attempt to make an application in the Chancery Division under s 30 LPA when divorce proceedings were pending was transferred to the Family Division since it was obviously within their remit).

You should bear in mind that the approach of the two statutes could not be more different:

- MWPA looks *back* to how property rights arose, MCA s 24 looks *forward* to needs and resources;
- MWPA is purely procedural and declaratory, MCA gives the court unfettered discretion within the s 25 considerations;
- MWPA declares and gives effect to existing rights, MCA alters them;
- MWPA considers conduct irrelevant, MCA considers conduct occasionally relevant;
- MWPA considers children's interests generally irrelevant, MCA gives first consideration to children;
- MWPA considers conjugal services irrelevant, MCA considers such contributions important.

Self-assessment questions

1 Why is it sometimes important to know which spouse owns particular property?
2 Who may apply under MWPA 1882 s 17?
3 What are the powers of the court under s 17?
4 How is ownership established for s 17 purposes?
5 What is the difference between a resulting and a constructive trust?
6 What is proprietary estoppel?
7 What is a contractual licence?
8 What are the rules about housekeeping allowances?
9 Who owns assets bought out of joint bank accounts?
10 Who owns wedding presents?

Section 6

Domestic violence injunction

Chapter 17

Domestic violence: remedies for the married and unmarried client

Introduction   17.1

For many years there have been four jurisdictions under which the client suffering violence or other anti-social conduct on the part of a spouse or cohabitee could seek various orders to restrain the behaviour complained of. These orders are of two types, ie:

- for *personal protection* or *non-molestation* (ie to protect both the threatened spouse and the children of the household from such behaviour whether at home or elsewhere); and/or
- for exclusion or ouster of the offending spouse from the home in such a way that that spouse was either restricted to a defined part of the home or actually excluded from it altogether.

These four jurisdictions have been found to be complex and confusing by successive cohorts of students, and it was therefore a great disappointment that the Domestic Violence Bill which was before Parliament in 1995 did not ultimately reach the statute book, especially as this was due to an ill informed campaign pressed by a tabloid newspaper. This was particularly unfortunate because the principal effect of the new statute was to unify the four existing jurisdictions so that all the remedies which they collectively made available could be sought throughout the triple tier of courts in which justice in the field of family law is now conveniently dispensed. The Family Law Act 1996 has retained most of the new law proposed in the 1995 Bill, but Part IV of the FLA, which contains the new domestic violence provisions, is not expected to be in force before autumn 1997.

As a result of this delay, you must for the moment learn the mass of complex detail comprised in the existing law, although it will at least now be possible to look forward to a more logical future.For the benefit of those going into a training contract towards the end of 1997, a summary of the new law which will probably come into force then is included at 17.7.

The four possible jurisdictions are:
- The Matrimonial Homes Act 1983 (MHA 1983);
- The Domestic Violence and Matrimonial Proceedings Act 1976 (usually abbreviated to DVA 1976);
- Domestic Proceedings and Magistrates' Courts Act 1978 (DPMCA 1978);
- The inherent jurisdiction of the court (ie to grant injunctions, in support of some legal or equitable right, pursuant to the Supreme Court Act 1981 s 37(1) in the High Court and the County Courts Act 1984 s 38 (as inserted by the Courts and Legal Services Act 1990 s 3) in the county court – the most common in the family law context will be where divorce proceedings have already been started or in wardship or ancillary to proceedings under the Children Act).

17.1.1   Which jurisdiction?

The need for this 'menu' all of which the lost Bill was going to repeal, and which Part IV of the FLA 1996 will replace, is because no one of these Acts can at present do *everything* that a client seeking protection from an anti-social spouse usually wants, and which the prudent solicitor will usually consider necessary for that spouse in the fraught (but usually temporary) circumstances often accompanying the breakdown of relationships.

The choice of jurisdiction will therefore depend on what remedy suits the precise situation:
- ouster and exclusion orders to remove or exclude a *spouse* from the *matrimonial* home must be applied for under the MHA 1983 because this is the statute which *regulates* the *occupation* of the home occupied by *married* people – so it follows that *cohabitees* can never use this statute.

However:
- one of the other jurisdictions must be used to obtain an order restraining the actual behaviour complained of since the MHA only regulates *occupation* not how married people behave towards each other!

There are also some restrictions depending on the *status* of the applicant:
- only *spouses* can use the DPMCA, which is the magistrates' court statute which combines some of the powers of the DVA and the MCA, though the DVA gives much wider powers than the

DPMCA which cannot exclude the anti-social spouse from the area as well as the actual home;

- *unmarried couples* must therefore used the DVA or the inherent powers of the court because that is all that is available to them (so they will have to use the High Court or county court);
- *legally aided parties* will usually have to use the DPMCA because the magistrates' court is cheaper than the county court (which is the court applying the DVA).

The MHA with the DVA is therefore a very powerful remedy since it provides the possibility of:

- exclusion from the house; plus
- exclusion from the area around; plus
- a personal protection order in the widest form, excluding every sort of molestation and harassment, as well as violence;

and this may be the best solution where there is a serious situation in which it is only a matter of time before very serious injury is caused unless the offender is kept right away from the applicant.

Note _____

The necessity to use the MHA to *exclude spouses from the home* was discovered in *Richards v Richards*, a case already mentioned, where there was certainly irretrievable breakdown but the husband's behaviour, although daft to a degree, was insufficient for Fact B: although unable for the time being to divorce him the wife then tried to get him out of the home but did not in fact succeed as the court said that besides the triviality of her complaints the husband was a good, affectionate father loved by his children and an exclusion order was inappropriate.

However, in considering the case, the House of Lords observed that since the MHA provided a statutory code for the occupation of the matrimonial home, an application to *exclude* a spouse, who was by definition a person who had a right of occupation until the court said otherwise, could only be made with reference to the statute in question.

At first this literally meant that a *separate originating application* had to be filed (since the originating summons asking the court to determine the matter is the procedure for invoking such a declaration) but ultimately applications came to be made simply by coupling the MHA with whatever other jurisdiction was being used and the FPR 1991 r 3.8(3) now provides that where matrimonial proceedings are pending application under the MHA is made by notice of application in those proceedings.

> This means that *one single notice of application* can now be used to seek an exclusion order under the MHA (for which the MHA was designed) *and* a non-molestation injunction (which the MHA cannot give).

Due to the idiosyncrasies of each of the relevant sources of orders, it will be convenient to examine the individual jurisdictions separately. In every case it is *possible* to obtain in respect of both personal protection or non-molestation orders and ouster or exclusion orders:

- an *emergency order* without notice to the other side (called an *ex parte* or *expedited* order, depending on the court in which it is sought); and
- a *power of arrest* to reinforce the order in appropriate circumstances;

though there are *stringent* conditions attached to the grant of each of these and neither is routine.

In every case, any *ouster* or *exclusion* order will last for no more than about three months since such orders are regarded as 'first aid' pending some more permanent solution being worked out in ancillary relief proceedings and effected by a property adjustment order under MCA s 24: thus, the orders themselves have no effect on property rights, although spouses sometimes mistakenly think that they do and that it would therefore be of tactical advantage in any ancillary relief proceedings to eject the other spouse from the property. Conversely, because there is no permanent effect on property rights, and because of the time limit on orders, what appear to be very harsh orders are sometimes made where there is no alternative, eg where both spouses have a high degree of need of the property and it is not possible to make an order in respect of part only, an order *may* nevertheless be made to exclude one spouse from the *whole* of the premises for the entire period of the order even where it is manifestly inconvenient because of a business being conducted on the premises. It is all a question of what the court *thinks* (the word used in s 1(3) of the Act) it is just and reasonable to do in the particular case.

17.2   The Matrimonial Homes Act 1983

This is available to non-owning or jointly owning spouses as well as to the legal owner of the house. It is *not* available to cohabitees and the only orders available are exclusion or ouster orders and *not* personal protection or non-molestation orders, for which the DPMCA or DVA will be required. Because the Act gives each spouse,

whether the owner or part owner or not an owner at all,
or where neither is an owner because the home is rented,
a statutory right of occupation (see 15.2) it permits the
court to regulate that occupation of the home by:

- declaring, enforcing, restricting or terminating
  the right of occupation;
- prohibiting, suspending or restricting the exercise
  by either spouse of the right to occupy;
- requiring either spouse to permit the exercise by
  the other of the right: s 1(2).

Note

The home must be a dwelling house (which includes a flat)
which is or has been occupied by the spouses as a matrimonial home: s 1(10). Thus it does not apply to holiday cot-
tages or other premises which are not 'the matrimonial
home', for the purposes of the protection provided by the
Act, although if the parties have more than one or even
several homes, any one which has been used as 'a matrimonial home' can qualify.

By s 1(3) the court may make 'such order as it thinks just
and reasonable' and in particular may:

- exclude a spouse from *part* of the home only, particularly from a part which is used by the other
  spouse in connection with a trade, business or
  profession: s 1(3)(a);
- order a spouse occupying the home or any part of
  it to pay an occupation rent to the other spouse:
  s 1(3)(b);
- order either spouse to repair and maintain the
  home or to pay for outgoings: s 1(3)((c).

Example

By s 1(3)(a) the court can make an order that the *husband* is
excluded from the house as a whole *except* for his studio in
the garden and that the wife is excluded from the studio
where the husband carries on his business as an architect.

The effect of the Act is therefore that the court can make
an *exclusion* order against a spouse (or complementary
orders against both spouses in respect of different parts
of the property) since the definition of the home in s 10
(1) includes 'any yard, garden, garage or outhouse
belonging to the dwelling house and occupied therewith'
but it cannot *under this statute* grant an injunction to keep
a spouse right away from the *area* in which the property
is situated as is possible under the DVA 1976, nor make a

personal protection non-molestation order, which can only be done under the DVA 1976 or the DPMCA 1978.

Where the MHA *must* be used, this difficulty is overcome by coupling the application with one under the DVA which can exclude from the area, so that the offender can be kept right away from the home and at the same time this will enable a *non-molestation* order to be made so that if the parties chance to meet outside the area from which the offender is prohibited, any conduct designed to take out the restrained person's frustration on the successful applicant for the orders will also be prohibited, provided of course the wording of the order was sufficiently wide to forbid any likely form that might take! This is the job of the person drafting the order for submission to the court – it is wise to ask for *all* forms of harassment, as well as actual violence, to be restrained, including the use of an agent to carry out the conduct which the injunction forbids to the spouse personally! In case the trainee should think this is over egging the pudding, it should be noted that experience has shown that *no one* is more juvenile than the parties to a failed relationship who have to be restrained by the court: they will often continue to bicker and attempt to score off each other indefinitely which is why precision in the wording of injunctions sought is so important.

17.2.1 Principles on which the court determines applications: MHA 1983 s 1(3)

Four considerations are laid down by s 1(3) on the basis of which the court will decide whether an ouster or exclusion order should be made:

- the conduct of the spouses in relation to each other and otherwise;
- their respective needs and financial resources;
- the needs of any children;
- all the circumstances of the case.

No one head is more important than any other: *Richards v Richards* already mentioned above.

It will be convenient to look at these four heads in detail since it has become accepted practice for a court making an ouster or exclusion order under any of the possible jurisdictions to use these MHA heads to determine the justice of making an order, *irrespective* of whether the parties before them are married or not. The trainee will no doubt readily grasp why this field of family law badly needed tidying up by the lost Bill!

The parties' conduct in relation to each other and otherwise

The case of *Elsworth v Elsworth* (1978) 9 Fam Law 21 shows that there must be some conduct complained of which is good reason to exclude the spouse wanting the injunction to seek it. In that case the wife left and refused to return till the husband left, but there was no identifiable reason for her objection to doing so and she did not get her injunction. The conduct must, moreover, not be trivial nor apparently a 'one off' incident, even when some conduct can be established: in the case of *Myers v Myers* [1982] 1 WLR 247, [1982] 1 All ER 776 there was one act of violence and a good deal of verbal abuse, but even this was not sufficient, partly because of the relative triviality and partly because it was not likely to be repeated.

In this sort of situation, the court is likely to look to see if the home could be divided for the period of any injunction, so as either to enable them to use their powers to exclude each spouse from a *part* of the home, or to make no order at all, as proved possible in the case of *Hall v Hall* [1971] 1 WLR 404, [1971] 1 All ER 762, where the house itself was large enough, there was no violence and the parties were relatively sensible and civilised, so that although the situation was unpleasant and tense, the court decided that no order was actually necessary.

However, where the home is small and where the parties are obviously not sufficiently sensible that an appeal may be made for adult behaviour, an order will usually be granted, as in the case of *Phillips v Phillips* [1973] 1 WLR 615, [1973] 2 All ER 423 where the home was a small council flat, the divorce had already been obtained and the situation was such that the wife said she and the son of the marriage would become psychiatric invalids (of which there was some medical evidence) if the order were not granted! The case of *Walker v Walker* [1978] 1 WLR 533, [1978] 3 All ER 141 was a similar situation where proof of a clinically depressive illness could be linked to the tension and friction present in the home and the injunction was therefore granted.

Nevertheless, it is *not* possible to grant an injunction to *prevent* a tense situation getting worse in the hope that a respite will lead to a reconciliation, as the judge attempted to do in the case of *Summers v Summers* [1986] 1 FLR 343 because an order cannot be granted unless it is *necessary*, which in this case it was held on appeal *not* to be although the parties were quarrelling loudly and upsetting the children, both being equally to blame, until the point was reached where the husband had to go and sleep on his grandmother's sofa, which had inspired the judge to grant a two month exclusion order to enable everybody to calm down! A similar two month order was set aside in the case of *Kadeer v Kadeer* [1987] CLY 1775 where the conduct complained of was the husband's excessive sexual demands following the wife's affair, which had led her to resort to sleeping on the study floor to escape his attentions and to the judge's idea that a short separation might settle the parties' differences! Basically, unless there is violence or provable damage to health an exclusion order is too draconian a measure for this type of situation.

However, proof of *violence* as such is *not* absolutely essential as is shown by the case of *Scott v Scott* [1992] 1 FLR 529, provided there is a sufficiently serious situation. In that case a divorce had been obtained but proceedings were pending to settle the future of the 15 year old daughter of the marriage, and the husband was already repeatedly in breach of a non-molestation order, since although never violent he did not accept that the marriage was over and continually pestered the wife about a reconciliation which she did not want. Clearly something had to be done since the parties could not live in the same house, so an exclusion order was granted and the husband's appeal, on the basis that it had been granted on insubstantial grounds, rejected.

More recently, the case of *Brown v Brown* [1994] 1 FLR 233 has confirmed this approach: in that case there was again no violence but the husband was so jealous, strict, stubborn and nasty that he had no need to resort to actual violence to make life intolerable for the wife and to the husband's surprise the court took the view that there was an immediate need for her to be protected by his exclusion.

Note

The cheek of some respondents to domestic violence applications in trying to take technical points which they think may assist them, is well illustrated by the recent case of *Khan v Khan* [1995] 2 FLR 221 (CA) where the husband, in claiming that no order should be made because of the wife's three month delay in applying, added that she could not really complain because he had been beating her up throughout their married life (50 years – they were married in 1945) so his violence was no worse than before, especially now that he was so old (75). The court said that this was 'an astonishing proposition'.

The parties' needs and resources

The court will require detailed information as to which party can best obtain and/or afford alternative accommodation, and how easy or difficult it is for either party to be rehoused, perhaps, if there are no relatives who could help out temporarily, by the local authority as in *Thurley v Smith* [1985] Fam Law 31. In this equation, often the woman has the edge if she has children as they will handicap her in finding accommodation as in the case of *Lee v Lee* [1984] FLR 243, and it may also be possible for her to 'score' under the next heading of 'children's needs' as happened in the *Lee* case, where there were two children of an unmarried couple, including a daughter who made allegations of indecency against the father as a result of which she had to stay with her grandmother while her mother was in hospital – the court gave occupancy of the jointly owned former council flat since the man on his own did not require extensive accommodation nor have such a high degree of need for it.

However, this does not always work to the woman's advantage, as was the case in *Wiseman v Simpson* [1988] 1 All ER 245, a leading case on the draconian nature of exclusion orders. In that case there was a young unmarried couple with a child where the woman clearly thought she was going to succeed merely because of the existence of the child, but where the court refused to make an order at all because, although there was an 'atmosphere', the man had done nothing of which the wife could legitimately complain, it being really a case, as the court observed, of 'two young people who had fallen out of love with each other'.

Note

In practice, however, where the other heads are satisfied and someone has to move out, this head will usually mean that the one who has the children will stay in the home because finding accommodation for children (whether babies who may be fractious, older children who may be unruly or teenagers who may be loud) as well as the ejected spouse will obviously be more difficult, besides which some landlords will not have had tenants with children.

However, that does not mean that no order will be made if the spouse *without* children to accommodate still has nowhere else obvious to go, though in that case the court may give the one who has to move out longer to do so before the order is effective.

Where both spouses have children (eg where both spouses have been married before and the cause of the disruption is that the *children as well as the spouses do not get on*) the court has a headache – this is really a housing and not a legal problem at all, which should be referred to the local authority, who should be reminded of their general duty to children in their area under s 17(1) of the Children Act 1989 (ie to promote their upbringing where possible in their own families) although the realities may mean that they can do no more than offer temporary accommodation under s 20 without taking such children formally into care: see above at 6.7.8.

Children's needs

It should be noted that children's needs are not paramount under s 1(3) of the MHA which must be contrasted in this respect with s 1(1) of the Children Act 1989 where they *are* paramount. They are not even *first* as under s 25(1) of the MCA 1973. Nevertheless, the reality of the situation is that the court will take their needs very seriously, will if necessary hear an application for a residence order under the Children Act concurrently with that for the exclusion order, and if the spouse with the children is not then adjudged to win outright under this head of children's needs, that spouse will usually get a second bite of the cherry under the fourth head of 'all the circumstances of the case'.

Note

Until the case of *Richards* in 1983 the needs of the children *were* considered to be paramount in exclusion cases, but the modern approach has more recently been confirmed in the case of *Gibson v Austin* [1992] 2 FLR 437, a depressing case of a cohabitational relationship where the man had children of an earlier relationship and there was also a baby who was a child of both parties. The parties were joint owners of a former council property. Despite threats by the man, armed with a knife, against the woman, the judge found that the parties were making arrangements to separate and sever their financial connections within a very short time, that the knife attacks were not as serious as alleged and that therefore there were no needs of the children which outweighed the other s 1(3) considerations.

A similar result was reached in the later case of *G v J (Ouster Order)* [1993] Fam Law 341 where an order was made excluding the woman so that the man and the child could live in the home on the basis that the child should not be exposed to matrimonial quarrels but this was over-

turned on appeal because the child's needs were insufficient to make a draconian order on the basis of no more
than the situation which had been insufficient in the case of
Wiseman v Simpson.

Where there are competing children's needs, eg where
the husband has a teenage son and the couple have a
baby who needs to be with the wife, as in the case of
Bassett v Bassett [1976] 1 All ER 513, and the home is very
small (in that case a two-roomed flat) the husband and
older child will often be regarded as being the ones more
likely to be able to find alternative accommodation, especially if the alternative is for the wife to live with parents
where she and the baby will be very overcrowded, as a
woman and a baby are not usually popular tenants of
any landlord, and the husband and son would at least be
able to be accommodated by the local authority on a bed
and breakfast basis. This conclusion tends to be reinforced where there is proof that the husband (as in this
case) drinks and is violent, or where the wife is enduring
disagreeable conditions elsewhere rather than try to
share a tiny property, as in the case of *Anderson v
Anderson* [1984] FLR 566 where the wife, who apart from
having a two year old was also pregnant again and living
in a hostel for battered wives.

Where the allegations of conduct under the first head
are the same as those in a divorce petition on which the
court has not yet adjudicated, the court hearing the
application for an exclusion order will not look into the
adequacy of the allegations in the petition, in order to
determine whether a party was justified in leaving, but
this will not stop them making an order on the basis of
the children's needs if those can be shown to exist, as was
the case in *Samson v Samson* [1982] 1 WLR 252, [1982] 1
All ER 178. However, if the children's needs are not alone
sufficient to secure the exclusion order sought, as in the
case of *Myers*, already mentioned above, where there was
only a one off incident of violence and some verbal
abuse, a spouse will *not* get an order merely because the
'children's needs' head has been proved.

All the circumstances of the case

This covers anything else which is not apparent under
the earlier three headings, such as where the husband
installs his mistress in the home in an attempt to preempt
the ultimate property settlement, as in *Jones v Jones* [1971]
2 All ER 737 and *Hadden v Hadden* [1966] 3 All ER 412,
where one spouse was trying to evict the other.

17.2.2   Procedural considerations

In order to invoke the protection afforded by the Act *without* coupling the application with any other Act, it used to be *technically correct* to apply to the High Court or county court by *originating summons* supported by affidavit on a minimum of 21 days' notice but as many applications are now *in existing or projected divorce proceedings* to which such applications should be attached if divorce is contemplated (undertaking to file the petition as soon as possible if it is not possible to file it immediately) *all* applications are now by simple notice and the 21 day period of notice to the respondent can be abridged in suitable cases. Thus normally the ordinary written application on Form N16A will be used in *all* cases even those in which *no matrimonial proceedings are pending* and where therefore the MHA jurisdiction is officially invoked by *originating application*: FPR 1991 r 3.8(2) and r 3.6(1). See below at 17.6.4.

Ex parte application (ie urgent application without giving notice to the other side) is allowed only in the most drastic circumstances, either because the case is particularly shocking or because the *ex parte* order is to be in force only for the briefest of periods, until a hearing can take place on notice, eg for 48 hours. Since the 21 day period of notice can be abridged in suitable cases there is really otherwise no justification for an *ex parte* order, as is demonstrated by the case of *G v G* [1990] 1 FLR 395, where an *ex parte* ouster was obtained by a husband against a wife together with a non-molestation order restraining her from assaulting him, but was set aside because:

- she was readily available for service;
- there was a conflict of evidence;
- the period granted *ex parte* was far too long and such an order should only be for a very short period pending a hearing on notice.

17.3   Domestic Violence Act 1976

This Act allows the court to grant either:

- a *non-molestation* order, ie to restrain a party to a marriage or one of a couple comprising a man and a woman who are living with each other in the same household as husband and wife from molesting the applicant, or a child living with the applicant: s 1(1) (a) and (b); or
- an *ouster* or *exclusion* order, ie (provided application is coupled with an application under the

MHA in the case of married persons) to exclude that person from the home or a part of the home or the area around the home, and/or to permit the applicant to enter and occupy the home or any part of it.: s 1(1)(c) and (d).

Note

The word *molestation* in this context does not bear its usual connotation, and various pleas have been made (including by the Joint Director of the Judicial Studies Board who as a London Divorce County Court judge hears endless domestic violence applications) for any new Domestic Violence Act which may eventually be passed not to use this term, but to change to the use of the word 'harassment'!

The DVA is the *widest* of the jurisdictions, especially when coupled with the MHA, particularly as *molesting* includes *harassing and pestering in any form: Vaughan v Vaughan* [1973] 1 WLR 1159, [1973] 3 All ER 449 where the husband was a perfect nuisance, always making unwelcome visits to his wife from whom he was separated. Similarly in *Horner v Horner* [1982] 2 WLR 914, [1982] 2 All ER 495 the husband continually made offensive telephone calls to the wife from whom he was separated, and in *Johnson v Walton* [1990] 1 FLR 350 one of the parties made embarrassing revelations (accompanied by photographs) to the newspapers about the other which brought down a plague of journalists on to the unfortunate victim! It follows that actual *violence* is not necessary, despite the word being in the title of the Act.

Note

Sometimes the conduct to be restrained can be *involuntary* as in the rather sad case of *Wooton v Wooton* [1984] FLR 871 a case of violence which was only brought on, Jekyll and Hyde-like, by epileptic fits.

Conditions for obtaining a DVA order   17.3.1

There is basically only one condition attaching to the grant of an order under this Act which is that if the parties are not still living together they *must have done so immediately before the incident* complained of even if one has had to leave the premises because of the violence before the application is made, and they *must not be intending to continue to live together*.

Note

If the parties have *never* lived together they cannot use this Act and must rely on the ordinary law of assault, although this was going to be changed by the lost Bill, which would have protected those who had had only a 'semi-detached' relationship, such as in *Harrison v Lewis* and *R v S* [1988] 2 FLR 339 where the women lived elsewhere and were harassed, threatened and subjected to violence by boyfriends. This does not really matter in fact, as it is now possible to obtain an injunction in support of an action in tort, to restrain the tort of 'harassment' as was established in the case of *Khorasandjian v Bush* [1993] 2 FLR 66 where the man continually annoyed the woman, with whom he had never cohabited, in various ways including making abusive telephone calls.

It is clear from s 1(1)(d) of the Act (which allows the court to order that an applicant be permitted re-entry to the home) that it is not necessary to be *living* in the premises by the time the application is made, a point taken in the case of *McLean v Nugent* (1980) 1 FLR 26 and not examined too closely where application is not made entirely promptly after one party has moved out, as in the case of *Davis v Johnson* [1978] 2 WLR 533, [1978] 1 All ER 1132 (HL) where the woman had moved out with her baby to a battered wives' hostel and had lived there in grossly overcrowded and insanitary conditions before being able to make her application to move back to live in the property without the man who had threatened to kill her, throw her into the river, chop her up and put her remains in the deep freeze. However, in the case of *O'Neill v Williams* [1984] FLR 1 the delay before application was six months which was held to be too long to permit application since s 1(2) of the Act actually refers to a man and a woman who 'are living with each other'. The longer the delay, the less likely the application is to be entertained.

This can however be interpreted fairly liberally as in the case of *Adeoso v Adeoso* [1980] 1 WLR 1535, [1981] 1 All ER 107, where the parties, who communicated only by notes, were living each in one room of a council flat, the respective doors of which they kept locked: they were still held to be living together as husband and wife due to the smallness of the accommodation.

Note

If they are going to continue to live together they cannot use the Act, as was the case in *F v F* [1989] 2 FLR 451 where the man was an alcoholic with whom the woman wanted to continue to live, but subject to the court's control of his violence towards her and the child, through the grant of an

injunction. However the court declined this supervisory
role! This case also provided a good definition of the type
of conduct which will be restrained as any conduct which
is sufficiently serious that it substantially interferes with
the applicant or a child, whether by violence or other
means, such as pestering, intimidation, harassment or
unwelcome offers of reconciliation.

Exclusion orders under the DVA

17.3.2

Where an *ouster* or *exclusion* order is sought under the
Act the same four heads under the MHA 1983 as are considered in married cases will be guide the court in deciding whether it is just and reasonable to make an order,
with the additional factor that pursuant to the decision in
Hennie v Hennie [1993] 2 FLR 351 (CA) the court is supposed to pay particular attention to the *urgency* of the
applicant's situation, the quality of the relationship and
the availability of alternative accommodation because
the DVA was originally a statute designed to give urgent
short-term relief.

Duration

While there is no duration specified for orders in the Act,
there is a *Practice Note* [1978] 2 All ER 1056 which lays
down a limit of three months in most cases, which has
been reinforced as generally applicable at least in the first
instance by cases such as *Hopper v Hopper* [1979] 1 All ER
181, though this can be exceeded where the couple are
not married and the applicant is the legal owner of the
property. In an appropriate case however, an unlimited
duration might be granted as in the case of *Galan v Galan*
[1985] FLR 905 (CA) where the judge at first instance
took the view that the husband was entirely to blame,
and that there was an ample continuing risk of violence,
and the Court of Appeal did not overrule him despite
confirming that in general a short-term would be appropriate. Because the Act does not specify a duration, an
injunction can be expressed to continue 'until further
order'.

Note

If circumstances change the respondent can always apply
to have the injunction discharged, eg if there is a reconciliation.

Emergencies: *ex parte* orders

Non-molestation orders can be granted *ex parte* without
too much difficulty wherever protection is either

genuinely so urgent that it cannot wait for notice to be given or it is desirable that the respondent should have no notice of the application as otherwise there would be likely to be an immediate incident, from which advance protection is required in the shape of an injunction already granted before the opportunity arises for the respondent to take out any frustration on discovering that hitting the applicant is now legally forbidden! However, as they preclude the court's hearing the respondent's side of the story, they are not available where there is a conflict of evidence or where the respondent is readily available for service, especially as only two days' notice is required.

Ouster and *exclusion* are more difficult to obtain *ex parte* as unlike the long period of notice required in the case of MHA applications, only two days' notice is required under the DVA, and accordingly, the scope for *ex parte ouster and exclusion* orders is correspondingly reduced. Soon after the Act came into force the case of *Ansah v Ansah* [1977] Fam 138 (CA) laid down the general rule that *ex parte* ouster and exclusion orders were only for real emergency in the interests of justice and where the protection of the applicant and/or a child required the court's immediate action, and this was subsequently confirmed in a *Practice Note* [1978] 2 All ER 919 identifying the indicator as 'real immediate danger of serious injury or irreparable damage'. Where an ouster or exclusion injunction is granted *ex parte*, the order must specify the date when it expires, and this will usually be when the hearing on notice will take place a few – generally not more than seven – days later. Basically, an *ex parte* ouster or exclusion order is only merited when there has been *violence*, preferably *recent* violence.

17.3.3

Power of arrest: DVA 1976 s 2

Where a *non-molestation* injunction restrains the use of *violence* or where there is an *exclusion* order either from the home or from a specified area around it, s 2 permits a power of arrest to be attached where the judge is satisfied that the respondent:

- has caused *actual bodily harm* to the applicant or a child mentioned in the injunction; *and*
- *is likely to do so again.*

The purpose of a power of arrest is to enable the police to arrest without warrant if the suspect the party restrained is in breach of the injunction: s 2(3). If arrested, such a person can be kept in custody and only brought before a judge at the end of 24 hours, and need not be released earlier without leave of the judge: s 2(4). This is an extremely practical and effective tool since the power of arrest is registered at the local police station when granted, so that only the most confrontational of respondents is likely to consider deliberately invoking the disagreeable consequences of breach of the injunction which it reinforces.

Moreover it was held in the case of *Lewis v Lewis* [1978] Fam 60 that this power of arrest can be attached to any injunction satisfying the s 2 conditions whether it is granted under the DVA or under the inherent jurisdiction of the court, eg in divorce proceedings although there is doubt as to whether it can be attached to an MHA order. Since this problem can be overcome by using both Acts, this query is not likely to be a substantive worry. The only slight problem which may arise in relation to attaching powers of arrest does not therefore in fact lie with the MHA, but in the fact that sometimes *undertakings* are accepted *in lieu of* injunctions being granted, and it is not possible to attach a power of arrest to an undertaking: *McConnell v McConnell* (1980) 10 Fam Law 214, *Carpenter v Carpenter* [1988] 1 FLR 121.

Note
_____

Powers of arrest are not *routine*, are restricted usually to cases of *recent personal violence*, and are *not usual* where the case is predominantly one of other forms of molestation and where the only violence is not recent. The idea is to restrain *persistent disobedience to orders and constant nuisance to the applicant and others*. In the *Lewis* case the court of Appeal held that more was required than forcing Mrs Lewis out of the house to a hostel (so the power of arrest was inappropriate in that case) and in *Kendrick v Kendrick* [1990] 2 FLR 107 where the wife was frightened but not actually physically injured a power of arrest was refused as the husband's only conduct was threats so she could only demonstrate psychological harm.

The Domestic Proceedings and Magistrates' Courts Act 1978

17.4

The DPMCA 1978 s 16 permits the magistrates to make a *personal protection order* or an *exclusion order*.

The *personal protection order* is now known as a *family protection order* and orders the respondent not to use or threaten to use violence against either the applicant or a *child of the family* (unlike under the DVA not simply a 'child living with the applicant') or both: s 16(2). By s 16(10) inciting or assisting another to do the same is equally forbidden. The order may only be made where:

- the respondent has *used* violence or *threatened* to use violence against the person of the applicant or a child of the family; and
- the order is *necessary* for the protection of the applicant or a child of the family;

and this is a question of fact.

The DPMCA 1978 s 88 defines a child of the family in the same way as the MCA 1973. By s 16(1) the relief is available under the DPMCA only on the application of a *party to the marriage*. This does *not* include cohabitees nor those spouses who are already *divorced*, and does not therefore permit a *child* to be protected *except* where the application is made by a *party to the marriage* irrespective of whether the *spouse* wants protection too.

Note

If it is desired to protect a *child* the application *must* therefore be made by the *spouse* who is that child's parent and *not* by the child independently although the order made *will* be expressed to protect the child.

The *exclusion* order can be made where the magistrates are satisfied that the respondent:

- has *used violence* against the person of the applicant or a child of the family; or
- has *threatened* to use violence against the person of the applicant or child of the family *and* has *used violence* against some other person; or
- has, *in contravention of a personal protection order, threatened to use violence* against the person of the applicant or child of the family; *and*
- the applicant or child of the family is in danger of being physically injured by the respondent or would be if the applicant or child were to enter the matrimonial home.

The case of *McCartney v McCartney* [1981] 2 WLR 184, [1981] 1 All ER 597 established that the danger of physical injury need not be immediate: in that case there were a number of assaults and then a lull of five months before the application was made which initially made the magistrates think that an order could not be granted, but on appeal this was held not to be the case although there must be *objectively observable danger*.

Moreover, by s 16(9) the order can be subject to exceptions or conditions, so that although the magistrates

cannot exclude from the area as the DVA in the county
court can, they can permit the use of part of the home, eg
a studio used for professional purposes by the respondent, as can be done under the MHA, or permit visits to
the home, eg to collect the children for contact.

Duration of exclusion orders is normally the same
three months as in the county court and High Court, and
as in the other courts such an order has no effect on title
to the property in question.

By s 18(1) a power of arrest may be attached where
there has been physical injury and it is likely to happen
again, and if such a power is not initially attached the
applicant can ask for it to be attached later at any time if
the respondent disobeys the order.

Note

Both exclusion orders and a power of arrest are draconian
orders for the magistrates, and if they attach a power of
arrest they should give reasons as was held in the case of
Widdowson v Widdowson (1983) 4 FLR 121.

By s 16(7) the magistrates can grant an *expedited order*.
This is the magistrates' version of the *ex parte* order in the
superior courts. It is made when there is imminent
danger of physical injury: s 16(6) and may be made by a
single magistrate, not necessarily from the domestic
panel: s 16(7). Once granted, it lasts for 28 days: s 16(8)
but is only effective when served.

Note

There is no power to make an *expedited exclusion order*
though a *power of arrest* may be attached to an *expedited personal protection order* which is a fairly effective brake on violence, and it is common to seek an expedited personal
protection order to avoid giving the respondent notice of
the application and thus inviting a violent reaction!
Alternatively the expedited personal protection order may
be used where the order is required so urgently there is no
time to serve the respondent, even though the non-expe-
dited application only needs 'reasonable notice' which
means one day.

The inherent jurisdiction of the court   17.5

The Supreme Court Act 1981 s 37(1) and County Courts
Act 1984 s 38 (inserted by the Courts and Legal Services
Act 1990 s 3) give the respective courts the power to
'grant injunctions in all cases in which it appears to the

court to be just and convenient to do so' and this is the origin of the power to grant injunctions ancillary to pending divorce proceedings, ie where a petition has already been filed or where a divorce is intended. In the latter situation an undertaking may be given to file such a petition so as to permit the grant of an immediate injunction in an appropriate case where the application is urgent, notwithstanding that the paperwork has not actually already been done. Technically, such injunctions are granted only in support of some recognised legal or equitable right, so that there must be a link between those proceedings and the injunction sought. Clearly in the case of divorce where there is violence and a need for protection of one of the parties and/or any children, this link is established.

Most divorce cases in which domestic violence injunctions are required will therefore be dealt with under the inherent jurisdiction ancillary to divorce proceedings. Where this jurisdiction is used, the court has the same powers as under the statutes which might otherwise have been used, provided the orders are really *necessary* to provide protection in relation to the main proceedings. Thus *ouster and exclusion orders* will only be made under this jurisdiction where *essential*.

Other cases in which the inherent jurisdiction can be used are where the protection is required for children which can include the adult living with them. This was possible prior to the Children Act 1989 as in the case of *Re W (A Minor)* [1981] 3 All ER 401. The well known case of *Ainsbury v Millington* [1986] 4 All ER 73 was an unsuccessful attempt to obtain a non-molestation order in support of a custody order under the guardianship of Minors Act 1971. The modern jurisdiction stems from the court's power to grant orders under s 8 of the Children Act 1989 and therefore, in any 'family proceedings' as defined by s 8(3) and (4), injunctions for the protection of both children who are the subject of the s 8 orders and of adults with whom those children reside.

17.6   Procedure

The first priority will be to decide which jurisdiction to use. This will depend on whether the client is *married* or *unmarried* and if the former, whether *divorce proceedings are pending* or not. It should be remembered that if divorce proceedings have not been started, but if a divorce is clearly desirable, an undertaking can be given to file a petition after grant of the injunction if the matter is urgent.

Married clients 17.6.1

If divorce *is* pending, application should be made ancillary to those proceedings.

If divorce is *not* pending or intended, then first consideration should be given to the magistrates' court under the DPMCA, if the client satisfied the rules, ie:

- is there violence or threatened violence against the client and/or a child of the family? (the magistrates cannot restrain molestation nor protect a child who is not a child of the family);
- will a simple ouster or exclusion order be sufficient? (They cannot exclude from the area around the home).

Note

The magistrates' court is the *cheapest and quickest* source of remedy, as the magistrates sit frequently and there is usually a court locally, whereas some distance may have to be travelled to the county court. It is also preferred by the Legal Aid Board, who will usually grant ABWOR (and may not want to grant legal aid for the county court).

If the family proceedings court is excluded, then the DVA 1976 coupled with the MHA will have to be used in the county court. This will be more expensive, but the county court protection is wider as it can exclude from the *area*, and if the client is going there anyway, and does not want a divorce, the MHA can be used to order payment of outgoings on the home!

Unmarried clients 17.6.2

The unmarried client must use the DVA 1976 in the county court, or the inherent jurisdiction if an application can be latched on to a Children Act application, eg where an unmarried mother seeks protection from a former cohabitee, she can obtain a s 8 residence order and a non-molestation order ancillary to those proceedings.

Unmarried clients *cannot* use the MHA or DPMCA.

Family Proceedings Court applications 17.6.3

This must be made in the family proceedings court most convenient to the applicant but within the magistrates' commission area where the applicant or respondent normally live: DPMCA 1978 s 30(1). Procedure is governed by the Family Proceedings Courts (Matrimonial Proceedings) Rules 1991. Application is on a prescribed form, with sufficient copies for service, except in the case of a s 16 application where no form is prescribed, it must be *in writing* (see below).

Except in the case of expedited orders where serving the respondent is not required, service must be effected and the copy served must indicate the hearing date and be accompanied by a notice indicating the court's powers: r 3(2)(a). As only 'reasonable notice' which has been held to be one day is required, service obviously needs to be speedy! Service can be:

- personally or by first class post: r 4(i)(a); or
- on the respondent's solicitor, if the respondent is known to be represented, by first class post, via the document exchange or by fax (apparently this must be 'legible'!): r 4(i)(b);

and the applicant must lodge a statement at court detailing the method of service employed: r 4(4).

Written statements of oral evidence are required to be filed prior to the hearing. Oral evidence is then given at the hearing and the magistrates must give reasons for their decision in writing. The hearing, being family proceedings, is in private. when drawn up the order must be served on both parties.

Expedited order procedure is obviously principally different in that no service is necessary. As there is no form prescribed the applicant should apply to the justices' clerk who will arrange a hearing, and it is usual for an statement to be made either orally or in writing to the effect that there is imminent danger of physical injury to the applicant and/or to a child of the family, whereupon there will usually be an immediate hearing at which an order may be made, if necessary by one justice not on the normal family panel: r 20(1) The order must be served personally on the respondent: s 20(2) and if not done immediately prior to the hearing, within 48 hours a formal application must be made in writing and a copy of that also served on the respondent: r 3(4).

Note

The order lasts only for a maximum of 28 days or until the substantive hearing on notice, and is not effective until served on the respondent. If the magistrates will not grant an order, the applicant can still apply to the county court under the DVA as was demonstrated in the case of *O'Brien v O'Brien* [1985] FLR 801. however, if the magistrates do grant an order and then a subsequent application is made

to the county court (eg because the client wants ultimately
to obtain the superior but slower protection of the DVA)
the magistrates' order should be discharged so there are
not two orders in force at once, as in the case of *Horner v
Horner* [1982] 2 WLR 914, [1982] 2 All ER 495.

County court applications

All applications are now made on *notice of application* on
Form N 16A, whether in divorce proceedings or not, and
this form must be supported by affidavit. The difference
between divorce proceedings applications and others is
that the petition (if there is a history of violence) will
usually already contain much of the information that
would otherwise have to go in the affidavit, so that the
affidavit in that case will be somewhat shorter since not
much background will be required. It is for this reason
that although behaviour petitions are normally somewhat restrained and laconic (see Chapter 4 above) a practitioner drafting such a petition where a domestic
violence application is anticipated or likely will usually
be somewhat more expansive about any violence in the
petition.

Where there has to be an undertaking to file a petition, because the application is urgent, a copy of the proposed petition should be available if at all possible.

The FPR 1991 govern applications on Form N16A.
The trainee should remember that even where there is an
originating application under the MHA this form is still
used: rr 3.8(2) and 3.6.(1). For an application under the
Children Act there is a simple application obtainable
from the Family Hearing Centre in the normal way for
Children Act applications.

The affidavit in support should set out the facts fully
and the application should be accompanied by a draft
Order in the form sought so that the precise protection
required is obtained from the court.

Legal aid is available and if legal aid is used the certificate must be filed together with a copy notice of issue
of the certificate, plus notice of acting if the solicitor is
not already on the record.

A hearing date will be given and the respondent must
be served with the appropriate notice unless the period
in question is abridged:
- ancillary injunctions, including under the MHA
  where a divorce suit is pending: two clear days:
  County Court Rules (CCR) 1981 Ord 13 r 1(2);

- MHA where no divorce suit pending: 21 clear days unless abridged: CCR 1981 Ord 7 r 10(5);

Note

The 21 days can be abridged if it is urgent to do so: CCR 1981 Ord 13 r 4.

- DVA 1976: two clear days: FPR 1991 r 3.9(5);
- CA 1989: 14 days unless abridged: FP(Amendment No 2)R 1992 r 8 and Schedule 1.

Note

Ex parte applications are governed by FPR 1991 r 4.4(4)

Service is usually effected personally, by an enquiry agent who should then file an affidavit of service which will be useful if the respondent fails to turn up to the hearing, as otherwise the court is unlikely to grant more than a non-molestation order.

The hearing will require the applicant's attendance to give evidence, accompanied by any witnesses, and affidavits should be sworn and served on the other side prior to this. Any medical evidence should also be sworn and the doctor should attend, unless the respondent accepts a doctor's letter which they tend not to do!

The applicant's solicitor will then open the case before the judge or district judge in Chambers and call witnesses. The applicant may not need to say much if she has enough bruises, scratches, black eyes etc! Witnesses are cross examined in the normal way. An undertaking may be accepted in lieu of an order since this is as effective as an injunction except that a power of arrest cannot be attached to it.

Note

The respondent's solicitor should be sure the respondent understands what he is agreeing to before the respondent gives any undertaking! Breach of it is punishable by committal in the same way as breach of an injunction since it is a solemn undertaking to the court breach of which is contempt.

The procedure is similar for *ex parte* applications, except that only one side will be present and so there will be no cross examination. In emergency a judge can always be found outside court hours, at home and if necessary available to grant an injunction over the telephone. An *ex parte* application is available under the Children Act: FPR 1991 r 4.4(4) and FPC(CA 1989)R 1991, r 4(4).

Both types of orders, on notice and *ex parte*, are effective immediately though they need to be served effectively to ensure enforcement in case of breach. A copy for service is available from the court office after the hearing.

Enforcement

17.6.5

In the Family Proceedings Court

A power of arrest attached to the order automatically brings the respondent back before the court for breach.

Otherwise a *warrant for arrest* will be needed if there is a breach. Sworn evidence is needed to obtain this and the magistrate must have reasonable grounds for believing that the respondent has disobeyed the order: DPMCA s 18(4).

The penalty will either be a fine of up to £2,000 or imprisonment for two months.

In the county court

The power of arrest position is the same as for the family proceedings court.

Otherwise the applicant will have to apply for an order for committal. It is essential to follow the procedure *exactly*. The procedure is set out in Order 29 r 1 CCR 1981 and will require:

- a copy of the injunction with a penal notice attached which has been personally served on the respondent;

Note

A penal notice warns the respondent that the order must be obeyed or that the consequences will be dire and is normally included on all pre-printed forms of order.

- the applicant must ask the court to issue a notice to the respondent to show cause why a committal order should not be made against him, on Form N78 County Court Forms;
- a hearing to be fixed endorsed on the notice and the notice sealed by the court: Ord 29 r 1(4);
- the notice served on the respondent personally at least two clear days before the hearing: CCR 1981 Ord 13 r 1(2).

The hearing is in open court before a judge. Both applicant and respondent and witnesses for each may give evidence. The judge can make an order for committal for up to two years. If there are earlier breaches and an earlier suspended period of committal is activated two years is still the maximum: *Villers v Villers* [1994] 2 All ER

149. The order will be for the issue of a warrant of committal: Form N 80, Ord 29 r 1(5) and the warrant will be enforced by the court bailiff.

However, it is unlikely that there will be a committal until there are repeated breaches, as the hearing is meant to be a warning to obey in future rather than punishment for past offences. a power of arrest is likely to be attached to the original order if there was no t one before, and the injunction might be amended (on application of the applicant) if necessary. The respondent might be fined. Alternatively the judge might either adjourn the application *sine die* again as a warning to the respondent, so the applicant can bring the respondent back to court if there are further problems, or there might be a suspended committal order, for a finite period as in the case of *Pidduck v Molloy* [1992] 2 FLR 202 though these orders have dangers for the respondent if the applicant enforces them thus removing the respondent to prison without being able to say anything about any defence! The court always prefers to investigate the full facts and therefore does not generally deal with an application for committal in the absence of the contemnor: *Benesch v Newman* [1987] 1 FLR 262.

17.7   The new law: Part IV of the Family Law Act 1996

Part IV of the Family Law Act 1996 codifies, improves and extends the existing law, providing a logical and comprehensive set of remedies which can be accessed in the unified framework of courts dispensing family law. All the various orders which can now be granted under the existing law remain available under the Act, but are divided by type into *occupation* or *non-molestation* orders, depending on their purpose. This ends the various terminologies appropriate to the distinct Acts at present in force, and provides a uniform vocabulary no matter to which court the application is made. It also ends any deliberation as to the relative merits of the orders available in the different jurisdictions – all forms of relief, achieving the same result no matter which court is applied to, will be available when an order is obtained. The only decision to be made will be whether a non-molestation order is sufficient, or whether an occupation order is also required.

Occupation orders

17.7.1

There are certain restrictions on the granting of the new occupation orders, depending on who precisely is applying, but generally the categories of potential applicants is now enlarged to include former spouses and former cohabitees (called 'cohabitants' in the Act) even where it is not 'entitled', ie there is no legal or beneficial right in the applicant to occupy, providing the property in question is or has been their home, or it was intended to be their home: ss 33–38. Different considerations are to be taken into account by the court in making such orders depending on whether the applicant falls into one category or the other, eg how recently the relationship has broken up.

Associated persons

17.7.2

The Act also creates a new category of 'associated persons' defined by s 62(3) and where an applicant is 'entitled' in relation to the property an occupation order may be obtained against any such 'associated person'. This category includes all relatives and any persons who have lived together in the same household otherwise than on a commercial basis, besides fiancés and former fiancés, and persons associated through parentage or parental responsibility for a child, or through family proceedings outside Part IV.

Modifications of the s 1(3) criteria under MHA 1983

17.7.3

The long established s 1(3) criteria are repeated by the Act and rewritten by s 33(6) to include the likely effect on health, safety or well being of the parties and any relevant child (ie of whether the order sought is granted or not). By s 33(7) a new *balance of harm* test is introduced into the court's decision as whether to exercise its powers.

Non-molestation orders

17.7.4

The provisions of the DVA 1976 and DPMCA 1978 are replaced by s 42 of the Act, and s 42(5) expressly permits non-molestation orders to be made to secure the health, safety or well being of any relevant child. By s 42(6) any conduct at all can be restrained. Fiancés and former fiancés can apply within three years of the termination of their engagement: s 42(4) though by s 44 applicants will have to produce defined proof that they were engaged. Otherwise non-molestation orders may be obtained by anyone who meets the definition of associated persons in s 62(3). A child under 16 may apply, with leave: s 43.

17.7.5 Matrimonial home rights

The Act continues its changes of existing terminology in creating *matrimonial home rights* in place of the *rights of occupation* with which we are familiar under the MHA 1983. The whole of the MHA 1983 will be repealed when Part IV of the FLA 1996 comes into force and ss 30–32 Schedule 4 reenact (and rewrite) the old sections of the MHA 1983 which gave spouses their rights of occupation as spouses. These new *matrimonial home rights* will make a potential spouse applicant for an occupation order under s 33 'entitled' although that section also expressly refers to 'matrimonial home rights'.

17.7.6 Powers of arrest

By s 47(2) attachment of a power of arrest is likely to be attached more frequently than under the existing law (where it is 'not routine'). The new power is *mandatory* if violence has already been used or threatened unless it appears not to be necessary. Moreover, it can be attached to a non-molestation or occupation order, and for a period shorter than that of the injunction (presumably to cater for instant adverse reaction to the order!)

17.7.7 *Ex parte* orders

By s 45 orders may be made where it is 'just and convenient'. By s 45(2) criteria are set out to assist the court to exercise its powers but in practice this is still likely to be regarded as a draconian measure. By s 46 the position remains that an undertaking may be accepted *in lieu of* making an order, but no power of arrest may be attached to such an undertaking.

Self-assessment questions

1 What are the existing jurisdictions for obtaining domestic violence injunctions?
2 Which apply to cohabitees?
3 What orders can exclude a violent spouse? In which courts?
4 Is violence necessary for an exclusion order?
5 What conduct is necessary for a non-molestation order?
6 Can a child be protected from violence as well as a spouse or cohabitee?
7 Under which Act can the court exclude from the area around the house?
8 Is an order available if the parties are not divorcing?
9 What is an associated person under the FLA 1996?
10 How will the existing s 1(3) criteria be modified under the FLA 1996?

Section 7

Cohabitation

Chapter 18

The unmarried family

Introduction

The prevalence of cohabitation and of births outside wedlock has led to the necessity to reconsider what precisely we understand by 'the family'. The Rowntree Foundation has been doing research on the contemporary concept of the family, which has now experienced such changes that inevitably the trainee will encounter significant numbers of unmarried clients and will need to be aware of their separate problems which will require a distinct approach. Already some steps have been taken to minimalise the effect for children of the fact that their parents are not married, eg in the application of the Child Support Act 1991 which catches both married and unmarried absent parents who are not maintaining their children in exactly the same way, and gradually the position has been reached that there as many similarities as differences between the two types of family.

Current initiatives

The trainee will be familiar, through study of the core subjects at the academic stage of training, with the range of property problems which arise where cohabitees buy and occupy property together, and through their LPC work with remedies available to cohabitees for domestic violence, the operation of the CSA in obtaining maintenance for children from their absent parents, and the provision made under the Children Act 1989 for unmarried fathers to obtain both parental responsibility and s 8 orders in respect of their children. Unfortunately, there is very little else apart from this small portfolio of remedies which is available to unmarried parties when a relationship breaks down. However, two other useful possibilities should be added:

- a Children Act Capital (Transfer of Property) Order, which may be obtained under the Children Act 1989 to enable an unmarried carer parent to secure the occupation of the former cohabitational home for that parent and the child or children;

- the Law Reform (Succession) Act 1995, which has improved the rights of cohabitees on the death of their partners.

Nevertheless, the law reform society JUSTICE has in recent years embarked on a campaign to inform cohabitees (especially *women*, who appear to suffer most from informal arrangements about property, particularly if they in respect of jointly acquired homes) of the possibility of entering into cohabitational contracts or at the very least of securing recognition of the respective property rights of the parties at the initial conveyancing stage, rather than later when the parties are separating, since there is no statutory provision similar to that under MCA 1973 s 24 to facilitate division of the cohabitational couple's assets on relationship breakdown, as is available to wives in a similar position on *marriage* breakdown.

18.3   Property disputes

Where cohabitees or former cohabitees cannot agree on property rights, a declaration of ownership can always be sought whether of real or personal property. This will of course *not* be under the Married Women's Property Act 1882, except in the case of formerly engaged couples as the parties are by definition not married, but is still obtainable under the strict rules of property rights applied under the ordinary law of property. Similarly, a cohabitee may also seek an order for sale under the LPA 1925 s 30. If these remedies are adopted, the law is basically the same for married or unmarried couples: see Chapter 16, especially 16.1.5 for resulting and constructive trusts

18.3.1   Declarations of ownership

A trainee advising a cohabitee about a declaration of ownership should therefore (as in the case of married parties):
- check the deeds for any express legal or equitable title;
- if the cohabitee was ever *engaged* to be married to the other party, apply for a declaration of ownership under s 17 of the MWPA 1882 together with a consequential order for sale, exactly as in the case of a married client, except that in the case of a former fiancé(e) it is necessary to make the application within three years of the termination of the engagement: see 16.1.1;

Note
_____

If the cohabitee has made any substantial improvements to the property, this may provide a share or an increased share under s 37 of the Matrimonial Proceedings and Property Act 1970, which former fiancé(e)s – but not other cohabitees – may use pursuant to the right given to them by the Law Reform (Miscellaneous Provisions) Act 1970 ss 2(1) and 2(2)

- If the cohabitee was *not* ever engaged to be married then it is only possible to apply to the court for a declaration under the LPA 1925 s 53(2).

LPA 1925 s 30   18.3.2

This is the normal jurisdiction for an order for sale where land is held on trust for the parties jointly and cohabitees may use this where the position is clear that the land is held jointly as in that case it is automatically held on trust for sale or where a declaration has been successfully sought. The court will then have the same discretion as to whether to order a sale as in the case of married people and the decision will depend on whether the trust for sale *has* or *has not* in fact come to an end: see 16.1.2, particularly the case of *Re Evers Trust* which is fairly typical of the cohabitational situation to which these remedies may apply.

Occupation to the exclusion of the other   18.3.3

The cohabitee has no rights similar to those of a spouse under the Matrimonial Homes Act 1983. There are however four ways of achieving sole occupation of the home for a cohabitee, either:

- under the domestic violence rules, currently the Domestic Violence Act 1976, the only existing domestic violence jurisdiction to apply specifically to cohabitees: see 17.3 above, or by establishing the newly discovered tort of *harassment*: *Khoransandijian v Bush* [1993] 3 All ER 669, which enables an injunction to be granted ancillary to those proceedings in tort, ie under the inherent jurisdiction of the court: see 17.5; or

Note
_____

The provisions of Part IV of the Family Law Act 1996, will replace all the existing domestic violence jurisdictions when it comes into force, which is thought to be likely towards the end of 1997.

- by establishing a licence to occupy either as a *contractual licence* or under the rules of *proprietary estoppel*: see Alternatives to a constructive trust at 16.1.5;
- by establishing an interest in the proceeds of sale which carries with it a right to occupy: *Bull v Bull* [1955] 1 QB 234;
- by obtaining a transfer of property order under the Children Act 1989 Schedule I whereby the property is held for the benefit of the minor child of the relationship.

Note

It may also be possible to obtain a domestic violence injunction for a short period only ancillary to a s 8 order under the Children Act.

Otherwise neither party can occupy the property to the exclusion of the other, and it is essential to obtain an exclusion order which must be in support of some recognised legal or equitable right: *Ainsbury v Millington* [1986] 1 All ER 73.

18.3.4   Trusts

All the usual rules of resulting and constructive trusts apply in determining cohabitees' interests There will usually be a rebuttable presumption of a resulting trust where money has changed hands as in any joint purchase but cases may sometimes be complicated where a cohabitee is also involved with other members of the family where it must be determined what is the precise status of payments made. Useful cases to look at which may provide arguments by analogy are the family cases of *Sekhon v Alissa* [1989] 2 FLR 94, and *Passee v Passee* [1988] 2 FLR 263.

18.3.5   Hazards

The cohabitee often has to contend with specious arguments to intended to rebut what is otherwise a fairly obvious case of a resulting trust, for example a claim that money spent was a 'loan' as in the case of *Risch v McFee* [1991] 1 FLR 105 and *Stokes v Anderson* [1991] 1 FLR 391, [1980] Fam Law 310, The cohabitee's situation will often share similarities in this situation as in the cases of other family members whose financial affairs have become entangled as *Re Sharpe* [1980] 1 WLR 219, [1980] 1 All ER 198 (where the loan was in fact from an aunt to a nephew) and 'family' cases are often of assistance in arguing for recognition of financial contributions which were *not* by way of non-proprietorial payments such as loans, rent etc.

The simplest cohabitational situation is where (as in the case of married couples) a 'joint venture' can be established, as happened in the case of *Bernard v Josephs* [1984] FLR 126 where both parties contributed and pooled their earnings, but had made unequal contributions to the deposit to buy their home. The court (in an exercise similar to that recently adopted in *Midland Bank v Cooke* above) deduced that there had been a joint venture and on separating they were held to own the house in equal shares On the other hand, in a similar case, *Walker v Hall* [1984] FLR 126, no joint venture was discernible and the woman received a quarter share.

The problem cases are those such as *Windeler v Windeler*, *Burns v Burns* and *Richards v Dove* (see 16.1.5) where no trust can be established according to strict property rules.

Maintenance of the partner in life   18.4

There is no direct obligation on a partner to maintain a cohabitee when the parties are not married unless there is some contractual arrangement between them, although indirect support may be obtained if there is a child support assessment where a percentage of the amount paid over is in fact a payment towards the expenses of the child's carer. Thus the only possible claim for support for a cohabitee is usually to make an ordinary application to the Benefits Agency for income support or other benefits, when there will nevertheless be only one claim per household. If the parties are still *cohabiting*, as is often the case when a relationship is breaking up, and the client is without funds, either the partner who is in work must provide support voluntarily, or if both parties are out of work one or other of them must make an application for benefits on behalf of both: see Chapter 13. Once they separate, each partner may make a separate application, and the whole range of benefits will be available: see Chapter 13.

Note _____

A female cohabitee with children will of course usually have child benefit and one parent benefit, and will make an independent claim for child support in respect of *her* children.

18.5   Maintenance of the partner after death

This is provided for by the Inheritance (Provision for Families and Dependants) Act 1975 s 1(1)(c) if the cohabitee can show that he or she '... immediately before the death was being maintained, either wholly or partly, by the deceased'. To use this section, the cohabitee must show that the deceased, '...otherwise than for full valuable consideration, was making a substantial contribution in money or money's worth towards the reasonable needs of that person': I(PFFD)A 1975 s 1(3). If these conditions are proved, the court may make an order under s 2.

The court has wide powers to grant periodical payments, lump sums, transfers or settlements of property and even acquisition of property for the benefit of the surviving cohabitee using assets from the estate to do so.

However, many cohabitees are unable to show the necessary dependence, eg where the reason that the parties did not marry was because the surviving cohabitee had independent means, such as a pension which would be forfeited on remarriage. The Law Reform (Succession) Act 1995 s 2 now provides for them, amending the I(PFFD)A 1975 to enable non-dependent cohabitees to apply, but at the same time requiring the court to have regard to a different set of guidelines from those applying to spouses, in particular the court will have to have regard to the:

- age of the applicant and the length of time during which the applicant lived as husband and wife with the deceased in the same household;
- contribution made by the applicant to the welfare of the family by the applicant, including any contribution made by looking after the home and caring for the family;

and the cohabitee applicant can only receive such provision as would be reasonable for maintenance, whereas spouses receive such provision as would be reasonable, whether or not it is required for maintenance.

18.6   Maintenance of children

Children of cohabitees are, however, in a much more advantageous position. They may obtain both maintenance from their natural parent, through the Child Support Agency: see above Chapter 7 and orders for capital provision; these are of two types:

- Lump sums up to £1,000 from the family proceedings court;
- Lump sums of any amount and orders for transfer or settlement of property for their benefit from the county court or High Court: Children Act 1989, s 15 and Schedule 1.

Note

A parent who is not married to the child's other parent and who is able to secure such an order for the benefit of the child is thus able indirectly to obtain financial assistance with the upbringing of the child beyond mere maintenance of the child, even including obtaining the right to remain in the family home, which may be transferred for the benefit of the child.

Establishing paternity 18.6.1

If it is necessary to establish paternity in order to invoke the maintenance provisions of the CSA 1991 or the relief obtainable under the Children Act 1989, it will be necessary to apply to the court for a declaration to establish relationship to the child: CSA 1991 s 27. The application may be made by either the carer parent or the Secretary of State. The carer parent, if on benefits, is required to authorise the Secretary of State to take such proceedings: CSA 1991 s 6(1). The carer's benefits will otherwise usually be reduced: CSA 1991 s 46. If, exceptionally, there is some good reason why this information should not be divulged, the carer may explain the position to the child support officer, eg if there is risk of violence or other undue harm or distress which is likely to be suffered. If benefit is reduced it will normally be for a maximum of 18 months

In some cases the child support officer may make a finding of paternity on the facts before him in which case the father may appeal to the Family Proceedings Court: Child Support Appeals (Jurisdiction of Courts) Order 1993, SI 1993/961.

Appeals against assessments as such go to the Child Support Appeal Tribunal.

Establishing paternity for other purposes 18.6.2

For the purposes of s 8 CA 1989 the natural father is treated as a 'parent', and therefore not requiring leave to apply for such an order, whether or not he has parental responsibility, which is a separate issue. If, however, the mother steadfastly refuses to recognise that the natural father is the child's father, and there is no proof one way or the other, then the father will probably have to obtain a declaration, although if the parties have cohabited and he has therefore lived with the child for three years he would then have a right to apply for a residence or contact order without leave anyway: CA 1989 s 10(7). Otherwise the Family Law Reform Act 1987 s 1 gives the unmarried father status as a parent in all cases where paternity is accepted or proved, including in all statutes where the word parent would otherwise include him if he were married to the mother.

18.7   Parental responsibility

The position is that the mother of a child has sole parental rights if not married to the father. However the father may acquire parental responsibility rights in a number of ways provided by CA 1989 s 4: see 6.2.1.

18.8   Cohabitation contracts

As a result of the above, there is now a modest growth rate in the provision of cohabitation contracts, which can provide for the parties whatever terms they wish to regulate their relationship, both while they are cohabiting happily and when it breaks down. They have a similar role to play for unmarried parties as separation and maintenance agreements do for married parties who separate, save that cohabitation agreements can sometimes hold the relationship together in the first place, while separation and maintenance agreements (for which see above at 14.6) usually provide a *modus vivendi* for those who know that they can no longer live together. In either case this is an opportunity for imaginative advice and creative drafting on the part of the solicitor. Cohabitation contracts are contracts like any other and are perfectly legal.

Many firms keep precedents in the word processor and suitable forms will also be found in some drafting encyclopaedias, besides which there is at least one specialist collection commercially available. In view of the high incidence of cohabitation and of births in families who do not fit the marital template, yet which are at least semi-permanent (or at least as permanent as some marriages!) further formalisation of cohabitational relationships is likely. Meanwhile the trainee must be prepared to use such law as is available to assist the unmarried client so as to provide such remedies as can be accessed when relationships break down, or better, to attempt to obviate problems by recommending a cohabitation contract and explaining to the client what will happen if one is not entered into.

Self-assessment questions

1 Can cohabitees use the MWPA 1882 to resolve their property disputes?
2 How does a cohabitee obtain a declaration of ownership of disputed property?
3 Can a cohabitee obtain exclusive occupation of the family home when the relationship breaks down?
4 Is there any way in which a cohabitee can obtain maintenance from a former cohabitee?
5 What is the effect of cohabitation on the right to welfare benefits?
6 What rights does a cohabitee have over the estate of a deceased partner?
7 How if at all is maintenance of a child affected by the fact that the child's parents are not married?
8 How if at all is the right to parental responsibility or s 8 CA 1989 orders affected by the fact that a father is not married to the child's mother?
9 How will a putative father's paternity be established for the purposes of the CSA 1991 if it is not admitted?
10 What is the purpose and effect of a cohabitation agreement?

The Solicitors Family Law Association – Introduction and Code of Practice

An SFLA solicitor believes that in resolving the problems arising at the end of family relationships or in family crises, it is preferable to promote a conciliatory atmosphere and to deal with matters in a sensitive, constructive and cost-effective way. To help put this into practice, SFLA members subscribe to a Code of Practice.

The Association was created in 1982 when there was widespread concern that too often solicitors and the court process were adding to the distress and anger that can arise on the breakdown of a family relationship. Our members believe that solicitors could and should deal with matters in a way designed to ensure that people's dignity is preserved, with every encouragement to reach agreement and avoid unnecessary litigation. The result will be to achieve the same or more satisfactory solutions but at less cost in terms of emotion and money.

Most importantly, they will be solutions that do not destroy the possibility of former family members dealing with each other in a civilised way, for example in parents agreeing arrangements for the benefit of their children notwithstanding their own differences. Experience shows that agreed solutions are more likely to be adhered to than those imposed by a court. Even where proceedings are inevitable so that a court has to decide matters, it is to the advantage of the whole family that proceedings are conducted in a constructive and realistic manner rather than as if in the midst of a war zone.

What the Association is

1. It is an association of solicitors and currently has over 3,000 members, each of whom subscribes to a Code of Practice. Most members undertake legal aid work. The Law Society recommends that all solicitors practising family law should follow the Code of Practice. Members should inform their clients of the Code as it will form the basis of the approach that they adopt.

2. Its administration has an office staffed by full-time personnel. Most areas of the country have a regional group.

3. It is also a representative body. It is actively involved in law reform both initiating improvements and responding to proposals for change.

4. It provides education for its members, to equip them to deal with both the legal and practical issues of family breakdown and the

emotional consequences. It encourages the use of mediation where appropriate.

5. Members vary in experience, from newly qualified to those qualified many years. Membership is not a guarantee of excellence or specialisation. Admission to the Association is on the basis of a commitment to the Code and confirmation that the solicitor will endeavour to ensure his work is carried out in accordance with the Code. Although members are proposed and seconded by fellow members, there is no test of legal ability.

What the Code is not

1. Adherence to the Code is not a sign of weakness nor does it expose the client to disadvantage. The approach adopted should be firm and fair. The solicitor is not prevented from taking immediate and decisive action where this is required. Even where there are ongoing discussion, they may often proceed in parallel with court proceedings, in case negotiations do not produce a settlement.

2. It is not a straight-jacket. The guidelines of the Code cannot be absolute rules in as much as the solicitor may have to depart from them if the law or professional rules or duties to the client so require.

CODE OF PRACTICE

1. GENERAL

1.1   At an early stage the solicitor should inform the client of the approach he adopts in family work.

1.2   The solicitor should advise, negotiate and conduct matters so as to encourage and assist the parties to achieve a constructive settlement of their differences as quickly as may be reasonable while recognising that the parties may need time to come to terms with their new situation.

1.3   The solicitor should ensure that the client appreciates that the interests of the children should be the first concern. The solicitor should encourage the client to see the advantages to the family of a constructive and non-adversarial approach as a way of resolving their differences. The solicitor should explain to the client that in cases where there are children the attitude of the client to the other family members in any negotiations will affect the family as a whole and may affect the relationship of the children with the parents.

1.4   The solicitor should encourage the attitude that a family dispute is not a contest in which there is one winner and one loser, but rather a search for fair solutions. He should avoid using words or phrases that imply a dispute when no serious dispute necessarily exists.

1.5   Because of the involvement of personal emotions in family disputes the solicitor should where possible avoid heightening such emotions in any way.

1.6   The solicitor should have regard to the impact of correspondence on the other party when writing a letter of which a copy may be sent to that party. he should also consider carefully the impact of correspondence on his own client before sending copies of letter to the client. The solicitor should avoid expressing personal opinion as to the conduct of the other party.

1.7   The solicitor should aim to avoid mistrust between parties by encouraging at an early stage full, frank and clear disclosure of information and openness in dealings.

2. RELATIONSHIP WITH CLIENT

2.1   The solicitor should ensure that his relationship with his client is such that his objectivity is preserved and his own personal emotions do not cloud his judgment.

2.2   Whilst recognising the need to advise firmly and guide the client, the solicitor should ensure that where the decision is properly that of the client, it is taken by the client and that its consequences are fully understood, both as to its effect on any children involved and financially.

2.3   The solicitor should always ensure that the client is fully aware of the impact of costs on any chosen course of action. The solicitor should throughout have regard to the cost of negotiations and proceedings.

2.4   The solicitor should ensure that the client is aware of the existence and range of all other services which may be of assistance in bringing about a resolution and helping members of the family through the process of family breakdown, such as mediation and counselling.

3. DEALINGS WITH OTHER SOLICITORS

3.1   In all dealings with other solicitors, the solicitor should show courtesy and endeavour to create and maintain a good working relationship.

3.2   The solicitor should not denigrate the other solicitors involved in the case to the client.

4. DEALINGS WITH THE OTHER PARTY IN PERSON

4.1   In dealings with another party who is not legally represented the solicitor should take particular care to be courteous and restrained. Special care should be taken to express letters and other communications clearly, avoiding technical language where it is not readily understandable to the layman or might be misunderstood.

4.2   Wherever any party is not legally represented, that party should, in the interests of both parties and the family, be advised to consult a solicitor.

5. COURT PROCEEDINGS

5.1   The taking of any action or proceedings which is likely to cause or increase animosity between the parties must be balanced against the likely benefit to the client and the family.

5.2   Where the purpose of taking a particular step in proceedings may be misunderstood or appear hostile, the solicitor should consider explaining it, at the first practical opportunity, to the other party or his solicitors.

5.3   Before filing a petition, the solicitor should consider with the client whether the other party or his solicitor should be contacted in advance as to the intention to petition, the 'facts' on which the petition is to be based and/or the particulars to be alleged, with a view to proceeding by agreement. A client should be advised that filing a petition and/or Statement of Arrangements without first attempting to agree the contents is likely to increase feelings of contentiousness and hostility, making any settlement much more difficult to achieve. It may also earn the disapproval of the Court and may have a bearing on the issue of costs.

5.4   The solicitor should advise the client that on receipt for approval from the other spouse of a Petition or Statement of Arrangements, and other than in exceptional circumstances, a client should not first file their own petition without giving their spouse at least five working days written notice of the intention to do so.

5.5   The solicitor should conduct family law proceedings, including the preparation, advocacy and implementation, in the most cost-effective manner and in such a way as not to increase hostility unnecessarily and as to allow reasonable opportunity for settlement.

6. CHILDREN

6.1   The solicitor should, in advising, negotiating and conducting proceedings, encourage both his client and other family members to regard the welfare of the child as the first and paramount consideration.

6.2   The solicitor should aim to promote co-operation between parents in decisions concerning the child, and should consider encouraging arrangements to be reached direct or through mediation.

6.3   Issues of arrangements for the children on the one hand and finance on the other must be kept separate. They should be referred to in separate letters.

6.4   The solicitor must remember that the interests of the child may not coincide with those of either parents, and in exceptional cases it may be appropriate for the child to be separately represented; this may be by the Official Solicitor, a Panel Guardian (in specified proceedings) or in the case of a 'mature' child by a solicitor direct.

7. THE CHILD AS CLIENT

7.1   A solicitor should only accept instructions from a child direct if the solicitor has the requisite training and expertise in this field. The solicitor should make a personal commitment to undertake all preparation and advocacy for the child and give the child the same respect afforded to an adult as client.

7.2   A difficult and continuing duty for the solicitor is to assess the child's capacity to give instructions.

7.3   The solicitor should ensure that the child has sufficient information throughout the proceedings to make informed decisions; advice and information should be presented in a clear and understandable form. The solicitor must be aware that certain information may be harmful to the child.

7.4   The child's solicitor should maintain a neutral approach as between each parent, the local authority and other parties.

7.5   Detailed guidelines have been drawn up by the SFLA for those members acting for children. Copies are available from the Secretary.

For further information about the SFLA contact the Permanent Secretary:

Mary I'Anson
SFLA
Box 302
Orpington
Kent BR6 8QX

For an address list of local SFLA members please send an SAE.

Grateful acknowledgment is given to the SFLA for permission to reproduce the Code.

Appendix 2

Petition – printed form and Notes for Guidance

(Various legal stationers produce printed forms of petition. All forms are not laid out identically. That following is a typical version.)

Before completing this form, read carefully the attached **Notes for Guidance**.

In the
County Court*

         * Delete as appropriate

In the Divorce Registry*   **No.**

(1)   On the   day of   19   the petitioner was lawfully married to (hereinafter called 'the respondent') at

(2)   The petitioner and the respondent last lived together as husband and wife at

(3)   The petitioner is domiciled in England and Wales, and is by occupation a   and resides at and the respondent is by occupation a and resides at

(4)   There are no children of the family now living *except*

(5)   No other child, now living, has been born to the petitioner/respondent during the marriage (so far as is known to the petitioner) *except*

(6)   There are or have been no other proceedings in any court in England and Wales or elsewhere with reference to the marriage (or to any child of the family) or between the petitioner and respondent with reference to any property of either or both of them *except*

(7)   There are or have been no proceedings in the Child Support Agency with reference to the maintenance of any child of the family *except*

(8)   There are no proceedings continuing in any country outside England or Wales which are in respect of the marriage or are capable of affecting its validity or subsistence *except*

(9)   (This paragraph should be completed only if the petition is based on five years' separation.) No agreement or arrangement has been made or is proposed to be made between the parties for the support of the petitioner/respondent (and any child of the family) *except*

(10)   The said marriage has broken down irretrievably.

(11)

(12)   Particulars

Prayer

The petitioner therefore prays

(1)   The suit

That the said marriage be dissolved

(2)   Costs

That the   may be ordered to pay the costs of this suit

(3)   Ancillary relief

that the petitioner may be granted the following ancillary relief:

(a)   an order for maintenance pending suit

a periodical payments order

a secured provision order

a lump sum order

a property adjustment order

(b)   For the children

a periodical payments order

a secured provision order

a lump sum order

a property adjustment order

Signed

The names and address of the person to be served with this petitioner are:-
Respondent:-

Co-Respondent (adultery case only):-

The Petitioner's address for service is:-

Dated this day of 19

Address all communications for the court to : The Chief Clerk, County Court,

The Court }
office at   }
is open from 10 a.m. to 4 p.m. (4.30 p.m. at the Principal Registry of the Family Division – Somerset House) on Mondays to Fridays.

In the

County Court*

*Delete as appropriate

No.

In the Divorce Registry*

Between

Petitioner

and

Respondent

Divorce Petition

Full name and address of the petitioner or
of solicitors if they are acting for the
petitioner

Divorce Petition

Notes for Guidance

Each of the notes below will help you to complete that paragraph in the divorce petition which has the same number as the note. You should not cross out any of the paragraphs numbered 1 to 11 unless the notes say that you should.

(1) You will find the information you need to complete this paragraph on your marriage certificate. You must explain any differences between the information given in your petition and that on your marriage certificate. If either you or the respondent have changed your name(s) since the marriage took place you must explain this, for example by adding: name changed by deed poll, now known as. Please give: the date of your marriage, your full name (the petitioner), the full name of your husband or wife (the respondent), the place of marriage. For example:

Where the marriage took place in a Register Office:

The Register Office, in the District of ....
in the County of ....

Where the marriage took place in a church: ....
Church, in the Parish of .... in the County ....

(2) Please give the last address at which you have lived with the respondent as husband and wife.

(3) Please give your occupation and current address and those of the respondent. If either you or the respondent are not domiciled (that is, you or the respondent do not live permanently) in England and Wales please give the name of the countr(y)(ies) in which you are domiciled (in which you do live). Where both of you are domiciled (live permanently) outside England and Wales, add the following paragraph, if it applies:

The petitioner (respondent) has been domiciled in England and Wales throughout the period of one year ending with the date of the presentation of the petition.

You should give the address(es) where you and the respondent lived during that year and the length of time lived at each address.

(4) If there are no children of the family cross out the word 'except'. If there are any children of the family give: their full names (including surname), their date of birth, or if over 18 say so, H the child is over 16 but under 18, say if he or she is at school, or college, or is training for a trade, profession or vocation, or is working full time.

(5) If no other child has been born during the marriage you should cross out the word 'except'.

If you are the husband, cross out the word 'petitioner' where it first appears in the paragraph, but do not cross out the words in brackets.

If you are the wife, cross out the word 'respondent', and cross out the words in brackets. If there is a child give:

- the full name (including surname);
- the date of birth, or if over 18 say so.

If there is a dispute whether a living child is a child of the family please add a paragraph saying so.

(6) If there have not been any court proceedings in England and Wales concerning:

- your marriage;
- any child of the family;
- any property belonging to either you or the respondent,

cross out the word 'except'.

If there have been proceedings please give:

- the name of the court in which they took place;
- details of the order(s) which were made;
- if the proceedings were about your marriage say if you and the respondent resumed living together as husband and wife after the order was made.

(7) If there have been no proceedings in a court outside England and Wales which have affected the marriage, or may affect it, cross out the word 'except'.

If there are or have been proceedings please give:

- the name of the country and the court in which they are taking/have taken place;
- details of the order(s) made;
- if no order has yet been made the date of any future hearing.

(8) If your petition is not based on five years separation, cross out this paragraph.

If your petition is based on five years separation but no agreement or arrangement has been made, cross out the word 'except'.

If your petition is based on five years' separation and an agreement or arrangement has been made with the respondent:

- about maintenance either for him or herself or for any child of the family;
- about the family property,

please give full details.

(9) If you are applying for a judicial separation please cross out this paragraph.

(10) Please write in, exactly as set out below, the paragraph (or paragraphs) upon which you intend to rely to prove that your marriage has irretrievably broken down.

Please note

You do not need to give the name of the person with whom the respondent has committed adultery unless you wish to claim costs against that person.

(a) The co-respondent has committed adultery with a [man] [woman] and the petitioner finds it intolerable to live with the respondent, or

The respondent has committed adultery with (give the name) ....

(called the co-respondent) and the petitioner finds it intolerable to live with the respondent.

(b) The respondent has behaved in such a way that the petitioner cannot reasonably be expected to live with the respondent.

(c) The respondent has deserted the petitioner for a continuous period of at least two years immediately preceding the presentation of this petition.

(d) The parties to the marriage have lived apart for a continuous period of at least two years immediately preceding the presentation of the petition and the respondent consents to a decree being granted.

(e) The parties to the marriage have lived apart for a continuous period of at least five years immediately preceding the presentation of the petition.

Particulars

(11) This space is provided for you to give details of the allegations which you are using to prove the facts given in paragraph 10. In most cases one or two sentences will do.

(a) If you have alleged adultery give:

• the date(s) and place(s) where the adultery took place.

(b) If you have alleged unreasonable behaviour give:

• details of particular incidents, including dates but it should not be necessary to give more than about half a dozen examples of the more serious incidents, including the most recent.

(c) If you have alleged desertion give:

• the date of desertion;

• brief details of how the desertion came about.

(d) & (e) If you have alleged either two or five years' separation give:

• the date of separation;

• brief details of how the separation came about.

Prayer

The prayer of the petition is your request to the court. You should consider carefully the claims which you wish to make. You should adapt the prayer to suit your claims.

(1) The suit

If you are asking for a judicial separation, cross out this paragraph and write in its place:

'that the petitioner may be judicially separated from the respondent'.

(2) Costs

If you wish to claim that the respondent or co-respondent pay your costs you must do so in your petition.

It is not possible to make a claim after a decree has been granted.

If you do wish to claim costs write in respondent, or co-respondent, or both, as appropriate.

If you do not wish to claim costs, cross out this paragraph.

(3) Ancillary relief

If you cross out this paragraph, or any part of it, and later change your mind, you will first have to ask the courts permission before any application can be made. Permission cannot be granted after re-marriage.

If you are asking for a property adjustment order, give the address of the property concerned.

(4) Children

The court will only make an order if it considers that an order will be better for the child(ren) than no order.

If you consider that a court will need to determine:

- where the child(ren) live (a Residence Order);
- with whom the child(ren) should have contact (a Contact Order);
- a Specific Issue Order;
- a Prohibited Steps Order

write in this space the order you will be seeking and the full name(s) of the child(ren) concerned. You must apply for the order on form C1. You can get this form from the court office. You may enclose the completed form with your petition or submit it later. If you wish to apply for any of these orders or any other orders which may be available to you under Part 1 or 2 of the Children Act 1989 you are advised to see a solicitor.

Finally, do not forget to:

- sign and date the petition;
- give the name(s) and personal address(es) of the person(s) to be served with the petition;
- bring or send your marriage certificate and fee to the court;
- complete a Statement of Arrangements if there are children of the family.

Draft petition

(A petition may be drafted from scratch if for some reason the printed form is not to be used. Such a draft will generally follow the printed form but the text will be typed out in full rather than filled in as the form would have to be.)

IN THE BUNBURY COUNTY COURT   **No.**

The petition of ANNE AMELIA SMITH shows that:

1.   On 1 January 1993 the Petitioner was lawfully married to John James Smith (hereinafter called the Respondent) at Bunbury Register Office, Town Hall Chambers, Bunbury, London N99.

2.   The Petitioner and the Respondent last lived together at 1 Lilac Avenue, Bunbury, London N99.

3.   The Petitioner is domiciled in England and Wales. The Petitioner is a housewife and resides at 10 High Road, Bunbury End, London N92, and the Respondent is a sales manager and resides at 1 Lilac Avenue, Bunbury aforesaid.

4.   There is one child of the family, namely Jeremy James Smith born on 1 December 1993.

5.   No other child now living has been born to the Petitioner during the said marriage.

6.   There are or have been no other proceedings in the court in England and Wales with reference to the said marriage or the said children of the family or between the Petitioner and the Respondent with reference to any property of either or both of them.

7.   There have been no proceedings in the Child Support Agency with reference to the maintenance of any child of the family.

8.   There are no proceedings continuing in any country outside England and Wales which are in respect of the marriage or are capable of affecting its validity or substance.

9.   The said marriage has broken down irretrievably.

10.   The Respondent has behaved in such way that the Petitioner cannot reasonably be expected to live with the Respondent.

PARTICULARS

(i)   From shortly after Easter 1993 the Respondent began to treat the Petitioner with extreme coldness and persistently claimed that she had tricked him into the marriage which he claimed had not turned out as he had expected.

(ii)   From the month of May 1993, when the Petitioner discovered that she was pregnant, the Respondent repeatedly pressed her to have an abortion because he claimed that he did not want children, to the great distress of the Petitioner.

(iii)   From the month of June 1993 until the birth of the child of the family Jeremy James Smith, the Respondent persistently neglected the Petitioner, refusing to come home for meals in the evening because he claimed that the Petitioner was a 'boring old cow' and going out with his friends during the entire weekend. He refused to help the Petitioner with any shopping or housework, despite the fact that she continued to work until the eighth month of her pregnancy.

(iv)   From the month of December 1993 when the child of the family was born, the Respondent persisted in his uncaring attitude, refusing the Petitioner any help with the baby as a result of which she was unable to return to work at the end of her maternity leave and subsequently lost her job.

(v)   In the month of March 1994 the Respondent took employment in Saudi Arabia and has since been home only once a year, usually for one month in the summer. During his absence he has written no letters to the Petitioner, has not telephoned her, has shown no interest in the child of the family and has sent her inadequate housekeeping to maintain herself and the said child. The Respondent has however sent generous presents to his mother and sisters with whom he normally spends most of his leaves, and has boasted to the Petitioner of how much he is earning.

(vi)   On 1 December 1996 the Respondent returned from overseas without warning accompanied by two males colleagues who despite the Petitioner's protests moved into the matrimonial home with the Respondent. In view of the foregoing the Petitioner has left the home and has since been forced to reside with her parents at 10 High Road, Little Bunbury aforesaid.

The Petitioner therefore prays:

1.   That the said marriage may be dissolved.

2.   That the court may order such payments by way of maintenance pending suit and make such orders for financial provision or adjustment of property as may be just.

3.   That the Respondent may be ordered to pay the costs of this suit.

The name and address of the person to be served with this petition is:

John James Smith
1 Lilac Avenue
Bunbury
London N99

The Petitioner's address for service is:
c/o Black and White, Solicitors
123 High Street
Bunbury
London N99

Appendix 3

Draft Answer

IN THE BUNBURY COUNTY COURT   **1996 D No 123**

BETWEEN   ANNE AMELIA SMITH   Petitioner

and

JOHN JAMES SMITH   Respondent

and

THOMAS TIDDLER   Party Cited

The Respondent in ANSWER to the petition filed in this suit says that:

1.   No other child now living has been born to the Petitioner during the said marriage, so far as is known to the Respondent.

2.   It is admitted that the said marriage has broken down irretrievably.

3.   It is denied that the Respondent has behaved in such a way as alleged in the petition or at all.

4.   Save as hereinafter expressly admitted, the Respondent denies each and every allegation contained in paragraph 10 of the petition.

5.   The Respondent denies that he treated the Petitioner with extreme coldness as alleged or at all. In so far as he may appear to have done so, this was entirely justified by the Petitioner's lack of ability as a housewife. The Petitioner made it clear that she was not prepared to discharge her domestic duties unless she was permitted to give up her employment, and required the Respondent to assume a disproportionate share of the housework, shopping and cooking. Naturally this was an intolerable burden for the Respondent to assume on top of his own onerous employment which it was important that he retained in order to defray the costs of purchasing and equipping the matrimonial home and to fund the generous household budget required by the Petitioner.

6.   The Respondent denies that he pressed the Petitioner to have an abortion. He merely suggested that since she found her existing domestic duties, for which she had no aptitude, too much for her that she might have difficulty in looking after a child as well.

7.   The Respondent denies that he refused to come home for meals in the evenings during the Petitioner's pregnancy; nor did he go out for the entire weekend with his friends. The Petitioner asked him to eat out so that she could go to bed early and also to have the weekends to rest as she found that working up to the eighth month of her pregnancy to be difficult, as the Respondent had already suggested to her it would be. The Respondent did not call the Petitioner a 'boring old cow'. He may have commented that she had become somewhat 'broody'.

8.   The Respondent denies that he refused to help the Petitioner with the child of the family, or that his lack of help caused her to give up her job. He offered repeatedly to help, but the Petitioner preferred to deal with the baby on her own and herself gave in her notice at her place of employment. The Respondent in no way contributed to the Petitioner's decision.

9.   The Respondent admits that he took employment in Saudi Arabia in March 1994. This was necessary due to the birth of the child of the family and the Petitioner's giving up work. The Respondent's employer offered him the opportunity upon hearing of his financial difficulties and the Respondent accepted the offer. He could not otherwise pay the mortgage on the matrimonial home and meet the other outgoings (which had been budgeted for on the basis that the Petitioner would continue to work) without requiring the Petitioner to move to more modest accommodation.

10.   The Respondent admits that he did not correspond with or telephone the Petitioner while overseas. He did initially do so but the Petitioner indicated that contact with him was an extra burden so at her express request he desisted and asked for news of his family from his parents who reside near the matrimonial home. The Respondent admits that during his annual leaves he spent a considerable time with his mother and sisters (and that he brought home present for them) but he always slept at home and absented himself only to assist the Petitioner in reducing her domestic burdens as she indicated that it was a nuisance to cook for him. The Respondent admits that he disclosed his salary to his parents and sisters and that he restricted the Petitioner's housekeeping but this was because of her extravagance and to enable him to save so that he might return eventually to live and work in the United Kingdom.

11.   The Respondent admits that on 1 December 1996 he returned from Saudi Arabia (although this was not without warning) and that on his arrival he was accompanied by two male colleagues whom he had agreed to put up in the spare room of the matrimonial home until they could find accommodation. His colleagues had offered to pay a good rental and the Respondent had resided in their house upon similar terms when first in Saudi Arabia. The Respondent was glad to

have the extra money and was embarrassed by the Petitioner's unreasonable response to this temporary arrangement which was for the family's financial benefit. However, the Petitioner insisted on leaving the home on the spot in order to go to reside with her parents, since when the parties have not resumed cohabitation.

12.   The Petitioner has committed adultery and the Respondent finds it intolerable to live with her.

PARTICULARS

(a)   The Petitioner committed adultery with Thomas Tiddler (hereinafter called the Party Cited) on a day or days unknown to the Respondent in about October and November 1996 at a place or places unknown to the Respondent but including 1 Lilac Avenue, Bunbury, London N99.

(b)   Since 1 December 1996 the Petitioner has committed adultery with Thomas Tiddler on a day or days unknown at a place or places unknown but including 10 High Road, Bunbury End, London N9 and that this adultery is continuing.

The Respondent therefore prays:

1.   That the prayer of the petition may be rejected.

2.   That the said marriage may be dissolved.

3.   That the Party Cited may be ordered to pay the costs of this suit.

[Signature]

Names, addresses etc as at the bottom of a petition.

A backsheet will be required in the same style as for a petition, taking the heading from the Answer.

Appendix 4

Instructions to Counsel

IN THE BUNBURY COUNTY COURT   No 1996 D 123

Between   ANNE AMELIA SMITH   Petitioner

and   JOHN JAMES SMITH   Respondent

INSTRUCTIONS TO COUNSEL TO ADVISE ON THE PETITIONER'S
CLAIM FOR ANCILLARY RELIEF AND TO DRAFT AN AFFIDAVIT
OF MEANS

Counsel has herewith copies of the following:

1. Statement of petitioner dated 20 December 1996

2. Petition for divorce of Anne Amelia Smith

3. Statement of Arrangements for the child of the family

4. Respondent's Acknowledgment of Service

5. Petitioner's affidavit in support of petition

6. (Decree Nisi if pronounced; Decree Absolute if granted)

7. (Relevant correspondence between Instructing Solicitors and petitioner)

8. (Relevant correspondence between Instructing Solicitors and respondent's solicitors)

9. Bundle of documents relating to petitioner's means as per the schedule on page one of the bundle

10. Petitioner's legal aid certificate.

Introduction

Instructing Solicitors act for the petitioner, Mrs Anne Smith , on her application for financial provision and property adjustment ancillary to divorce. The petitioner has been granted legal aid to make the application (certificate number ...., enclosure 10).

Instructing Solicitors are advising and assisting Mrs Smith in relation to her divorce proceedings under the Green Form Scheme. (Directions for trial under the Special Procedure have been applied for) [Decree Nisi was pronounced on ....] [and made absolute on ....] (enclosure 6).

Claims for all forms of ancillary relief were included in the petition. Counsel is referred to the petitioner's Statement, Petition and Statement of Arrangements (enclosures 1, 2 and 3) for the facts of the matter. Briefly, the facts are these:

History of the marriage

The parties married on 1 January 1993.

The petitioner is aged 25. Her occupation is mother and housewife. She was formerly a receptionist. She presently lives with the child of the family, Jeremy James Smith, at her parents residence, 10 High Road, Bunbury End, London N92, and the respondent lives in the former matrimonial home, 1 First Avenue, Bunbury, London N99.

The respondent is aged 32. He is a sales manager in a firm of engineers. He has recently returned from Saudi Arabia where he worked and lived alone throughout a short-term contract which ran for just under two years.

The one child of the family is Jeremy James Smith (aged two).

The former matrimonial home is a three bedroomed house jointly owned by the parties. Its current value is estimated to be £90,000, subject to a mortgage securing an outstanding amount of nearly £30,000. The petitioner did not contribute to the purchase but she did work during the first 11 months of the marriage and contributed to the household budget.

Financial history

The parties met in June 1992. At the time, the petitioner was working as a receptionist at the respondent's firm, supporting herself but living with her parents. The respondent was a sales manager with the firm with good prospects.

The respondent and the petitioner set up house in October 1992 in the matrimonial home which was bought for the purpose and three months later they married. Initially the petitioner provided significant financial support for the household and worked until Jeremy was born in December 1993. The petitioner re-signed from her employment before Jeremy's birth and has not returned to work since.

Subsequently the family was supported entirely by the respondent's income from his employment as a sales manager. In he was sent by the firm to Saudi Arabia, sending the petitioner housekeeping money on which she and the child lived.

Petitioner's present income and resources

(This information may be presented in a schedule)

The petitioner has an annual income of approximately £ ..... of which £ ..... derives from her child benefit. The respondent presently pays £..... per week for her and the minor child of the family.

In addition to her half share of the equity in matrimonial home, the petitioner owns some National Savings Certificates worth £500 approximately and a half share (£.....) of the parties' joint savings in the Bunbury Building Society.

The petitioner could possibly work part-time, but prefers not to do so until the child is older. (He is now only three).

Petitioner's plans for the future

The petitioner hopes to return to and to remain in the matrimonial home, caring for the child. She intends to return to part-time work when he reaches six years of age. The petitioner will then be aged 31. She has no plans to remarry or cohabit with another partner.

Respondent's present income and resources

{This information may be presented in a schedule]

The information in the petitioner's statement regarding the respondent's means has not been verified by disclosure. Moreover as it seems that the parties have not dealt openly with each other over financial matters, we cannot expect the information to be reliable.

The petitioner estimates the respondent's annual income at £ ..... His salary and bonuses from his employers are in the region of £..... pa, although this figure has been higher in previous years (as much as £ .....) when he was in Saudi Arabia and can still be expected to increase as he is promoted. He has further income of £..... dividends on shares in the company employing him and £..... interest on savings in the Building Society account mentioned above.. The respondent owns shares worth £..... , a car worth £ ....., and a half share (£.....) of the joint savings.

Respondent's plans for the future

So far as the petitioner is aware, the respondent has no plans to remarry or cohabit. She thinks he hopes to purchase a flat or small house as a home and to facilitate the child staying with him.

The petitioner hopes to have the matrimonial home transferred into her sole name, with periodical payments for herself until the child reaches the age of 13, as well as maintenance for the child.

It is the view of Instructing Solicitors that a claim for maintenance for herself is not *per se* unreasonable although she thinks the respondent may attempt to obtain an order for limited term maintenance. Counsel will no doubt be aware of the case of *Waterman v Waterman* [1989] 1 FLR 380, where the wife, a secretary with care of the parties' five year old child, was granted maintenance for a five year term (a restriction on extension of the term being lifted on appeal), and the case of *Evans v Evans* [1990] 2 All ER 147, where the wife who was retraining was granted maintenance for three years, to take account of her responsibilities to the younger child of the family (aged nine) until his removal to boarding school.

Instructing Solicitors consider that these cases indicate the court's willingness to award maintenance to a party caring full time for children of the family, at least till secondary school age. It is less certain that the maintenance awarded will enable the petitioner to pay for the outgoing of the home, with which she has struggled during the respondent's absence. Counsel will please indicate a view on this matter.

Regarding the matrimonial home, Instructing Solicitors consider that unless the respondent proves particularly generous, an outright transfer is unlikely to be agreed alongside maintenance for the petitioner, especially as the marriage is of only three years duration (although the existence of a young child would appear to cancel out any such consideration).

A *Martin v Martin* arrangement would appear to be the most advantageous alternative for the petitioner. Instructing solicitors consider that the petitioner would be advised to accept a restriction on extension of the term of periodical payments in order to gain agreement to a *Martin* order. (Counsel is no doubt familiar with the view of Lloyd LJ in *Clutton v Clutton* [1991] All ER 340, that such an order 'could only be said to offend against the principle of the clean break in the most extended sense of that term'.)

However, given the limited capital of the parties and the potential earning capacity of the petitioner, Instructing Solicitors consider that the respondent, if well advised, is likely to insist on a *Mesher v Mesher* arrangement. Counsel will please indicate if this conforms to his/her view.

Counsel is accordingly requested to advise on the following matters:

(Here specify the legal questions, including questions of quantum and evidence, on which you would like counsel's opinion, eg:)

(i) On the basis of the limited information available, is counsel of the opinion that the petitioner's suggestion of periodical payments for herself with transfer of respondent's share of the matrimonial home to her realistic?

(ii) If so, what does counsel assess to be the range within which the periodical payments might reasonably be expected to fall?

(iii) If not, what terms of financial provision and property adjustment can the petitioner reasonably expect to obtain by agreement, in line with her wishes?

(iv) generally.

Counsel is further requested to settle an affidavit of means on behalf of the petitioner in support of her application for ancillary relief.

Should counsel require further information or wish Instructing Solicitors to arrange a conference with the petitioner, counsel will please inform Instructing Solicitors accordingly. If counsel has any queries he/she is invited to contact the writer.

In the Bunbury County Court

Between

Anne Amelia Smith Petitioner

and

John James Smith Respondent

INSTRUCTIONS TO COUNSEL TO
ADVISE ON THE PETITIONER'S
CLAIM FOR ANCILLARY RELIEF
AND TO DRAFT AN AFFIDAVIT OF
MEANS

A Counsel
River Court Chambers
Inn Temple
London EC4

LEGAL AID

Black & White, Solicitors
123 High Street
Bunbury
London N99
Tel: (071) 320 1500
Ref: ABC/123

[date of instructions]

Appendix 5

Affidavits of means

(There are two forms (i) the pre-printed form, reproduced below, often used for maintenance pending suit and in very straightforward ancillary relief claims; and (ii) the affidavit individually drafted from scratch for each case. The former will only be used for a very simple case; the latter is more likely to be suitable for a full scale ancillary relief claim unless a client's affairs are very simple. Like pre-printed petition forms there are many different stationers producing these forms commercially and they will differ slightly depending on the stationer.)

In the Bunbury County Court

BETWEEN

ANNE AMELIA SMITH		Petitioner
	and	
JOHN JAMES SMITH		Respondent

I ANNE AMELIA SMITH of 10, High Road, Bunbury End, London N92, MAKE OATH and say that the answers to the questions below are true to the best of my knowledge information and belief and that they are a full and accurate statement of my means. Save as set out in the said answers I have no capital or income.

1. What is your present occupation?

If you are not now employed, give details of your last employment and any trade or professional qualifications.

2. What is our current gross income from:

    (a) your employment, trade or profession

        (i) normal per year (month) (week)

        (ii) overtime or other special receipt per year (month) (week)

    (b) pension or annuities

(c) interest on bank or savings deposits

(d) building society interest

(e) dividends

(f) any other source

(So far as possible show all receipts in respect of the same period of time: ie. give all weekly, all monthly or all annual amounts. Show all receipts as gross amounts before deduction of tax where possible; where not possible indicate that the amount shown is the net amount received.) Do you receive any benefits in kind, such as free accommodation, use of car, etc, etc? If so, give details.

3. What National Insurance contributions are paid by you?

4. Are there any, and if so what, other expenses, which are necessary to enable you to earn the income set out above?

5.   (a) What was your gross taxable income during the complete tax year (6 April to 5 April) from employment, trade or profession including overtime, other special payments and taxable benefits?

    (b) What was your income tax liability during complete tax year?

Where figures for the last complete tax year are not available, give them for the last year for which they are available. (In the case of a fluctuating income give also the figures for two or more preceding years.)

6. What do you claim to be your necessary expenses of providing yourself with a place to live in, such as rent, rates, rate, mortgage interest and repayments premium on endowment insurance used as collateral etc?

7. What maintenance payments (if any) do you make/receive from your (former) wife/husband including payments to or for any child including school fees?

8. Are any payments to which question 7 refers made

   (a) under a Court order (give Court, date and order)

   (b) under an enforceable agreement (give date and details)

   (c) voluntarily?

9. What payments (if any) do you receive from the Benefits Agency by way of income support or family credit?

10. What family allowance (if any) do you receive for a child or children?

11. Was the former matrimonial home

   (a) rented

   (b) owned

   (i) by you

   (ii) your (former) husband/wife

   (iii) jointly by you and your (former) husband.

12.   (a) Is the former matrimonial home still occupied by you or your (former) wife/husband or by both of you?

       (b) If it is owned by you or your (former) husband/wife or by both of you jointly, at what do you estimate its present value?

       (c) Is it subject to a mortgage? If so, give details of the mortgage, including the rate of repayment, the amount outstanding and the date in which repayment will be completed. If there is any collateral security in the form of an endowment assurance, state the surrender value of the policy.

13. Do you own any car(s)?

If yes, what is its (their) make, model and year of manufacture and what do you estimate its (their) present value?

14. What other assets do you have, such as cash at bank, savings bank accounts, premium savings bonds, building society account, stock and shares, reversionary interests, etc? (Give details and present value). Include any house property owned or in which you have any interest, jointly held property and articles of substantial value such as jewellery or furniture.

15.   (a) Apart from any liability set out in the answers to questions 8 and 12 what other unpaid debts are at present due and payable by you including hire purchase debts? Also give particulars of any judgments against you.

    (b) Do you have any life or endowment assurance policy other than any set out in the answers to questions 6? If so, give details including amount of annual premium and date of maturity.

16. (To be answered only by respondents to applications for financial provision.)

If a decree absolute has been made, have you re-married?

If a decree has not been pronounced or made absolute, do you intend to re-marry?

If one is made do you provide for your intended wife/husband by way of accommodation, living expenses or otherwise?

Do you provide for any other person?

If so, give particulars.

In either case, has the wife/husband, intended wife or other person any means?

If so, state briefly what they are.

17. Are you a member of any pension or superannuation scheme (other than State Insurance)?

(a) Give details:

(b) Would your (former) husband/wife have been entitled to any benefits at your death in the absence of a decree absolute?

18. Is, to your knowledge, your husband/wife a member of such a scheme?

If so, do you think you will lose any benefits by reason of decree absolute, and if so, what?

19. Is there any other reason which you wish to urge against paying maintenance or are there any other matter you wish to raise in connection with this application?

(A suitable template for a form of answer to this question appears on the next page).

DRAFT SUITABLE TO COMPLETE PARAGRAPH 19 OF THE PRINTED FORM OF AFFIDAVIT OF MEANS OF Anne Amelia Smith

(1)   I wish to draw the attention of the Court to the fact that the minor child of the marriage will reside with me and his welfare is my first consideration. He must have a secure home and suitable living conditions during his minority. The Respondent is has recently been residing overseas and residing there and has no need of the home for accommodation. The home should not therefore be sold now or in the foreseeable future and the Respondent should be required to contribute to maintenance for me and the maintenance of the said child.

(2)   I urge the Court to have regard to the fact that while my marriage to the Respondent lasted only three years I have a young child. I looked after the home during the entire period of the marriage, during most of which the Respondent resided abroad, and I have been shouldering almost the entire burden of the day-to-day care of the child since his birth as the Respondent was rarely home. Further I worked part time when I could (up to the eighth month of my pregnancy) and my earnings have contributed to the welfare of the family.

(3)   I would ask the Court to make an order securing the occupation of the former matrimonial home for myself and the child of the family. I could not otherwise accommodate myself and the child since my family responsibilities preclude my working other than part time during school terms once the child of the family is older and established at school and even then to work longer hours or throughout the year would prevent my discharging my responsibilities to him in a manner consistent with his welfare. I would further ask the Court to order that upon eventual sale of the former matrimonial home I should receive at least three-quarters of the sale proceeds as I would not otherwise be able to rehouse myself when the child is grown up as my domestic responsibilities will preclude my accumulating capital, whereas the Respondent already has substantial savings, stocks and shares and a valuable vintage car which is likely to increase further in value.

(4)   I have no plans to remarry or cohabit with any person.

(5)   I would therefore ask this Honourable Court to make an order in the terms proposed above and also such further orders as are thought fit for my benefit in view of the fact that I will be continuing to shoulder all the burden of day-to-day care of the child of the family, whose interests will continue to take priority over any professional work I am able to do.

Dated, etc.

IN THE BUNBURY COUNTY COURT   Petitioner: A Smith

1st. 3. 2 .97

BETWEEN   ANNE AMELIA SMITH   Petitioner

and

JOHN JAMES SMITH   Respondent

I, ANNE AMELIA SMITH, of 10 High Road, Bunbury End, London N92, MAKE OATH and say as follows:

1.   I am the above named Petitioner, and I make this affidavit in support of my application for financial provision and a property adjustment order. In so far as the content of this affidavit is within my personal knowledge it is true and in so far as it is not within my personal knowledge it is true to the best of my knowledge and belief.

Background

2.   I was married to the Respondent on 1 January 1993. There is one child of the marriage, namely Jeremy James Smith, born on 1 December 1993 and Judith.

3.   The marriage was happy for a short period but very quickly became increasingly unhappy and I was obliged to leave the matrimonial home in December 1996, since when we have lived separate and apart. On 16 February 1996 I obtained a decree nisi of divorce because of the Respondent's behaviour.

Income and earning capacity

4.   Prior to our marriage I worked as a receptionist and after we married I was able to continue working until I was eight months pregnant with our child, so that we were able to use my earnings to complete the furnishing of our home and to buy essential equipment for the baby. l am now aged 28 and will be at least 31 before the child of the family is established at primary school I am able to resume work even part time. Although I would like to revert to part time work, I am obviously unable to do so for the foreseeable future. Thus my only income now is Child Benefit and One Parent Benefit of £..... per month.

Capital

5.   I own a half share of the matrimonial home but have virtually no other capital or resources, apart from a half share of our joint savings in the Bunbury Building Society, the precise amount of which I do not know since the Respondent has the book. There was approximately £..... in the account when last I had access to it.

Expenditure

6.   My expenditure each month is £..... for food for myself and the child of the family, £..... per month for clothes, and £..... per month mortgage interest and repayments. My council tax is £..... and the water rate is £..... per month. The other utility bills come to £..... per month. Miscellaneous items, including nominal pocket money for myself, coming to £...... .

The matrimonial home

7.   The matrimonial home was purchased in 1992 for £90,000. It has 3 bedrooms and is registered at HM Land Registry under Title Number A12345. The down payment of £10,000 and legal costs of £ came from wedding gifts from both sets of parents and our joint savings of £500. The balance was raised on mortgage from the Bunbury Building Society. There is currently £..... outstanding on the mortgage which will be paid off in the year 2013.

The position of the Respondent

8.   The Respondent is employed as Sales Manager at the Smart Engineering Company. He earns about £..... a year in salary and bonuses. However, he has never revealed to me full details of his income but it has always appeared to support a good basic standard of living for the family. He is now only 37 and should have the potential to increase his earning capacity even further.

9.   Since December 1996 the Respondent has been living in the matrimonial home and I have resided with my parents. The child of the family lives with me. I urgently require to return to the matrimonial home as my parents cannot house me indefinitely and I have no other means of finding a home for myself and the said child of the family.

The future

10.   The Respondent has an ample income to provide himself with accommodation, and in any event he generally works overseas where subsidised accommodation is provided by the company and can have no need of the matrimonial home for this purpose. Moreover, the breakdown of our marriage is entirely attributable to his behaviour and this has left me solely responsible for the future upbringing of the child of the family, whose welfare is my first concern. I myself have no plans to remarry or cohabit with any person.

Conclusion

11.   In all the circumstances, I would ask the Court to make an order for periodical payments in my favour and for a transfer of the Respondent's share of the matrimonial home to me to provide secure accommodation for the child of the family and myself. I would otherwise be unable to provide for myself, even if I return to part time work in due course. I shall require periodical payments until I am able to return to part time work when the child of the family is established at primary school after which I shall use my best endeavours to contribute to the family budget in so far as I can do so without endangering the health and security of the said child.

Sworn, etc.

Consent orders

Consent order based on rule 2.61 statement of information providing
- periodical payments to spouse for child
- lump sum to spouse
- transfer of property
- certificate for the purpose of Civil Legal Aid (General) Regs

In the Bunbury County Court   **No 1996 D 123**

Between   ANNE AMELIA SMITH   Petitioner

and

JOHN JAMES SMITH   Respondent

DRAFT/CONSENT ORDER

UPON the basis of the statement of information filed herein pursuant to the Family Proceedings Rules 1991 rule 2.61.

AND UPON the Petitioner undertaking to use all reasonable endeavours to procure the release of the Respondent from all liability in respect of the mortgage in favour of the Orion Building Society over the former matrimonial home known as 1 Lilac Avenue, Bunbury, London and pending such release to indemnify him against any future liability in respect of the said mortgage.

BY CONSENT IT IS ORDERED THAT:

1.   The Respondent shall make or cause to be made to the Petitioner periodical payments for the benefit of the child of the family Jeremy James Smith (born 1 December 1993), with effect from 1 June 1997 until such time as he shall attain the age of seventeen years or shall cease to receive full-time education or to undergo training for a trade, profession or vocation, whichever shall be the later, or until further order at the rate of £..... a year payable monthly in advance.

2.   The Respondent shall forthwith upon Decree Absolute pay or cause to be paid to the Petitioner the sum of £5,000.

3.   The Respondent shall within 28 days of the date of this order transfer or cause to be transferred to the Petitioner all that his right and interest in the property known as 1 Lilac Avenue, Bunbury, London, registered at HM Land Registry with Title Number A 12345 subject to the mortgage in favour of the Bunbury Building Society.

4.   Upon compliance by the Respondent with paragraphs 2 and above all the Petitioner's claims for periodical payments, secured periodical payments, lump sum or sums and further or other property adjustment orders shall stand dismissed (and it is directed that the Petitioner shall not be entitled to make any further application in relation to the marriage for an order under section 23(1)(a) or (b) of the Matrimonial Causes Act 1973).

5.   Neither party shall on the death of the other be entitled to apply for an order under section 2 of the Inheritance (Provision for Family and Dependants) Act 1975.

6.   There shall be liberty to each party to apply.

7.   There shall be no order as to costs save legal aid taxation of the Petitioner's costs.

8.   It is certified for the purpose of the Civil Legal Aid (General) Regulations 1989 that the property known as 1 Lilac Avenue, Bunbury, London has been recovered and preserved for the Petitioner for use as a home for herself.

Dated the   day of   1997.

We consent to an order in the above terms.

....
Petitioner   Greenback & Co
                                                Solicitors for the Respondent

Solicitous & Co
Solicitors for the Petitioner

....
Respondent
[signature]

* Note that in order to achieve a complete 'clean break', parties should make claims for all forms of relief, so that the court may dismiss those claims in the order.

Consent order based on

- fixed term periodical payments (with variation excluded)

- *Mesher* order

In the Bunbury County Court   **No 1996 D 123**

Between   ANNE AMELIA SMITH   Petitioner

and

JOHN JAMES SMITH   Respondent

UPON hearing counsel for the Petitioner and the Respondent and upon reading the affidavit of the Petitioner sworn on [date] and the affidavit of the Respondent sworn on [date] and upon hearing the oral evidence of the Petitioner and the Respondent

AND UPON the Petitioner undertaking promptly to make all payments due in respect of the mortgage in favour of Bunbury Building Society in respect of the former matrimonial home the property described below and promptly to discharge all outgoings and expenses on the property including council tax, water rates, buildings insurance, contents insurance and gas, electricity and telephone accounts until such time as the property is sold or further order and to keep the property in good repair, the cost of repair to be borne equally by the Petitioner and Respondent.

IT IS ORDERED THAT:

1.   The Respondent shall make or cause to be made to the Petitioner with effect from 1 June 1997 for a period of five years or until her remarriage or further order periodical payments at the rate of £...... a year payable monthly in advance (and it is directed that the Petitioner shall not be entitled to make any further application in relation to the marriage for an order under section 23(1)(a) or (b) of the Matrimonial Causes Act 1973 or to apply under section 31 of the Matrimonial Causes Act 1973 for an extension of the term specified above).

2.   The property known as 1 Lilac Avenue, Bunbury, London registered at HM Land Registry under Title Number A12345 (the Property) shall be held by the Petitioner and the Respondent on trust for sale for themselves as beneficial tenants in common on the following terms:

(i)   the Petitioner shall be entitled to occupy the Property to the exclusion of the Respondent until sale;

(ii)   the trust for sale shall not be enforced without the Petitioner's consent until the Petitioner remarries, dies or voluntarily leaves the Property or the child of the family reaches the age of 18 or finishes full-time education if later (whichever occurs first) or until further order of the Court;

(iii) upon sale, the proceeds of sale shall be applied towards redeeming the mortgage and paying the costs of and incidental to the sale and the balance remaining shall be divided in the proportion two thirds to the Petitioner and one third to the Respondent.

3.   There shall be liberty to each party to apply.

4.   There shall be no order as to costs.

Dated, etc.

Consent order based on

- periodical payments to the wife (nominal order)

- no periodical payments for the child (therefore to be assessed by the CSA)

- *Martin* type order for the home

In the Bunbury County Court   **1996 D No**

Between   ANNE AMELIA SMITH   Petitioner

and

JOHN JAMES SMITH   Respondent

UPON hearing counsel for the Petitioner and the Respondent and upon hearing the oral evidence of the Petitioner and the Respondent

AND UPON the Petitioner undertaking promptly to make all payments due in respect of the mortgage in favour of the Bunbury Building Society in respect of the former matrimonial home the property described below and promptly to discharge all outgoings and expenses of the property including council tax, water rates, buildings insurance, contents insurance and gas, electricity and telephone accounts until such time as the property is sold or further order and to keep the property in good repair, the cost of repair to be borne equally by the Petitioner and the Respondent

IT IS ORDERED THAT:

1.   The Respondent shall pay to the Petitioner during their joint lives or until such time as the Petitioner shall remarry or until further order periodical payments at the rate of 5p a year.

2.   The Petitioner and the Respondent shall continue to hold the property known as 1 Lilac Avenue, Bunbury, London, registered at HM Land Registry with title number A12345 (the Property) on trust for sale for themselves as beneficial tenants in common on the following terms:

(i)   the Petitioner shall have the sole right to occupy the Property until sale;

(ii)   the trust for sale shall not be enforced without the Petitioner's consent until the Petitioner dies, remarries or voluntarily leaves the Property whichever occurs soonest;

(iii)   upon sale the proceeds of sale shall be applied in redeeming the mortgage in favour of Bunbury Building Society dated
and paying the costs of and incidental to the sale and the balance remaining shall be divided between the two parties in the proportions

three fifths to the Petitioner and two fifths to the Respondent* (*or insert whatever alternative proportions are preferred).

3.   There shall be liberty to each party to apply.

4.   The Respondent do pay the costs of this action including the costs of negotiation in connection therewith.

Dated, etc.

Consent order based on a clean break

- limited term periodical payments
- *Martin* order for the home
- dismissal of all future claims

In the Bunbury County Court   **1996 D No 123**

Between   ANNE AMELIA SMITH   Petitioner

and

JOHN JAMES SMITH   Respondent

UPON the Petitioner and the Respondent agreeing that the provision referred to hereafter is accepted in full and final settlement of all claims the Petitioner and the Respondent may have against each other for income, capital and other property adjustment including all such claims arising under the Matrimonial Causes Act 1973 (as amended), the Married Women's Property Act 1882 (as amended) or any claim which each may have against the estate of the other under the Inheritance (Provision for Family and Dependants) Act 1975.

AND UPON the Petitioner undertaking promptly to pay all outgoings of the former matrimonial home including council tax, water rates, buildings insurance, contents insurance and all bills for gas, electricity, and telephone until such time as the property is sold and to keep the property in good repair the cost of repair, the cost of repairs to be borne by the Petitioner.

AND UPON the Petitioner and the Respondent mutually acknowledging and agreeing that:

(a)   the contents of the former matrimonial home at 1 Lilac Avenue, Bunbury, London shall be the absolute property of the Petitioner;

(b)   the following to be the absolute property of the Respondent

(i) the Peugeot 405 motor car registration number N123 ABC

(ii) the balance in the Bunbury Building Society account number 12345678.

IT IS ORDERED THAT:

1.   The Respondent shall pay to the Petitioner for three years with effect from 1 June 1997 or until such time as the Petitioner shall remarry if that be sooner periodical payments at the rate of £..... a year.

2.   The Petitioner and the Respondent shall continue to hold the property known as 1 Lilac Avenue, Bunbury, London, registered at HM Land Registry with title number A12345 (the Property) on trust for sale for themselves as beneficial tenants in common on the following terms:

    (i) the Petitioner shall have the sole right to occupy the Property until sale;

    (ii) the trust for sale shall not be enforced without the Petitioner's consent until the Petitioner dies, remarries or voluntarily leaves the Property whichever occurs soonest;

    (iii) upon sale the proceeds of sale shall be applied in redeeming the mortgage in favour of the Bunbury Building Society dated and paying the costs of and incidental to the sale and the balance remaining shall be divided equally between the two parties.

3.   Neither party shall upon the death of the other be entitled to apply for an order under section 2 of the Inheritance (Provision for Family and Dependants) Act 1975.

4.   There shall be no order as to costs.

5.   Liberty to apply.

Dated, etc.

Index